THE BIBLE IN MEDIEVAL TRADITION

GENERAL EDITORS

H. Lawrence Bond†
Philip D. W. Krey
Ian Christopher Levy
Thomas Ryan

The major intent of the series THE BIBLE IN MEDIEVAL TRADITION is to reacquaint the Church with its rich history of biblical interpretation and with the contemporary applicability of this history, especially for academic study, spiritual formation, preaching, discussion groups, and individual reflection. Each volume focuses on a particular biblical book or set of books and provides documentary evidence of the most significant ways in which that work was treated in the course of medieval biblical interpretation.

The series takes its shape in dialogue both with the special traditions of medieval exegesis and with the interests of contemporary readers. Each volume in the series comprises fresh translations of several commentaries. The selections are lengthy and, in most cases, have never been available in English before.

Compared to patristic material, relatively little medieval exegesis has been translated. While medieval interpretations do resemble their patristic forebears, they do not simply replicate them. Indeed, they are produced at new times and in new situations. As a result, they lend insight into the changing culture and scholarship of the Middle Ages and comprise a storehouse of the era's theological and spiritual riches that can enhance contemporary reading of the Bible. They, therefore, merit their own consideration, to which this series is meant to contribute.

D1591135

The Book of
JEREMIAH

Translated and edited by

Joy A. Schroeder

WILLIAM B. EERDMANS PUBLISHING COMPANY

GRAND RAPIDS, MICHIGAN

Wm. B. Eerdmans Publishing Co.
2140 Oak Industrial Drive NE, Grand Rapids, Michigan 49505
www.eerdmans.com

Published 2017
Printed in the United States of America

26 25 24 23 22 21 20 19 18 17   2 3 4 5 6 7 8 9 10

ISBN 978-0-8028-7329-3

Library of Congress Cataloging-in-Publication Data

A catalog record for this book is available from the Library of Congress

Contents

CONTENTS

Editors' Preface

The medieval period witnessed an outpouring of biblical interpretation, which included commentaries written in Latin in a wide array of styles over the course of a millennium. These commentaries are significant as successors to patristic exegesis and predecessors to Reformation exegesis, but they are important in their own right.

The major intent of this series, THE BIBLE IN MEDIEVAL TRADITION, is to place newly translated medieval scriptural commentary into the hands of contemporary readers. In doing so, the series reacquaints the church with its rich tradition of biblical interpretation. It fosters academic study, spiritual formation, preaching, discussion groups, and individual reflection. It also enables the contemporary application of this tradition. Each volume focuses on the era's interpretation of one biblical book, or set of related books, and comprises substantial selections from representative exegetes and hermeneutical approaches. Similarly, each provides a fully documented introduction that locates the commentaries in their theological and historical contexts.

While interdisciplinary and cross-confessional interest in the Middle Ages has grown over the last century, it falls short if it does not at the same time recognize the centrality of the Bible to this period and its religious life. The Bible structured sermons, guided prayer, and inspired mystical visions. It was woven through liturgy, enacted in drama, and embodied in sculpture and other art forms. Less explicitly ecclesial works, such as Dante's *Divine Comedy,* were also steeped in its imagery and narrative. Because of the Bible's importance to the period, this series, therefore, opens a window not only to its religious practices but also to its culture more broadly.

Similarly, biblical interpretation played a vital role in the work of medieval theologians. Among the tasks of theological masters was to deliver ordinary lectures on the Bible. Their commentaries — often edited versions of their public lectures — were the means by which many worked out their most important theological insights. Thus the Bible was the primary text for theologians and the center of the curriculum for theology students. Some, such as the authors of *summae* and sentence commentaries, produced systematic treatises that, while not devoted to verse-by-verse explication, nevertheless often cited biblical evidence, addressed apparent contradictions in the scriptural witness, and responded under the guidance of nuanced theories of interpretation. They were biblical theologians.

Biblical commentaries provided the largest reservoir of medieval interpretation and hermeneutics, and they took a variety of forms. Monastic perspectives shaped some, scholastic perspectives still others. Some commentaries emphasized the spiritual senses, others the literal. Some relied more heavily on scholarly tools, such as dictionaries, histories, concordances, critical texts, knowledge of languages, and Jewish commentaries. Whatever the case, medieval commentaries were a privileged and substantial locus of interpretation, and they offer us fresh insight into the Bible and their own cultural contexts.

For readers and the church today, critical engagement with medieval exegesis counteracts the twin dangers of amnesia and nostalgia. One temptation is to study the Bible as if its interpretation had no past. This series brings the past to the present and thereby supplies the resources and memories that can enrich current reading. Medieval exegesis also bears studying because it can exemplify how not to interpret the Bible. Despite nascent critical sensibilities in some of its practitioners, it often offered fanciful etymologies and was anachronistic in its conflation of past and present. It could also demonize others. Yet, with its playful attention to words and acceptance of a multiplicity of meanings and methods, it anticipated critical theory's turn to language today and the indeterminacy characteristic of its literary theory.

What this series sets out to accomplish requires that selections in each volume are lengthy. In most cases, these selections have never been available in English before. Compared to the amount of patristic material, comparatively little medieval exegesis has been translated. Yet, the medieval was not simply a repetition of the patristic. It differed enough in genre, content, and application to merit its own special focus, and it applied earlier church exegesis to new situations and times as well as reflected the changing culture and scholarship in the Middle Ages. The series, therefore, makes these resources more widely available, guides readers in entering into medieval exegetical texts, and enables a more informed and insightful study of the church's biblical heritage.

PHILIP D. W. KREY
IAN CHRISTOPHER LEVY
THOMAS RYAN

Abbreviations

ACCS   Ancient Christian Commentary on Scripture. 29 vols. Downers
        Grove, IL: InterVarsity Press, 2000–10.
CCCM   Corpus Christianorum, Continuatio Mediaevalis. Turnhout:
        Brepols, 1966–.
CCSL   Corpus Christianorum, Series Latina. Turnhout: Brepols, 1953–.
LCL   Loeb Classical Library. Cambridge, MA: Harvard University Press.
MGH   Monumenta Germaniae Historica.
NRSV   New Revised Standard Version Bible.
PG   Patrologia Graeca. 166 vols. Ed. J.-P. Migne. Paris, 1857–86.
PL   Patrologia Latina. 221 vols. Ed. J.-P. Migne. Paris, 1844–55.
SC   Sources Chrétiennes. Paris: Éditions du Cerf, 1941–.
Vulg.   Vulgate.

Introduction

Medieval readers of the book of Jeremiah encountered a challenging text. Jeremiah is filled with words of warning, messages of judgment, and nightmare scenarios of slaughter. In Jeremiah's prophecies, the defeated city of Jerusalem becomes desolate, and the landscape is strewn with the unburied bodies of Judeans massacred by the invading Babylonian army. Graves of priests and princes are looted, and their bones are exposed to the elements. Captives are forced into exile. Those who escape slaughter or captivity suffer disease and starvation, envying the dead. The earth itself laments as cultivated land reverts to wilderness. The same book contains hopeful promises of healing, restoration, and return from captivity, inspiring subsequent generations of Jews and Christians who studied Jeremiah's words.

The Hebrew prophet Jeremiah lived during a turbulent time for the residents of Jerusalem and other inhabitants of Judah. Judean leaders struggled to navigate a path of political and national survival as the kingdom of Judah was caught in the power struggles between Egypt and the Babylonian Empire, which was emerging as a superpower. The Assyrian Empire, which had conquered the northern kingdom of Israel more than a century earlier, in 721 BCE, collapsed in the year 612, defeated by the Babylonians.[1] During Jeremiah's lifetime, there were shifting alliances and a sequence of Judean kings, some of whom are identified by several different names in Scripture.[2]

---

1. William L. Holladay, *Jeremiah: Reading the Prophet in His Time—and Ours* (Minneapolis: Fortress, 1990), 6.

2. In certain cases, the ruler has a name given at birth and a throne name. For instance,

1

According to the opening verses of Jeremiah (1:1–2), the prophet's call to ministry occurred in the thirteenth year of the reign of Josiah (627 BCE), a Judean king who undertook religious reforms and ultimately died in battle against the Egyptians in 609 BCE (2 Chr 35:20–25).[3] Josiah was succeeded by his son Shallum, also called Jehoahaz, who reigned only three months before Pharaoh Neco deposed him, kept him confined in Egypt, and set up Shallum's brother Jehoiakim (Eliakim) as king of Judah (2 Kgs 23:28–37). Meanwhile, the "two great riverine kingdoms [Egypt and Babylon] seesawed in relationship to one another" until Babylon's pivotal victory at the battle of Carchemish (ca. 605) "usher[ed] in the long rule of Babylonian Nebuchadnezzar with disastrous consequences for Judah and others in the neighborhood."[4] In Judah, Jehoiakim reigned eleven years (608–598 BCE), switching allegiances several times prior to his death, which took place as Nebuchadnezzar besieged Jerusalem for several months in retaliation for aligning with Egypt. Jehoiakim was succeeded by his son Jehoiachin, also known in the book of Jeremiah as Coniah (2 Kgs 24:6–17). Jehoiachin and other elites of Judah were deported to Babylon in what became known as the first exile (597 BCE). The Babylonians (whom the biblical text calls "Chaldeans," the name of one of the empire's ethnic groups) appointed Josiah's son Zedekiah (Mattaniah) as king, resulting in the situation of "two Davidic kings alive and heading distinct communities: one in Babylon and one in Judah."[5]

A substantial portion of the book of Jeremiah (including chapters 21–24, 27–34, 37–39) is set during the time of Zedekiah, the prophet's "primary royal partner."[6] Barbara Green describes the situation at the time of Zedekiah's reign: "Zedekiah's court will have had its pro-Egyptian faction and its pro-Babylonian adherents, with each hoping that the king would successfully play one of those major powers off against the other, to the gain of Judah."[7] After Zedekiah's rebellion against Babylon (2 Kgs 24:20), Nebuchadnezzar laid siege to Jerusalem for over a year, conquering the city

---

in 2 Kgs 23:34, Pharaoh Neco places Eliakim son of Josiah on the throne and changes his name to Jehoiakim.

3. For debates about whether Jeremiah began to preach in 627 BCE (the prevailing view) or whether the reference to the thirteenth year of King Josiah's reign pertains to Jeremiah's birth year, see Holladay, *Jeremiah*, 9–14.

4. Barbara Green, *Jeremiah and God's Plans of Well-Being* (Columbia: University of South Carolina Press, 2013), 7.

5. Green, *Jeremiah and God's Plans*, 6.

6. Green, *Jeremiah and God's Plans*, 7.

7. Green, *Jeremiah and God's Plans*, 7.

in 587. Zedekiah was apprehended trying to escape from the city. The king was forced to witness the execution of his family before being blinded and taken to Babylon in chains (2 Kgs 25:1–7).

These political and military events are the context for Jeremiah's ministry and the biblical book that bears his name. The book of Jeremiah is filled with third-person narrative, first-person autobiographical accounts, diatribes, oracles addressed to listeners in the name of God, and the prophet's own laments and struggles with God. Through poetic words, prophetic actions, vivid imagery, and object lessons, God and the prophet endeavor to call the people away from idolatry and back to the worship of the Lord. The biblical text characterizes the Judean people and their leaders as frustrated with Jeremiah's preaching. It describes Jeremiah's lively confrontations with false prophets and erring political leaders. It recounts the conflicted sentiments of King Zedekiah, the siege by the Babylonian army, the drought that afflicted the people, Jeremiah's imprisonment in the cistern, and his subsequent rescue.

Jeremiah reports his own struggles to keep the Judeans faithful to the God of Israel who had brought them from Egypt and established a covenant with them. He castigates those who follow other gods. He regards the Babylonian siege of Jerusalem to be punishment for Judean idolatry and their refusal to trust in the Lord alone. Jeremiah also voices complaints to God (12:1–4) and curses the day of his birth (20:14). Diane Jacobson and Robert Kysar observe: "Most notable in Jeremiah is the presence of personal laments. Through the laments, the private anxiety of the prophet and his struggle and relationship with God become part of the message of the book."[8] Biblical scholars have identified five of these personal laments or "confessions," which are found in 11:18–12:6; 15:10–21; 17:14–18; 18:19–23; and 20:7–18.[9]

Chapters 30–33, commonly called Jeremiah's "Book of Consolation," constitute the most hopeful section of the book. God promises restoration, healing, return from exile, and a new covenant written on the people's hearts (31:31–33). As a prophetic sign of hope during the time of the siege of Jerusalem, Jeremiah purchased a field from his cousin and carefully described the process entailed in the real estate transaction, including the gathering of witnesses and the writing of the deed (32:6–15). He declared that, when the

---

8. Diane L. Jacobson and Robert Kysar, *A Beginner's Guide to the Books of the Bible* (Minneapolis: Augsburg, 1991), 55.

9. See Michael D. Coogan, *A Brief Introduction to the Old Testament: The Hebrew Bible in Its Context* (New York: Oxford University Press, 2009), 303.

Lord restored the fortunes of Judah, the land would no longer be desolate. Fields would once again have value, purchases of this sort would resume, and deeds would be written (32:43–44).

Medieval Christian commentators approached the complex text of the book of Jeremiah in various ways, seeking understanding of the text and its pastoral applications for their own times. Some scholars harvested and collated the exegetical work of the church fathers and other predecessors. Several Christian authors turned to Jewish sources for solutions to puzzling passages. A number of authors developed imaginative—even fanciful—reflections on the text and applied them in ways that Jeremiah could never have envisioned. For instance, in the commentary of the thirteenth-century Dominican Hugh of St. Cher, the bones of the Judean priests desecrated by Babylonian grave robbers (Jer 8:1–2) represent the sins of a bishop that come to light after his death and scandalize the faithful.[10] Most Christian commentators looked for parallels between Jeremiah and Christ: both of them were sanctified in their mothers' wombs (Jer 1:5); both of them preached and suffered in Jerusalem; both of them prophesied the destruction of the city.

Medieval Christians inherited and expanded on a tradition that identified multiple senses of Scripture. In addition to a literal or historical sense, there were mystical or spiritual senses that could include allegory, anagogy (images related to heaven, hell, judgment, and the soul's final rest), and moral readings (also called tropologies).[11] For instance, in Jeremiah 7:29, God tells the prophet to shave his hair and scatter it to the wind, as an image of the Judean people scattered after the destruction of Jerusalem—an image of punishment and desolation. However, in a moral reading of this verse, shaving one's hair means to cast off earthly things, something that has a positive connotation for Hugh of St Cher.[12]

Most medieval commentators on Jeremiah sought first to discern the literal sense of the text, endeavoring to understand what the biblical text meant in its historical context.[13] Attention to the literal sense, or "letter," of

---

10. See Hugh of St. Cher's comments on Jer 8:1–3, translated in this volume.

11. See the discussion in Frans van Liere, *An Introduction to the Medieval Bible* (New York: Cambridge University Press, 2014), 120–23.

12. See Hugh of St. Cher's comments on Jer 7:29–31, translated in this volume.

13. The patristic and medieval understanding of the "literal sense" differs from what some present-day "biblical literalists" mean by a literal interpretation. The literal sense included many of the things that modern-day text critics study, such as philology and historical context. The literal sense allowed for hyperbole, exaggeration, and symbolic use of language. It also allowed for cases where the medieval interpreter could conclude that historical events

the text included the tasks of clarifying obscure vocabulary, explaining ancient customs, establishing chronological sequence, and considering alternative translations, such as the Septuagint and other ancient Greek translations. Also included in the literal sense is the challenging task of discerning who is speaking in the text—Jeremiah, God, or the Judean people. For instance, commentators note that the words of Jeremiah 8:18, "My sorrow is above sorrow," could be the speech of either God or the prophet, voicing compassion and distress for the people.[14] Another method used in literal interpretation, especially in the thirteenth and fourteenth centuries, was *divisio textus* (textual division), the process of dividing the biblical text into thematic units and subunits, as an organizational technique.

Allegorical readings, part of the "spiritual sense," generally viewed the prophet Jeremiah and his sufferings as a prefiguring of Christ and his passion. Of particular note, early and medieval Christian interpreters perceived the cross of Christ in the Latin translation of Jeremiah 11:19: "Let us throw wood on his bread, and let us erase him from the land of the living." The original Hebrew reads, "Let us destroy the tree with its bread [i.e., fruit]." Following the Septuagint, Jerome had translated the text as "throw wood on his bread," believing that Jeremiah's enemies had tried to poison the prophet's food with wood from the toxic yew tree.[15] Many early and medieval commentators on this passage asserted that, interpreted according to the spiritual sense, this verse shows that the "bread" of Christ's body suffered on the "wood" of the cross.[16] The same passage could yield other readings, such as the claim that "bread" signifies Jeremiah's and Christ's teaching. Opponents threw "wood" on the "bread" when they regarded such teaching to be like a shepherd's menacing wooden rod rather than wholesome nourishment offered in loving-kindness.[17]

Allegorical and moral readings of biblical texts were frequently used

---

occurred in a different sequence than that reported in Scripture. Furthermore, according to the literal sense, a reference to David or Solomon (for instance) might actually be a reference to Christ rather than to the Old Testament figure; a reference to Jerusalem might be about the church rather than the Judean city. See the discussion in Joy A. Schroeder, ed. and trans., *The Book of Genesis*, The Bible in Medieval Tradition 3 (Grand Rapids: Eerdmans, 2015), 4–5; and Deeana Copeland Klepper, *The Insight of Unbelievers: Nicholas of Lyra and Christian Reading of Jewish Text in the Later Middle Ages* (Philadelphia: University of Pennsylvania Press, 2007), 35.

14. See Hugh of St. Cher's comments on Jer 8:18, translated in this volume.

15. See the discussion of this passage in Jerome, *Commentary on Jeremiah*, trans. Michael Graves, ed. Christopher A. Hall, Ancient Christian Texts (Downers Grove, IL: IVP Academic, 2011), 75n302.

16. See Thomas Aquinas's comments on Jer 11:18–23, translated in this volume.

17. See Albert the Great's comments on Jer 1:5b, translated in this volume.

in medieval preaching. One such homiletic application of Jeremiah is found in a late-twelfth-century vernacular Old English sermon on Jeremiah's imprisonment in the cistern (Jer 38:6), *Hic dicendum est de propheta* (This should be said regarding the prophet). The anonymous author, interpreting the text morally, writes: "Dear men, we find in holy book *[sic]* that Jeremiah the prophet stood in a pit and in the mire up to his mouth; and when he had stood there awhile then his body became very feeble, and they took ropes and cast unto him for to draw him out of this pit."[18] In this homily, Jeremiah represents the sinner who has not yet confessed one's mortal sins: "The pit denotes deepness of sin, for as long as we lie in [deadly sins] all of that time we stand in the pit and also the mire . . . up to the mouth, as these men do that lie in adultery and gluttony, and perjury and pride, and in other foul sins."[19] The harsh ropes lowered down to Jeremiah symbolize the harshness of confession and penance, but these are softened by the cloths, representing prayers, sent from the king's house, the church (Jer 38:11-12).

Medieval Christians interpreters, like their early Christian counterparts, regarded Jeremiah as a divinely inspired prophet, recipient of revelations, and powerful spokesman for God. Sanctified in his mother's womb, he was appointed as "prophet to the nations" (Jer 1:5). When treating the book of Jeremiah, a number of biblical commentators, especially beginning in the thirteenth century, discussed the nature of prophecy and the means by which prophets receive revelation and foreknowledge of coming events. For instance, thirteenth-century Dominican interpreter Albert the Great offered a definition of prophet: "For a prophet, who is also called 'soothsayer,' is said to be one who 'speaks from afar' or 'speaks for others' by the power of the mind, because that person utters mysteries to others by the power of a mind illuminated by divine revelation."[20] Albert believed that God implanted within prophets the "mirror of eternity" (*speculum aeternitatis*), which was "a created representation of the divine eternity."[21] The biblical prophets' knowl-

---

18. *Hic dicendum est de propheta*, in *Old English Homilies and Homiletic Treatises (Sawles warde, and þe wohunge of Ure Lauerd: Ureisuns of Ure Louerd and of Ure Lefdi, &c.) of the Twelfth and Thirteenth Centuries*, ed. Richard Morris, Early English Text Society, First Series, 29 (London: Trübner, 1868), 46. For a discussion of this text, see Joseph Hall, ed., *Selections from Early Middle English 1130–1250*, part 2, *Notes* (London: Oxford University Press, 1920), 421–27.

19. *Hic dicendum est de propheta*, 48.

20. See Albert the Great's comments on Jer 1:5c, translated in this volume.

21. Carl J. Peter, *Participated Eternity in the Vision of God: A Study of the Opinions of Thomas Aquinas and His Commentators on the Duration of the Acts of Glory*, Analecta Gregoriana 142 (Rome: Gregorian University Press, 1964), 53.

edge was finite compared to God's infinite knowing; nevertheless they received significant divine revelation by gazing into this mirror. Albert states: "The prophets read from this mirror when they received revelation."[22]

In the prologue to his commentary on Jeremiah, Thomas Aquinas writes: "God's prophets are those who receive illumination from God about future events through the mediation of angels."[23] Thomas distinguishes true prophecy from false prophecy, which is mediated through demons and—during Old Testament times—was conveyed to the prophets of Baal and other idols. True prophets are endowed with prophetic gifts and are united with God.[24] Both Albert and Thomas quoted Wisdom 7:27, asserting that God's Spirit of wisdom "conveys itself into holy souls and makes them friends of God and prophets."[25] Thomas also emphasized that prophets such as Jeremiah serve as a mediator between God and the people.[26] Jeremiah received some of his revelations through dreams and visions, and he conveyed his message through "similitudes and figures."[27] Commentators such as Hugh of St. Cher found it significant that Jeremiah saw the fall of Jerusalem "not only through spiritual revelation" but also "with his bodily eyes."[28] Thus Jeremiah was foreteller of the event as well as eyewitness to the destruction that he had predicted. Medieval commentators generally believed that he was the author of Lamentations, which describes the fall of Jerusalem in poignant verse.[29]

Authors and Texts

In this volume I provide selections from seven commentators, representing a chronological range of over six hundred years and a variety of medieval approaches to biblical interpretation. To the best of my knowledge, none of

22. See Albert's comments on Jer 1:5c, translated in this volume.

23. Thomas Aquinas, "Prologue," in *On Jeremiah*, in *Opera Omnia* (Parma: Fiaccadori, 1863), 14:577.

24. Thomas Aquinas, "Prologue," 577–78.

25. See Albert's comments on Jer 1:5c, translated in this volume; and Thomas Aquinas, "Prologue," 578.

26. Thomas Aquinas, "Prologue," 578. Here Thomas cites Moses's words to the Israelites in Deut 5:5: "I was the mediator and stood between God and you."

27. Thomas Aquinas, "Prologue," 578.

28. Hugh of St. Cher, "Prologue," in *On Jeremiah*, in *Opera Omnia in Universum Vetus & Novum Testamentum: Tomi Octo In Libros Prophetarum, Isaiae, Ieremiae, & eiusdem Threnorum, Baruch* (Lyon: Ioannes Antonius Huguetan and Guillielmus Barbier, 1669), 4:175v.

29. See, for instance, Hugh of St. Cher, "Prologue," 355.

these selections has yet been translated into English. These commentators are Rabanus Maurus (ca. 780–856), Rupert of Deutz (ca. 1075–1129/1130), Albert the Great (ca. 1206–1280), Hugh of St. Cher (ca. 1200–1263), Thomas Aquinas (ca. 1225–1274), Nicholas of Lyra (ca. 1270–1349), and Denis the Carthusian (1402–1471).

Monastic, mendicant, and university approaches to biblical interpretation are represented in this selection of authors. Rabanus Maurus, a Benedictine scholar in the Carolingian period, compiled an enormous Jeremiah commentary composed largely of patristic texts.[30] The Benedictine theologian Rupert focused on the place of Jeremiah and the fall of Jerusalem in salvation history, identifying parallels between the life and ministries of Jeremiah and Jesus.[31] Thirteenth-century Dominicans are well represented in this volume.[32] I include Albert the Great's comments on the call of Jeremiah (1:4–10), the only portion of his massive Jeremiah commentary that is still extant.[33] This fragment contains a scholastic discussion of the different "stages" of Jeremiah's calling and provides a ranking of the prenatal consecrations of the Virgin Mary, John the Baptist, and Jeremiah. The Dominican postill (commentary) of Hugh of St. Cher, excerpted here, was most likely a collaborative effort by friars working under Hugh's direction, offering literal and moral interpretations that frequently addressed thirteenth-century clergy misconduct.[34] Another Dominican, Thomas Aquinas, attended primarily to the literal meaning of the text, interpreting chiefly through an orderly "division of the text."[35] I include portions of the literal commentary of Nicholas of Lyra, a fourteenth-century Franciscan famed for his attention

30. Rabanus Maurus, *Exposition on the Prophet Jeremiah*, PL 111:797–1272.

31. Rupert of Deutz, *On the Holy Trinity and Its Works: On Jeremiah*, ed. Hrabanus Haacke, CCCM 23 (Turnhout: Brepols, 1971), 1571–91.

32. Thirteenth-century Dominican biblical scholars were especially prolific. Andrew Sulavik asserts that, between the years 1230 and 1275, Dominican masters produced more postils on Scripture than any other group in Paris; introduction to William of Luxi, *Opera*, ed. Andrew T. Sulavik, CCCM 219 (Turnhout: Brepols, 2005), x.

33. A fragment of Albert the Great's *Postillae super Ieremiam* is preserved in Codex Bruges, Bibl. du Séminaire 103/129, with a critical edition edited by Henricus Ostlender, printed in *Opera Alberti Magni* (Monasterii Westfalorum: Aschendorff, 1952), 19:633–37.

34. Hugh of St. Cher, *On Jeremiah*, in *Opera Omnia*, 4:175r–282r. The word *postill* is probably a composite of *post* (after) and *illa* (those, i.e., those words). See Ian Christopher Levy, Philip D. W. Krey, and Thomas Ryan, trans. and eds., *The Letter to the Romans*, The Bible in Medieval Tradition 2 (Grand Rapids: Eerdmans, 2013), 50.

35. The text is found in Thomas Aquinas, *On Jeremiah*, in *Opera Omnia* (Parma: Fiaccadori, 1863), 14:577–667.

to the Hebrew text and Jewish sources.[36] His comments translated in this volume focus on Christological readings of "the righteous branch of David" (23:5) and other messianic promises. Early printed editions of Nicholas's postills regularly include exegetical comments added by Paul of Burgos (née Solomon ha-Levi), a Spanish rabbi who converted to Christianity and later became archbishop of Burgos. I have included his additions in this volume. Finally, Denis the Carthusian, a fifteenth-century scholarly monk belonging to a contemplative religious order, offers both literal and spiritual interpretations of the text.[37] These sources represent virtually every medieval Latin Jeremiah commentary currently available in print, apart from the twelfth-century *Glossa ordinaria* (which draws heavily on Rabanus Maurus) and a thirteenth-century commentary *Super Ieremiam* (*On Jeremiah*) that claims to be the work of the twelfth-century apocalyptic abbot Joachim of Fiore but was probably written during the thirteenth century by admirers of Joachim (perhaps members of the Florensian order that he founded), with later additions by other devotees.[38] The *Scholastic History* of Peter Comestor (d. ca. 1178) does include events from Jeremiah's life and ministry in its summary and explanation of 2 Kgs 22–25, but it does not treat the book of Jeremiah in a sustained way.[39]

In his *Commentary on Jeremiah*, the scholarly church father Jerome wrote about the challenges of keeping his commentary brief: "The vast length of the book [of Jeremiah] itself can be a deterrent to readers. How much

---

36. Nicholas of Lyra, "Prologue," in *Literal Postill on Jeremiah*, in *Postilla super Totam Bibliam*, vol. 2 (Strassburg, 1492; repr., Frankfurt am Main: Minerva, 1971), unpaginated.

37. Denis the Carthusian, *Exposition on Jeremiah*, in *Opera Omnia* (Monstrolii: Typis Cartusiae Sanctae Mariae de Pratis, 1900), 9:5–312.

38. Robert Moynihan, "The Development of the 'Pseudo-Joachim' Commentary 'Super Hieremiam': New Manuscript Evidence," *Mélanges de l'Ecole française de Rome, Moyen-Age, Tempes modernes* 98 (1986): 109–42. The Pseudo-Joachim commentary will be discussed later in this introduction. Regarding the *Glossa ordinaria*, E. Ann Matter writes: "In the case of Jeremiah, it seems that the *Glossa Ordinaria* is quoting Hrabanus quoting Jerome"; "The Church Fathers and the *Glossa Ordinaria*," in *The Reception of the Church Fathers in the West: From the Carolingians to the Maurists*, ed. Irena Doreta Backus (Leiden: Brill, 1997), 1:101. Other medieval Jeremiah commentaries not yet in a printed or critical edition include a postill, extant in several manuscripts, composed by thirteenth-century Dominican commentator William of Luxi, also known as William of Alton. See Timothy Bellamah, *The Biblical Interpretation of William of Alton*, Oxford Studies in Historical Theology (New York: Oxford University Press, 2011), 169. There is a critical edition of the prologue to William's Jeremiah postill in William of Luxi, *Opera*, 131–32.

39. Peter Comestor, *Scholastic History—The Book of 2 Kings*, PL 198:1416–27.

more if the book is discussed by us too extensively!"[40] The book of Jeremiah is fifty-two chapters, and most medieval commentators offered lengthy explanations on each verse. Space limitations prevented me from covering all of Jeremiah in this volume. Therefore I selected chapters of particular interest to preachers and biblical scholars. All chapters of Jeremiah found in major western Christian lectionaries are included here, so that ministers can consult this volume as part of sermon preparation. Additionally, I consulted several biblical scholars to see which chapters would be considered essential for researchers interested in the history of interpretation. Contained in this volume are comments on twenty-four chapters. It is material that includes Jeremiah's call (Jer 1), numerous warnings and calls to repentance (Jer 2–4, 7–9), his preaching in the gate (Jer 7), most of the "confessions of Jeremiah" (Jer 11, 15, 17, 18, 20),[41] the prophet's prayer for the people during the drought (Jer 14), his visit to the potter's house (Jer 18), messianic promises (Jer 23), Hananiah's prophecy and his breaking of the chains that Jeremiah had been wearing as a prophetic sign (Jer 28), Jeremiah's letter to the exiles in Babylon (Jer 29), his purchase of a field (Jer 32), the "Book of Consolation" (Jer 30–33), the burning of the scroll (Jer 36), Jeremiah's imprisonment and his descent into the cistern (Jer 37–38), and the siege and fall of Jerusalem (Jer 39). Though I was not able to cover every passage that might be of interest to scholars and religious leaders, it is my hope that the resulting selection provides a generous "sampler" that introduces the reader to the fascinating variety of medieval approaches to biblical interpretation.

Space limitations likewise prevented me from offering multiple authors' interpretation of the same passages, apart from Jer 1, which is here covered by two commentators, Rupert of Deutz and Albert the Great, whose extant commentaries deal chiefly with the prophet's opening chapter. With the exception of these selections from Albert and Rupert, I have organized the translations chronologically, so that readers can observe the development of exegetical methods and see how later authors drew on (or reacted to) earlier authors. For instance, Nicholas of Lyra frequently takes issue with Hugh of St. Cher, and Denis the Carthusian regularly cites Nicholas of Lyra. A limitation to this approach—breadth of coverage rather than multiple treatments of the same text—is that it precludes side-by-side comparisons

40. Jerome, *On Jeremiah* 7:32–33, ed. Sigofredus Reiter, CCSL 74 (Turnhout: Brepols, 1960), 85.
41. Apart from Jer 12:1–6, which is a portion of Jeremiah's first lament, all of the material identified as "confessions" is included in this volume.

of different authors on the same chapters and verses. However, it is my hope that this collection of substantial excerpts, organized chronologically, will nevertheless help the reader gain a good sense of the hermeneutical methods not only of these particular writers but also of medieval Christian interpreters in general. As the reader will observe, medieval commentators on Jeremiah labored earnestly to penetrate the depths of Jeremiah's message, endeavoring to understand the biblical text in its historical context and to find contemporary theological and pastoral applications.

Patristic Interpretations of Jeremiah

Relatively few of the church fathers wrote sustained commentaries on the book of Jeremiah.[42] Apart from a few fragments from Cyril of Alexandria (d. 444) and Ephrem (ca. 306–373), or Pseudo-Ephrem, preserved in catenae (collections), commentaries or sermon collections from only a handful of early authors are extant.[43] These writings include twenty sermons by Origen of Alexandria (ca. 185–ca. 254) preserved in Greek; fourteen of his sermons, translated into Latin by Jerome, also survive.[44] Working in the 440s, Theodoret of Cyrrhus (ca. 393–ca. 458) wrote a commentary in Greek.[45] Also in existence is a commentary spuriously attributed to John Chrysostom.[46] A Syriac commentary on Jeremiah by the theologian and poet Narsai (399–502) has been lost.[47]

Interpretations of particular passages from Jeremiah are found in other early Christian writings.[48] For instance, in his *Moralia on Job*, Gregory the

---

42. Seth B. Tarrer, *Reading with the Faithful: Interpretation of True and False Prophecy in the Book of Jeremiah from Ancient Times to Modern*, Journal of Theological Interpretation Supplements 6 (Winona Lake, IN: Eisenbrauns 2013), 5. Also see Dean O. Wenthe, ed., *Jeremiah, Lamentations*, ACCS Old Testament 12 (Downers Grove, IL: InterVarsity Press, 2009), xxii–xxvi.

43. David Balás and D. Jeffrey Bingham, "Patristic Exegesis of the Books of the Bible," in Charles Kannengiesser, *Handbook of Patristic Exegesis: The Bible in Ancient Christianity* (Boston: Brill, 2006), 313–14.

44. Origen, *Homilies on Jeremiah*, ed. P. Nautin and P. Hussen, SC 232, 238 (Paris: Éditions du Cerf, 1976–1977); PL 25:583–692.

45. Theodoret of Cyrrhus, *Interpretatio in Ieremiam*, PG 81:496–805. See Jean-Noël, "Theodoret of Cyrus," in Kannengiesser, *Handbook*, 890.

46. Pseudo-Chrysostom, *Fragmenta in Ieremiam*, PG 64:740–1037.

47. Joseph Chalassery, *The Holy Spirit and Christian Initiation in the East Syrian Tradition* (Rome: Mar Thoma Yogam, 1995), 69.

48. See the numerous examples offered in Wenthe, *Jeremiah, Lamentations*, 1–271.

Great (ca. 540–604) said that the ropes used to lift Jeremiah out of the cistern (Jer 38:12–13) symbolized the Lord's commands, which bind believers tightly and draw them up, away from situations of evildoing. Since the strong, demanding ropes of the divine commands might offer injury to frail followers of Christ, they—like Jeremiah—should cushion their arms against the strain of the ropes by using the old rags, which represent the examples of the ancient ancestors that offer support to those who are weak.[49] In his eighth hymn for the feast of the Epiphany of Christ, the poet Ephrem the Syrian compared baptism to the sanctification of the prenatal Jeremiah (Jer 1:5). If, in the womb, Jeremiah could be sanctified and taught by God, how much more are Christians purified in the womb of baptism.[50]

By far, the most influential patristic treatment of Jeremiah in the western church was the work of Jerome (ca. 345–420), who wrote a Latin commentary on the first thirty-two chapters.[51] A scholarly monk living in Bethlehem, he spent the years 391–405 translating the Old Testament from Hebrew into Latin, creating the text that he called *iuxta Hebraeos* (according to the Hebrews) and which came to be called the Vulgate.[52] As a mature man, in his late sixties, Jerome most likely commenced work on the Jeremiah commentary in 414. He died before he could complete the volume.[53] Jerome dedicated the commentary to Eusebius of Cremona, an influential abbot who raised funds for a hostel for pilgrims in Bethlehem.[54] Most of Jerome's commentary treats the text *ad litteram* ("literally," "according to the letter" of the text). Jerome offers explanations and answers to confusing matters arising from the text, such as the question of who is speaking in a particular passage—God or the prophet?[55]

As is apparent from the portions of Jerome's commentary used by Rabanus Maurus in the selection translated in this present volume, Jerome's comments on Jeremiah are highly lexical and philological. Jerome defines Hebrew words and discusses the variances between the Hebrew text and the

49. Gregory the Great, *Moralia on Job* 25.7, PL 76:329.

50. Chalassery, *The Holy Spirit and Christian Initiation*, 56.

51. Jerome, *On Jeremiah*, ed. Sigofredus Reiter, CCSL 74 (Turnhout: Brepols, 1960).

52. Michael Graves, "Translator's Introduction," in Jerome, *Commentary on Jeremiah*, xxvii.

53. Michael Graves, *Jerome's Hebrew Philology: A Study Based on His Commentary on Jeremiah*, Supplements to Vigiliae Christianae 90 (Boston: Brill 2007), 10.

54. Tarrer, *Reading with the Faithful*, 12.

55. "Jerome was keenly aware of how difficult it could be to identify the speaker, especially in the prophets"; Graves, *Jerome's Hebrew Philology*, 34.

different Greek translations of Jeremiah. While living in Palestine, Jerome
had opportunity to learn from and consult Jewish scholars about the Hebrew
text of Jeremiah, in conversations that were likely conducted in Greek.[56] As
he worked on his Jeremiah commentary, Jerome regularly consulted the
Septuagint (LXX) translation of Jeremiah, a Greek translation made by Jews
living in Egypt in the second century BCE.[57] He also had access to the Greek
translations of Symmachus, a second-century-CE Ebionite (Jewish Christian) or Samaritan who converted to Judaism, and Theodotion, a second-
century-CE Jewish translator. Jerome similarly consulted the Greek revision
of the Septuagint made by Aquila, a second-century-CE convert to Judaism.[58]

Jerome's commentary provides the reader with Latin translations of the
Hebrew text and of the significant Greek variants.[59] Sometimes he explains
that the Septuagint varies from the "Hebrew Truth" (*Hebraica veritas*) and is
less accurate than Aquila, Symmachus, and Theodotion. Yet Jerome also asserts the value of the Septuagint translation, which was "the church's regnant
text in his day."[60] For instance in his discussion of Jer 2:23, about whether
a phrase should be translated "swift runner" or "swift dromedary," Jerome
notes: "In this passage the Septuagint edition is significantly different from
the Hebrew Truth, but each has its own meaning."[61] Jerome tended to use the

---

56. Graves, *Jerome's Hebrew Philology*, 95.

57. For background on the LXX and its significance in early Christianity, see Timothy
Michael Law, *When God Spoke Greek: The Septuagint and the Making of the Christian Bible* (New
York: Oxford University Press, 2013); see page 53 for the dating of LXX translation of Jeremiah.

58. For information on the Greek translations and revisions of the Old Testament, see
Ernst Würthwein, *The Text of the Old Testament: An Introduction to the "Biblia Hebraica,"* rev.
and expanded by Alexander Achilles Fischer, trans. Erroll F. Rhodes (Grand Rapids: Eerdmans,
2014), 106–10, 145–48. For a discussion of Jerome's access to and use of Greek translations of
Jeremiah, see Graves, *Jerome's Hebrew Philology*, 92–106.

59. For a detailed discussion of the LXX text of Jeremiah, including its substantial
variances from the Hebrew Masoretic text, see Marvin A. Sweeney, *Form and Intertextuality in
Prophetic and Apocalyptic Literature* (Tübingen: Mohr Siebeck, 2005), 65–77; Albert Pietersma
and Marc Saunders, "To the Reader of Ieremias," in *A New English Translation of the Septuagint*,
ed. Albert Pietersma and Benjamin G. Wright (New York: Oxford University Press, 2007),
876–81; and Law, *When God Spoke Greek*, 28–30, 52–53. Law argues: "The differences between
the Greek and Hebrew Bible are often not only to do with small details. The new consensus, but
one that some commentators have still not fully appreciated, is that the Septuagint is not merely
a guide to understand the Hebrew Bible better, but is sometimes our only source preserving
alternative versions of the Hebrew scriptures" (*When God Spoke Greek*, 21).

60. Tarrer, *Reading with the Faithful*, 11.

61. Jerome, *On Jeremiah* 2:23c–24, CCSL 74:23. See the entire passage from Jerome, as
quoted in Rabanus Maurus, *Exposition on Jeremiah* 2:23c–24, in this volume.

Hebrew text to treat the literal sense of Scripture, such as historical events and philological matters. He looked for spiritual and allegorical meanings in the Septuagint.[62] Jerome's tendency to associate the spiritual sense with the Septuagint was likely inspired by Origen of Alexandria, whose work he knew well.[63] In his Jeremiah commentary, Jerome treated a verse or two at a time, first providing textual variants when applicable, followed by historical explanation. Then, particularly when treating passages about divine judgment against the Judeans, Jerome frequently asserted that the same passage could be directed against heretics, false teachers, or corrupt church leaders of his own day. Thus Jeremiah's words to the people of Jerusalem were appropriate for ecclesiastical correction. Since Rabanus Maurus, writing in the early Middle Ages, draws heavily on Jerome's commentary on Jeremiah, the reader of this volume can see Jerome's attention to the "Hebrew Truth," the Greek variant translations, and his pastoral applications of Old Testament prophecies of judgment in that commentary.

Rabanus Maurus and Carolingian Interpretation

Maxentius Rabanus was born circa 783 to noble parents in the Frankish walled city of Mainz. His name Rabanus (also spelled Hrabanus and Rhabanus) means "raven" or "crow."[64] In 788, Rabanus's parents dedicated their child to the Benedictine monastery of Fulda, ninety miles from Mainz. The young monk studied at the cloister school at Fulda and was ordained a deacon in 801. The following year he continued his studies of theology and the liberal arts at the abbey of Saint Martin's at Tours. There the renowned scholar Alcuin of York (ca. 740–804), who had previously headed Charlemagne's Palace School at Aachen, served as abbot and shepherded a circle of talented scholars. At Tours, Rabanus was introduced to "the precocious court culture of Charlemagne's reign, in which gifted students sought out esoteric knowledge from manuscript sources."[65] Alcuin, who described himself as a mother bird feeding the student-chicks with learning and piety in his "beloved nest" at Tours, gave Rabanus the nickname *Corvulus* (little crow).

---

62. Graves, *Jerome's Hebrew Philology*, 198.

63. For a discussion of Origen's desire to interpret the Septuagint and "understand positively the divergences with the Hebrew text," see Law, *When God Spoke Greek*, 145.

64. Lynda L. Coon, *Dark Age Bodies: Gender and Monastic Practice in the Early Medieval West*, The Middle Ages (Philadelphia: University of Pennsylvania Press, 2011), 14–16.

65. Coon, *Dark Age Bodies*, 17.

Alcuin also called him Maurus, after St. Benedict's beloved disciple—a sign that the close relationship between Alcuin and Rabanus resembled that of Benedict and Maurus.[66]

After his studies in Tours, Rabanus returned to Fulda, where he served as master of the cloister school at Fulda. He was ordained to the priesthood in 814 and was elected abbot in 822.[67] Under Rabanus, the monastic school became famous for its scholarship, impressive library, and literary output.[68] A number of celebrated scholars, including Walafrid Strabo (ca. 808–849), studied there.

Rabanus was among the most prolific and influential of the Carolingian biblical scholars. His works include poetry and a book of instruction for the clergy (*De clericorum institutione*).[69] He wrote commentaries on most of the Old Testament books and a number of New Testament books (Matthew, the Pauline Letters, and the Letter to the Hebrews), dedicating them to prominent individuals, especially the Frankish emperors. Empresses received commentaries on the books of Judith and Esther.[70] Mayke de Jong comments: "Beginning with Charlemagne, generations of Carolingian rulers were offered the choice fruits of the exegetical labour of the most learned men of the realm. These were rulers who measured themselves against the kings and leaders of the Old Testament—David, Solomon, Moses, Joshua, Josiah—and who took a lively interest in biblical commentary, particularly if it dealt with Old Testament 'history.'"[71] Expert readers (*peritissimi lectores*) apparently read the biblical commentaries aloud at the emperor's court.[72] For Rabanus, dedicating commentaries to rulers was a form

---

66. Coon, *Dark Age Bodies*, 16.

67. Priscilla Throop, introduction to Rabanus Maurus, *De Universo: The Peculiar Properties of Words and Their Mystical Significance*, trans. Priscilla Throop (Charlotte, VT: MedievalMS, 2009), 1:x.

68. Janneke Raaijmakers, *The Making of the Monastic Community of Fulda, c. 744–c. 900* (New York: Cambridge University Press, 2012), 189.

69. Rabanus Maurus, *Carmina*, ed. Ernst Dümmler, MGH Poetae 2 (Berlin: Weidmann, 1844), 159–244; Rabanus Maurus, *De institutione clericorum*, ed. Detlev Zimpel, Freiburger Beiträge zur mittelalterlichen Geschichte: Studien und Texte 7 (Frankfurt: Peter Lang, 1996).

70. Mayke de Jong, "Exegesis for an Empress," in *Medieval Transformations: Texts, Power, and Gifts in Context*, ed. Esther Cohen and Mayke B. de Jong, Cultures, Beliefs and Traditions: Medieval and Early Modern Peoples 11 (Boston: Brill, 2001), 69, 73.

71. De Jong, "Exegesis for an Empress," 71.

72. Mayke de Jong, "Old Law and New-Found Power: Hrabanus Maurus and the Old Testament," in *Centres of Learning: Learning and Location in Pre-modern Europe and the Near East*, ed. Jan Willem Drijvers and Alasdair A. MacDonald (New York: Brill, 1995), 165.

of political expression. In the midst of a rebellion by the three oldest sons of Emperor Louis the Pious in 833, Rabanus showed his support for Louis by creating a compilation of biblical texts commending sons' obedience to fathers and subjects' obedience to leaders.[73] At a time of stormy struggles for succession following Louis's death in 840, Louis's eldest son, Lothar, commissioned commentaries on Ezekiel and Jeremiah. Rabanus honored Lothar's request. Presentation of these works was a public way for Rabanus to assert his view that Lothar was the legitimate successor. Rabanus's preface to his *Exposition on the Prophet Jeremiah,* which was finished in 841, included a vow of lifelong faithfulness to Lothar.[74] De Jong suggests that the timing of the Jeremiah commentary was purposeful: "There was nothing arbitrary about Hrabanus' choice of specific biblical commentary for male rulers: to send the Emperor Lothar an exposition of Jeremiah lamenting the destruction of a kingdom at a time when he was still at war with his brothers was an appropriate and seasonal gift."[75]

In 842, after Lothar's military defeat at the hands of his brother Louis the German, Rabanus concluded his service as Fulda's abbot—either because he was removed from his post due to his support of Lothar or because he withdrew into voluntary retirement.[76] The Treaty of Verdun (843) divided the Frankish empire between the brothers, and Louis was given control of the eastern portion, where Fulda was located. For five years Rabanus lived in scholarly retreat on abbey grounds, about two miles from the abbey, and devoted his time to writing biblical commentaries and the completion of *De rerum naturis,* a magisterial scientific work dedicated to Louis the German, with whom Rabanus eventually made peace.[77] With Louis's support, Rabanus became archbishop of Mainz in 847. In this capacity he dealt with a number of public disputes, including a controversy with his former student, Gottschalk of Orbais (ca. 804–ca. 869), regarding predestination.[78] Rabanus served as archbishop until his death in 856.

73. De Jong, "Exegesis for an Empress," 72.
74. Rabanus Maurus, preface to *Exposition on the Prophet Jeremiah,* PL 111:795.
75. De Jong, "Exegesis for an Empress," 72.
76. Coon, *Dark Age Bodies,* 34–35.
77. Rabanus Maurus, *De rerum naturis,* PL 111:9–614. See Coon, *Dark Age Bodies,* 37. Louis the German also received commentaries on Daniel and the Maccabees, as well as other exegetical works. See de Jong, "Old Law and New-Found Power," 168.
78. See Gottschalk of Orbais, *Gottschalk and a Medieval Predestination Controversy: Texts Translated from the Latin,* ed. and trans. Victor Genke and Francis X. Gumerlock (Milwaukee: Marquette University Press, 2010), 29–31, 36–38.

Introduction

As was the case with most of the Carolingian biblical scholars who were his contemporaries, Rabanus created commentaries by carefully selecting excerpts from patristic authors and other predecessors. His *Exposition on the Prophet Jeremiah* draws primarily from Jerome's *Commentary on Jeremiah*, which includes philological matters, the historical meaning of the text, and moral application. Rabanus also uses Origen's *Homilies on Jeremiah* (which Jerome had translated into Latin), Gregory the Great's *Moralia on Job* and *Pastoral Rule,* the *Conferences* of John Cassian (ca. 360–ca. 435), and other patristic sources. Rabanus (or monks under his direction) had carefully combed through works such as Gregory's *Moralia* to discover references to and discussions of biblical quotations—material that could be retrieved and placed in commentaries. For instance, explaining how God can cry out, "My belly, my belly" (Jer 4:19), Rabanus includes a quotation from Gregory, who had referenced Jer 4:19 to explain Job 30:27 ("My belly is in turmoil") to demonstrate that "belly" can mean "mind," since "thoughts are contained in the mind the way food is contained in the belly."[79] Occasionally this approach resulted in inaccuracies, such as several instances when Rabanus's commentary claimed to be quoting Isaiah, when in fact the biblical passage quoted was simply a slightly different translation of the very verse from Jeremiah under discussion, gleaned from Jerome's *Commentary on Isaiah.*[80] At various points in the *Exposition on the Prophet Jeremiah,* Rabanus does include some of his own words, which offer moral exhortation, allegory, or other commentary on the text. When composing his commentaries, Rabanus instructed his scribes to note the source material by writing the original authors' initials in large letters in the margins—"A" for Augustine, "B" for Bede, and so forth. He explained that an "M" in the margins signaled his own composition: "When divine grace deigned to permit me to dictate something original, I took care to note it at the outset with the letter 'M,' referring to the name 'Maurus,' which my teacher Albinus [Alcuin] of blessed memory conferred on me."[81]

Since Rabanus and his Carolingian contemporaries interpreted scripture chiefly through compilation, their work has frequently been dismissed as derivative, uninteresting, and unoriginal. However, recent scholars have pointed out the enormous intellectual and creative effort required to gather and assemble the scholarly output of their predecessors. This sort of com-

79. Gregory the Great, *Moralia on Job* 12.55.64, CCCM 143A, ed. Marcus Adriaen (Turnhout: Brepols, 1979), 668. See Rabanus's comments on 4:19, included in this volume.

80. See Rabanus's comments on Jer 2:28a and 2:30a, included in this volume.

81. Rabanus Maurus, "Letter 14," in *Hrabani (Mauri) Epistolae,* ed. Ernst Dümmler, MGH *Epistolae* 5 (Berlin: Weidmann, 1899), 403.

pilation entailed conscious choices about what material to include and how
to arrange it. Frans van Liere argues that by "selecting, paraphrasing, and
rearranging the old materials, these scholars were creating a new type of
commentary."[82]

The excerpt of Rabanus's commentary translated in this volume treats
Jer 2–4, which contains the prophet's condemnation of the Judeans' idolatry
and faithlessness. Jeremiah castigates their priests, false prophets, teachers
of the law, and wicked "shepherds" (Jer 2:8). For this section of his commentary, Rabanus selects pertinent passages from Jerome, Origen, Gregory the
Great, and Cassian. For each verse or short unit of verses, Rabanus begins
with the appropriate passage from Jerome's commentary, which usually offers philological and historical information, followed by Jerome's pastoral
application of the passage to the church of his day. For instance, Jeremiah's
condemnation of the Judeans' "wicked shepherds" elicits Jerome's statement
that these words can also be rightly directed toward the false teachers within
the church: "These words should be employed against teachers in our ranks
who devour God's people like a serving of bread."[83] The destruction of Judah
and its reduction to wilderness (Jer 4:23–25) refer to the church when it falls
into sin: "Everything we have said about Jerusalem and Judah according
to the historical sense we can apply to God's church when it offends God.
Where there once was an entire choir of virtues and gladness, there now
dwells a multitude of sins and sorrows."[84] Then, when a pertinent passage
from Gregory or another church father is available, Rabanus appends it to
the material from Jerome. Usually these passages deal with teaching and
behavior within the church—condemnation of heretics and false teachers,
criticism of corrupt clergy, and admonishment of the laity for being lax in
their devotion. The cumulative effect of gathering these patristic comments
together is that the text of Jeremiah is treated as scripture that is especially
directed toward *the church* as admonishment. When the scriptural passage
condemns the sins of the Judean people and their religious leaders, Rabanus's
commentary makes clear that Jeremiah is also—or *especially*—addressing the
sins of church members and Christian clergy. In several instances, however,
Rabanus softens Jerome's harsh rhetoric by adding his own material that
emphasizes God's forgiveness. For instance, Rabanus's discussion of Jer 4:4–5
includes Jerome's sharp warning that vices provoke God's anger. Rabanus

82. Van Liere, *Introduction to the Medieval Bible*, 148.
83. See Rabanus Maurus's comments on Jer 2:8, translated in this volume.
84. See Rabanus Maurus's comments on Jer 4:23–25, translated in this volume.

then adds several statements of his own, reminding his readers that God does not desire the death of sinners (Ezek 18:23) but, rather, offers pardon to all who repent.[85]

In his own day, Rabanus was celebrated as the leading biblical scholar. Lothar I, writing to Rabanus around 854, compared him with Jerome, Ambrose, Augustine, and Gregory the Great.[86] Rabanus's *Exposition on the Prophet Jeremiah* is extant in thirty-seven manuscripts.[87] His Jeremiah commentary also provided the essential groundwork for the treatment of Jeremiah in the *Glossa ordinaria*, the most popular biblical-study resource in the Middle Ages. Dante placed Rabanus in the company of Bonaventure, Anselm, and Aquinas in the fourth heaven of *Paradiso*, the sphere of the sun.[88]

Rupert of Deutz

Born around 1075 near Liège, Rupert entered the Benedictine abbey of St. Lawrence as a child oblate. There he became a monk, was ordained to the priesthood, and spent most of his life before his election to the office of abbot of the monastery at Deutz, near Cologne, in 1120, where he lived the remainder of his life.[89] Between the years 1112 and 1117, Rupert composed a theological commentary on the Scriptures titled *De Sancta Trinitate et operibus eius* (*On the Holy Trinity and Its Works*). His brief commentary *On Jeremiah*, excerpted in this volume, is set within *On the Holy Trinity*, which treats all of Scripture and salvation history.

Rupert's discussion of Jeremiah opens with a prologue, setting the biblical book into its chronological sequence, at the "dawn of the fifth age of the world."[90] Drawing on Augustine and other patristic interpreters, Rupert divides chronological time into seven ages, corresponding to the stages

---

85. See Rabanus Maurus's comments on Jer 4:4–5, in this volume.

86. Rabanus Maurus, "Letter 49," in *Epistolae*, 504. See Coon, *Dark Age Bodies*, 13.

87. Raymund Kottje, *Verzeichnis der Handschriften mit den Werken des Hrabanus Maurus*, MGH Hilfsmittel 27 (Hannover: Hahnsche Buchhandlung, 2012), 243.

88. Coon, *Dark Age Bodies*, 13, citing Dante, *Paradiso* 12.139.

89. For biographical details, see John H. Van Engen, *Rupert of Deutz* (Berkeley: University of California Press, 1983); Wanda Zemler-Cizewski, "The Literal Sense of Scripture according to Rupert of Deutz," in *The Multiple Meaning of Scripture: the Role of Exegesis in Early-Christian and Medieval Culture*, ed. Ineke van 't Spijker (Boston: Brill, 2009), 203–5; and Schroeder, *Book of Genesis*, 16–17.

90. Rupert of Deutz, *On Jeremiah*, CCCM 23:1572.

of human life.[91] The seven ages of the world were compared to stages in a human lifespan. After the world's infancy (the time between Adam and the great flood), childhood (the time beginning with God's covenant with Noah), adolescence (the period that includes Abraham's call and receiving the "discipline of the law" through Moses), young adulthood (which includes the kingship of David), the fifth age—full maturity—began with Jeremiah's prophetic work and lasted until the incarnation of Christ.

Rupert reads the book of Jeremiah both literally (*ad litteram*) and typologically. Finding parallels between Jeremiah and Christ throughout the book, Rupert interprets the biblical prophet as a "type" or image of Christ. God's words to Jeremiah, "Before I formed you in the womb I knew you" (1:5), can be applied to Christ, who, as the eternally begotten Son coexisting with the Father, was indeed known by God before his incarnation and formation in the Virgin Mary's womb.[92] Like Jesus, Jeremiah undertook a preaching ministry, spoke in the temple, and encountered resistance. Jeremiah predicted the fall of Jerusalem at the hand of the Babylonians, prefiguring Jesus's warnings about the Roman destruction of the city, which occurred in 70 CE. Each, in some sense, "preached" to the Gentile nations.[93] Each survived destruction—Jesus through resurrection and Jeremiah through rescue from the cistern.[94]

Wanda Zemler-Cizewski observes: "Rupert's interpretation of Scripture is essentially Trinitarian and Christological, and his reading of the Old Testament frequently conveys an explicit or implicit polemic against its Jewish interpreters."[95] Indeed, Rupert's exegesis of Jeremiah is filled with odious and offensive anti-Jewish sentiments.[96] Jeremiah's conviction that the impending fall of Jerusalem resulted from Judean disobedience prompted a comparison with the Judeans of Jesus's time. Rupert, like many medieval Christians, regarded the destruction of Jerusalem by the Romans, and the subsequent dispersion of the Jews, to be retribution for their rejection of

91. For a discussion of this tradition, see Peter Darby, *Bede and the End of Time* (Burlington, VT: Ashgate, 2012), 23.

92. Rupert of Deutz, *On Jeremiah*, CCCM 23:1576.

93. Jer 46–51 is composed of oracles against the nations.

94. Rupert of Deutz, *On Jeremiah*, CCCM 23:1574.

95. Zemler-Cizewski, "The Literal Sense of Scripture," 206.

96. For a discussion of anti-Judaism in Rupert's works, see Wanda Zemler-Cizewski, "Rupert of Deutz and the Law of the Stray Wife: Anti-Jewish Allegory in *De Sancta Trinitate et Operibus Eius*," *Recherches de Théologie et Philosophie Médiévales* 75 (2008): 257–69; and Anna Sapir Abulafia, "The Ideology of Reform and Changing Ideas concerning Jews in the Works of Rupert of Deutz and Hermanus Quondam Iudeus," *Jewish History* 7 (1993): 43–63; and Schroeder, *Book of Genesis*, 19.

Christ. Particularly harsh is Rupert's conclusion that the marginalization of the Jews of his own day was the result of appropriate divine judgment. Unlike the Babylonian exile, in which an entire people was transported to one place and remained united despite their captivity, the Roman destruction of Jerusalem resulted in a complete dispersion. Now in his time, says Rupert, Jews reside scattered in tiny villages or in small urban enclaves. The words to Jeremiah, "You shall uproot and destroy, you shall scatter and disperse, you shall build and plant" (1:10), summon Christ to inflict brutal vengeance against Jews, who will be destroyed body and soul.

> How shall you uproot and destroy them? Let the Romans come as your avengers. Let them seize their land and the people. Then let their souls, after being ripped from their bodies by the physical sword, become "prey for foxes" (Ps 63:10)—that is, for evil spirits. And you shall scatter and disperse. So you shall not only uproot them, so that you would, at least, permit them to be carried into one place of captivity but instead you shall scatter them among all the peoples and disperse them into little village footpaths or small sections of cities. And you shall build and plant. Whom? Not the aforementioned people, but others in their place.[97]

Translated for this volume are Rupert's prologue and introduction to the book of Jeremiah and his commentary on the first chapter. In the remainder of his treatment of Jeremiah, which offers cursory attention to selected verses from chapters 2 to 18, Rupert highlights aspects of the text that reinforce his conviction that God has abandoned and driven out the Jews. The words of Jer 7:11, echoed in Mark 11:17, that God's house has become "a den of robbers," prompt a discussion of Jesus's use of a whip to drive the buyers, sellers, and sacrificial animals from the temple (John 2:13–16). For Rupert, the cleansing of the temple signifies Jesus's disdain for animal sacrifices and prefigures the expulsion of the Jews from Jerusalem and the temple: "The things that follow this tearful message or speech especially foretell their expulsion, which is signified by the whip that we just mentioned. I assert that this is the expulsion in which they were handed over to the power of the Romans' sword and suffered the irrevocable destruction of the city and temple."[98] As I read and translated these texts, I was dismayed by the hostility found in Rupert's interpretation, but I include this excerpt as an illustration

97. Rupert of Deutz, *On Jeremiah,* CCCM 23:1577.
98. Rupert of Deutz, *On Jeremiah,* CCCM 23:1582.

of anti-Jewish sentiments found among many Christians throughout medieval Europe, as well as an example of typological exegesis that regarded the prophet Jeremiah as a "type" or prefiguring of Christ.

Albert the Great

Albertus Magnus (ca. 1206–1280), a Dominican theologian of knightly German descent, was known for his extensive study of science, philosophy, and theology. Even during his life, he received the appellations "the Great" (*Magnus*) and "universal doctor" (*doctor universalis*). Albert's birthplace is unknown. Since he referred to himself as "Albert of Lauingen," it is possible that he was raised in the small town of Lauingen, located on the Danube, near Ulm. On the other hand, Lauingen may be a family name.[99] Many biographers believe he studied the liberal arts at Padua and there was drawn to the Dominican order by the charismatic preacher Jordan of Saxony (ca. 1190–1237).[100] Albert continued his studies at the Dominican priory at Cologne. He served as *lector* (lecturer) at several different Dominican houses of study (Hildesheim, Freiburg, Regensburg, and Strasbourg). As *lector,* he had responsibilities for lecturing on the Bible. He was sent to Paris, where he became a Master of Theology in 1245. For several years he held one of the Dominican chairs in theology at the University of Paris before returning to Cologne.[101] Thomas Aquinas, who met Albert in Paris and followed him to Cologne, was his most famous student. From 1254 to 1257, Albert served as Provincial of the Order of Preachers in Germany. He served as bishop of Regensburg for several years (1260–1262) and then briefly spent time as a papal envoy. His final years were spent teaching at Dominican houses in Würzburg, Strasbourg, and Cologne. Throughout his life as an administrator and teacher, he was required to deal with various ecclesiastical and theological controversies, academic disputes, internal Dominican struggles, and political conflicts. Albert is renowned for

99. Simon Tugwell, "Albert the Great: Introduction," in *Albert and Thomas: Selected Writings*, trans. and ed. Simon Tugwell, Classics of Western Spirituality (Mahwah, NJ: Paulist, 1988), 3.

100. Karlfried Froehlich, "Christian Interpretation of the Old Testament in the High Middle Ages," in *Hebrew Bible / Old Testament: The History of Its Interpretation*, vol. 1, part 2, ed. Magne Saebø (Göttingen: Vandenhoeck & Ruprecht, 2000), 533; Francis J. Kovach and Robert W. Shahan, introduction to *Albert the Great: Commemorative Essays,* ed. Francis J. Kovach and Robert W. Shahan (Norman: University of Oklahoma Press, 1980), ix.

101. Tugwell, "Albert the Great," 11.

his public disputation, held at the papal court in 1256, against philosophical ideas attributed to the Muslim scholar Averroes (1126–1198).[102]

Albert's substantial written corpus includes works of theology, philosophy, natural history, and commentaries on Pseudo-Dionysius.[103] Albert composed commentaries on the four Gospels, Isaiah, Jeremiah, Lamentations, Baruch, Ezekiel, Daniel, the twelve Minor Prophets, and Job.[104] Karlfried Froehlich argues that Albert's biblical commentaries probably date from the latter part of his life, around 1264–1274, and draw on his considerable experience as a lecturer.[105]

Albert's commentaries on Isaiah and Jeremiah were massive, but unfortunately most of Albert's *Postillae super Ieremiam* (*Postills on Jeremiah*) have been lost. Only a fragment—a few pages on the "Call of Jeremiah" (Jer 1:4–10)—remains. The fragment, translated in this volume, attends primarily to the "literal" or historical meaning of the text. As a scholastic interpreter, Albert worked to find a structure in the biblical text, dividing it into parts and subparts—using multiples of three whenever possible. Regarding Albert's scholastic approach, Froehlich observes: "Albert's hermeneutics were fully in tune with contemporary scholarship. One of his major methodological procedures was the logical division of textual units, including numbered chapters; his exegetical exploration focused deliberately on the literal sense."[106]

In the passage translated in this volume, Albert describes the threefold "perfection" of Jeremiah that readied him to serve as a prophet. This perfection (*perfectio*) consisted of consecration (*consecratio*), illumination (*illuminatio*), and strengthening (*confortatio*). Then the consecration itself is divided into three parts, and Albert's text continues in this vein. Treating the statement in Jer 1:5b, "before you came out of the womb I sanctified you," Albert is concerned to rank the eminence (and relative sinfulness or sinlessness) of the biblical individuals known to have been sanctified in their mother's wombs. The Virgin Mary holds first place, followed by John the

102. Tugwell, "Albert the Great," 14.

103. See the essays in James A. Weisheipl, ed., *Albertus Magnus and the Sciences: Commemorative Essays, 1980*, Studies and Texts—Pontifical Institute of Mediaeval Studies 49 (Toronto: Pontifical Institute of Mediaeval Studies, 1980).

104. Froehlich, "Christian Interpretation," 534. See Albert Fries, "Zur Entstehungszeit der Bibelkommentare Alberts des Grossen," in *Albertus Magnus: Doctor Universalis 1280/1980*, ed. Gerbert Meyer and Albert Zimmermann, Walberberger Studien: Philosophische Reihe 6 (Mainz: Matthias-Grünewald-Verlag, 1980), 119–65.

105. Froehlich, "Christian Interpretation," 534.

106. Froehlich, "Christian Interpretation," 534–35.

Baptist, and then Jeremiah who, despite being ranked third, "nevertheless did not lack status."[107] Albert believed that the prophet received grace in utero so that, despite the abiding presence of original sin following his prenatal sanctification, Jeremiah would not succumb to some serious temptation or sin that could hinder the reception of God's prophetic spirit.

Albert read extensively and employed a wide range of sources—Christian and non-Christian—in his interpretive work. This is apparent even in the brief portion of the Jeremiah postill that has been preserved. Sources included Plato, Aristotle, Horace, Jerome, Boethius (ca. 480–ca. 524), John of Damascus (ca. 655–ca. 750), and the *Glossa ordinaria*. Aristotle's theories of perception and optics provided Albert with a conceptual framework to understand and explain how prophecy occurred. Albert and many of his contemporaries believed that there was, implanted within prophets, the "mirror of eternity," in which prophets could view past or future events in a partial or limited way.[108] Much of Albert's interpretive work entailed the fairly exhaustive study of various biblical themes, vocabulary, and terminology. For instance, drawing on Jerome, Albert provides the reader with a comparison of the calls of Isaiah (whose lips were purified with a burning coal), Ezekiel (required to eat a scroll), and Jeremiah, whose mouth was touched by God's hand. This is followed by an extensive listing of biblical passages that use the language of God "touching" or activating people's lips to speak forth prophecy. Thus, in this fragment from Albert, translated here in its entirety, the reader receives a representative sample of Albert's approach to biblical interpretation.

Hugh of St. Cher and the Dominican Postill

Hugh of St. Cher (ca. 1200–1263) was born in southeastern France and studied at the University of Paris.[109] A Dominican friar, he served as Provincial for the Order of Preachers in France. He was made a cardinal priest in 1244.[110]

107. See Albert's comments on Jer 1:5b, in this volume.
108. Peter, *Participated Eternity*, 53.
109. For a discussion of Hugh's time as a student and his early years in the Dominican order, see Jacque Verger, "Hugh des Saint-Cher dans le contexte Universitaire Parisien," in *Hugues de Saint-Cher (†1263), bibliste et théologien*, ed. Louis-Jacques Bataillon, Gilbert Dahan, and Pierre-Marie Gy, Bibliothèque d'Histoire Culturelle du Moyen Âge 1 (Turnhout: Brepols, 2004), 13–16.
110. Pierre-Marie Gy, "Hugues de Saint-Cher Dominicain," in Bataillon, Dahan, and Gy, *Hugues de Saint-Cher,* 24–26.

During his time in Paris, probably working together with "a consortium of Dominicans," Hugh created or supervised a massive commentary on the entire Bible that offered literal, allegorical, and moral readings intended to provide pastoral counsel for individuals pursing religious vocations.[111] It is generally agreed that, under Hugh's direction, these *Postillae in totam Bibliam* (Postills on the entire Bible) were prepared by the friars at the Dominican house of St. Jacques in Paris between 1230 and 1236.[112] Spencer E. Young, discussing scholarly community at the University of Paris, notes that sometimes a "master and his students functioned together as a kind of intellectual atelier . . . to compose works that would then circulate under the master's name."[113] Though scholars usually use "Hugh" as a "term of convenience" when referring to the authorship of the works disseminated under his name, most agree that the postill was the product of a collaborative effort.[114] For this reason, some scholars prefer to use the term "Dominican Postill" to refer to the commentary.[115] Internal evidence, such as conflicting opinions within the same postill, supports the prevailing view that it was created by multiple authors.[116] Other works produced under Hugh's supervision were a substantial concordance to the Bible and a *correctorium*, which was a collation of textual variants compiled for the purpose of establishing a faithful text of Scripture.[117]

During Hugh's time, the primary study aid employed by university students, teachers, and preachers was the gloss. In fact, there were a num-

111. Robert E. Lerner, "Poverty, Preaching, and Eschatology in the Revelation Commentaries of 'Hugh of St. Cher,'" in *The Bible in the Medieval World*, ed. Katherine Walsh and Diane Wood (Oxford: Basil Blackwell, 1985), 181–83.

112. Athanasius Sulavik, "Hugh of St. Cher's Postill on the Book of Baruch: The Work of a Medieval Compiler or Biblical Exegete?," in Bataillon, Dahan, and Gy, *Hugues de Saint-Cher*, 155.

113. Spencer E. Young, *Scholarly Community at the Early University of Paris: Theologians, Education and Society, 1215–1248* (New York: Cambridge University Press, 2014), 78.

114. Robert E. Lerner, "The Vocation of the Friars Preacher: Hugh of St. Cher between Peter the Chanter and Albert the Great," in Bataillon, Dahan, and Gy, *Hugues de Saint-Cher*, 215. For challenges to Lerner's claims and a reassessment of Hugh's authorship of the postill, see Lesley Smith, "Hugh of St. Cher and Medieval Collaboration," in *Transforming Relations: Essays on Jews and Christians throughout History in Honor of Michael A. Signer*, ed. Franklin T. Harkins (Notre Dame: University of Notre Dame Press, 2010), 241–64.

115. Froehlich, "Christian Interpretation," 518, 522.

116. Lerner, "Vocation of the Friars Preacher," 215.

117. See Cornelia Linde, *How to Correct the "Sacra Scriptura"? Textual Criticism of the Latin Bible between the Twelfth and Fifteenth Century*, Medium Ævum Monographs 29 (Oxford: Society for the Study of Medieval Languages and Literature, 2012), 255–56.

ber of glosses in circulation, but the standard resource, created in Laon, in northern France, in the early twelfth century, was the *Ordinary Gloss* (*Glossa ordinaria*). It contained the Vulgate text with "glosses," or comments, in the margins, excerpted from church fathers and other earlier sources, together with the interlinear gloss, which consisted of short comments and explanations inserted between the lines of the Vulgate text.[118] Hugh and his colleagues endeavored to provide students and preachers with study aids, "the best of what the twelfth and early thirteenth century had to give biblical interpretation."[119] The postill created under his direction was likely intended to supplement the *Ordinary Gloss*.[120]

In Hugh's postill, the Latin biblical text was provided for the reader, marked with letters (*a, b, c,* and so forth) that divide each sentence into tiny units, usually consisting of brief phrases. In the text of the commentary, comments or glosses on each lemma (the phrase or word commented on) were introduced by the corresponding letters. At a time when chapters were not yet divided into verses, this offered ease of reference for the reader, whose eye could move from the biblical text to the corresponding comment, or vice versa.[121] The large size of the quarto page, such as that used for the printed edition of Hugh, meant that the lemma and its commentary could usually be on the same page.

The postill begins its discussion of each chapter by dividing it into thematic sections. This is followed by literal and moral comments on the biblical text. Some moral commentary provided material that preachers could develop for use in their homilies; other moral interpretations sharply attacked greed and corruption found among the clergy of their day.

Comments on the literal sense were chiefly explanatory, elucidating unfamiliar vocabulary, ancient customs, and other details that might be puzzling to the reader. Regarding Jeremiah's denunciation of the family activity of baking cakes for the Queen of Heaven (7:18), the reader is told that the

118. For a brief account of the creation of the *Glossa ordinaria*, see van Liere, *Introduction to the Medieval Bible*, 152–56. The authorship of the gloss on Jeremiah is uncertain. It may have been the work of Gilbert the Universal (Gilbert of Auxerre, d. 1134). See Matter, "The Church Fathers and the *Glossa Ordinaria*," 100.

119. Stephanie A. Paulsell, "Hugh of St. Cher," in *Dictionary of Major Biblical Interpreters*, ed. Donald K. McKim, 2nd ed. (Downers Grove, IL: IVP Academic, 2007), 554.

120. Paulsell, "Hugh of St. Cher," 555.

121. Though the chapter division in use today has its roots in the twelfth century, chapters were not divided into verses until the sixteenth century. See van Liere, *Introduction to the Medieval Bible*, 43–45.

Queen of Heaven is either the moon or the heavenly "army" of stars.[122] The commentator offers an etymology for the word *placenta* (cake), which he says is related to *placere*, "to please," since the cakes were intended to placate the female deity.[123] He also explains that a *placenta* is wheat bread known in French as *foisse*, which the reader would recognize as a flat hearth-baked loaf of focaccia bread. In the literal discussion of the roles of children, fathers, and mothers, the commentator explains each family member's involvement. Children are young and vigorous, with strength to gather the wood for the fire. The fathers use their fire-building skill and experience to kindle the flames. Though the Masoretic Hebrew text says that women "knead the dough,"[124] the Latin translation reports that the women "sprinkle the fat" (*conspergunt adipem*), a puzzling detail that the commentator explains: the women were sprinkling fat onto the fire as an offering, committing an idolatrous act condemned by Leviticus 3:16-17, which instructs the Israelites that fat is to be offered to the Lord alone. At the moral level, the story serves as a warning for indulgent parents. The "wood" gathered by the children "signifies wicked desires with which the devil's fire is kindled in the hearts of sinners." Fathers "kindle" their children's bad behavior, not only letting it continue unchecked but even encouraging them by giving them "clothing, money, and other opportunities for them to collect this 'wood'—that is, harmful desires—more easily."[125] Mothers "sprinkle the fat" by pampering their children too much—even "cooking" their children through their maternal leniency and indulgence, causing their offspring to be kindled and consumed by harmful desires. Interpreted morally, offering cakes to the Queen of Heaven refers to offering one's body to "the moon"—which represents the sin of extravagance—by attending too many parties.

The literal sense of Scripture includes zoological and ornithological

122. When speaking of the "Queen of Heaven," Jeremiah was referring to the Assyro-Babylonian astral goddess Astarte, also known as Ishtar. Hugh's assertion that the queen of heaven may refer to the army of stars probably derives from the LXX, which says "army [*stratia*] of heaven" rather than "queen of heaven." See William L. Holladay, *Jeremiah 1: A Commentary on the Book of the Prophet Jeremiah Chapters 1-25*, Hermeneia (Philadelphia: Fortress, 1986), 251; and J. A. Thompson, *The Book of Jeremiah*, New International Commentary on the Old Testament (Grand Rapids: Eerdmans, 1980), 284-85.

123. In fact, the Latin *placenta* derives from the Greek *plakoūs*, which refers to a flat cake. Charlton T. Lewis and Charles Short, eds., *A Latin Dictionary* (New York: Oxford University Press, 1984), 1382.

124. For a discussion of the Hebrew text and a detailed explanation of the ancient Near Eastern practices condemned in Jer 7:18, see Holladay, *Jeremiah 1*, 254.

125. Hugh of St. Cher, *On Jeremiah 7:18*, translated in this volume.

information. Jer 8:7a, "The kite in heaven has recognized its time," occasions comments on migratory birds that travel to warm, calmer climates to avoid stormy winters. "The turtle dove, and the swallow, and the stork have observed the time of their coming" (Jer 8:7b) is information that prompts the commentator to note that there are two kinds of turtle doves: one is migratory and other is present year round. The commentator also observes that variant translations mention different bird species: "Where our text has 'kite,' another text reads 'heron.' Where we have 'swallow,' the Septuagint reads 'sparrows of the field.'" Additional zoological information is used to explain Jer 8:17, "Behold I will send you terrible serpents." The reader learns that, instead of "serpents," an ancient Greek translation said "basilisk," referring to a mythological reptile whose deadly breath is able to strike down birds in flight. Read literally, "basilisk" is an image of the brutal Babylonians about to attack Jerusalem. At the moral level, it refers to the deadly attack of demons who use temptation to "slay contemplatives" by interfering with their attempts to ascend through virtue. Or, according to the commentator, the passage could refer to a demonic attack against bishops and high-ranking clergy who use their "wings of vices" to ascend to high offices and positions.

The commentary provides a glimpse into some of the ecclesiastical controversies of the day and Hugh's desire to reform the clergy. Hugh was known for his outspoken criticism of corrupt clerics.[126] The postill's moral interpretations are filled with concern about clergy failings, especially the greed, financial malfeasance, and bad behavior of high-ranking clergy. The commentary is interspersed with criticisms of thirteenth-century clergy. God's question, "Has this house, in which my name has been called on, become a den of robbers?" (7:11), occasions the commentator's criticism of nepotism and the buying and selling of church offices. The birds that devour the unburied corpses of the Judeans (7:33) represent clergymen who "rush from church to church" to acquire profitable ecclesiastical offices; the beasts that scavenge human carcasses represent resident clergy who "consume" everyone through their bad example and "eat" the offerings and revenues given to the church on behalf of the dead. Jeremiah's warning that the bones of the priests will be unearthed and cast out of their graves (8:1) can be understood literally in terms of the Babylonians—and later the Romans—desecrating graves in search of treasure, but at the moral level this means that the devil

126. R. F. Bennett, *The Early Dominicans: Studies in Thirteenth-Century Dominican History* (New York: Russell & Russell, 1971), 12.

tries to uncover and reveal the sins of bishops after their deaths in order to scandalize the laity.

Some of the commentary offers encouragement to members of the Order of Preachers. The example of Jeremiah shows that preachers should not become disheartened when listeners do not respect them or pay attention to their sermons: "Therefore the preacher should not cease preaching even if the listeners are disobedient. Nor should the preacher take offense if they do not heed him, or if they regard the preacher as unworthy."[127]

The commentator encourages readers to engage in salutary devotional activities. A moral reading of the grim statement that unburied bones will be "as dung on the surface of the earth" (8:2) yields an exhortation to confess sins contritely. When unconfessed sins accumulate, they rot and stink like a pile of dung; but, when one confesses these sins, the metaphorical dung is scattered like fertilizer to nurture the penitent's good works. Hugh piously exhorts his readers: "Let us fertilize the field of our minds." God's message to the Judeans, "Rising up early, I spoke to you" (7:13), prompts an excursus on the benefits of early morning prayer, as well as the testy statement that this verse should not be used to suppress preaching that takes place after breakfast—even if early morning sermons are better! Finally, in the postill's coments on Jer 8:14 ("for our Lord has made us become silent"), we receive a delightful glimpse into Hugh's world when the text charmingly asserts: "It is possible to direct this statement to theologians at Paris who study so much all day."

Thomas Aquinas

Thomas Aquinas is perhaps the most renowned theologian of the Middle Ages, but his extensive work as a biblical commentator is far less widely known. In fact, he composed commentaries on the Psalms, Job, Isaiah, Jeremiah, Lamentations, the Gospels, and the Epistles of Paul.[128] Born into an aristocratic family near Aquino in the kingdom of Naples around 1225, Thomas studied at the prestigious Benedictine abbey at Monte Cassino and the University of Naples. He joined the Order of Preachers (Dominicans), who sent him to study at the University of Paris in 1245. In Paris he met Albert the Great, who became his teacher and mentor. Thomas followed Albert to the University of Cologne in 1248. There, as a *baccalaureus biblicus,* he

127. Hugh of St. Cher, *On Jeremiah* 7:27, translated in this volume.
128. Eleonore Stump, *Aquinas* (New York: Routledge, 2003), 455.

lectured on Scripture at the Dominican house of studies, commenting on biblical books chapter by chapter, verse by verse, as was the custom. Thomas later returned to Paris, received his master of theology, and held a number of teaching appointments.[129] Thomas's literary output, which included his famous *Summa theologiae* and his commentaries on Aristotle, was massive.[130]

Thomas's *Super Ieremiam* (*On Jeremiah*) dates from the time he served as *baccalaureus* lecturing on Scripture.[131] The unfinished commentary, which covers Jer 1:1–42:1, is extant in five manuscripts.[132] The lectures on Jeremiah were probably delivered during Thomas's first two years at Cologne, around 1251–1252, during the time that he also lectured on Lamentations and Isaiah.[133] Thus we have the work of Thomas as a young man, approximately twenty-four years of age. Historian Jean-Pierre Torrell, speaking of the Isaiah commentary extant in Thomas's own hand, characterizes this early exegetical work as lecture notes, originally "set down on parchment, day after day, by the young bachelor. He did this with an eye to the lectures that he had to give in a few hours. They bear all the marks of hasty work."[134] Thomas's nearly exclusive attention to the literal text, appropriate and customary for cursory lectures by a thirteenth-century *baccalaureus biblicus,* caused later figures such as theologian Sixtus of Siena (1520–1569) to question Thomas's authorship of the Isaiah, Jeremiah, and Lamentations commentaries due to their "doctrinal poverty" (*sterilitas doctrinae*).[135] However, Torrell defends Thomas's early exegetical work (specifically the Isaiah commentary), saying that "even if it sometimes leaves us a little hungry for more, it possesses great riches on certain points."[136]

129. He served as regent master in theology at the University of Paris, and he oversaw the studies at Dominican houses in Naples, Orvieto, and Rome. Stump, *Aquinas,* 3.

130. See the chronological listing of Thomas's works in Stump, *Aquinas,* xvi–xx.

131. Stump, *Aquinas,* xvi; Jean-Pierre Torrell, *Saint Thomas Aquinas,* vol. 1, *The Person and His Work,* rev. ed., trans. Robert Royal (Washington, DC: Catholic University of America Press, 2005), 25.

132. Froehlich, "Christian Interpretation," 543.

133. Torrell, *Saint Thomas Aquinas,* 27.

134. Torrell, *Saint Thomas Aquinas,* 29. In this quotation, Torrell is specifically referring to Thomas's *Super Isaiam,* chapters 34–50, written in Thomas's own hand, found in manuscript *Vaticanus latinus* 9850. See Torell, *Saint Thomas Aquinas,* 28–29n42. Later works, such as Thomas's Romans commentary, are *reportationes* ("reports") recorded by secretaries, sometimes later reworked by Thomas and corrected. An example is the *correctio* of the first eight chapters of Romans. See Ian Christopher Levy, Philip D. W. Krey, and Thomas Ryan, introduction to *Letter to the Romans,* 41.

135. Torrell, *Saint Thomas Aquinas,* 27–28.

136. Torrell, *Saint Thomas Aquinas,* 27.

Included in this volume are Thomas's comments on chapters 9, 11, 14–15, 17–18, and 20, material that contains nearly all of Jeremiah's "confessions." The most prominent feature of *On Jeremiah* is Thomas's practice of dividing scripture passages into units and subunits. Thomas divides the biblical passage (usually a chapter) under study, subdivides it, and then subdivides it further. The divisions are generally multiples of two or three, with ever smaller sections "nested" in larger sections.[137] He often uses multiples of two for his division of the text into points or subpoints, though sometimes he identifies three or four subpoints in a given passage. The practice of textual division (*divisio textus*), an approach that can be confusing to the modern reader, is "a highly schematized approach to biblical interpretation" used by Thomas "to organize his work based on the biblical text under study and to introduce the issues that he will address later on."[138]

A second prominent feature of Thomas's interpretation is his extensive quoting of other scripture passages that contain vocabulary, imagery, and themes similar to the words or ideas found in the verse being considered. Frequently, this is to help his listener or reader understand a particular Latin word or phrase that might be ambiguous or unclear. For instance, commenting on Jer 11:22, "I will visit upon them" (*ego visitabo super eos*), he quotes Ps 89:32 ("I will visit their iniquities with a rod") to make clear that here God's "visitation" refers to punishment.[139]

Thomas opens his Jeremiah commentary with a prologue introducing the prophet Jeremiah and his significance. He structures his discussion of the prophet around the themes found in 2 Macc 5:14, words spoken by the priest Onias, who saw Jeremiah in a vision during the Maccabean Revolt (167–160 BCE), several centuries after Jeremiah's death: "He is a lover of his brothers and sisters, and of the people of Israel. This is he who prays much for his people and for the entire holy city, Jeremiah, the prophet of God." The various qualities and attributes of Jeremiah ("lover of his brothers and sisters," "who prays much," and so forth) exemplify the characteristics and actions of a genuine prophet.[140]

137. Speaking about Thomas Aquinas's use of this practice in his Psalms commentary, Thomas Ryan writes: "To summarize, Thomas's comments on individual words and phrases of the Psalm are carefully nested within layers of divisions"; Thomas F. Ryan, *Thomas Aquinas as Reader of the Psalms,* Studies in Spirituality and Theology 6 (Notre Dame: University of Notre Dame Press, 2000), 27.
138. Levy, Krey, and Ryan, introduction, 41.
139. See Thomas's comments on Jer 11:21, in this volume.
140. Thomas of Aquinas, "Prologue," 577–78.

Throughout *On Jeremiah,* Thomas attends chiefly to the literal meaning of the text, providing historical explanations when needed. The reader learns that the reason why "the gates have fallen" (14:2), prior to the Babylonians' attack, is that the city wall was crumbling due to the drought described in chapter 14; the water shortage prevented the people from making the appropriate repairs. Or, says Thomas, this was a reference not to the gates themselves but to the downfall of the judges who had been accustomed to sitting at the gates to render judgment.[141] When Jeremiah cries out, "Call for the mourning women" (9:17), Thomas describes the biblical custom of hiring female mourners, with reference to the women of Jerusalem who followed behind Jesus while weeping and beating their breasts (Luke 23:27–28). Or, regarding the phrase, "The wild donkeys stood on the rocks, they inhaled the wind like dragons" (Jer 14:6 Vulg.), Thomas explains that wild donkeys can go a long time without drinking, so their behavior here is a sign of the drought's severity. He provides the additional zoological information that dragons inhale wind to cool their thirst.[142]

Thomas's interpretation included Christological readings of the text. Prophecies about Jeremiah's suffering applied not only to Jeremiah himself but also to Christ. Jeremiah's suffering also serves as a prefiguring or prophecy about Christ's suffering. Explaining that portions of chapter 11 refer simultaneously to Jeremiah and to Christ, Thomas writes:

> This passage [Jer 11:18–23] shows how they transgressed by sinning against the prophet himself, and, indeed, what is said pertains, according to the literal sense, to Jeremiah, who became hated by the people because of the evil events that he announced. But Jeremiah's persecution prefigures Christ's passion. . . . Now when it says that we should regard this as applying to the person of Christ rather than Jeremiah, it seems to contradict the earlier statement, etc. However, all the prophets prefigure Christ to a great extent, so something that is fulfilled in Jeremiah during his time was also prophesied regarding Christ in the future.[143]

Of particular interest is Thomas's examination of the ethical concerns raised by Jeremiah's final "confession" (20:7–18), especially when the prophet voices curses against the day of his own birth and against the person who

141. See Thomas's comments on Jer 14:2, in this volume.
142. See Thomas's comments on Jer 14:6, in this volume.
143. Thomas Aquinas, *On Jeremiah* 11:18–23, in *Opera Omnia* 14:607.

brought news of Jeremiah's birth to his father rather than killing the unborn Jeremiah in his mother's womb (Jer 20:14–18). The hypothetical objector might ask whether Jeremiah should not have rejoiced in his tribulations as Paul did in Rom 5:3. And since a day is a good creation of God, is it not sinful to curse it? Furthermore, since a day is something transitory, is it not stupid or foolish to apply a curse to it? Finally—and most seriously—did the prophet not sin by cursing the innocent person who brought the announcement of Jeremiah's birth to his father and did not kill the unborn infant? Responding to these objections, Aquinas defends and explains Jeremiah's words. Even though tribulations can serve a good purpose, just as painful surgery can cure a disease, the events themselves may be inherently bad. Jeremiah did not curse the day per se, but only in connection with the evil occurring on it. Particularly with regard to the curses against individuals connected with Jeremiah's birth, the reader should not interpret the curses literally, for "in order to express his own sense of revulsion, [Jeremiah] speaks hyperbolically about the misery of his life."[144] Regarding that same passage, Thomas deals with Jeremiah's blunt accusation that God seduced and overpowered him (Jer 20:7), language that contains connotations of sexual violence.[145] The Latin text uses *seducere* (to seduce, to entice, to lead astray) to characterize God's treatment of Jeremiah. Thomas provides scripture references to explain how God can be said to "seduce" by using persuasion, "luring" individuals with soothing words or even guile when necessary, as when Paul lovingly used guile to "capture" the Corinthians (2 Cor 12:16). The Lord overpowers or "prevails" (*invalere*) by administering correction, diverting people from harm, and restraining them through love.[146] Thus, with these explanations, a reader confused or disturbed by the biblical language is guided toward an appropriate understanding of God's interactions with humans.

At times, Thomas offers moral readings, such as his comments regarding the statement that Jeremiah "went down" to the potter's house (Jer 18:3). After attending to the literal sense, explaining that the artisans worked in the lower section of the city, Thomas says that Jeremiah's descent signifies that "the Lord's words are revealed to the one who descends into reflection about one's own weakness."[147]

---

144. See Thomas's comments on Jer 20:14–18, in this volume.
145. Thompson, *Book of Jeremiah*, 459.
146. Thomas Aquinas, *On Jeremiah* 20, in *Opera Omnia* 14:627.
147. See Thomas's comments on Jer 18:1–6, in this volume.

At the conclusion of each of the seven chapters translated in this volume, there are one or more paragraphs that offer meditations on or pastoral applications of themes arising from the biblical chapter. They consist primarily of scripture citations suggested by the vocabulary or themes found in the chapter being treated. Torrell suggests that these are preliminary notes toward "a spiritual or pastoral expansion of his literal commentary."[148] These comments were probably originally in the margins of the Jeremiah commentary, written in outline form, next to the specific verse being commented on—such as is found in Thomas's autograph copy of the *Super Isaiam*. The comments are introduced by the words *nota* (note) or *notandum* (one should note) and signal that "the author is changing registers, passing from the literal to the spiritual sense."[149] Though it is not known what term, if any, Thomas used to refer to these pastoral expansions, Jacobinus of Asti, who transcribed Thomas's Isaiah commentary at the end of the thirteenth century, called these comments "collations" (*collationes*).[150] Following suit, I have used the word "collation" as a title for these comments in this volume. In his study of the collations in Thomas's Isaiah commentary, P.-M. Gils writes: "The *collationes* of the *Super Isaiam* are *assemblies* of scriptural quotations, connections that a given word in Isaiah suggested, that do not find a place in a strictly literal commentary, but that inspire spiritual or moral applications of the text."[151]

Usually a collation involves some sort of pastoral application prompted by word association. For instance, chapter 11 includes a collation occasioned by Jer 11:16, which describes God's people as an olive tree. The collation assembles passages that connect to olive wood and olive oil, such as the olive wood of the carved cherubim and the oil of an anointed messiah. Thomas assembles these passages to discuss how the attributes of an olive tree correspond to virtues in the holy person. The "richness" of olive oil is the holy person's devotion. The luster from its oil is contemplation. The tree's fruitfulness is the holy person's abundance of good works.

The prophet's statement that "their land will be given up to desolation and to a perpetual hissing" (Jer 18:16) prompts a collation on good and bad hissing. Thomas provides a word study of the use of *sibilus,* which can mean

<hr />

148. Torell, *Saint Thomas Aquinas,* 29.

149. Torrell, *Saint Thomas Aquinas,* 27.

150. Torrell, *Saint Thomas Aquinas,* 29.

151. Pierre-Marie Gils, "*Les Collationes* marginales dan l'autographe du commentaire de S. Thomas sur Isaïe," *Revue des sciences philosophiques et théologiques* 42 (1958): 255, quoted and translated in Torrell, *Saint Thomas Aquinas,* 30.

"whistle" or "hiss," and which has various connotations in the biblical text. Positive connotations include God's "whistling" as an image of divine inspiration (Zech 10:8), as well as a hissing of human compassion (Jer 49:17). Negative connotations include a "hissing of wicked persuasion" (Wis 17:9) and the insulting hiss (Lam 2:15). Another collation is prompted by Jer 9:23 ("Let not the wise boast in their wisdom; let not the strong boast in their strength; and let not the rich boast in their riches"). Thomas here provides a biblical meditation on the transitory nature of wisdom, strength, and riches.[152] Thus we see, in Thomas's commentary, "the spiritual concern that animates the literal analysis."[153]

Nicholas of Lyra

Between the years 1322 and 1332, Franciscan exegete Nicholas of Lyra composed a magisterial literal postill on the entire Bible.[154] Nicholas was born in Lyre (Normandy) around 1270, joined the Franciscan order in 1300, and studied at the University of Paris, where he lectured on the Bible during the first decade of the fourteenth century. The lectures were the basis for his commentary, which he continued to work on while also assigned to administrative duties, including service as Franciscan provincial minister in Burgundy.[155]

Nicholas's literal commentary is noteworthy for its employment of Jewish sources. Nicholas was one of a very small number of medieval Christians who had facility with the Hebrew language.[156] It is not known how he gained this proficiency. He may have learned Hebrew from one or more baptized

---

152. Thomas Aquinas, *On Jeremiah* 9, in *Opera Omnia* 14:602.

153. Torrell, *Saint Thomas Aquinas*, 30. Also see the reflections by Ryan in *Thomas Aquinas as Reader of the Psalms*, 145-49.

154. Nicholas, who often provides dates for his commentaries, does not do so for his Jeremiah postill, so the dating is uncertain. Henri Labrosse provides known dates for Nicholas's postills on prophetic books in "Oeuvres de Nicholas de Lyre," *Études franciscaines* 19 (1908): 165-68.

155. For background on Nicholas's life and work, see "Nicolas de Lyre franciscain," in *Nicolas de Lyre: Franciscain du XIVe siècle exégète et théologien*, ed. Gilbert Dahan, Collection des Études Augustiniennes, Série Moyen Âge et Temps Modernes 48 (Paris: Institut d'Études Augustiniennes, 2011), 17-28; Levy, Krey, and Ryan, *Letter to the Romans*, 50-51; Ian Christopher Levy, ed. and trans., *The Letter to the Galatians*, Bible in Medieval Tradition 1 (Grand Rapids: Eerdmans, 2011), 69-71; and Schroeder, *Book of Genesis*, 30-32.

156. Gibert Dahan, "Nicolas de Lyre: Herménetique et méthode d'exégèse," in Dahan, *Nicolas de Lyre*, 115.

Jews, since converts were "the main channel through which Jewish knowledge percolated into the Christian world."[157] In the excerpt included in this volume, we see Nicholas's familiarity with Jewish sources, which included Rashi (Rabbi Solomon ben Isaac of Troyes, 1040–1105), Moses Maimonides (1135–1204), and the Babylonian targum on Jeremiah, which is an Aramaic paraphrase that may date as early as the fourth or fifth century CE.[158] Nicholas calls this targum "the Chaldean translation," and he frequently uses this text to refute medieval Jewish sources, since he sees in the targum evidence of the Messiah's divinity.

Nicholas's attention to the Hebrew text and his familiarity with Jewish sources caused him to become "the Christian Bible commentator of first resort" for succeeding generations of biblical scholars in the Middle Ages and early Modern period.[159] In 1429, eight decades after Nicholas's death, the Spanish-born bishop Paul of Burgos (d. 1435), known as Rabbi Solomon ha-Levi prior to his conversion from Judaism, wrote marginal notes in a copy of the postill, critical of the work on a number of points, including Nicholas's use of Rashi as an authoritative source.[160] These "additions" are frequently included in printed editions of the postill, and I have translated his comments for this volume.[161]

Nicholas is noted for his application of the literal and the "double-literal" senses of Scripture. When a passage is interpreted according to the literal sense, a particular person, image, or event mentioned in the Old Testament Scriptures may refer to the individual or thing mentioned in the text; or, instead, it may be a reference to Christ, the church, or New Testament event. In a passage that has a "double-literal" meaning, the literal sense can be applied to each. For example, a particular prophecy about King David might refer only to the historical David (literal sense); or it may refer only to Christ and *not* David (also the literal sense); or it may refer to *both* Christ and David (the double-literal sense).[162]

---

157. Ari Geiger, "A Student and an Opponent: Nicholas of Lyra and His Jewish Sources," in Dahan, *Nicolas de Lyre*, 31.

158. Robert Hayward, trans., *The Targum of Jeremiah,* The Aramaic Bible 12 (Wilmington, DE: Michael Glazier, 1987), 34–35.

159. Klepper, *Insight of Unbelievers,* 5.

160. Klepper, *Insight of Unbelievers,* 124.

161. Franciscan exegete Matthias Döring (d. 1435) defended Nicholas by writing rebuttals to Paul of Burgos's comments. These were printed together with the bishop's "additions." There are no rebuttals from Döring on the chapters covered in this volume.

162. See the discussion in Klepper, *Insight of Unbelievers,* 35.

Nicholas opens his *Literal Postill on Jeremiah* with a prologue discussing authorship of the book, the nature of prophecy, and the distinction between true and false prophets. Using philosophical terminology in his discussion of authorship of Jeremiah, he says that the book's "principal cause" was "God revealing all the things contained in this book," while Jeremiah, who "wrote that book" (*scripsit librum istum*), was its "instrumental cause," the means by which the book was written.[163] Nicholas distinguished between true prophets, who are inspired by divine revelation, and false prophets, who manufacture prophecies from their own imaginations or, in other cases, are inspired by demons.[164]

In his *Literal Postill on Jeremiah,* Nicholas attends almost solely to the literal-historical meaning of the text, which, for him, includes messianic prophecies. In the selection provided for this volume, Jer 23 and 28–30, Nicholas usually avoids the double-literal sense. He is insistent that the Davidic references are about Christ and not about mortal Judean kings or leaders. In most cases, references to the restoration of Jerusalem are about the church rather than about the rebuilding of the city following the Judean return from exile in 537 BCE (see Ezra 1–3). For instance, when God says, "And I will build you again" (Jer 31:4), this is, in Nicholas's literal reading of the text, a reference to Christ's establishment of the church.[165]

In chapter 23, Jeremiah's prophecy—generally grim and foreboding—shifts to a particularly hopeful key, at least for several verses (23:3–8). There the reader encounters promises that the Lord would gather the remnant of the flock together, set up good shepherds (*pastores*), and raise up for David a "righteous branch" to serve as king. Nicholas perceived that the good shepherds were Christ ("the leader of the shepherds"), the apostles, and their successors. The righteous branch of David is Christ. The flock, once scattered, is the church, gathered together from among Jews and Gentiles.

The sixth verse of chapter 23, "And this is the name they will call him, 'The Lord, our just one,'" prompted a lengthy discussion attacking Hugh's Dominican postill as well as medieval Jewish interpretations of the passage. Hugh had glossed this passage by asserting that "Jews gave the names of God to their children."[166] Hugh's postill also asserted that the "righteous branch of David" was Zerubbabel, who led a group of Judeans back to Judah

163. Nicholas of Lyra, "Prologue," n.p.
164. Nicholas of Lyra, "Prologue," n.p.
165. See Nicholas's comments on Jer 31:4, translated in this volume.
166. Hugh of St. Cher, *On Jeremiah* 23:6, in *Opera Omnia* 4:233r.

after the Babylonian captivity.[167] Fueled not only by the traditional rivalry between Dominicans and Franciscans, but also by his outrage over uninformed, inaccurate exegesis, Nicholas lambastes Hugh's identification of the righteous branch with Zerubbabel rather than Christ, since the prophecy announced that the righteous branch would reign as king (23:5b)—a claim that could be made only about Christ, not Zerubbabel. Since the Chaldean targum and medieval Jewish interpreters identified the "righteous branch" with the Messiah, Nicholas concludes that "these [Christian] interpreters Judaize more than the Jews."[168] (Thereby he includes a slur against the Jews whom he himself is citing as authorities.)

In the same discussion of the twenty-third chapter, Nicholas refutes Hugh's "fictitious and baseless" assertion that Jews customarily gave God's names to their children. Nicholas's readers receive a lesson about the "Tetragrammaton name of the Lord" (YHWH), which Jerome translated with the epithet *Dominus* (Lord). Nicholas explains that the Tetragrammaton was regarded by Jews as so holy that the name could be applied only to the Most High Creator and was never uttered aloud except by priests in the temple.[169] As evidence of Jewish practice, he cites "Rabbi Moses" (Maimonides), who says that the Tetragrammaton refers to the "bare divine essence."[170] For Nicholas, the divine name YHWH applied to the righteous branch of David is Old Testament evidence of Christ's divinity—something that Jews denied and that Hugh's postill wretchedly overlooked in its treatment of this passage.

Nicholas regards chapters 28 (Hananiah's false prophecy) and 29 (Jeremiah's letter to the exiles) to be chiefly about the Babylonian exile and return. However, chapters 30 and 31 (part of the Book of Consolation) are, according to the literal sense, primarily prophecies about Christ's incarnation and the salvation offered through him. "It is not possible to interpret this passage suitably in any other way than to apply it to the time of Christ," he writes.[171]

167. Hugh of St. Cher, *On Jeremiah* 23:3–5, in *Opera Omnia in Universum Vetus & Novum Testamentum: Tomi Octo In Libros Prophetarum, Isaiae, Ieremiae, & eiusdem Threnorum, Baruch*, Vol. 4 (Lyon: Ioannes Antonius Huguetan and Guillielmus Barbier, 1669), 233r.

168. See Nicholas's comments on Jer 23:3a, in this volume. For medieval Jewish interpretations of this passage, see *Jeremiah: A New English Translation*, translation of text, Rashi, and commentary by A. J. Rosenberg (New York: Judaica Press, 1985), 1:186. Also see Hayward, *Targum of Jeremiah*, 111.

169. See Nicholas's comments on Jer 23:3a, in this volume.

170. Moses Maimonides, *The Guide for the Perplexed* 1.61, trans. M. Friedländer, 2nd ed. (New York: Dover, 1956), 89.

171. Nicholas of Lyra, *Literal Postill on Jeremiah* 30:1.

God's promise to "restore the captivity of my people Israel and Judah" (Jer 30:3) cannot apply to the Judean return from Babylonia or any other subsequent temporal deliverance since the people of Israel, the northern kingdom, have not been restored. Indeed, says Nicholas, the Jews themselves do not expect Israelite return from captivity until the coming of the Messiah.[172] Thus the prophecies in this portion of Jeremiah must pertain to Christ. Nicholas uses a talmudic saying to explain why the events prophesied in Jer 30 (the antichrist's persecution of the church) and 31 (the establishment of the church, Herod's slaughter of the holy innocents, and Emperor Hadrian's expansion of Jerusalem's boundaries in the second century CE) do not follow historical sequence: "As Hebrew scholars say, 'There is no earlier and later in the law,' by which they mean that, in the Old Testament, the sequence in which things are described does not follow chronological order."[173]

In Matthew's account of Herod's slaughter of the innocent children of Bethlehem (Matt 2:16–18), the gospel writer quoted Jer 31:15: "A voice was heard in the height, of lamentation, of mourning and weeping, of Rachel weeping for her children." Nicholas explains that, although the Hebrew word *Ramah* (height) could be taken to refer to the town near Gibeah by that name, geographical considerations require that the word be translated "height," to "indicate the magnitude of the cry of the women whose children were slaughtered."[174] Nicholas said that Rachel could be called "mother" of the slaughtered innocents since her burial near Bethlehem made her the patron of the city of Bethlehem and the entire region, "just as, among us, saints whose bodies rest in churches are called patrons not only of these churches but also the cities and adjacent territories."[175] Nicholas criticizes the "fictitious" story found in Jewish tradition that, as the Judeans walked past Rachel's tomb while they were led captive to Babylon, a voice came forth from the tomb begging God for compassion on the exiles.[176]

---

172. See Nicholas's comments on Jer 30:3.

173. Nicholas of Lyra, *Literal Postill on Jeremiah* 30:1. A commonly repeated rabbinic maxim, derived from the Babylonian Talmud, states: "There is no earlier and later in the Torah." Pesaḥim 6b, in I. Epstein, ed., *The Babylonian Talmud, Seder Mo'ed*, trans. H. Freedman (London: Soncino, 1938), 25.

174. Nicholas of Lyra, *Literal Postill on Jeremiah* 31:15b. In his comments, Nicholas notes that the town of Ramah is some distance from Bethlehem, and Jerusalem is situated between the two towns.

175. Nicholas of Lyra, *Literal Postill on Jeremiah* 31:15b.

176. See the rabbinic comments on Jer 31:14 in Rosenberg, *Jeremiah: A New English Translation*, 2:248.

The accurate interpretation, says Nicholas, is found in Christian exegesis, which identifies Rachel's cry as the cry of the mothers of Bethlehem weeping for their massacred infants, for "Rachel is said to weep through her daughters."[177] The promise that "they will return out of the land of the enemy, and there is hope" (Jer 31:16–17) refers to the martyred children's release from hell's limbo when Christ descended to the dead and led them forth to heaven.

Nicholas says that Jer 31:38–40, a description of the rebuilding of Jerusalem, can be taken as a prophecy about the establishment of the church, but it is chiefly a prediction of Emperor Hadrian's rebuilding of Jerusalem and expansion of the city walls to encompass the site of Christ's sepulchre, previously outside the city.[178] Other parts of chapter 31 are best applied to the church. The promise in 31:12, that the people will gather to Mount Zion to receive grain, wine, and oil, refers to the Eucharist—the sacrament "confected under the species of bread and wine." The oil is the grace conveyed through this sacrament.[179] (Paul of Burgos registered his disagreement about the meaning of the oil since, in a literal interpretation of the passage, the oil is obviously the matter used for the sacraments of confirmation and extreme unction![180]) The promise that virgin Israel will be "furnished again with your tambourines" (Jer 31:4a) refers, in a literal way, to the church bells that summon worshippers to gather and give praise to God.[181] Nicholas's concern not to give license to ribald revelry evinces a clarification that offers a charming glimpse into his enjoyment of music. Interpreting the phrase "you will go forth in the chorus of those who make merry" (Jer 31:4b), he adds, "not dissolutely, but devoutly, just as when one choir cheerfully sings counterpoint to another choir."[182]

177. Nicholas of Lyra, *Literal Postill on Jeremiah* 31:15b. Though he does not specifically use the phrase *ad litteram* in this section of his commentary, this is an example of Nicholas's literal reading of the text—that the only proper literal interpretation of Rachel weeping for her children is to understand it as a reference the slaughter of the innocents at the time of Christ's birth. In his comments on Jer 31:15a, Nicholas states that this passage mentions "things pertaining to the incarnation."

178. Nicholas of Lyra, *Literal Postill on Jeremiah* 31:38–40.

179. Nicholas of Lyra, *Literal Postill on Jeremiah* 31:12.

180. Paul of Burgos, "Addition to Lyra's Comments on Jeremiah 31:12," translated in this volume.

181. Nicholas of Lyra, *Literal Postill on Jeremiah* 31:4.

182. Nicholas of Lyra, *Literal Postill on Jeremiah* 31:4.

Introduction

Denis the Carthusian

Born in the small village of Rijkel (in what is now Belgium) in 1402 or 1403, Denis de Leeuwis (Denys Van Leeuwen) apparently was named for Dionysius the Areopagite, a saint who had been converted by the preaching of the Apostle Paul (Acts 17:34).[183] Kent Emery suggests that perhaps "his name piously predisposed him to his later predilection for the teaching of his namesake, Dionysius the Areopagite."[184] Denis studied at the abbey school in the nearby town of Sint-Truiden. When he outpaced his Latin teacher, he enrolled in the city school of Zwolle, where he received an excellent education in classical Latin writers such as Cicero, Seneca, and Virgil, as well as Christian authors. In Zwolle, he was also influenced by the *Devotio Moderna* and the Brothers and Sisters of the Common Life, a group celebrated for its piety and devotion to religious study.[185] In his late teens—age seventeen or eighteen—he applied to enter the Carthusian charterhouse in Roermond. Since the minimum age for entrance was twenty, the prior of the charterhouse made arrangements for him to attend the University of Cologne as intellectual preparation for his time as a monk. Denis studied there from 1421 to 1424, receiving the master of arts degree.[186] Finally, in 1425, he entered the charterhouse of Roermond in the Netherlands.[187] Apart from several occasions when he was dispatched to attend to administrative matters for his order, he spent the remainder of his life in the charterhouse. There, dwelling in a community of twelve monks, Denis engaged in copious study and writing, which he regarded to be part of his contemplative vocation. Emery observes: "The narrow confines and physical stability of his life accentuate, in contrast, the vast world of thought wherein his mind wandered and dwelt."[188]

Denis wrote numerous works, including commentaries on Pseudo-Dionysius and Boethius.[189] A major project, which occupied him from 1434

183. Kent Emery Jr., "Denys the Carthusian: The World of Thought Comes to Roermond," in *The Carthusians in the Low Countries: Studies in Monastic History and Heritage*, ed. Krijn Pansters (Leuven: Peeters, 2014), 257. For biographical information, also see Schroeder, *Book of Genesis*, 35–36.

184. Emery, "Denys the Carthusian," 257. A set of mystical treatises written in the fifth or sixth century CE circulated in Dionysius's name. See Pseudo-Dionysius, *The Complete Works*, trans. Colm Luibhéid and Paul Rorem, Classics of Western Spirituality (Mahwah, NJ: Paulist, 1987).

185. Emery, "Denys the Carthusian," 257.

186. Emery, "Denys the Carthusian," 257–59.

187. Emery, "Denys the Carthusian," 263.

188. Emery, "Denys the Carthusian," 255.

189. Emery, "Denys the Carthusian, 274. For a summary list of his major writings, see

to 1457, was his massive line-by-line commentary on the entirety of the Scriptures.[190] The Scripture commentaries include significant attention to the literal sense, which for Denis included Christological predictions that he perceived in Old Testament prophecies. Following his extensive treatment of the literal sense of each chapter, Denis usually offered a shorter "mystical"—moral or allegorical—interpretation. Denis's writings made use of his extensive research into a wide variety of sources, a fact observed by later devotees, who coined the motto: "Whoever reads Denis, reads everything."[191] In his *Exposition on Jeremiah,* Denis employs Jerome, Peter Comestor, and Nicholas of Lyra (with whom he frequently disagreed). In the passage excerpted in this volume, he also quotes Aristotle and Boethius.

In his treatment of chapter 32, about Jeremiah purchasing a field as a prophetic sign about eventual return from captivity, Denis offers clarifying historical details about ancient customs. The prophet's cousin Hanamel—who Denis believes was guided by divine inspiration—offered Jeremiah the opportunity to purchase land in the territory of Benjamin, saying, "For it is your right to buy it, because of your close kinship" (Jer 32:7). Denis explains the applicable biblical property and inheritance laws, providing the scripture references.[192] When Jer 32:9–15 meticulously describes the complicated ritual of purchase, Denis offers an explication of the process, including the documents used, the clay jar the documents were stored in, and the seals applied both to the documents and to the outside of the clay jar. During the course of his literal exposition, Denis draws a lesson from this detailed account: "It is clear from this that all legal requirements for wills and contracts should be observed and proceed in a methodical way."[193] In his spiritual interpretation of the chapter, Denis identifies "the spiritual fields in the land of Judah" with the everlasting dwellings that believers

---

L. A. Shoemaker, "Denys the Carthusian," in McKim, *Dictionary of Major Biblical Interpreters,* 363.

190. This time frame is inclusive of a decade-long interruption in the 1440s when his prior forbade him to continue work on his Scripture commentaries. Though some Carthusians questioned the compatibility of academic studies with the contemplative vocation, the prior's motivation may have been, instead, concern that Denis had a master of arts degree, not a master of theology. Without studies under the direction of a faculty of theology, he may not—from his prior's perspective—have had license to "comment on the Scriptures magisterially"; Emery, "Denys the Carthusian," 278; see pages 274–78 for a thorough discussion of this dispute.

191. Terence O'Reilly, introduction to Denis the Carthusian, *Spiritual Writings,* trans. Íde M. Ní Riain (Dublin: Four Courts Press, 2005), xii.

192. See Denis's comments on 32:6–7, in this volume.

193. Denis the Carthusian, *Exposition on the Prophet Jeremiah* 32:11–15.

should endeavor to obtain (Luke 16:9). Various components and parties in Jeremiah's ritual transaction have corresponding elements related to eternal salvation: "And the names of the buyers are written in the book of the living. They are sealed with the sign of the cross. And all the choirs of the blessed ones are called as witnesses."[194]

Denis says that chapter 33, the promise of Jerusalem's restoration and healing, *began* to be fulfilled when the Judeans returned from Babylon, but "complete healing from the wound of sin was accomplished through Christ's incarnation and passion."[195] All of the things promised in this chapter—the voice of the bridegroom (33:11), the shoot of justice (33:15), the Davidic king on the throne (33:17), the restoration of the priesthood (33:18), and the eternal covenant (33:19-26)—refer, in a literal way (*ad litteram*), to Christ and his accomplishments. In the biblical text, God promises that the deserted land will once again be inhabited by sheep and shepherds, and "the flocks shall once again pass under the hand that counts them" (33:13). Denis explains that believers will be brought, "one by one . . . to their shepherd [Christ] for inspection."[196] After citing evidence from John's Gospel that Christ is the shepherd and his followers are the sheep, Denis reinforces his insistence that this is a literal interpretation by repeating information from Nicholas of Lyra that "a certain scholar, preeminent among the Hebrews," understands sheep, livestock, and herds to refer to humans. The Jewish scholar, unnamed by Denis, is Rashi, credited by name in Nicholas's text.[197] Denis is frequently critical of Nicholas's employment of Jewish sources.[198] Thus he needs to justify his own citation of this source: "I am sharing this so that no one supposes that [my own] explanation is merely spiritual rather than literal."[199]

Denis's treatment of chapters 36 (the scroll dictated to Baruch), 37-38 (Jeremiah's imprisonment and his descent into the cistern), and 39 (the fall of Jerusalem) attends primarily to the literal sense of the events that occurred in these passages. Baruch's answer to the princes about Jeremiah's dictation of the scroll that he had read to them, that Jeremiah "spoke these words as

194. Denis the Carthusian, *Exposition on the Prophet Jeremiah* 32.
195. Denis the Carthusian, *Exposition on the Prophet Jeremiah* 33:4-7.
196. Denis the Carthusian, *Exposition on the Prophet Jeremiah* 33:12-13.
197. Nicholas of Lyra, *Literal Postill on Jeremiah* 33:10. Nicholas says that his source is Rabbi Solomon (Rashi). Denis's point is that the Jewish explanation of "sheep" as humans reinforces Denis's identification of sheep with the human followers of Jesus.
198. Klepper, *Insight of Unbelievers*, 124.
199. Denis the Carthusian, *Exposition on the Prophet Jeremiah* 33:12-13.

though he were reading them to me" (36:18), prompts an observation about how the writing process often benefits from divine assistance:

> This was an indication of heavenly instruction. For there is no difficulty or delay in learning when the mind is illuminated by the Holy Spirit, whose grace knows nothing of slow exertions or lengthy efforts. For that reason many people, when they write, compose or give explanations while assisted by the Holy Spirit, are able to produce everything very quickly due to their minds being, in some sense, filled.[200]

After the episode with the scroll, the Lord hid Jeremiah and Baruch from the angry king (36:26). Denis explains that this was supernatural protection. They were likely rendered invisible in the same way that Christ hid himself and departed from the temple unscathed (John 8:59). "Certainly Christ did not hide himself behind a pillar! Instead he made himself appear invisible to his enemies."[201] Or perhaps, instead of making the prophets invisible, God miraculously conveyed Jeremiah and Baruch to a nearby hiding place.[202]

In the discussion of Jeremiah's grim circumstances while imprisoned in the cistern, Denis praises the piety and patience of the prophet: "See how much this most holy man suffered because of his integrity. Our own miserable impatience should blush with shame."[203] In contrast, the wavering king Zedekiah is no worthy exemplar. Though internally "favorably disposed or even friendly toward Jeremiah," the king relied too much on his princes, so that "his downfall was caused by the wicked advice of others, just as it happens with rulers all the time."[204] At one point the king confined Jeremiah to a somewhat more comfortable section of the prison (37:20–21):

> This shows there was a certain degree of piety in Zedekiah, but he nevertheless ought to have acted in accordance with genuine justice and released Jeremiah, who was completely innocent. But he did not want to offend his princes, so he confined the prophet in the prison's entrance. There are many such people who wish to serve two masters (Matt 6:24), pleasing both God and the world, and they try to appear agreeable in every

200. Denis the Carthusian, *Exposition on the Prophet Jeremiah* 36:14–18.
201. Denis the Carthusian, *Exposition on the Prophet Jeremiah* 36:21–26.
202. Denis the Carthusian, *Exposition on the Prophet Jeremiah* 36:21–26.
203. Denis the Carthusian, *Exposition on the Prophet Jeremiah* 38:4–6.
204. Denis the Carthusian, *Exposition on the Prophet Jeremiah* 37:3–4.

circumstance. It is certain that these people wander and stray from the path of impartiality quite frequently.[205]

The fall of Jerusalem concludes with the horrific account of Zedekiah forced to witness the slaughter of his sons before being blinded and transported in chains to Babylon (Jer 39:5–7). At the moral level, this represents wicked bishops and leaders of the church under the control of the devil: "When they give in to his temptation, they and their spiritual children or subjects are killed by him. The devil also put out the eyes of Zedekiah and bound him with shackles, for he thoroughly blinds the hearts of wicked bishops and leaders of the church, and binds them with the chains of impiety, and sends them to hell."[206] Thus (just as we have seen in Hugh of St. Cher's postill) a gruesome biblical account offers an opportunity to critique the shortcomings of unworthy religious leaders of Denis's day.

Medieval Apocalyptic and Women's Visionary Interpretations of Jeremiah

Several other works, not included in this volume, warrant discussion in this introduction, so that the reader can receive a fuller picture of medieval reception of Jeremiah: namely, the thirteenth-century Pseudo-Joachim *Super Ieremiam* (*On Jeremiah*) and the writings of visionary women Birgitta of Sweden, Hildegard of Bingen, and Mechthild of Magdeburg, who offered brief interpretations of Jeremiah in their works.

The Pseudo-Joachim Commentary

The *Super Ieremiam*, a commentary that is strikingly different from those included in this volume, claims to be written by the controversial abbot Joachim Fiore (ca. 1135–1202). Joachim, born in Sicily, spent time as a monk in the Cistercian order before departing and founding the stricter order of San Giovanni, also known as the Florensian order due to the monastery's location in Fiore in the Calabrian mountains.[207] Joachim wrote esoteric

---

205. Denis the Carthusian, *Exposition on the Prophet Jeremiah* 37:20.
206. Denis the Carthusian, *Exposition on the Prophet Jeremiah* 37.
207. For biographical information about Joachim, see Henry Bett, *Joachim of Flora*

apocalyptic works that sharply critiqued the abuses, moral laxity, greed, and corruption that he perceived in the church of his day. Through his study of Scripture and history, he devised a threefold division of the ages of the world. These were overlapping stages or states (*status*) corresponding to the Father (beginning with Adam, coming to fruition with Abraham, and ending at the time of Christ), the Son (beginning at the time of King Uzziah, coming to fruition at the time of John the Baptist's father Zechariah, and ending at the time of Joachim of Fiore), and the Holy Spirit (commencing with the sixth-century monastic founder Benedict, and—from Joachim's perspective—about to come to fruition in the near future).[208] Joachim's teachings about the Trinity were condemned by the Fourth Lateran Council and Pope Innocent III in 1215, more than a decade after his death.[209] Works written by Joachim, as well as those written in his name, gained popularity in the decades and centuries following his death, and Dante's *Paradiso* mentions "the Calabrian abbot Joachim" and Rabanus Maurus in the same lines.[210]

The *Super Ieremiam*, which was written in Joachim's name and went through several recensions, seems to reflect the concerns of Joachim's devotees in the decades following his death. It is generally dated to the early 1240s.[211] Various arguments have been made for Florensian, Franciscan, or Cistercian authorship.[212] The esoteric text requires of its reader some knowledge of thirteenth-century ecclesiastical and secular politics. Structured as a commentary on the book of Jeremiah, it sees the historical events of Jeremi-

---

(Merrick, NY: Richwood, 1976); and Bernard McGinn, *The Calabrian Abbot: Joachim of Fiore in the History of Western Thought* (New York: Macmillan, 1985), 18–30.

208. Brett Edward Whalen, *Dominion of God: Christendom and Apocalypse in the Middle Ages* (Cambridge, MA: Harvard University Press, 2009), 107.

209. Stephen E. Wessley, *Joachim of Fiore and Monastic Reform* (New York: Peter Lang, 1990), 102.

210. Bett, *Joachim of Flora*, citing Dante, *Paradiso* 12.139–41. For Joachim's enduring impact, see Marjorie Reeves, *Joachim of Fiore and the Prophetic Future* (New York: Harper, 1977).

211. For discussions of the complicated manuscript history of this text, see Wessley, *Joachim of Fiore and Monastic Reform*, 114–20; and Robert Moynihan, "The Development of the 'Pseudo-Joachim' Commentary 'Super Hieremiam': New Manuscript Evidence," *Mélanges de l'École Française de Rome, Moyen âge–Temps modernes* 98 (1986): 109–42. Moynihan argues that a "core" of the Jeremiah commentary originates with Joachim himself, but this view is not generally accepted. For criticisms of Moynihan's argument, see David Morris, "The Historiography of the *Super Prophetas* (also known as *Super Esaiam*) of Pseudo-Joachim of Fiore," *Oliviana* 4 (2012): 15n25, http://oliviana.revues.org/512; and Wessley, *Joachim of Fiore and Monastic Reform*, 119.

212. Wessley, *Joachim of Fiore and Monastic Reform*, 123.

ah's life and ministry as containing prophecy that is fulfilled in a twofold way. First, the content of the book of Jeremiah foretells New Testament events. Second, it foretells political and ecclesiastical events that occur in the early 1200s and beyond. The persecution of the Old Testament prophet is reca- pitulated in the sufferings of Christ and again in the struggles of medieval individuals, orders, and movements struggling to follow Christ faithfully. For instance, the conspiracy of the "men of Anathoth" who try to kill Jeremiah (Jer 11:21) is an event that foretells the collusion of the high priest Caiaphas and Jesus's other enemies (John 11:50), as well as "Cistercian abbots, priors, and monks" who were adversaries of the *doctor* (teacher) Joachim.[213] An- other conspirator is the "pope who will come after Celestine," a reference to Innocent III, who condemned Joachim's writings.[214] Stephen E. Wessley notes that "what concerns our author most are the tribulations in the Church since the year 1200."[215] A particularly significant passage, referenced several times in the *Super Ieremiam,* is the king's cutting and burning of the scroll in Jer 36, a specific reference to the condemnation of Joachim's teachings at the Fourth Lateran Council. (In the biblical text the king is Jehoiakim. The *Super Ieremiam* mistakenly refers to him as Zedekiah.). The king represents Caiaphas the high priest and Pope Innocent.

> For it will come to pass that Caiaphas the high priest will intrude upon the truth so that one person is condemned, that is, the *doctor* dies for the people, so that be the entire race does not perish in error. Thus Zedekiah rises up against Jeremiah. He condemns the book. He cuts the Trinity from the unity, cutting the opinion of the *doctor* using the knife of the scribe.[216]

Containing references to the prophecies of Merlin the magician and filled with eschatological themes, the text remained popular among readers inter- ested in apocalyptic speculation, and "it was, it seems, quite as well known as any of Joachim's generally recognized authentic works."[217]

213. Pseudo-Joachim of Fiore, *Super Ieremiam* [*Abbatis Ioachim Divina prorsus in Iere- miam Prophetam Interpretatio*] (Cologne: Alectorius and haeredes Soteri, 1577), 151.
214. Pseudo-Joachim, *Super Ieremiam,* 150.
215. Wessley, *Joachim of Fiore and Monastic Reform,* 105.
216. Pseudo-Joachim, *Super Ieremiam,* 150. The cutting and burning of the scroll is also discussed in *Super Ieremiam,* 368–69.
217. Moynihan, "Development of the 'Pseudo-Joachim' Commentary," 110.

Visionary Women's Interpretations of Jeremiah

Though there are no extant female-authored medieval commentaries on Jeremiah, a number of women offered brief interpretations of passages from Jeremiah in their visionary works. For instance, Birgitta of Sweden (ca. 1303–1373), writing shortly before her death, used fiery rhetoric to apply Jeremiah's story to the political and ecclesiastical situation of her day. She reports that she received a divine revelation regarding Pope Gregory XI, who was residing in Avignon, where popes had reigned since 1309—a situation that scandalized many. Birgitta had repeatedly urged Gregory to move his papal court to Rome, but her pleas and warnings were thus far unsuccessful. She laments that the king of France, the cardinals, and others were putting obstacles in the pope's way, and that "many people have arisen there saying that they have God's Spirit and receive divine revelations and visions that they use as a pretext to dissuade him from coming."[218] God revealed to her that the situation was similar to that of King Zedekiah, who had listened to false prophets rather than to Jeremiah.

> God answered: "You have heard it read about how Jeremiah lived in Israel in those days and had God's Spirit for prophecy, and how there were many at the time who had the spirit of dreams and lies. The wicked king put his trust in them, which is why both the king himself and his people fell into captivity. If the king had put his trust in Jeremiah alone, my anger would have been withdrawn from him. So it is now as well. Sages arise or dreamers or friends not of the spirit but of the flesh, and they use their persuasion on Pope Gregory and dissuade him from the opposite course of action. Nevertheless, I, the Lord, shall still prevail over them and bring the pope to Rome against their encouragement. However, whether you will see him come or not, that is not permitted for you to know."[219]

Two other visionary women treated Jeremiah in a more devotional vein. The Benedictine nun Hildegard of Bingen (1098–1179), whose writings are filled with imagery of trees and "greenness" to describe God as the source of life and fecundity, commented on the prophet's vision in the opening

218. Birgitta of Sweden, *Liber Caelestis* 4.141, in *The Revelations of St. Birgitta of Sweden*, trans. Denis Searby, introduction and notes by Bridget Morris (New York: Oxford University Press, 2008), 2:253.

219. Birgitta of Sweden, *Liber Caelestis* 4.14, trans. Searby, 2:253–54. Birgitta died in 1373, fewer than four years before Gregory XI moved to Rome in 1377.

chapter of Jeremiah. The "rod watching" witnessed by the prophet refers to humanity: "O Divine Brightness of that brightness which shines within Your creation, You are the root that sent forth many branches. . . . For in the beginning, You fashioned a root and made it watchful with the breath of life [Gen 2:7], and when You said to Jeremiah, 'What seest thou, Jeremiah,' he replied to You, 'I see a rod watching' [Jer 1:11]."[220] Finally, the beguine Mechthild of Magdeburg (ca. 1260–ca. 1282), writing in Middle Low German, praises Jeremiah as one of "five lights," five prophets who illumine the book she wrote. "Jeremiah illumines also for his part when he speaks of the intimate secrets of our Lady," for his statement that "a woman will encompass a man" (Jer 31:22) was generally seen as a prophecy of the incarnation of Christ in the Virgin Mary's womb.[221] Thus we see the importance of the prophet Jeremiah for medieval Christian interpreters, both male and female.

About This Translation

I endeavored to make this translation both readable and accurate. Attending to contemporary concerns regarding gendered language for humans, I translated *homines* as "humans" and *viri* as "men." *Filii* was translated as "children" unless the context called for the masculine "sons." In the Latin text, in sentences where there is no name or pronoun as subject of the sentence, the deity is frequently the unnamed subject of the verb. In these cases, I frequently used the name or title (e.g., "God," "Lord") that was the antecedent in that biblical passage. Other times, particularly to avoid awkward verbal constructions (such as Godself), I used the masculine pronoun, reflecting medieval usage that assigned grammatical (though not ontological) gender to the deity.

The book of Jeremiah deals extensively with the suffering of the people of Judah, the *Iudaei*, at the time of the Babylonian siege and destruction of Jerusalem. The noun *Iudaei* can be translated either as "Judeans" or as "Jews," English terms that have distinct (if overlapping) connotations. When the text referred to the residents of Judah at the time of Jeremiah, I usually translated the word as "Judeans." When a given commentator was clearly referring to

220. Hildegard of Bingen, "Letter 389," in *The Letters of Hildegard of Bingen*, trans. Joseph L. Baird and Radd K. Ehrman (New York: Oxford University Press, 2004), 3:182.

221. Mechthild of Magdeburg, *The Flowing Light of the Godhead* 3.20, trans. Frank Tobin, Classics of Western Spirituality (New York: Paulist, 1998), 127 and 351n45. The other prophets are Moses, David, Solomon, and Daniel.

Jews of his own day or to adherents to the religious tradition Judaism in the postexilic period, I used "Jews." Nevertheless, the reader should be aware that this distinction would not necessarily have been present to medieval writers and readers of these commentaries, though the interpreters excerpted in this volume often used *Hebraei* (Hebrews) when speaking of Jews (especially Jewish scholars) of their own day. In a context where there was widespread suspicion of Jews, the Christian author or reader of a passage that criticized the *Iudaei* who rejected Jeremiah's message may also have had in mind the European *Iudaei* who lived in nearby communities, studying and worshipping at local synagogues.

I have used the Vulgate numbering system for the chapters and verses of Jeremiah commented on in these excerpts.[222] For other biblical passages, for ease of reference, I employed chapter and verse numbering found in contemporary translations such as the New Revised Standard Version. Though verse numbers were not used in the medieval texts, I have included these to assist the reader. I also used the modern designations for 1 Samuel through 2 Kings, instead of naming them as 1–4 Kings. In most cases, I used NRSV spellings for biblical names. When the medieval biblical commentary included transliterations of Hebrew words, I used the spelling found in the Latin text; transliterations employed in explanatory footnotes use the Society of Biblical Literature style.[223] Since the authors translated here were commenting on the Latin text (even in cases where the commentator consulted the Hebrew text), the biblical passages used as the lemmas are translated from the Vulgate, so that the reader can see the text that the commentator had before him. Significant variations from the Hebrew text are often signaled in the commentary itself, especially by Nicholas of Lyra or when commentators employed Jerome, who dealt with this topic at length. Readers may find it helpful to consult the Douay-Rheims Bible, an English translation of the Vulgate published in stages between 1582 and 1610.[224] Though my own translations of the Vulgate frequently are based on Douay-Rheims, I translated the scripture text according to the sense understood by the particular commentator whom I was treating, even when that translation differed significantly from Douay-Rheims.

222. Chapters were not divided into verses until the sixteenth century. See van Liere, *Introduction to the Medieval Bible*, 43–45.

223. For the transliteration of Hebrew words in material that Rabanus Maurus excerpted from Jerome, I followed the spelling used in the critical edition of Jerome, *On Jeremiah* (CCSL 74).

224. *The Vulgate Bible: Douay-Rheims Translation*, vol. 4, *The Major Prophetical Books*, ed. Angela M. Kinney (Cambridge, MA: Harvard University Press, 2012).

In conclusion, I wish to acknowledge those who have supported me in the process of preparing this volume. I thank the Bible in Medieval Tradition series editors, Philip D. W. Krey, Ian Christopher Levy, and Thomas Ryan, for their expert guidance. I thank Linda Bieze, senior project manager at Wm. B. Eerdmans Publishing Company, for her skillful assistance. I am grateful to the librarians at Trinity Lutheran Seminary's Hamma Library, especially Carla Birkhimer, Kathy Nodo, and Ray Olson, and the library staff at Capital University's Blackmore Library, especially Scott Bates, Matthew Cook, and Elizabeth Woods, for helping me obtain necessary sources. I express my thanks to all of the faculty and staff at both institutions for their collegiality and friendship. I especially appreciated inspirational conversations about this project with Jonathan Loopstra, Wray Bryant, and Alan Katchen. Much of the work on this book was completed during a sabbatical year, for which I thank the board of trustees at Capital University and the board of directors at Trinity Lutheran Seminary. Encouraging my ongoing progress was a group of colleagues who gathered weekly to set scholarship goals: Erica Brownstein, Suzanne Marilley, Cheryl Peterson, and Sally Stamper. I am grateful for the advice of biblical scholars Jeremy Hutton, Rodney Hutton, and Mary E. Shields regarding which chapters in Jeremiah to include. Michael Brunner was a helpful and capable research assistant. Julie A. Kanarr was my diligent proofreader. Maureen McCann and Melanie Garrabrant provided valuable office assistance. Finally, I thank John Birkner, who has supported my work in numerous ways.

RUPERT OF DEUTZ

On the Holy Trinity and Its Works: On Jeremiah

Jeremiah 1

CCCM 23

Prologue: Jeremiah's Prophecy
and the Dawn of the Fifth Age of the World

The dawn of the fifth age of the world is the prediction of the Babylonian captivity and the destruction and burning of the city and temple, which the prophet Jeremiah foretold and would also see with his own eyes. Here it is appropriate to ask what was happening in the world so that it could now rightly be called or reckoned "the fifth age," with a clear, fixed boundary, after the fourth age was completed. The reason exists on account of the preceding events. For in the first age, before the flood, the world was like an infant left to itself, free from paying attention to God's teaching.[1] In the second age, the world was like a child learning the first basics of instruction through the covenant that God made with Noah. In the third age it was like an adolescent when it received, in Abraham, the promise of the blessed offspring, and, in Moses, the discipline of the law. In the fourth age, like a young person, the world heard in David the promise of Christ's reign. So now, at this time, what did the world hear or receive more fully so that one could rightly consider it to be like the fifth age of a fully grown or fully developed man? It indisputably received the promise of Christ's priesthood. For the one who was promised as *human*

---

1. Drawing on the writings of Augustine (354–430), medieval Christians commonly divided chronological time into six "ages" or periods corresponding with the lifespan of a human. See Peter Darby, *Bede and the End of Time* (Burlington, VT: Ashgate, 2012), 23.

in Abraham and as *king* in David was promised as *priest* in the prophets at this time. Here Christ's priesthood is prefigured through events and made known by prophetic words.

Certainly in an earlier age it was said about him: "You are a priest forever, according to the order of Melchizedek" (Ps 110:4). And it was said to the priest Eli, as an image of the downfall of the Jews' priesthood, which would be succeeded by the faithful priesthood of Christ and the church: "Behold the days are coming when I will cut off your arm, and the arm of your father's house, so there shall be no elders in your house" (1 Sam 2:31). But here the cause and effect of Christ's priesthood are both represented together, much more fully and much more blessedly, and the time of his coming is determined. The Babylonian captivity of one nation undoubtedly signifies the reason, shared by all peoples, why such a priest was needed for the entire human race. The return of the captives under the great priest Jeshua (Ezra 3:2) symbolizes the remission of our sins, by which we are freed through our leader and liberator Jesus Christ, the great high priest. Furthermore, the time of his coming is determined in this way: "O Daniel, consider the word and understand the vision. Seven weeks are shortened for your people and for your holy city, so that transgression may be finished, sin may be ended, iniquity may be abolished, everlasting justice may be instituted, vision and prophecy may be fulfilled, and the Holy of Holies may be anointed," etc. (Dan 9:22–24).

Furthermore, at the dividing point that marks the end of this [fifth] age, the entire promise regarding this priest is fulfilled when the angel said to Mary's husband Joseph, "She will give birth to a son, and you will name him Jesus, for he will save his people from their sins" (Matt 1:21). It should be clear that this very priest is God, who alone is able to save people from sins and "did not need to offer sacrifices daily for his own sins as other priests did before then, offering sacrifices for the people" (Heb 7:27). Indeed, evangelical authority established these dividing points of the ages by saying, in the Book of the Genealogy of Jesus Christ [Gospel of Matthew]: "So all the generations from Abraham until David are fourteen generations; and from David until the migration to Babylon are fourteen generations; and from the migration to Babylon until Christ there are fourteen generations" (Matt 1:17). We rightly understand that the following is said only about the generation of Jesus Christ: He is truly human, according to the promise made to Abraham, "In your offspring I will bless all nations" (Gen 22:18). He is also king, according to the promise made to David, "I will put offspring from your loins upon your throne" (Ps 132:11). And Christ is undoubtedly priest in office and God in his authority, according to the promise made to Mary's husband Joseph, "For he himself will save his people from their sins" (Matt 1:21).

Now this is the beginning of the fifth age, which contains remarkable works of God just like the fifth day of the creation of the world, corresponding to the Spirit of Counsel, which is the fifth [gift of the Spirit] and precedes the Spirit of the Fear of the Lord.[2] For divine counsel permitted God's beautiful and noble temple—which was the only one in the whole world at that time, and very rich with gold, marvelously constructed, and renowned for its sanctity—to be burned with fire by Babylon, plundered, profaned, and covered with the blood of the slaughtered, along with the palace and city of David and Solomon. For while it was young and self-indulgent, the world was instructed not to think that God, who dwells in heaven, takes delight in the gold of a human-made temple or the wealth of cities rather than in the faith and good deeds of humans, who have God's temple prepared in their souls; only here does God take delight and deem it worthy to appear and have his presence recognized. Without [faith and good deeds], one seeks God in vain in outward things, in the stones and gold of a human-made temple. This fifth age also has some resemblance to the fifth day of the world's creation. For just as not all things were lifted up into the air, because one kind of creature arises from the waters, so not all of the captives said: "By the waters of Babylon, there we sat and wept" (Ps 137:1). Those of them who said this were the ones who remembered Zion, where there was the holy temple of the Lord's name, where it was appropriate to worship the one and only true God, unimpeded by the Babylonian king. These sorts of people certainly were not engulfed under the waters of the river of Babylon, but they rose above them like the birds that the waters produced at God's command, prepared for flight as soon as they heard the edict of release from Cyrus, king of the Persians. The rest, who remained in Babylonian luxury spending time in the arms of Babylonian wives, which was forbidden by the law, preferred their captivity to the freedom offered to them. They were like little fish, whose every pleasure is sunken beneath the waters and who do not know how to fly. But now we should proceed to the matter at hand.

---

2. Throughout his work, Rupert aligns the seven days of creation with the seven ages of the world, the seven stages in human life, and the seven gifts of the Spirit (Isa 11:2–3). For instance, in his discussion of Gen 1:20–21, Rupert explained how the Spirit of Counsel, which he regarded as the fifth gift of the Spirit, was symbolized by the birds that God created on the fifth day, since birds take special care or counsel to tend their young; Rupert of Deutz, *On Genesis* 1.48, ed. Hrabanus Haacke, CCCM 21 (Turnhout: Brepols, 1971), 175.

Introduction: Jeremiah's Prophetic Ministry
Foreshadows Christ's Prophetic Role

To begin with, Jeremiah—which means "exalted Lord," for he is the exalted Lord's prophet—foreshadows the Lord's prophetic character in every respect.[3] Undoubtedly, when Jeremiah was sanctified in his mother's womb and was told, **"Before I formed you in the womb I knew you, and before you came out of the womb I sanctified you"** (Jer 1:5), this was said to foreshadow the one who was "God with God" (John 1:1) before he was conceived as human from the Virgin's womb.

Jeremiah also foreshadowed our Lord when he preached to his people, calling to repentance a people that refused to listen when he predicted the future destruction of the temple and the city. Though he was struck down, he survived this destruction, and then he evangelized the nations and left the Judeans in blindness. This prophet prophesied against the city, urging it to repentance while it turned against him with obstinate contempt. He predicted the arrival of the Babylonian army and the imminent burning of the temple and city. And although he endured many trials, he survived the burning and prophesied to foreign nations when King Zedekiah was captured and his eyes were put out. Now let us enumerate how many times the word of the Lord came to Jeremiah before the siege of the city, and let us follow the sequence of the message of the gospel, which is clear and well-known, according to the order and sequence of the prophecy:

First, it is written: **And the word of the Lord came to me, saying: "Before I formed you in the womb I knew you, and before you came out of the womb I sanctified you and made you a prophet to the nations"** (1:4–5).

Second: **And the word of the Lord came to me, saying, "What do you see, Jeremiah?" And I said, "I see a rod watching"** (1:11). Again: **"What do you see?" And I said, "I see a boiling kettle, and it is faced away from the north"** (1:13). These two sayings are rightly considered one word of the Lord since they each have the same message. The rod that is watching is the discipline of repentance to those who receive it and the boiling kettle is the judgment of eternal damnation for the impenitent.

Then, in a third place: **And the word of the Lord came to me, saying: Go and cry in the ears of Jerusalem, saying, "Thus says the Lord: I have**

---

3. The etymology comes from Jerome, *Interpretation of Hebrew Names* 15.18, ed. Paul de Lagarde, CCSL 72 (Turnhout: Brepols, 1959), 127.

remembered you, pitying your youth and the love when you were a bride, when you followed me in the wilderness in a land that is not sown, etc." (2:1–2), and much more, in which he recalls Jerusalem's own sins in a lengthy sermon and calls her to repentance.

After this, in the fourth place: **The word that came to Jeremiah from the Lord, saying: Stand in the gate of the house of the Lord and proclaim this word and say, "Hear the word of the Lord, all people of Judah who enter through these gates to worship the Lord. Thus says the Lord of Hosts, the God of Israel: Make your ways and your actions good, and I will dwell with you in this place. Do not trust in lying words, saying, 'This is the temple of the Lord, the temple of the Lord, the temple of the Lord'"** (7:1–4).

Then, in the fifth place: **The word that came to Jeremiah from the Lord, saying: Hear the words of this covenant and speak to the men of Judah and the inhabitants of Jerusalem, and you shall say to them, "Thus says the Lord, the God of Israel: Cursed is the man who will not heed the words of this covenant that I commanded to your ancestors"** (11:1–4). And a little later: **The house of Israel and the house of Judah have made void my covenant that I made with their ancestors** (11:10).

Then in the sixth place: **The word of the Lord that came to Jeremiah concerning the messages about the drought: Judah has mourned and its gates have fallen and lie covered in the ground. Nobles sent their inferiors to the water. They came to draw water and, finding none, they carried their vessels back empty** (14:1–3).

After these things, in the seventh place: **The word that came to Jeremiah from the Lord, saying: "Arise, and go down to the potter's house, and there you shall hear my words." And I went down into the potter's house, and behold he was doing work at the wheel. And the vase that he was making of clay with his hands was ruined. And turning it, he made it into another vessel, as it seemed good in his eyes to make. Then the word of the Lord came to me, saying, "O house of Israel, can I not do with you as this potter has done? See, just like clay in the hand of a potter, so you are in my hand, O house of Israel"** (18:1–6). Immediately after these words, every prophecy is entirely about the imminent destruction of this city and temple.

Chapter One

Jeremiah's Call Prefigures Christ's Incarnation

Now let us see how the progression of this kind of prophecy is similar to the gospel of Christ. First, what is said here may also be said, in some sense, about a holy person:

1:5 Before I formed you in the womb I knew you, and before you came out of the womb I sanctified you.

1:9–10 And God put forth his hand and touched my mouth. And the Lord said to me: See, I have placed my word in your mouth. Look, today I have set you up over the nations and over the kingdoms, so that you shall root up and destroy, you shall scatter and disperse, you shall build and plant. It is clear that this declares the thorough anointing, obedience, and glorification of the Holy of Holies. For who else, other than him, did God the Father know before he was formed in the womb? Who else, before he came out of the womb, did God sanctify and set up as prophet over the nations? Indeed, this is the truly spoken cry of each and every child of Adam: "See, I was conceived in iniquity, and in sin my mother conceived me" (Ps 51:5). But the word "sanctified" can be understood in two ways. In one sense, someone can be called "sanctified" by being free of the infection of sin. No one can be "sanctified" in this sense except through Christ's grace. In another sense, the term refers to being set apart from public or common usage for a holy use or ministry (Lev 10:10). This sort of sanctification can be broadly construed, so that firstborn livestock can be called "sanctified to God" (Exod 13:2) because they are legally set apart for use, by lawful right of the ministers of the holy altars. In the same way, God's knowledge, about which it here says, **Before I formed you in the womb I knew you,** can likewise be understood in several ways. In one way, God knew his only begotten Son before he was formed in the womb; in another way, God knew one of his own chosen ones before he was formed in the womb. God knew the former through coexistence with him; God knew the latter through firm and certain foreknowledge. So, indeed, in a certain sense, God knew this prophet [Jeremiah] before forming him in the womb, and before he came out of the womb God sanctified him. For he was a type of the Prophet and Lord of the Prophets, his only begotten Son, the only one whom God knew in a unique way, sanctifying him when he was made human, was formed in the womb, and came out of the womb. Regarding the statement that God knew him, the Son himself says: "No one has known the Son except the Father" (Matt 11:27). Moreover, the statement that God knew him before forming him in the womb, and sanctified him before he came out of the womb, is a true belief, rightly held by all devout people. For he was conceived not by the male semen but by the Holy Spirit, and he was sent as a prophet to the nations, not only to the Jews but also for the salvation of the Gentiles. God says: **See, I have placed my word in your mouth,** which you shall obediently say and speak in the world. The Son himself says this in a certain place: "Because I have not spoken from myself, but the Father who sent me has given me a command regarding what to say and what to speak" (John 12:49). **Look, I have set you up over the nations and over the kingdoms.** Because you have become obedient unto death, even death on the cross, I will set **you up over nations and over kingdoms,** as the psalmist sang about you: "You have made him a little less than angels and have crowned him with glory and honor; and you have set him over the works of your hands, and you have subjected all things under his feet" (Ps 8:5–6).

    So that you shall uproot up and destroy. This means: **You shall uproot** the things that are wickedly rooted, and **you shall destroy** the things wickedly built, especially the gatherings of the scribes and Pharisees that have their roots planted deeply in the soil of greed, and also are like sepulchers of the dead that outwardly appear pleasing to humans but inside are filled with dead peoples' bones (Matt 23:27). How shall you **uproot and destroy** them? Let the Romans come as your avengers.[4] Let them seize their land and the people. Then let their souls, after being ripped from their bodies by the physical sword, become "prey for foxes"—that is, for evil spirits (Ps 63:10). **And you shall scatter and disperse.** So **you shall** not only **uproot** them, so that you would, at least, permit them to be carried into one place of captivity, but instead **you shall scatter** them among all the peoples **and disperse** them into little village footpaths or small sections of cities. **And you shall build and plant.** Whom? Not the aforementioned people, but others in their place. **You shall build** nations that have been forsaken until now. "In the land of the living" you shall plant the nations that, until now, did not have a place in God's covenant (Ps 27:13).

---

4. Here Rupert regards Jeremiah's prophecy to be fulfilled by New Testament events and by the Roman destruction of Jerusalem and the temple in 70 CE.

The Vision of the Watching Rod and the Boiling Kettle

Next we should understand that this Holy of Holies (Dan 9:24) is coming in the following manner: his first coming shall be a fatherly rod of correction to all those who receive him and, for that reason, are made children of God (John 1:12); his second coming will be the judgment of damnation for the impious and the unbelievers.

1:11–13 "What do you see, Jeremiah?" and I said, "I see a rod watching." And the Lord said to me, "You have seen well, for I will watch over my word in order to perform it." [And the word of the Lord came to me a second time, saying:] "What do you see?" and I said, "I see a boiling kettle and it is faced away from the north." Clearly, when these things were spoken, evils were being prepared—evils that would be poured out on all who dwelled in the land of Judah—coming from the north, from Babylon whose land was located north of them. There is no doubt that this very same evil of captivity would be a rod for some and a boiling kettle for others. This captivity did not lead to the same results for Daniel and the companions who were with him as it did for all the others. This exalted Lord, the Holy of Holies, Christ—who is all the more preeminent and solicitous—sees **a rod watching** for us who believe and **a boiling kettle faced away from the north** for the impious and the despisers. This means he sees for us **a rod watching,** which refers to the necessary fear of future judgment and eternal punishment. Just as Daniel and his companions were with those against whom God was angry because of their idolatry, so all of us—the pious with the impious, the faithful ones with the unfaithful—are kept in the same place of captivity on account of Adam's guilt. Each and every one of us will die, for we are all mortals. But for the pious and faithful, this captivity or mortality is a rod that we can endure temporally so we may be trained in the discipline of humility, since we fell through pride. So Christ says in the beginning of his preaching, "Repent, for the reign of God is at hand" (Matt 4:17). Furthermore, the discipline of repentance is sometimes difficult and other times pleasant and voluntary. Regarding the discipline imposed as something difficult, it is written: "If his children forsake my law and do not walk according to my judgments, I will visit their transgressions with the rod and their sins with beatings" (Ps 89:30–32). For it is unpleasant to be visited with God's rod of adversity or sickness, about which it is also written elsewhere: "The Lord disciplines those whom he loves and beats every child whom he accepts" (Heb 12:6). But this very same difficulty shall be made fruitful through patience, for it will not be devoid of the fruits of repentance (Matt 3:8). Moreover there are different kinds of repentance. One is universal, the other individual. An example of universal repentance is when we confess our sins and are baptized into the death of Christ Jesus. Individual repentance is when someone puts to death one's members on earth, just as the Apostle says (Col 3:5). For the pious and faithful, the Lord sees a **rod watching. Watching** means hastening and rousing us to every good work. On the other hand, when it says he sees **a boiling pot,** this pertains to the unrepentant impious people. For example, John [the Baptist] says: "Every tree that does not bear good fruit is cut down and thrown into the fire" (Matt 3:10). And again, when Christ declares what he himself will say, "You cursed ones, go into the eternal fire that has been prepared for the devil and his angels" (Matt 25:41).[5]

5. Rupert's commentary does not treat Jer 1:14–19.

ALBERT THE GREAT

Postill on Jeremiah

Jeremiah 1

Chapter One

The Call of Jeremiah

1:4 And the word of the Lord came to me. Here we have a prophecy that is divided into two parts, set apart from one another by the placement of the heading.[1] The first of these parts describes the prophet being perfected in order to prophesy. The second part describes the series of revelatory visions, in 2:1: "And the word of the Lord came to me saying, 'Go and cry out.'" The prophet is perfected in three ways, and so three things are discussed in the first part: the prophet's consecration and the prophet's illumination when he says, "The word of the Lord came to me, saying, 'What do you see?'" (1:11), and the prophet's encouragement to prophesy when he says, "Therefore gird up your loins" (1:6).[2] Regarding the first of these [the consecration],

---

1. That is, "And the word of the Lord came to me" is a "heading" or serves as the opening passage of two different prophetic passages (1:4 and 2:1).

2. Scholastic theologians frequently looked for a structure in biblical passages, and they provided labels—often nouns with similar endings—to help the reader. According to Albert, the material in the opening chapter of Jeremiah describes a "threefold" perfection (*perfectio*), consisting of consecration (*consecratio*), illumination (*illuminatio*), and encouragement or strengthening (*confortatio*). The consecration of Jeremiah is divided into three parts: the consecration itself, the removal (*ablatio*) of his impediment, and the gathering (*collatio*) of his power. The first of these, the consecration itself, is subdivided into two parts: the deity's confirmation (*confirmatio*) and the consecration of the prophet to perform holy acts.

three things are mentioned: his consecration and removal of his impediment where he says, "And I said, 'Ah, ah, ah'" (1:6), and the gathering of his power where he says, "See, I have set you over nations and kingdoms" (1:10). In the first of these, two things are mentioned: the deity's confirmation and the prophet's consecration for an act of such exceptional holiness. Regarding the first, he says: **And the word,** which was uncreated and not made, **came** from God the Father.[3] The phrase "the word came to me" [*verbum ad me est factum*] means it was inspired by divine action. Luke 2:15: "Let us see this word that has come to pass [*verbum quod factum est*], which the Lord has done and shown to us."

1:5a Before I formed you [in the womb, I knew you]. God says three things that pertain to the consecration: the foreordaining of predestination, the conferring of grace, and the gathering of his power or rank. Regarding the first of these God says: **Before I formed you** with a rational soul, which is the human "form" that I placed in the human race, **I knew you.** By the light of predestination, I foreordained you for grace and glory. Now God did not know in a human fashion. Humans gain knowledge of something by encountering it, and this understanding never lacks experience, because to encounter something is to experience it. God knows things by the light of his own wisdom, by establishing them in their forms and by giving approval to what comes into existence. Genesis 1:31: "God saw all the things that he had made and they were very good." Thus God knows with the eyes of one who is well pleased—the eyes with which God provides grace and glory. Exodus 33:12: "You have found grace in my sight, and I know you by name." Second Timothy 2:19: "The Lord knows those who are his." So when in Matt 7:23 the opposite is said about wicked people, those to whom God did not provide grace and glory, "I will swear to them, 'I never knew you,'" it does not mean that he did not previously see the wicked people or notice them in the way "sight" is commonly understood. Rather, it means that he did not pour out on them the light of grace from his gracious eyes, just as it states in the Psalm [32:8] regarding the saints: "In the way in which you will go, I will fix my eyes on you." Second Samuel 19:38: "Chimham will go with me and I will set my eyes on him." According to this reasoning, then, God's knowledge of things

---

3. In Jer 1:4 and other points in the book, the Vulgate text reads: *Et factum est verbum Domini ad me.* A natural translation is: "And the word of the Lord came to me," but it also could also be translated as, "And the word of the Lord was made [*factum est*] to me." Albert is explaining that this should not be read as the making or creation of the Word, the Son, who according to the Nicene Creed was "begotten, not made."

is not dependent on encountering these things. Rather, God's knowledge brings about their very existence. Therefore God knows things in the same way before they exist and after they have been made. Romans 4:17: "He calls the things that are not, as though they are the things that are." Now there were heretics among the philosophers who are called Stoics who used this passage as an excuse for error. On account of these and similar words, they said that souls have existed from eternity or were created at the same time as the beginning of the world; they said that this is how God knew Jeremiah before he was born, since God knows each and every soul. The *Gloss* refutes them, saying: "It is not that he existed before his conception, as the heretics suppose, but because the Lord knew he would come to exist. To the one for whom things are *about* to be made, they are already made, for 'he calls the things that are not, as though they are the things that are.'"[4]

1:5b And before you came out of the womb [I sanctified you]. God mentions the conferring of grace that the one who is formed in the womb receives before coming forth to the light, and this is what God means when he says: **I sanctified you.** This means: I cleansed you by the grace that makes you acceptable. Now it is one thing to be made holy, and it is another thing to be holy. Something sanctified is made holy through an act. Something holy is not necessarily something that has been sanctified. It is in this sense that Christ was holy in the womb. Luke 1:35: "The Holy One that will be born from you will be called the Son of God." When something is sanctified through the form and effect of something holy, that holy thing is not made from something that was already holy; for instance, we are all made holy in baptism through the holiness of our holy Lord Jesus Christ. Now it is granted to a few, who are chosen for service to Christ by a special privilege, that they are sanctified in the womb without receiving any sacrament.

Since he suffered and prophesied about [Christ's] passion, which confers holiness through all the sacraments, Jeremiah especially prefigured that passion, even more than Isaiah, who—though he predicted the passion clearly—nevertheless is not said to have prefigured it. Indeed, Jeremiah suffered verbal opposition, plots were devised against him, and he was betrayed by men who had been friendly toward him, as he laments in 11:19: "[I did not know that they had devised plots against me, saying:] 'Come, let us throw wood on his bread,'" and many other things that he says there. This is the same thing that Christ said about himself in John 13:18: "The one who eats

4. *Glossa ordinaria* on Jer 1:5, PL 114:9.

my bread will lift up his heel against me." Psalm 41:9: "The peaceful person, in whom I trusted, has acted with extreme deceit toward me." John the Baptist prepared the way for Christ's grace and so received an even greater sanctification. But the Blessed Virgin provided an example of this and every grace, and so she received a sanctification that was greater than all the preceding ones.

Now Jeremiah was consecrated from his mother's womb: from the womb, so that he would not be impeded by a contrary disposition; and consecrated, so that he would not be rejected as unfit due to sin. When a contrary disposition has sprung forth in someone, that person does not purely, freely, or suitably receive an aptitude for illumination. When a contrary disposition does not impede it, illumination does not encounter any obstacle, and so illumination conveys itself boundlessly into a pure subject, making that person a prophet. Wisdom 7:27: "Through the nations [Wisdom] conveys herself into holy souls and makes them friends [of God] and prophets." The person who is impeded by a contrary disposition is not yet free, and so the soul is free when it has received the grace of illumination before it has been polluted by active sin. As Horace says: "For a long time the pitcher will retain the smell of what first filled it when it was new."[5] Lamentations 3:27: "It is good for a person to have borne the master's yoke beginning in one's youth." Because of this purity, Isaiah 8:18 says regarding the prophets: "Behold, I and my children whom the Lord gave me as a sign and portent to the house of Israel." For such people are still suitable when no stain of active sin has rendered them unworthy. Psalm 25:21: "The innocent and the upright have adhered to me." Therefore those who have this from their mother's womb are preeminent.

Consecration refers to the Holy Spirit's anointing that Jeremiah received while in the womb. Although the Blessed Virgin had the highest degree of this sanctification, with which she showed forth this grace, nevertheless the forerunner [John the Baptist] ranked next to her in degree of sanctification; for though he had sin, nevertheless we do not read that he was tempted with mortal sin. Matthew 3:14: "I ought to be baptized by you." The *Gloss* says this was "to be cleansed from sin."[6] So John had at least venial sin. Now Jeremiah, as someone who showed what grace is, nevertheless experienced the impediment of sin even though he had received sanctification in the womb. For when he said, "I am a child" (Jer 1:6), he meant, "I am

5. Horace, *Epistles* 1.2.69–70, in *Satires, Epistles, and Ars Poetica*, trans. H. Rushton Fairclough, LCL 194 (Cambridge, MA: Harvard University Press, 2005), 266.

6. *Glossa interlinearea* on Matt 3:14.

inadequate because of immaturity." This immaturity presented such a great impediment that he admitted that he did not know how to speak.

Now the Blessed Virgin, who found special grace in the sight of God, is ranked first. Second is the forerunner, who prepared the way for grace. Third is the prophet Jeremiah, who was the foreteller of this grace. And if some were to ask why other prophets did not receive the same sort of sanctification even though they, too, were foretellers of grace, we should say that, in word, deed, and suffering, no one except Jeremiah was a foreteller of the highest grace that was shown by taking away sin through [Christ's] passion. Jeremiah is the one who predicted the passion through his speech, demonstrated it through the courage of his spirit, and prefigured it through the similarity of his own suffering. Jeremiah 11:19: "Come, let us throw wood on his bread, and let us cut him off from the land of the living, and let his name be remembered no more."[7] His "bread" refers to the bread of knowledge with which Jeremiah fed the people and Christ fed the disciples. The "wood" refers to wood used for punishment. "Wood is thrown on bread" when, while someone's bread is eaten, the bread is considered to be like punishment inflicted by a shepherd's wooden rod, even though the person's bread is offered as an act of loving-kindness. This is what some thought about Jeremiah and our Lord Jesus Christ. This is not said to have happened to any other prophet. Therefore Jeremiah received a special sanctification and consecration for this, and that is why it says he was consecrated—sanctified in his mother's womb to the prophetic office through the Holy Spirit's anointing. First John 2:27: "The anointing will teach you about all things." A prophet is sanctified in this way, Deut 18:15: "The Lord will raise up from your own people a prophet like me. Listen to that person." It is not remarkable that some people received a sanctification in the womb that surpassed others. Through word and action, these people were appointed to a special office to serve the one who was holy in the womb: the Blessed Virgin was to bring him forth, the forerunner was to prepare the way, and the prophets were to prefigure and predict him. And though the Virgin was privileged to receive the highest office, and the forerunner also received an office next in rank, nevertheless the prophet Jeremiah did not lack status.

1:5c [And I gave you as a prophet to the nations], a **prophet** illuminated with prophetic inspiration. For a prophet reveals things by divine inspiration,

7. See Thomas Aquinas's discussion of the Vulgate's rendering of Jer 11:19 ("Let us throw wood on his bread") below.

not describing the history of events or grasping knowledge by human arguments; instead, purely through prediction, the prophet foretells the things that God has foreordained to occur. Second Peter 1:21: "Prophecy never occurred at any time through human will, but the holy people of God spoke, inspired by the Holy Spirit." For with history, the memory of past events directs the human's perception. With learned arguments, logic leads to the truth. But with prophecy, only the divine Spirit foretells the things that will happen in the future, and therefore prophecy is the most accurate. For all the words of the prophets are not established on the fallacious human spirit but on the Spirit of God, which cannot be mistaken. First Corinthians 2:12: "We have not received the spirit of this world but the Spirit that is from God, so that we may know the things that are given to us by God." Ecclesiasticus 36:16: "Your prophets are found to be faithful." Amos 3:7: "[God] does nothing without revealing it to his servants," the prophets.

And note that, so that Jeremiah would be more suitable for prophesying, he was sanctified in the womb even before he was born, so that much of the fault of original sin was removed, and much of the inclination toward evil was weakened, so that nothing would develop that could present an impediment to such great sanctity. Isaiah 49:1: "The Lord called me from the womb." **To the nations,** so that he would not only prophesy to the children of Israel but also to the nations. Isaiah 49:6: "I gave you as a light of the nations." For a prophet, who is also called "soothsayer," is said to be one who "speaks from afar" or "speaks for others" by the power of the mind, because that person utters mysteries to others by the power of a mind illuminated by divine revelation.

Now God says, **"And I gave you,"** because prophecy is a gift of God, as we read in 1 Cor 12:10. Now this is a mode of giving [prophecy], because the light of divine understanding can be received in two ways. One way is to receive it directly within oneself, and thus it is one and singular in form. Or it is possible for it to be received in a delimited way, constituted of things in the form of *genera, species,* and discrete individual things, and this is the mode of revelation, as Jerome writes.[8] In this mode, the word of God is "reason" and "reckoning," and it is the cause of individual things, through which

8. For a discussion of Albert the Great's scholastic views on the modes of prophecy, see G. Meersseman, "De S. Alberti Magni Postilla inedita super Ieremiam," *Angelicum* 9 (1932): 236–37. Jerome's commentary on this verse, describing a parallel between Paul and Jeremiah, quotes Gal 1:15–16, which says that God set Paul apart in the womb in order to *reveal* the Son in the apostle. Jerome, *On Jeremiah* 1:4–5, ed. Sigofredus Reiter, CCSL 74 (Turnhout: Brepols, 1960), 4.

individual things exist. To infuse this word into the soul is to give the gift of prophecy. This is the same way that light can be viewed in two modes. The first is as an occurrence of brightness, and this is one and singular in form. The other mode is when it is dispersed in the surfaces of circumscribed objects, made up of colors, appearing in *genera* and *species* and discrete beings; and, in this mode, light is perceived by the eye through the perception and appearance of all the colors. Therefore Aristotle states: "In a circumscribed object, color is the exterior part of what is perceived."[9] And elsewhere he says: "Color is sight moved by an act of brightness."[10] In the aforementioned mode, such understanding is said to be contained, ever since ancient times, within the mirror of eternity, which was able to be perceived. The prophets read from this mirror when they received revelation.[11] In this way, therefore, God establishes prophets by perfecting them inwardly. Wisdom 7:27: The Spirit of wisdom "conveys itself into holy souls and makes them friends of God and prophets."

1:6 And I said, "Ah, ah, ah." This verse treats his claim of having an impediment and the removal of his impediment. The claim is so he can be excused [from his prophetic calling], and the removal of the impediment is to forestall this claim. In the claim he says: **And I said, "Ah, ah, ah,"** because I was frightened of this office and was aware of my weakness. The weakness was threefold: darkness due to the guilt of sin, the burden of his body, and the inexperience of his age. Therefore he says, **"Ah, ah, ah."** Job 37:19 says about the darkness of sin: "Indeed we are covered in darkness." And in Tob 5:10: "I sit in darkness and do not see the light of heaven." Concerning the burden of the body, Wis 9:15 states: "The body, because it is corrupted, weighs down the soul." Regarding the inexperience of his age, which causes desire to be present, it says in 2 Tim 2:22: "Flee youthful desires." Psalm 25:7: "Do not remember the failures of my youth," and so forth, because the psalmist

9. Aristotle, *De sensu et sensibilis* 3.439b, in Aristotle, *De Sensu and De Memoria*, ed. and trans. G. R. T. Ross (Cambridge: Cambridge University Press, 1906), 56.

10. Aristotle, *On the Soul* 2.7.418a–b, trans. W. S. Hett, LCL 288 (Cambridge, MA: Harvard University Press, 1995), 102–4.

11. Many scholastic theologians believed that prophets had within themselves "a created representation of the divine eternity (*speculum aeternitatis*)" implanted by God, though their knowledge was limited compared to God's infinite knowing; Carl J. Peter, *Participated Eternity in the Vision of God: A Study of the Opinions of Thomas Aquinas and His Commentators on the Duration of the Acts of Glory*, Analecta Gregoriana 142 (Rome: Gregorian University Press, 1964), 53.

blames his youthful failures on lack of experiential knowledge. Ecclesiasticus 34:10–11: "The one who has had no experience, what does that person know?" Therefore he says: **Ah, ah, ah, Lord God.** He says **"Lord God"** as an invocation. When he says **"Lord,"** it signifies power. When he says **"God,"** it signifies wisdom. Damascene says that, in Greek, *theos* is derived from *theoro, theoras,* which is "I see, you see."[12] It is as if he were saying: Lord, you are powerful, and God, you are knowledgeable. Look! I do not have skill in speaking. He claims an impediment by asserting the reason. The impediment is noted when he says: **Look! I do not know how to speak.** For a human who is near the outstanding Light is rendered irrational. As Dionysius states in chapter 7 of *The Divine Names:* "When we have approached God, we have found perfect irrationality."[13]

He does not claim to have a speech impediment like Moses in Exod 4:10: "I have had even more impediment of tongue since you spoke to your servant." Neither does he assert that he is unworthy, as in Isa 6:5: "I am a man of unclean lips, and I dwell in the midst of a people that has unclean lips." Rather, he claims that his age is an impediment. This is why he adds, **"For I am a child,"** which, though it would be an impediment for most people, is nevertheless unable to obstruct the Holy Spirit. Daniel 13:45: "God stirred up the spirit of a young boy."[14] In the same way Samuel received illumination through the voice of the Lord and began to prophesy even though he was a child, as we read in 1 Sam 3:1–21, and therefore Jerome asserts: "He begs not to be given this office, saying he is unable to assume it due to his age, and he speaks with the same modesty shown by Moses, who also said his voice was meager and poor. But Moses was taken [into service], as it were, when he was older and stronger, while Jeremiah is granted the grace of childhood, which is adorned with bashfulness and modesty."[15] Such youths are "gray-haired" in their understanding even though they are sometimes frail due to their age. First Corinthians 14:20: "Be children in evil, but be adults in thinking." Wisdom 4:8: "Venerable old age is not based on length of time, nor is it counted by the number of years." For this reason, as Plato reports, an elderly Egyptian argued that Greeks did not lack age but lacked sense, saying: "Greeks, you are children, and you do not have any gray-haired

---

12. John of Damascus, *Exposition of the Orthodox Faith* 1.9, PG 94:836–37.

13. Pseudo-Dionysius, *Divine Names* 7.2, PG 3:869.

14. This is from the Greek additions to Daniel, found in the Septuagint and included in the Vulgate.

15. Jerome, *On Jeremiah* 1:6, CCSL 74:5.

wisdom."[16] And the Philosopher said in the *Ethics:* "It makes no difference whether someone is childish in years or childish in character. The defect is not because of age but because of passion."[17] The Septuagint reads this way: "O Lord God, I am unskilled in speaking because I am youthful."

1:7 And the Lord said to me. This is the removal of the impediment, and it includes three things: the refutation, the reason for the refutation, and the removal of the impediment. Therefore God says: **Do not say, "For I am a child."** It is as if God were saying: Even though you are a child in age, when you obey my spirit you are not a child. For God poured into him the wisdom of venerable aged people. John 14:26: "He will teach you all things and advise you." For this reason the elders said in Dan 13:50: "Sit among us and show us, because God has given you the honors of old age." So for this reason God says: **Do not say, "For I am a child."** Psalm 8:2: "Out of the mouths of infants." This is demonstrated in John 12:13 by the children of the Hebrews, whose understanding surpassed that of more mature people, who were inferior to them due to wickedness.[18] Proverbs 1:4: "Let shrewdness be given to little ones, and knowledge and understanding to youths." In the same way, since he is called *puer* [child] because of his purity, he is more suited for the divine Spirit.[19] Isaiah 8:18: "Behold, I and my children, whom the Lord gave me."

Now when God says, **Do not [say, "For I am a child"],** God's will remains affirmed, and this is what the statement means: You should not wish to say, **"For I am a child,"** for someone whom God fills with his own Spirit cannot be considered a child. Luke 21:15: "I will give you a mouth and wisdom, which none of your enemies will be able to oppose." **For you will go,** in obedience to the commands, **to all the things,** namely, all the tasks, **to which I will send you**—tasks that grown men are sent to do. Therefore Eph 4:13 says: "Let us all attain to the perfect man, to the measure of the age of the fullness of Christ." Job 38:3: "Gird up your loins like a man. I will question you, and you must answer." Therefore, **Do not say, "For I am a**

---

16. Plato, *Timaeus* 22b–c, trans. R. G. Bury, LCL 234 (Cambridge, MA: Harvard University Press, 1999), 32.

17. Aristotle, *The Nicomachean Ethics* 1.3, trans. H. Rackham, LCL 73 (Cambridge, MA: Harvard University Press, 2003), 8.

18. Though Albert here cites John 12 (probably from memory), the parallel story in Matt 21:15–16 is the version of the entry into Jerusalem in which Jesus quotes Ps 8:2.

19. In *Etymologies* 11.2.10 (PL 82:416), Isidore of Seville claims that the word for child (*puer*) is derived from the word *puritas* (purity).

child," for being busy with God's tasks is not something done by children. **And everything that I command you,** which requires a strong memory, a keen intellect, a well-organized ability to reason, and powerful eloquence, **you shall speak** to them, speaking forth in a logical and discerning way to everyone who encounters you. Ezekiel 2:7: "You shall speak my words to them." Job 29:22: "My speech dropped on them." For the Spirit and wisdom were poured into his heart, and the power of speech was poured into his mouth. Acts 6:10: "They were not able to withstand the wisdom and the Spirit that spoke."

1:8 Do not be frightened. This is the encouragement, which follows from the things already spoken. In the first part God gives encouragement. In the second part, God gives the reason for the encouragement. God gives encouragement when he says: **Do not be frightened by their countenance.** "Countenance" refers to an arrogant expression that exhibits anger and rage. Ezekiel 3:8: "Behold, I have made your countenance stronger than their countenance." For virtue in a good person is more enduring than vice in a bad person. **Because I am with you.** The reason for the encouragement is fourfold: the promise of divine help, the removal of his impediment, the gathering of power for speaking, and his establishment in a position of power. And this is **because I am with you.** Jerome says: "It is only by your willingness that you are going forward. You will have me as a companion. You will complete all these things with my help."[20] Isaiah 50:7: "The Lord is my helper. Therefore I am not confounded." Exodus 4:12: "Just go forth, for I will be with you." Psalm 56:9b, 11: "God is with me. I will not fear what humans can do to me." The Lord says, **"with you,"** because God is not ashamed to work together harmoniously with us, even though God is the principal actor in the deed. Hebrews 11:16: "God is not ashamed to be called their God." Romans 8:31: "If God is for us, who is against us?" **So I may rescue you, says the Lord.** That is, **So I may rescue you** from enemies. Second Corinthians 1:10: "God has rescued us from such great dangers. In him we place our hope that he will rescue us again." Psalm 91:15: "I will rescue him, and I will honor him." **Says the Lord.** This is the confirmation of the message, since everything the Lord said has come to pass.

1:9 And God put forth his hand. This deals with the removal of the impediment. For Isaiah, as a man of unclean lips, since he was fully grown, was

20. Jerome, *On Jeremiah* 1:7–8, CCSL 74:5.

purified with a burning coal; that is, with the remedy of severe penance (Isa 6:5–7). And Ezekiel, because he had not yet attained reason, was perfected by eating a book, in Ezek 3:1. Now Jeremiah, because he was a child, had not been stained with the pollution of human society. Given as prophet to the nations by the illumination of his intellect away from youthful things, which are small and excusable matters, he is purified by a simple touch of the hand. When he says **"and he touched my mouth,"** with a physical touch, it means that God changes what he touches. The same thing is found in Matt 8:3, where it reads: "He touched him, saying, 'I wish it. Be cleansed.'" For the touch of power makes an impression. Whatever divine power imprints is unable to remain imperfect. Luke 8:46: "Somebody touched me, for I know power went forth from me." Psalm 104:32: "Touch the mountains and they will smoke." Matthew 14:36: "And they asked him to let them touch the fringe of his garment." **And the Lord said to me.** This is the conferring of Jeremiah's skill for speaking when it says: **See, I have placed my word,** the ability to speak my words, **in your mouth,** so that your mouth will be the instrument and I will move it. Exodus 4:12: "Go forth. I will be in your mouth." Psalm 45:1: "My tongue is the pen of the scribe." Job 32:8: "There is a spirit in humans and the inspiration of the Most High gives understanding." Therefore Matthew 10:20 says: "It is not you who speak but the spirit of your Father that speaks in you." Mark 13:11: "It is not you who shall be speaking, but the Holy Spirit." Second Corinthians 13:3: "Do you seek a proof that Christ speaks in me?" Wisdom 10:21: "Wisdom opened the mouth of the mute and made the tongues of infants eloquent."

1:10 See, I have set you. This is the gathering of power. By saying, **"this day,"** God indicates the present illumination with which the prophet is enlightened and perfected in power. Similarly God says to Moses in Exod 7:1: "I have set you as god over Pharaoh." This is indicated when God says, **"over the nations."** The word **"over"** denotes eminence and subjection, because, according to the literal sense, Jeremiah prophesies difficult things to the nations, just as Isaiah also does, and for this reason the nations turn to the Lord. Isaiah 49:6: "I have given you to be a light to the nations." **And kingdoms,** that is, the kingdoms' powers. Jeremiah prophesies that these powers are about to be overturned. Hebrews 11:33: "By faith the saints conquered kingdoms, administered justice, obtained promises." Isaiah 60:12: "The nation and the kingdom that will not serve you shall perish." **So that you shall root up** the roots of sins; **and you shall destroy** the act and indictment of sin; **and you shall scatter** the opportunities and occasions for sins; **and**

you shall disperse sins' fortifications, which are sins' excuses, defenses, and enticements. Those four things are noted in Job's arguments (Job 3:11–12): "Why did I come out of the vulva? Why did I not perish as soon as I came out of the womb? Why was I received on the knees? Why was I nursed at the breasts?" For "vulva" is said to be from the word *volendo* [wishing], since the vulva always wishes [*vult*] because of insatiable lusts; and it represents the roots of sins.[21] "Coming out of the womb" represents the act and indictment of sin. Being "placed on the knees" represents the opportunities and occasions for sins. "Being nursed at the breasts" represents enticements and defenses of sins. Isaiah 14:22: "And I will destroy the name of Babylon, and the remnant, and the sprout, and the offspring." And since, as Boethius says, vices must first be rooted out so that virtues can then be planted,[22] it continues: **And you shall build and you shall plant. You shall build** buildings of virtues. Exodus 1:21: "Because the midwives feared the Lord, he built houses for them." **You shall plant** the sprouts of God's word as an enduring fruit. Isaiah 4:2: "In that day the Lord's sprout shall be magnificent and glorious, and the fruit of the land shall stand tall." First Corinthians 3:9: "You are God's building, you are God's field." The Canticle [of Moses]: "You planted them on the mountain of your inheritance" (Exod 15:17).

---

21. Medieval theologians generally regarded women as more inclined to lust than men. For a discussion of medieval beliefs regarding the physiology of women's supposed concupiscence, see Dyan Elliott, "The Physiology of Rapture and Female Spirituality," in *Medieval Theology and the Natural Body*, ed. Peter Biller and A. J. Minnis, York Studies in Medieval Theology 1 (Rochester, NY: York Medieval Press, 1997), 157–59.

22. Boethius, *Consolation of Philosophy* 3, prose 4, PL 63:735.

RABANUS MAURUS

Exposition on Jeremiah

Jeremiah 2–4

PL 111

Chapter Two

The Lord Calls Judah to Repent

2:1–2a And the word came to me, saying: Go and cry in the ears of Jerusalem, saying. [Jerome:] This is not found in the Septuagint, but it is added under asterisks from Theodotion's edition.[1] But the Hebrew word *carath*, which we have said means "cry out" or "preach," is translated by Theodotion as "read."[2] This word, because of its ambiguity, means "a reading," "a shout,"

---

1. Rabanus Maurus usually provided the name of his sources, from which he usually copied with little or no change. The majority of Rabanus's *Exposition on Jeremiah*, even portions not specifically indicated, is derived from Jerome, *On Jeremiah*, ed. Sigofredus Reiter, CCSL 74 (Turnhout: Brepols, 1960). See the introduction to this volume for a discussion of Rabanus's use of sources. His own original contributions were marked with an "M" for "Maurus." Jerome had access to the Hebrew text and four Greek translations from Aquila, Symmachus, the Septuagint, and Theodotion. Origen of Alexandria sometimes used the text of Theodotion, a second-century-CE Jewish translator or reviser of a Greek version of the Hebrew scripture, to fill in gaps in the Septuagint. These additions from Theodotion were indicated by asterisks. For more information on the Greek translations, see Ernst Würthwein, *The Text of the Old Testament: An Introduction to the "Biblia Hebraica,"* rev. and expanded by Alexander Achilles Fischer, trans. Erroll F. Rhodes, 3rd ed. (Grand Rapids: Eerdmans, 2014), 95–117.

2. For the transliteration of Hebrew words in material excerpted from Jerome, I have normally followed the spelling used in the critical edition of Jerome, *On Jeremiah* (CCSL 74). The Hebrew text used by Jerome was very close to the Masoretic text but contained no

and "preaching." We should understand "the ears of Jerusalem" to mean "the ears of its inhabitants."

2:2b Thus says the Lord: I have remembered you, pitying your youth and the love you had when you were a bride, when you followed me in the wilderness in a land that is not sown. The Septuagint reads: "Thus says the Lord: I have remembered your youthful compassion and your love when you were grown." This is discussed more fully in Ezekiel when the Lord unites with Jerusalem in matrimony, embracing and joining with Jerusalem, who is personified as his wife (Ezek 16:6–14). Or, in order to indicate even stronger fondness, the Lord calls her a girl, and a young woman, and betrothed. For the more we are unable to obtain something, the more we desire to obtain it. The Lord says: "And when you followed me in the wilderness, I gave you the jewels of the law and the necklace of my words, as the equivalent of a dowry and wedding gifts."[3] The Lord credits this not to her merit but to his own compassion. She followed him because of this compassion and love. Furthermore, the phrase we provided, **in the wilderness in a land that is not sown,** is not found in the Septuagint.

2:3 Israel is holy to the Lord, the first-fruits of his harvest. All who devour it will be considered guilty; evils will come upon them, says the Lord. When he says that Israel is the Lord's firstfruits, he shows that the people were gathered together out of the nations ever since the beginning. As it is written in another place: "Remember your congregation, which you have established from the beginning" (Ps 74:2). Furthermore, first-fruits are owed to the priests, and not to enemies. The part that follows, **All who devour it will be considered guilty; evils will come upon them, says the Lord,** means: Just as those who devour the first-fruits when they are not from the priestly class are held accountable for the crime, in the same way those who defile Israel will be subjected to evils. As the holy person says in Ps 26 [27:2], "When the wicked approach me to eat my flesh, my enemies who trouble me are themselves made weak and have fallen." But the ones who execute God's sentence will not be immune from punishment, and evils will come

vowel pointing, which developed centuries later. The Masoretic text equivalent of the Hebrew words transliterated in this excerpt can be found in the footnotes of Jerome, *Commentary on Jeremiah,* trans. Michael Graves, ed. Christopher A. Hall, Ancient Christian Texts (Downers Grove, IL: IVP Academic, 2011).
3. This is Jerome's interpretative paraphrase of Ezek 16:11.

upon them. "Temptations must come, but, nevertheless, woe to the person by whom the temptations come" (Matt 18:7).

2:4-5 Hear the word of the Lord, O house of Jacob and all families of the house of Israel. Thus says the Lord: What wrong did your ancestors find in me, that they departed from me and went after worthless things and have themselves become worthless? Another prophet also makes a declaration with this same meaning: "My people, what have I done to you? How have I harmed you? Answer me, for I brought you out of the land of Egypt and delivered you from the house of slavery" (Mic 6:3-4). The names **Jacob** and **Israel** are both used, not as the name Israel is used when speaking of the two tribes [Judah] and the ten tribes [Israel], but to refer to the entire people, since Jacob himself was later called "Israel" (Gen 32:28). He mentions the offense committed by the ancestors not because the children should be charged with the sins of their parents but because the children are just like their parents and should be punished for their own sin, which their parents also committed. We often read that God has compassion on children because of their saintly parents. However, the ancestors of this sinful people had forsaken God, and not briefly, but for a long time. They followed worthless things instead of God: idols, which were made in their worshippers' image and offered no help to their worshippers at all. As it is written: "Let those who make [idols] become like them, and so also all who trust in them" (Ps 115:8).

2:6 And they have not said: "Where is the Lord, who made us come up out of the land of Egypt, who led us through the desert, through an uninhabited land that is impassable, through a land of thirst and the image of death, a land through which no man had walked and no human had dwelled?" Instead of "human," the Septuagint translates it as "the Son of Man."[4] And instead of "the image of death," Theodotion has "shadow of death." Since the historical sense is clear, we should look at it anagogically. While we are in this age and are being led out of Egypt, we ascend gradually. First we pass through deserted places and an **uninhabited land** where a holy person ought not to dwell. **Impassable** refers to the difficulty of the journey. **Through a land of thirst** means that when we constantly desire the greater things, we are not content with the present things. The **image,** or shadow, **of death** means that we always remain in danger and the devil sets up his snares

---

4. The Latin reads *filius hominis* (child of humanity), which I have translated "Son of Man" for its Christological resonances, which Jerome develops in this paragraph.

everywhere. **A land through which no man**—a person of mature age in Christ—**had walked;** we will all be raised "as a mature man, to the measure of the full maturity of Christ" (Eph 4:13). Not that the one who is a person of God—or Son of Man—ever dwelled in these places. Instead, he always hurried on to greater things. From this it is clear that one does not achieve perfection when on the journey, but instead, at the end of the journey, in the mansion prepared in heaven for the saints. About this it is said: "You who stand in the house of the Lord, in the courts of the house of our God" (Ps 135:2). Therefore the new heresy—which comes from an old one—believes in vain that victory can be perfectly achieved here, where there are strife, struggle, and uncertainty about the future outcome.[5]

The Lord Reproaches Judah's Idolatry

2:7 And I brought you into the land of Carmel to eat of its fruit and its good things. And when you entered, you defiled my land, and you made my inheritance an abomination. Because of the effort of the difficult journey, I gave you an abundance of everything. This is what is signified by "Carmel," which is *chermel* in Hebrew, and in our language it means "recognition of circumcision." Just as this people polluted and defiled the Holy Land and all its fertility with idolatry, so also we, when we have received knowledge of our true circumcision, eat its fruit. If carelessness creeps in, we pollute God's land and make God's inheritance an abomination.

2:8 The priests did not say, "Where is the Lord?" Those who handle the law did not know me, and the shepherds transgressed against me. The prophets prophesied by Baal, and they followed idols. After receiving such great benefits, they treated their honorable privileges with contempt, so that the priests did not seek the Lord. The scholars of the law, who ought to have been teaching others, did not know him. The preachers have become sinners through negligence. The prophets who preach among the people do not speak from God, but from an idol, and they worship images that they themselves had made. These words should be employed against teachers in

---

5. Jerome is referring to the teachings of Pelagius (ca. 354–418), which many fourth- and fifth-century opponents argued was an outgrowth of the teachings of Origen of Alexandria. See Dominic Keech, *The Anti-Pelagian Christology of Augustine of Hippo* (Oxford: Oxford University Press, 2012), 43.

our ranks who devour God's people like a serving of bread (Ps 53:4) and who, because of their evil deeds, do not call on God. [Gregory:] Truth complains that they do not know her. She protests that she is unacquainted with the leader of those who are ignorant. As it says in the gospel: "Depart from me, you evildoers. I do not know who you are" (Matt 7:23). Certainly the wicked, when they do not know the things belonging to the Lord, are not known by the Lord. Paul attests to this when he says: "If someone does not know, that person will not be known" (1 Cor 14:38). Undoubtedly this unskillful-ness of the shepherds often matches the failings of their followers. Though it is the shepherds' own fault that they do not have the light of knowledge, nevertheless a severe judgment is administered, such that—because of the shepherds' ignorance—those who follow them also stumble. For this reason the one who is the Truth speaks in the gospel: "If a blind person leads a blind person, both will fall into the pit" (Matt 15:14).[6]

2:9 Therefore I will still contend in judgment with you, says the Lord, and I will dispute with your children. [Jerome:] Instead of appearing to attack them by force, the Lord contends with them using reason, as though they were equals, just as David sings and the Apostle quotes: "So that you are justified in your words and may triumph when you are judged" (Ps 51:4; Rom 3:4). The fact that the Lord says "**still**" bears witness to the fact that they have done this often. And by adding the phrase "**and with your children,**" the Lord shows that a comparable stubbornness is also found in the children of these wicked people. In a hidden way, it also signifies that, at the coming of the Lord, their descendants followed in their parents' ancient denial of God.

2:10-11 Cross to the islands of Chettim and look. Or send to Kedar and examine diligently. See if such a thing has ever been done. See if a nation has ever changed its gods—though certainly these are not gods. My peo-ple changed their own glory into an idol, into something that does not profit. For the sake of comparison the Lord introduces something that is not comparable, contrasting the true God with the false ones. The Lord says: **Cross to the islands of Chettim,** which we should interpret as either the islands of Italy or the islands of the western regions, since near the land of Judah is the island of Cyprus, which has a city by this name. Zeno, founder of the Stoics, was from there. Now Kedar is a region of wilderness belonging

6. Gregory the Great, *Pastoral Rule* 1.1, ed. Floribert Rommel, SC 381 (Paris: Éditions du Cerf, 1992), 130–32.

to the Ishmaelites, who are now called Saracens. Toward the very last part
of this prophet, there is an oracle composed against Kedar (Jer 49:28–32).
And David makes mention of it, saying, "I have dwelled with the residents
of Kedar. My soul has wandered much" (Ps 120:5–6). This is what the passage
means: Travel to the east, or depart to the wilderness, and see if any nation
has ever done what you have done. None of them spurned their own gods.
Nor did they exchange wooden or stone gods for those of gold. Instead, they
followed their ancient error, holding on to what they received from their
ancestors. They did this even though their god was nonexistent and was only
a handmade human likeness. But my people exchanged truth for falsehood
and preferred an idol to me—an idol that was unable to help them in time of
need. We are also able to speak these words against those who follow vices
with greater zeal than they follow virtues. The Apostle admonished them,
saying, "I speak in human terms, because of the weakness of your flesh. For
just as you have yielded your members to serve uncleanness and wickedness,
leading to wickedness, so now yield your members to serve justice, leading
to sanctification" (Rom 6:19).

[Maurus:] You should also know that it is impermissible to make an
object of prayer out of something physical, introduced or fashioned to represent divine majesty, which is the anthropomorphite heresy. It is reported
in the *Collations* that Serapion, an ancient monk, was deluded by this error.[7]
Since God is spirit, whoever worships God ought to do so in spirit (John
4:24). [Cassian:] We should not be surprised that a very simple person, who
has received virtually no instruction about God's substance and nature, could
be diverted and led astray even until now. For such a person lacks sophistication and is accustomed to following an ancient error. Or, to speak more
accurately, the individual persists in the original error that was not brought
about by some new demonic illusion but by former pagan ignorance. Since
they were previously accustomed to honoring demons fashioned into human
likeness, even now they think that the incomprehensible glory of the true
Name should be worshipped under the limitations of some sort of image.
For they believe that they can grasp and hold nothing if they do not have

7. In his *Collationes*, also called the *Conferences*, John Cassian (ca. 360–ca. 435) tells the
story of Serapion, a pious but naive monk. A convert from paganism, Serapion had understood
Gen 1:27 ("Let us make humanity after our image and likeness") too literally, imagining God to
have a human appearance. Convicted of his error, Serapion changed his ways. John Cassian,
Conferences 10.3–5, ed. E. Pichery, SC 54 (Paris: Éditions du Cerf, 1958), 76–79. On the anthropomorphite dispute, see Paul A. Patterson, *Visions of Christ: The Anthropomorphite Controversy
of 399 CE*, Studien und Texte zu Antike und Christentum 68 (Tübingen: Mohr Siebeck, 2012).

some sort of image set before them, which they continually address while in prayer, carrying the image around in their minds and always holding it fixed before their eyes. The following passage may fittingly be used against their error: "And they changed the incorruptible glory of God into the likeness of the image of a corruptible human" (Rom 1:23). Jeremiah 2:11 also says: "My people changed my glory into an idol." This error—though it is engrained in the notions of some people because of the [pagan] origin we just spoke about—is just as present in the hearts of those who have never been tainted with pagan superstition, who use this passage as a pretext: "Let us make humanity according to our image and likeness" (Gen 1:26). This error came about through ignorance and lack of sophistication, such that a heresy actually emerged—the anthropomorphite heresy—which was caused by this hateful interpretation that claims with stubborn perverseness that the immeasurable and simple substance of divinity is fashioned with our human features and form. All who have been instructed in catholic doctrine will abhor this as heathen blasphemy. They will attain to prayer that is pure, in which effigies or physical features of the deity do not contaminate one's supplications (something that is a sin even to speak of). Instead, such pure prayer will not allow in itself even the memory of a spoken word, or the appearance of a deed, or the outline of any sort of character.[8]

2:12-13 Be astonished at this, you heavens. And, [heaven's] gates, be desolate! says the Lord. For my people have committed two evils. They have forsaken me, the fountain of living water, and they dug for themselves cracked cisterns that can hold no water. [Jerome:] The Septuagint reads: "Heaven was astonished at this and violently shuddered beyond measure." The rest [of this verse in the Septuagint] is similar. Heaven—to whom it was said, "Listen, O heaven, and I will speak" (Deut 32:1), and, "Hear, O heaven, and give ear, O earth" (Isa 1:2)—shuddered and could not hide its bewilderment when it saw God's commands trampled underfoot. All creation groans and grieves over humanity's sins (Rom 8:22). For God's people committed two acts of defiance. First, they deserted God, who is the fountain of life and who gave them the command: "I am the Lord your God, who brought you out of the land of Egypt" (Exod 20:2). Second, the matter written about in the same passage: "You shall have no other gods before me" (Exod 20:3). Instead of following God, they followed demons, which the verse calls **cracked**

---

8. This entire passage from Cassian's *Collationes* is placed in the mouth of Abbot Isaac, who explains the cause of the monk Serapion's error. Cassian, *Conferences* 10.5, SC 54:78-79.

cisterns because they are unable to contain God's commandments. And take note of this: God is a living fountain and holds living waters. Cisterns and reservoirs, on the other hand, are filled up from the ground and from rains, such as rushing streams and muddy waters.

[Maurus:] Thus Isaiah speaks about these waters that spring forth from the fountain of living water: "And on every high mountain and on every elevated hill there shall be rivers of running water" (Isa 30:25). And again: "I will open flowing streams on the upper hills and fountains in the midst of the plains" (Isa 41:18). Let us interpret "mountains" and "hills" to mean those who are lifted up to the heights because of their virtue, people who hunger and thirst for righteousness, those whom God calls to drink. Whoever drinks from the Lord's waters will never thirst (John 4:14). For this reason we read in the Psalm: "Bless the Lord from the fountains of Israel" (Ps 68:26). And it says in the gospel that rivers of living water shall flow forth from the belly of all who drink from Jesus's waters (John 7:38). And the holy person says to God: "For with you is the fountain of life," out of which flows a very pure river (Ps 36:9). Scripture again says about this: "The rushing of the river makes glad the city of God" (Ps 46:4). And in another place: "The river of God is filled with water" (Ps 65:9). And it says in Isaiah: "He will drink water from the Savior's fountains" (Isa 12:3). The Psalms sing about these fountains: "Bless the Lord God from the fountains of Israel" (Ps 68:26). And it says that God turned the desert into pools of water and an impassable land into streams of water (Isa 41:18). The Savior spoke about these waters in a mystical discourse in the gospel: "Whoever drinks from the water that I give to them will never thirst; instead, the water that I give them will become in them a fountain of water springing up into everlasting life" (John 4:14). And again: "Let anyone who is thirsty come to me and drink. Rivers of living water will stream forth from the belly of all who drink from the water that I give" (John 7:37–38). The gospel writer says: "He spoke this about the Holy Spirit, which those who believed in him were about to receive" (John 7:39).

[Jerome:] And it mentions the gates of the heavens, about which it is written in Ps 23 [24:7]: "Lift up your heads, O gates, and the king of glory will enter in." The Septuagint translates this as: "Lift up your gates, O princes." This will be discussed more fully in the appropriate place.[9] No one should be troubled that Aquila and Symmachus translated it "heavens" while the

---

9. Jerome, *Brief Comments on the Psalms* 23:7 [24:7], ed. Germani Morin, CCSL 72 (Turnhout: Brepols, 1959), 200.

Septuagint and Theodotion translated it "heaven."[10] For the Hebrew word *semaim* is of common number.[11] For "heavens" and "heaven" designate the same word. It is the same with Thebes, Athens, and Salonae.[12]

God's Judgment on Judah

2:14a Is Israel a slave or a home-born servant? I think that it is due to this verse that the Judeans, exalted with pride, said to the Savior: "We are Abraham's offspring and we have never been slaves to anyone. How can you say to us, 'You will be made free'?" (John 8:33). For they did not know that everyone who sins is a slave to sin (John 8:34) and that all people are bound to whomever they serve. Though they were born from Abraham, the friend of God (Jas 2:23), they have been made like the children of Ham, to whom it was said: "Cursed be Canaan. He will be a slave to his brothers" (Gen 9:25).

2:14b–15 Why has he become prey? The lions have roared over him and have raised their voice. They have made his land a wilderness. His cities are burned down, and there is no one to dwell in them. The divine word asks the question so that it can give the answer. **Lions** refer to the princes of Babylon who turned the land into a wilderness and devastated its cities with fire. Or certainly we can understand "**lions**" anagogically as adversarial powers or the leaders of heretics who lay waste to the church's land and devastate all its cities with heretical fire. It is written about this fire: "They are all adulterers. Their hearts are like a furnace" (Hos 7:4, 6). For these people certainly do raise their voice. And when they cry out, this same prophet describes them as a partridge: "They gather what they did not hatch. They amass wealth that is not theirs by right" (Jer 17:11). Therefore their cities have been devastated and destroyed because they did not have God as an inhabitant. As scripture says: **And there is no one to dwell in them.**

10. Aquila, a second-century-CE convert to Judaism from Asia Minor, produced a revision of the Septuagint. Symmachus, a second-century Ebionite (Jewish Christian) or Samaritan who converted to Judaism, produced a Greek translation from the Hebrew. See Würthwein, *The Text of the Old Testament*, 106–10.

11. The Hebrew *šāmayîm* (heavens) is in the dual form.

12. Jerome's examples are cities whose Latin names occur in grammatically plural form (*Thebae, Athenae, Salonae*).

2:16-17 The children[13] of Memphis and Tahpanhes have violated you, even up to the top of the head. Hasn't this been done to you because you forsook the Lord your God at that time, while he led you along the way? The phrase we have translated as "**at that time, while he led you along the way**" is not in the Septuagint. The verse mentions Memphis and Tahpanhes, Egypt's two greatest cities. Their children are said to have violated Israel all the way to the top of the head. The expression should be understood in the same sense used by Isaiah: "There is no health therein, from the sole of the foot even up to the top of the head" (Isa 1:6). There was so much lust in the Egyptians, who were very carnal, such that none of them could deny their members.[14] Instead, they defiled everything. According to the literal sense, this refers to the Egyptians' idols. According to the spiritual sense, it refers to teachers of perverse doctrine, those who pollute the church's purity with their own depravity. Therefore these things shall occur because the church abandoned the Lord its God precisely at the time it most needed to follow the Lord as its guide. According to the tropological sense, being violated **even up to the top of the head** is to be seduced in the lofty matter of faith after enjoying a wicked activity. For when all the evil spirits involve the soul in depraved deeds but are not able to violate the integrity of one's faith, it is as though they are contaminating only the lesser parts of the body but do not yet reach the top of the head. But whoever is seduced in the matter of faith is now violated all the way to the top of the head. For a malicious spirit extends its reach from the lesser members to the highest ones when, having contaminated the active life, it then corrupts faith's inviolate heights with the infection of disbelief.

2:18 And now why do you go on the way to Egypt to drink the water of Sior? And why do you want to go the way of the Assyrians to drink the water of the river? [Jerome:] We have translated *Sior* as "muddy," which is what the Hebrew word means, instead of *Gihon*, which is found in the common edition.[15] Since the passage previously mentioned the children of Memphis and Tahpanhes, who defiled Israel up to the top of the head, it now more clearly designates Egypt itself. There is no doubt that the Nile has

13. *Filii*, which I have translated as "children" following Douay-Rheims, might also be translated as "sons," since the verb *constupraverunt* denotes rape or sexual violation.

14. *Membrum*, which can refer to a limb or body part, often referred to male genitals.

15. The "common edition" refers to the Old Latin translation of the Septuagint (and related Greek texts), in circulation at the time of Jerome. See Würthwein, *The Text of the Old Testament*, 140–48.

muddy waters and that the river of the Assyrians refers to the Euphrates, since Scripture says that the promised land would extend from the torrent of Egypt to the great river Euphrates (Gen 15:18). All who forsake Christ, the fount of life, dig reservoirs of heresy for themselves. Those who turn their land into wilderness and destroy all the churches need to be subjected to lions. And they should be defiled to the top of the head, and they should drink muddy waters and the flooded streams of the river of Assyria and of the north, from where evil things erupt upon the earth.

2:19 Your own wickedness will reprove you—or, ***your own transgression will instruct you***—**and your apostasy will rebuke you.**[16] **Know and see that it is an evil and bitter thing for you to have forsaken the Lord your God and that fear of me is not with you, says the Lord God of hosts.** Note that after **wickedness** (or ***transgression***) sates the transgressor, it brings the individual to the point of nausea—as happened with the quails (Num 11:19–20)—so that it teaches the transgressor to repent. Such people are commanded to see what they have forsaken, what they have followed, and how they have rejected the good and sweet things, choosing what is evil and bitter. All this took place because they forsook the Lord their God, and the fear of God is not with them. "The fear of the Lord is the beginning of wisdom" (Prov 9:10). Since they lack this, they are handed over to evil and bitterness.

2:20 Long ago you broke my—or, ***your***—**yoke, you burst my**—or, ***your***—**chains, and you said, "I will not serve." For on every high hill and under every leafy tree you were prostrated on the ground like a prostitute**—or, ***there you were spread out in fornication.*** God addresses Israel as though it were a prostitute since Israel broke the marriage covenant and said, "**I will not serve** my master or husband." Instead Israel was prostrated in idolatry **on every high hill and under every leafy tree,** for the places dedicated to idols are always beautiful and elevated. It is also possible to direct this passage to someone who, as a Christian, initially received some instruction in sacred writings but later desired secular literature (signified by "hills") and beautiful eloquence (represented by "leafy trees"). Such a person has prostrated himself before demons, who use education and lofty knowledge as an opportunity to contaminate the souls of believers, making them spread their feet to all who pass by.

16. In the lemma, Jerome often gives the reader the alternative translations and variant readings. The second option, placed in bold italics in this volume, usually (but not always) reflects the Septuagint. See the comments by Michael Graves in Jerome, *Commentary on Jeremiah*, 13n110.

[Maurus:] After a rebuke in which the Lord reproaches the Judeans for changing their glory into an idol, forsaking the font of living water, and digging for themselves cracked cisterns unable to hold water, the Lord prompts their memory by using another example so they could recall how they had been chosen when their ancestors were chosen, and that they were planted like a vineyard in the promised land. As the psalmist attests: "You brought a vineyard out of Egypt, drove out the nations, and planted it. You made a way before it. You planted its roots and it filled the land" (Ps 80:8–9). Now the Lord also speaks about this through Jeremiah.

Judah's Rebellion

2:21 Yet I planted you as a choice vineyard, all true seed. How then were you changed into something distorted for me, O alien vineyard? The Septuagint reads: "I planted you as a fruit-bearing vine, all true. How then were you changed into a bitter alien vine?" [Jerome:] Instead of a "choice" or "fruit-bearing vineyard," the Hebrew has *sorec,* which is also found in the song of Isaiah (Isa 5:2). This is the best species of vine, from whose shoot the Lord said that Israel was planted. And the Lord was amazed that the true seed and choice vineyard had been changed into something bitter, thus becoming an alien vineyard. In fact, no one can be safe if the Lord's own planting—a true seed and *sorec* vineyard—is transformed so much by its own wickedness that it withdraws from the Lord because of its bitterness and becomes an alien vine. [Maurus:] Regarding this vineyard, discussed above, it is written in Isaiah: "I will sing to my beloved the song my cousin sang about his vineyard. 'My beloved vineyard was established on a hill in a fruitful place'" (Isa 5:1). The prophet mournfully sings this song, which he composed, to the people Israel. It is written about this in the gospel: "When he saw it"—the passage is clearly referring to Jerusalem—"he wept over it and said, 'If only you had known the things that bring you peace. The days are coming upon you when your enemies will set up ramparts around you, surround you, and destroy you and your children'" (Luke 19:41–44). And again: "How often I wished to gather your children together as a hen gathers her chicks under her wings, and you were not willing. See, your house shall be left to you, desolate" (Matt 23:37–38). Thus this prophetic message mourns Jerusalem and sings about its destruction. Now a different song is appointed for the church and the people who were previously from the Gentiles: "Sing to the Lord all the earth. Announce his salvation from day to day. Declare his glory among the nations, his wonders among the peoples" (1 Chr 16:23–24). And again: "Sing a new song to the Lord, for he has done marvelous things" (Ps 98:1). [Jerome:] And the Creator's mercy is seen in the fact that the one who said in the gospel, "I am the true vine" (John 15:1), also granted to his disciples and the people who believe in him that they might become a "choice" or "true" vine, if they wish to remain in him who was planted.

2:22 Though you wash yourself with lye and use much of the *borith* plant, you are stained in my sight because of your wickedness, says the Lord. Instead of "***borith* plant**," which is found in the Hebrew and we have transliterated it here, the Septuagint translated it as *póan* [grass], to designate a plant used for cleaning, which grows in wet, verdant places.[17] It has the same strength as lye and is used in the province of Palestine to wash away filth. However, *our* lye and cleansing plant is repentance. And our ecclesiastical message, which reproves, rebukes, and reproaches the transgressor, is like stinging lye. Whoever is spotted with a light stain of sin is cleansed by lighter warnings. But the serious sins that lead to death cannot be washed away by lye or the *borith* plant; instead, they require more severe torments. For "fire will test the work of every single person, showing what sort of work it is, and it will be revealed in fire" (1 Cor 3:13). And the passage appropriately includes the words, **You are stained in my sight because of your wickedness,** which means: Even if you appear clean in the eyes of humans, you are not clean to me, for I know the consciences of each and every individual. For this reason it says in another passage: "No living person shall be justified in your sight" (Ps 143:2).

2:23a In vain you say, "I am not polluted, and I have not walked after the Baals." Look at your ways in the valley. On the other hand, **valley,** which in Hebrew is *ge,* is also translated by the Septuagint as *polyandrion,* which in our language can be rendered as "tomb of a multitude." **In vain,** he says, for you are not willing to confess your crimes. You boast about your cleanness, though you are polluted with the filth of idolatry. You shamelessly deny that you have worshipped the idols of the Baals. Look at the valley of the children

---

17. *Borith* refers to a substance derived from the soda plant (*Salsola kali*). When burned, the plant's ashes become an alkali that was used for cleansing. See William L. Holladay, *Jeremiah 1: A Commentary on the Book of the Prophet Jeremiah, Chapters 1–25*, Hermeneia (Philadelphia: Fortress, 1986), 99.

of Hinnom (Jer 32:35), which is watered by the springs of Siloam. There you can see the shrine of Baal, which you venerated when you forsook the Lord.

2:23b By adding, "**Know what you have done,**" he opens the closed eyes of those who are in denial, so they can see what they are ashamed to look at. Interpreting this tropologically, let us rebuke the deeds of those who have a "shameless forehead" (Jer 3:3), refusing to admit their own crimes. For such people do not walk in the straight and narrow road that leads to life but in the wide and broad road, through which many enter, but it leads to death (Matt 7:13–14). This is what the name *polyandrion* [tomb of a multitude] means symbolically; or, according to the historical sense, it means that a multitude of people were killed and utterly destroyed there through the wickedness of idolatry.

2:23c–24 Like a swift runner pursuing her course, a wild donkey accustomed to the wilderness in her soul's desire, inhales the breath of her lover. None will turn away from her. None who seek her will be disappointed. They will find her in her menstrual discharges. The Septuagint reads: "Her voice howled in the evening. She has extended her ways over the waters of the desert. She was carried in the wind by the desire of her soul. She was handed over. Who will turn her back? None who seek her will toil. They will find her in her humiliation." In this passage the Septuagint edition is significantly different from the Hebrew Truth, but each has its own meaning. Since they said above, "I am not polluted" (2:23a), the Lord describes their fornication and speaks as though addressing a woman who conducted herself shamefully. Where it says, "Like a swift roe doe," we have used the more general term "swift runner." Aquila, Symmachus, and Theodotion more accurately translate it: "Like a *dromas kouphē* [nimble dromedary] pursuing its course, quickly running ahead, and like a wild donkey accustomed to the wilderness, she inhales the wind in the air, or the breath of her lover."[18] For, among the Hebrews, "wind" and "breath" are designated by the same word, *ruha*. So, because of so much passion, Israel or Jerusalem was drawn to the object of her lust. She thoroughly burned with love for her idols. No one was able to turn her away from this passion through their warnings. This was not because of any lack of prophets' abilities. Rather it was because of the perverse wickedness of the one feeling the desire. He says, "None who seek her will struggle with a difficult work, and they will find her in her menstrual

18. The Greek word *dromas* can mean "camel" or "runner."

discharges and in impurity." Where Aquila used the word *neomēnia*, that is, *Kalends*, Symmachus rendered it *mensis* [month, menstrual flow]; the Septuagint and Theodotion translated it "degradation."[19] This is the meaning given by the Septuagint: The prostitute Jerusalem, like the woman described in Proverbs, cried out with her voice in the evening and incited her lovers to lust (Prov 7:10–27). She uncovered the ways of her shamelessness and spread her feet to all who passed by. It was a place that had pleasant flowing waters. The place was especially delightful since it was surrounded by wilderness so no one could see her fornicating. The Septuagint says, "In her spirit's desire, *epneumatophoreito*," which can mean, "she was led by a perverse spirit," or "she drew in the refreshment of love," or "she sang the songs of her shamefulness." It says, "She was handed over to her vices and lust. No one could make her turn back." All who wished to go in to her would find her in the degradation of her wickedness. It was not possible to satisfy her love of sensual pleasure.

[Gregory:] For a wild donkey is an undomesticated ass. In this book, heretics who have been let loose in their pleasures and are strangers to the fetters of faith and reason are rightly compared to wild donkeys. Indeed the **wild donkey is accustomed to the wilderness** since, when one does not cultivate the land of one's heart with the virtue of discipline, one dwells where there is no fruitfulness. **In her soul's desire, she inhales the breath of her lover** means that the things conceived in the mind from a desire for knowledge are able to puff up, not build up. Concerning those people it is said: "Knowledge puffs up, but love builds up" (1 Cor 8:1).[20]

2:25 Keep your foot from being bare and your throat from thirst. And you said, "I have lost hope. I will not do it. For I have loved strangers and I will walk after them." The Septuagint reads: "Turn your feet from the rugged path and your throat from thirst. She said, 'I will act vigorously, for I have loved strangers and have walked after them.'" [Jerome:] When the Passover was about to occur, the people were commanded to have sandals on their feet (Exod 12:11). And the Apostle preaches that those who are prepared by the gospel should have sandaled feet (Eph 6:15) so that, while walking through the wilderness of this age, they are not vulnerable to venomous

19. *Kalends*, normally used for the first day of the Roman month, can also mean "month."

20. Gregory the Great, *Moralia on Job* 16.47.60, ed. Aristide Bocognano, SC 221 (Paris: Éditions du Cerf, 1975), 228.

animals that should be trampled and crushed by the evangelical foot. We keep our throat from thirst when we take up the commands of the Savior, who said, "Whoever thirsts should come to me and drink" (John 7:37-38). Out of desperation, because of her evil deeds, she refused to do what the Lord had commanded. She explained the reason: **"I have loved strangers and I will walk after them,"** thinking she would avoid accusations due to her shameless confession. Moreover, according to the Septuagint, the path of sinners is a rugged one that the Lord can turn into a level path. Whoever follows heretics should be admonished by the saying in these verses: **I have lost hope,** or I will act vigorously in my evil intention and am comfortable in my error. It is necessarily the case that whoever follows a doctrine foreign to the church loves strangers and follows their tracks—whether the ones they follow are demons or are leaders of heretics, who are strangers to God.

2:26-27a As a thief is confounded when apprehended, so are the houses of Israel confounded—they and their kings, princes, priests, and prophets, who say to a piece of wood, "You are my father," and to a stone, "You gave me birth." Though the face of a thief may be shameless and insolent, nevertheless the thief blushes in shame when caught in the act of theft. In the same way, when Israel said **to a piece of wood, "You are my father," and to a stone, "You gave me birth,"** the very ones who fashioned them and called them "parents" were confounded when apprehended in their own idolatry. So that we do not think this is being said about the common people, it says: **their kings, princes, priests, and prophets.** Let us use this testimony whenever our own princes and those who are considered rulers in the church are apprehended in vile sins.

2:27b They have turned their back to me and not their face. When a teacher gives an order, it is an indication of obedience if one listens with a bowed head, facing the teacher. Turning one's back on someone is a sign of contempt, as it is written in another passage: "They turned a retreating shoulder to me" (Zech 7:11). Those who reject God's messages turn their back to God rather than their face. God says, "They have so much contempt for my commandments that they do not wish to hear them. Instead, they display their spiritual arrogance through a bodily gesture."

2:27c And in the time of their affliction they will say, "Rise up and deliver us." Those who have not acknowledged God when receiving blessings will acknowledge God during times of suffering.

2:28a Where are your gods you have made for yourselves? Let *them* rise up and deliver you in the time of your affliction. It is a shameless request, in a time of need and difficulty, to ask for help from the one whom they despised in times of peace. This should be read with a tone of reprimanding: Let **your gods you have made for yourselves** deliver you. When humans try to create a god—even though God is the creator of humans—let this time of need demonstrate just what those whom you worshipped in the past, when you were untroubled, are able to do for you! It is written about this in Isaiah: "Where are the gods you made for yourselves? Let them rise up and make you safe during the time of your troubles!"[21] Therefore, this is properly spoken to the Judeans because the clamor of their synagogues is not able to deliver them at the time of the siege.

2:28b For the number of your gods was as many as the number of your cities, O Judah. [Jerome:] Each of the cities worshipped gods. In some cases the same gods were worshipped. In other cases cities worshipped their own various gods. Thus we see that they did not have agreement even in impiety; instead, superstition contending against itself followed a diversified error. And the Septuagint added the following: "And their sacrifices to Baal were as many as the number of Jerusalem's streets."

2:29 Why do you wish to contend with me in judgment? All of you have forsaken me, says the Lord. Human perversity is prone to excusing itself. They would have it seem that what they are suffering deservedly is actually unwarranted. They ascribe to God's court of justice the guilt that is actually their own. Thus it is saying: In vain you make charges and contend that the judge is unfair, for what you suffer is the result of your own impiety. Similarly, the following is added by the Septuagint: "And you all acted unjustly against me."

2:30a In vain I struck your children. They accepted no correction. Instead of this, the Septuagint reads: "*You* accepted no correction." The Hebrew text means: Those who were struck did not wish to accept correction. The meaning of the Septuagint is: Therefore I struck your children, so that you

---

21. This sentence and the following one are from Jerome, *Commentary on Isaiah* 57:12, PL 24, 555. The quotation, which Maurus says is found in the book of Isaiah, is actually a different translation of Jer 2:28c, provided by Jerome as commentary on Isa 57:13 ("Let your collection [of idols] deliver you").

might be instructed by their death. And so that you do not say to me, "You are unwilling to reprove sinners," learn from the blows that I dealt to your children that I am eager to treat you with even harsher medicine. Regarding this it says in Isaiah: "In vain I struck your children. You did not accept correction."[22] Enraged, God spoke through Hosea: "I will not visit punishment upon your daughters when they commit fornication, or upon your wives when they commit adultery" (Hos 4:14). And through Ezekiel: "And my jealousy shall depart from you and I will no longer be angry with you" (Ezek 16:42). And we read in the Psalms: "The blows they receive are not strong. They do not endure what other humans do, nor will they be whipped as other humans are" (Ps 73:5).

2:30b Your sword has devoured your prophets. They were not my prophets but **your prophets.** Nor was it my sword but **your sword**—which you took up on account of your sins—that **devoured** them. The Septuagint does not say "**your**." Instead, it is simply translated: "The sword has devoured your prophets," to indicate either "the sword of the enemy" or "my sword, with which I stabbed your sins."

2:30c–31a Your generation is like a ravaging lion. The Septuagint reads: "Like a ravaging lion, and you were not afraid." This verse means: The sword that devoured your prophets—doubtlessly referring to the soothsayers of Baal or perhaps the soothsayers of the idols—will lay waste to everything, like a lion; but your entire generation, which ought to have amended its ways after the slaying of a few people, nevertheless persisted in villainy. Now the meaning of the Septuagint is: The sword of the Lord—which refers to the sword of the enemies—devoured and tore apart your false prophets, just as a lion greedily tears apart the prey it has caught. And yet you could not be converted to better things, through your prophets' punishment.

2:31b See the word of the Lord: Have I become a wilderness to Israel, or a land of late blooming? Why, therefore, did my people say, "We have departed. We will come to you no more"? The Septuagint reads: "Hear the word of the Lord. The Lord says: Have I become a wilderness or a land full

---

22. This sentence and the rest of the commentary on verse 30a are from Jerome, *Commentary on Isaiah* 57:13, ed. Marcus Adriaen, CCSL 73 (Turnhout: Brepols, 1963), 11. The quotation, which Maurus says is found in the book of Isaiah, is actually a translation of the Septuagint on Jer 2:30, provided by Jerome as commentary on Isa 1:5 ("Why should I strike you any more, you who increase transgressions?").

of thorns, since the people say, 'We will not serve, nor will we come to you'?"
Moses also "saw" the voice of God.[23] And the Apostle John says he "saw"
and "touched" the word of God (1 John 1:1). The Lord is astonished that the
people Israel regarded God as a wilderness while they followed idols the way
people follow crowds in the cities. **A land of late blooming** is one that does
not receive the rainwaters of doctrines or the discipline of the gospel. And
it is "full of thorns" because it was not cultivated. The people at that time
were particularly cursed in God's sight because they departed from the Lord
and they no longer wished to return to their God. It is a great insult to be
unwilling to appease the one whom you have offended.

**2:32 Can a virgin forget her jewelry or a bride forget her breast sashes? My
people have forgotten me, days without number.** Through these things we
learn that Christ is the groom of the virgin church, which has neither spot
nor wrinkle (Eph 5:27). Now if Christ himself is the bridegroom, then the
words spoken by John the Baptist are about him: "The one who has the bride
is the bridegroom" (John 3:29). Those who depart from the Lord "ruin their
jewelry," and they lose their understanding of doctrines, which is signified
by "breast." For the evangelist John reclines on the Lord's breast (John 13:23).
And the breast portion—along with other parts—of sacrificed animals was
separated out for the priests (Lev 7:30–36). The more times we forget God,
the greater the punishment for our sin will be, since the sin was unable to
be controlled for such a long time.

**2:33–34 Why do you try to show that your way is good, in order to seek
my love, you who have taught that your evils are your ways, and on your
wings**—or, *on your hands*—**is found the blood of the souls of the poor
and innocent? I have not found them in ditches but in all these places,** or,
under every oak tree. He is saying: In vain you wish to defend yourself with
skillful words and show that your deeds are good, in order to win my love.
Furthermore you have even taught your ways to others and offered everyone
an example of evil deeds. **And on your wings**—or *on your hands*—**is found
the blood of the innocent,** whom you sacrificed to idols, or whose souls you
destroyed as though they were sacrifices. From the Hebrew we have used
the word "poor," which is not found in the Septuagint. The Lord is saying:
I have not found the poor and innocent dead in ditches, which happens to

---

23. The Hebrew text of Exod 20:18 speaks of the Israelites seeing the thunder and sound
of the trumpet when the Lord spoke to Moses on Sinai.

most people who are ambushed by bandits, **but in all these places**—or, *under every oak tree,* which, in Hebrew, is called *ella,* which can mean "these," so that it would mean "in all these places." Or it can mean: under the oak and terebinth trees, beneath whose shade and leafy branches, in a pleasant location, you enjoyed the crimes of idolatry.[24]

2:35-36a You said, "I am sinless and innocent. Therefore let your anger be turned away from me." See, I will contend with you in judgment, because you said, "I have not sinned." How incredibly worthless you have become—or, *you have shown so much contempt*—**repeating your ways again.** These words should be used against those who refuse to recognize their own sin and then, in times of suffering and difficulty, they say that what they are enduring has been inflicted unjustly. And so they provoke God to even greater wrath when they do not express grief for what they did but, instead, offer empty excuses for their sins. God says: **I will contend with you in judgment** when you say, **"I have not sinned,"** for, in some sense, it is an even greater sin to have something on one's conscience but to say something different with one's words. Let the new heresy learn from the old one: God's wrath is greatest when someone refuses to confess sin humbly but, instead, shamelessly boasts about having righteousness.[25]

2:36b-37 And you will be put to shame by Egypt just as you were put to shame by Assyria. For you will go forth from that place and your hands will be on your head. For the Lord has crushed your confidence—or, *hope*—**and you will not prosper from it.** In order to deflect the attack by the Egyptians, they fled to the Assyrians, whose protection was useless. For we read that the Assyrians were defeated by the Egyptians.[26] And then, on the other hand, to flee the wrath of the Assyrians, they relied on the help of the Egyptians, who, according to the historical record, were overcome by the Assyrians (2 Kgs 17:1-6; 18:21). Therefore they are reproached because they lost faith in God and relied on human assistance that was completely crushed and overthrown so that it was not of any use. Therefore he says: **You will go**

24. The word *'ēlleh* (Masoretic text) means "these," and *'ēlāh* (the interpretation chosen by the Septuagint) means "oak." See Graves's comment in Jerome, *Commentary on Jeremiah,* 18n144.

25. The "new heresy" is Pelagianism. See Michael Graves, "Translator's Introduction," in Jerome, *Commentary on Jeremiah,* xxxi.

26. Josephus, *Jewish Antiquities* 10.14-23, ed. and trans. Ralph Marcus, LCL 326 (Cambridge, MA: Harvard University Press, 1995), 156-70.

forth from that place, from Egypt, in the same way you went forth from the Assyrians. **And your hands will be on your head.** You will mourn the fact that you looked in vain to the Egyptians for protection. Let us remember the story of the time Tamar was violated and defiled by her truly wicked brother Amnon. She put her hands on her head, which she had sprinkled with ashes, and in this way she returned to her own house (2 Sam 13:19).

Chapter Three

The Faithlessness of God's People

3:1a It is commonly said (the Septuagint translated it simply as, *It is said*), **"If a man sends his wife away and she leaves him and takes another husband, shall he return to her any more? Will not that woman**—or, *land*—**be polluted and defiled?"**[27] **But you have fornicated with many lovers**—or, *shepherds.* For the word *rehim,* which is written with the four letters *res, ain, iod, mem,* means both "lovers" and "shepherds." If we read *reyim,* it means "lovers." If we read *rohim,* it means "shepherds."

3:1b Nevertheless, return to me, says the Lord—or, *You returned to me, says the Lord.* For in the Hebrew text, the Lord is willing to receive the one who is repentant, even after her fornication, and exhorts her to return to him. In the Septuagint, the Lord does not call her to repentance but instead denounces the prostitute's impudence because she dares to return to her husband after her adultery. And for, **Will not that woman be defiled?** where we read *land* in the Hebrew text, the Lord abandons the metaphor and speaks more clearly about the land of Israel, which is compared to an adulterous woman. Let us use this testimony against those who, after departing from the Lord's faith and binding themselves to the errors of heretics, and after committing many fornications and misleading souls, pretend they are returning to the pristine truth—not to get rid of the poison in their hearts but to introduce it to others.

[Gregory:] So, concerning the woman who committed fornication and was deserted, an argument for justice is put forward. Yet we are shown mercy rather than justice when we return after falling. We should certainly

---

27. In this verse, Jerome follows the Septuagint ("woman") and gives the Hebrew ("land") as the alternative.

conclude from this that we commit a very great sin if we do not return following our transgression, since we sinners are spared because of so much mercy. What pardon there will be for the wicked, from the one who does not stop calling us after we have sinned! Certainly this mercifulness—God calling sinners following a transgression—is expressed well through another prophet, addressing people who had turned away: "And your eyes will see your teacher and your ears will hear the word of the one behind your back, admonishing you" (Isa 30:20–21). Indeed, the Lord admonished humanity to its face when, in paradise, the Creator declared to the human, who was in a state of free will, what he should and should not do. But humanity turned its back on God's face when it arrogantly showed contempt for God's orders. Yet God did not desert humanity when it was arrogant, for God gave the law to call humans back. God sent angels to exhort us. And God appeared in our mortal flesh. Therefore, standing behind our back, God admonished us, for, despite being treated with contempt, God called us to the recovery of grace. Thus what could be said generally about all people alike must especially be understood to pertain to each individual. Indeed, all people hear the words of God's admonition—as though face-to-face with God—when they understand the precepts of God's will before committing the sins. For if people are still standing before God's face, they have not yet shown contempt for God by sinning. But, when they forsake the good of innocence and freely desire wickedness, individuals turn their back on the face of God. But look! God follows and admonishes them, even behind their backs. God still persuades them to return to him after sin. God summons back those who are turned away, by overlooking transgressions and opening a merciful bosom to those who return. So we are heeding the voice of the one admonishing us if, after our sins, we at least return to the Lord who is inviting us. Therefore, even if we refuse to fear God's justice, we at least should feel ashamed because of God's mercy. For it is an even more serious act of wickedness to scorn the one who, though despised, still does not disdain to call us.[28]

3:2a Lift up your eyes on high and see if there is anywhere you have not been lain with. You sat waiting on the roads like a bandit in the wilderness—or, *like a deserted crow.* [Jerome:] Where we wrote "bandit" and "crow," the Hebrew uses the word *arabe,* which can mean "Arab," a people

---

28. Gregory the Great, *Pastoral Rule* 3.28, ed. Floribert Rommel, SC 382 (Paris: Éditions du Cerf, 1992), 458–62.

prone to banditry.²⁹ Even up to the present day, they make incursions into the borderlands of Palestine, and they lie in wait along the roads for those who go down from Jerusalem to Jericho. In the gospel, the Lord makes reference to this sort of occurrence (Luke 10:30). So lift up **your eyes, O Jerusalem. Look around everywhere and see if there is any place where you have not been lain with** in fornication. For just as bandits are accustomed to planning ambushes against travelers in deserted places in the evening, so also you sit in the roads in the evening like the promiscuous woman (Prov 7:6–12), in order to destroy the souls of those fornicating in your bed. For this reason the entire land is polluted with your fornications. Clearly, according to the anagogical sense, this passage commands those who promise to abandon their heretical errors to lift up their eyes on high. For until they begin to see what is upright, they are not able to condemn their former depravity.

3:2b–3a You have polluted—or, *you have destroyed*—**the land with your fornications and with your wickedness. Therefore the showers of rain have been withheld and there were no late-season rains**—or, *in your stumbling, you had many shepherds.*³⁰ The land is destroyed, or polluted, because of the destruction of those who perished due to the fornication of idolatry. For this reason, the blessing on all things was taken away, so that they suffered a drought of God's word. Or, they had shepherds, through whom they offended God, so that those who ought to have been teachers keeping others from error actually became the authors of wickedness. [Gregory:] Sometimes in holy scripture, the brightness of preachers is represented by the word "sun," just as it is said through John: "And the sun became [black] like a sackcloth of hair" (Rev 6:12). In the end times the sun is shown to be like a "sackcloth of hair," because the shining life of the preachers is presented as rough and contemptible to those who are lost. The preachers are also represented by the brightness of stars, because they enlighten the shadows of our night when they preach correct things. So when the preachers are taken away, it is said through the prophet: "The stars of the rains are withheld" (Jer 3:2).³¹ The sun shines by day, and the stars brighten the night's darkness.

29. The same Hebrew letters can be construed as "Arab" or as "crow" (*'ōrēb*). Many ancient people stereotyped Arabs as bandits. See Graves's comment in Jerome, *Commentary on Jeremiah*, 20n153.

30. Graves notes: "The preserved LXX matches Jerome; the alternative rendering ('destroyed') could have been in Jerome's copy of the LXX"; Jerome, *Commentary on Jeremiah*, 20n156.

31. Gregory (or his source) reads *stellae* (stars), rather than *stillae* (showers) for

Frequently in holy scripture the eternal homeland is signified by the word "day" and our present life is signified by "night." Holy preachers become the sun to our eyes when they open to us a view of the true light. They shine like stars in the darkness when, in an active life, they manage earthly matters to offer assistance for our needs.[32]

3:3b You had a prostitute's forehead. You refused to be ashamed. The Septuagint reads: "You had the face of a prostitute. You have been shameless before all." [Jerome:] Since she said above, "I have not sinned" (Jer 2:35), she sinned all the more by denying her crimes. Therefore the Lord now offers a reproach, as though to a woman who is insolent and has such shamelessness that she shows her insolent expression not only to a few people, but she blushes before no one. We can use this passage against the assembly of heretics who glory in their own errors.

3:4–5a Therefore, at least, call to me from now on: "You are my father, the guide of my virginity. Will you be angry forever, or will you continue to the end?" Let the heretics—those who do not wish to be converted to better things or return to the Father their creator—be ashamed and listen: **At least, call to me from now on: "You are my father, the guide of my virginity."** With his embraces, the Lord himself has made marriage promises to our soul and teaches our soul how it ought to pray and do penance. The more merciful the Lord is—the one who shows the way of salvation after fornication—the more wretched is the prostitute who does not accept healing after being wounded.

3:5b See, you have spoken and done evil things, and you have been capable. Instead of words of repentance you have committed blasphemy with words of arrogance. You have carried out your evil plans. And you have shown your strength against men, showing that you are able to do what you said.

The Metaphor of Two Sisters

3:6–10 And the Lord said to me in the days of King Josiah: Have you seen what rebellious Israel has done? She has gone out onto every high

Jer 3:2. Gregory the Great, *Moralia on Job* 9.7, ed. Marcus Adriaen, CCCM 143 (Turnhout: Brepols, 1979), 461.

32. Gregory the Great, *Moralia on Job* 9.7, CCCM 143:460–61.

mountain and under every leafy tree and committed fornication there. And, when she had done all these things, I said, "Return to me," but she did not return. And her sister, false Judah, saw that I sent rebellious Israel away because of her adulteries and gave her a certificate of divorce, but she was not afraid. Instead she herself also departed and committed fornication. She polluted the land because she took her fornication so lightly, committing adultery with stone and timber. And in the midst of all these things, her sister, false Judah, did not return to me with her whole heart, but in pretense, says the Lord.** The torments of some people are the remedies for others. When murderers are punished, they receive punishment for what they themselves have done, but others are deterred from crime. So when the ten tribes that were called Israel were captured by the Assyrians and taken away to the land of the Medes, the two tribes Judah and Benjamin, which ought to have feared a similar fate and returned to the Lord with their whole mind, outdid the crimes of the ten tribes. They followed after idols so much that they even set up a statue of Baal—which Ezekiel calls an "idol" (Ezek 8:3)—in God's temple, provoking the Lord's jealousy and sense of rivalry. The Lord uses the metaphor of two sisters, since they were descended from the single lineage of Abraham, Isaac, and Jacob. He calls the first one "rebellious" and the next one "false." For the former utterly rebelled against God immediately, by worshipping golden calves at Dan and Bethel (1 Kgs 12:28–29). The latter, who had the temple and the religion of the true God, departed from the Lord gradually, in imitation of her sister. Therefore she is called "false," since anagogically it is a prophecy about heretics. For, through heretical subtlety, they prefer to acquire the knowledge of a false name. They climb up the mountain of pride, and—enticed by its carnal pleasures—they display their fornication beneath every leafy and pleasant tree. Though they are "handed over to the devil for the destruction of the flesh" (1 Cor 5:5), it often happens that—as with the house of Judah, which is the "true confession" or "true faith"—they are not deterred by seeing an example. Instead they commit much worse things and pollute the land of the church by treating the matter of their fornication so lightly. They commit adultery with stone and tree by following doctrines that are opposed to God. But if a churchman [*ecclesiasticus vir*] wishes to correct those who err, endeavoring to cut off the rotting flesh and draw back to repentance those who followed falsehood, and if those individuals nonetheless follow the original error under the guise of ecclesiastical truth, the following can be said about them: **In the midst of all these things, false Judah did not return to me with her whole heart, but in pretense.**

Now this prophecy occurred during the time of Josiah, the just king, under whom Jeremiah began to prophesy.

[Origen:] If you have considered the two peoples to represent Israel and the Gentiles, consider Israel's exile to refer to the Judean people.[33] It is written regarding this: "I sent her away and gave her a certificate of divorce." For God indeed sent away the people of Israel and gave them a certificate of divorce so that, by abandoning Israel, God would make the lesson stronger. If a woman is displeasing, the law of Moses commands that her husband give her a certificate of divorce and send her away (Deut 24:1-2). Then the man was permitted to take another wife. According to this understanding, you must recognize that the Judeans received a certificate of divorce and were completely forsaken by God. For where now are their prophets? Where are their signs of power? Where is the manifestation of God? There is no temple. There are no sacrifices. Nor are there any of the other rituals set forth in the scrolls of the law. They have been cast out of their own territories. In this way the Lord gave Israel a certificate of divorce. After these things, we who are called "Judeans" in the scriptures turned to the Lord. (We are called Judeans on account of the tribe of Judah, from whose lineage the Savior is descended.) And our final days—if only they were not coming to pass in our own time—will be the same as or worse than what happened to false Judah because of its sins.

So that you may believe the things that are about to happen to us at the end of this age are worse than what befell the Judeans, listen to what the Savior proclaims in the gospel: "When lawlessness increases, many people's love will grow cold. But the one who perseveres to the end will be saved" (Matt 24:12-13). And in another passage: "There will be signs and omens in heaven and on earth, to lead astray—if possible—even the chosen ones" (Luke 21:11; Matt 24:24). There will be so much disbelief among the entire human race that our Savior, because he knew what would take place, said: "When the Son of Man comes, do you think he will find faith on earth?" (Luke 18:8). Indeed, if we examine our faith honestly rather than considering the large number of people gathered, and if we take into account the people's intentions and not the size of their assemblies, we will see that it is difficult to find a faithful person even among so many churches. There were truly faithful people back then, when they became martyred victims, when we

33. In Origen's spiritual reading of the text, the first sister, Israel, represents the Jewish people (Judah and Israel) and the second sister, Judah, represents the Gentile church. This lengthy excerpt is from Jerome's translation of Origen, *Homily 14 on Jeremiah*, PL 25:688-92.

mourners returned to the church after following behind the blood-soaked funeral procession. And there was an entire multitude of powerful people, when catechumens—experiencing their first comprehension of the faith— were instructed by those who distinguished themselves through martyrdom. It was a time when mere women, the weaker sex, remained fearless unto death. At that time there were truly signs from heaven and portents on the earth. At that time they were few in number but they were truly faithful, entering the tight and narrow path that leads to life (Matt 7:14). Now, when we have become greater in number, "many are called but few are chosen" (Matt 22:14). Out of so many people professing the same faith in Christ, only a few are found to have faith that merits true blessedness.

When God first says, "I sent Israel away because of her sins and left her in peril, and when Judah heard what happened to Israel, she did not want to return to me," God is speaking about the sins of those of us who, when we read what the Judean people suffered, do not become fearful and say: "If God did not spare the natural branches, how much less will God spare us! Since they deserved it, Christ—who is the gentle and most merciful God—rooted out those who gloried that they were the good olive branch from the root of the patriarchs Abraham, Isaac, and Jacob. So how much more will Christ refrain from sparing *us* if we do similar things!"

See God's kindness and severity. For God is not so kind that he is not also severe. Nor is God so severe that he is not also kind. If God were too kind, we would scorn his kindness. If God were too severe, despair about our salvation—on account of the sins we committed—would cast us headlong into vices. Now we humans need kindness when we repent and severity when we fail; so God is both severe and kind. When we, who are Judah, read the sacred volumes and find there all the ways that the territory of Israel committed adultery, and when we see that God sent her away and gave her a certificate of divorce, then—because of the things that they suffered—we ought to be converted to better ways and take heed, because they were de-livered into captivity, killed by their enemies, and their cities were burned with fire because of their sins. Then, as we have said, we ought to consider these words to apply to ourselves: "If God did not spare the natural branches, how much less will God spare us" (Rom 11:21). If, on account of sins, God sent away those who were descended from the race of the patriarchs, what will *we*, who were called from the Gentiles, have to suffer? Have we given this no consideration? We were called so that the freeborn children may be incited to jealousy (Rom 11:11) when they see that those who were once low-born slaves are now God's children. So if they have suffered so much, how much worse will be our suffering if we commit sins! If someone who was recently purchased enters into the house of the one who is buyer and master, he asks a fellow slave what previous slaves did to offend their master. The slave who wishes to continue in the master's house takes care not to do the things he heard were done by those who deserved beatings, punishments, and restraints. Then, after carefully asking what was done by the slaves who earned freedom from their master, he exerts every effort to do the things that he learned that those individuals did. And so we, who were not slaves of God but slaves of idols and demons, were later gathered from the nations and came to believe in Christ.

Let us read Scripture and see who is righteous and who is displeasing to the Lord. Paying close attention, let us strive to do the things that we read that the just people did. And let us be warned by the things that befell those who were handed over to captivity and banished from God's inheritance. It says that false Judah did not fear; she herself departed and committed fornication (Jer 3:8). After Israel first ruined herself with fornication, Judah also committed fornication. Her fornication was worthless, and she committed adultery with tree and stone (Jer 3:9). When we sin against God with a hardened heart, we are doing nothing other than committing fornication with "stone." And when we sin in our will, we are committing adultery under every leafy tree. **And in the midst of all these things, false Judah did not return to me with her whole heart, but in pretense.** Now the text is not silent after the words: **false Judah did not return to me.** Instead it says: **False Judah did not return to me with her whole heart, but in pretense.** This was to show that those who have returned have done so only in pretense and not in truth if they have not returned their heart. Therefore let us read the Old Testament histories and prophets. When we find those who became righteous, let us imitate the things that caused them to become righteous. Let us read the Gospels and the entire New Testament. Let us read the Apostle Paul's letters. And let us write all these things in our hearts, living according to the heavenly commandments, so that we are not handed a certificate of divorce but may be made heirs with Christ Jesus.

3:11 And the Lord said to me: Rebellious Israel has justified her soul in comparison with false Judah. [Jerome:] It says that Israel is more just in comparison with Judah because Israel perished immediately at the outset. Judah could have changed her ways because of Israel's sufferings. Let the new heresy pay attention because of the old heresies, observing that Israel is called "justified" in comparison with the one who is worse. Nor is it remarkable that this is the case with sisters from one nation since Sodom also receives the name "just" in comparison with Jerusalem when the Lord says through Ezekiel that Sodom "has become justified because of you" (Ezek 16:52). Compared to the Pharisee, the tax collector was just (Luke 18:14).

God Calls Israel to Return

3:12–13 Go and proclaim—or, *read*—**these words toward the north, saying: Return, rebellious Israel, says the Lord, and I will not turn my face away from you**—or, *harden my face against you*—**since I am holy**—or, *merciful*—**says the Lord, and I will not be angry forever. Nevertheless, acknowledge your sin, because you acted falsely**—or, *acted impiously*—**toward the Lord God, and you scattered**—or, *poured out*—**your ways to strangers under every leafy tree, and you did not hear my voice, says the Lord.** The Hebrew word *carath* means "call" or "**proclaim**," as well as "read." For this reason Aquila and Symmachus translated it "cry out" and the Septuagint and Theodotion translated it "read." The message is directed to the north, against Babylon and the Assyrians, and to the ten and two tribes, announcing their return. The Lord says: **I will not turn my face away from you,** or, *I will not harden my face against you,* so that I will not receive you with harsh judgment but with the face of compassion. For **I am holy** and merciful, so I will not remember your sins any longer or recall that you departed from the Lord in favor of the idols that delighted you, and that you committed fornication under every shady, leafy tree. It is certainly fitting to direct these words to heretics and to negligent people in the church, who are called to repentance each day by churchmen. The words "**and you did not hear my voice**" can properly be applied to these people. For every heretic dwells "in the north" and has lost the heat of faith. The heretics are unable to hear what the Apostle says, "be burning in spirit" (Rom 12:11), because they handed themselves over to sensual pleasures and departed from the Lord. "Scattering their ways" to strange doctrines, they followed after pleasure. For there is no heresy that is not founded on gluttony and lust, to lead astray "weak women laden with sins" who are "always learning but never attaining to the knowledge of truth" (2 Tim 3:6–7). Concerning these [heretics] it is truly said: "They devour my people like a loaf of bread" (Ps 14:4). And Christ's apostle writes that they "devour widows' houses" (Mark 12:40). The Lord is saying: And when I have pity on you, do not think that you are righteous. Instead, you should remember and acknowledge your sins. Since you committed fornication against the Lord, bow down your proud necks. Thus you who offended God through arrogance may appease God through humility. On the other hand, what we said above, *I will not harden my face against you*,[34] aligns with the prophetic word: "Turn your face away from my sins and blot out all my iniquities" (Ps 51:9).

3:14-16 Return, my rebelling—or, *wandering and departing*—children, says the Lord, for I am your husband—or, *I will rule over you*. And I will take you, one from a city and two from a family, and I will bring you into Zion. And I will give you shepherds after my own heart. They will nourish you with knowledge and instruction. And when you have multiplied and increased, in those days, says the Lord, they will no longer say, "The ark of the Lord's covenant—or, *testament*." It shall not come to mind, nor will they remember it. Neither shall it be visited. It shall not be made again.
The Jews think this was fulfilled after the return from Babylon under Cyrus, king of Persia, and Zerubbabel, son of Shealtiel, even though not everyone was returned, which is signified by the phrase: **I will take you, one from a city and two from a family.** But the passage better refers to Christ's coming, when a remnant was saved, as the Apostle explains: "If the Lord of Hosts had not left offspring for us, we would have been like Sodom and would have been made to resemble Gomorrah" (Rom 9:29). Then they were brought to Zion, about which it is written: "Glorious things are spoken about you, city of God" (Ps 87:3). And they were given shepherds after the Lord's heart— apostles and apostolic men who fed a multitude of believers, not with Jewish ceremonies but with knowledge and instruction about Christ. By preaching the gospel, they have fathered children throughout the whole world. They will not put their trust in the Lord's ark, which was the container for the law of Moses. Instead, they themselves will be God's temple, not the way the erring Nazarenes are devoted to the sacrifices that have been abolished, but they will observe a spiritual worship.[35] Others believe this passage refers to the end of time, when all Israel will be saved through the ingathering of the full number of the Gentiles (Rom 11:25).

3:17 At that time they will call Jerusalem "the throne of the Lord," and all nations will be gathered to it in Jerusalem in the name of the Lord.

34. Septuagint translation of Jer 3:12.
35. Fourth-century Christians used the name "Nazarenes" to refer to Jewish-descent Christians living in Syria who observed many Jewish practices. Jerome probably encountered them during his time in Palestine. See Jerome, *De viris illustribus* 3.2, ed. Claudia Barthold (Mülheim: Carthusianus Verlag, 2010), 164.

And they will not follow the depravity in their evil heart. The Lord—to whom the people previously said, "Shine forth, you who are seated upon the cherubim" (Ps 80:1)—will definitely not be seated on the ark of the covenant and on the cherubim. Instead, all who believe with a perfect mind will be God's throne. Or, in fact, it is even better to understand this as referring to the entire church when all nations are gathered together in the Lord's name, in Jerusalem, where there is a vision of peace. And they are not following **the depravity in their evil heart,** doing whatever they desire. Nor are they following their own errors. Rather, they say with the prophet, "My soul has clung to you. Your right hand has upheld me" (Ps 63:8).

3:18 In those days the house of Judah will go to the house of Israel, and they will come at the same time from the land of the north to the land that I gave to their ancestors. This was fulfilled particularly through the coming of Christ, when some members of the twelve tribes believed in the gospel **at the same time.** Abandoning the land of the harsh, cold north and departing from the devil's dominion, they regained the promised land that had been promised to their ancestors Abraham, Isaac, and Jacob. I recently published a booklet about the promised land.[36]

3:19 But I said: How shall I place you among the children and give you a pleasant land, the splendid inheritance of the armies of the nations? And I said: You shall call me Father and shall not cease to follow me. Instead of **the splendid inheritance of the armies of the nations,** which the Septuagint translated "the chosen inheritance of Almighty God of the nations," Theodotion translated it more accurately as "the renowned inheritance of the strength of the most powerful nations," referring to Christ, who is commander and Lord of all the nations that believe in his name and suffering. For Christ himself said to Israel: **You shall call me Father.** And: "Whoever believes in me believes in the Father" (John 12:44). Christ himself promised: **I shall place you among the children,** among the number of my children, among the people of the nations who believed in me, those to whom I have given **a pleasant land.** For "as many as received him, he gave them power to become children of God" (John 1:12).

3:20 But as a woman despises her lover, so has the house of Israel despised me, says the Lord. This is Christ's voice to the Jewish people, to whom he

---

36. Jerome, *Letter* 129, "To Dardanum, On the Land of Promise," PL 22:1099–1107.

had said: "I shall place you among the children and give you a pleasant land," and, "You shall call me Father and shall not cease to follow me" (3:19). He says: **As a woman despises her lover,** and not her husband, when, after having intercourse, she saw that her lover was serving her lusts and that the law of nature had been inverted—the law under which she was previously subjected to her husband, when the Lord said, "And her desire will be for you" (Gen 3:16, paraphrased). So also the house of Israel, the Jewish people, despised the Lord their Savior, to their own downfall.

3:21–22a A voice was heard in the highways—or, *on the lips*—**wailing for the children of Israel because they made their way wicked and have forgotten the Lord their God. Return, you rebellious children, and I will heal your rebellions**—or, *griefs.* Symmachus translated this word as "turnings." The Lord eagerly receives those who are penitent, running to the child who experienced poverty and squalor, clothing the child with clean garments, and restoring the former glory of the one who has returned, as long as the child returns with weeping and wailing (Luke 15:20–23). For such people have made their way wicked with vice and forgot the Lord their God and Father. This prophetic message is now directed to those people: **Return, you rebellious children.** I call you "children" because you are acknowledging your sins by returning to your parent with weeping and wailing. It says: And when you have returned to the Lord, he will heal all your griefs, or the **rebellions**—or, indeed, the turnings—with which you departed from the Lord. For, although we may return voluntarily, nevertheless it is not possible for us to be saved unless the Lord draws us forth and strengthens our eagerness with his help. We should understand this passage to refer to the Jewish people, and also to the heretics who forsook the Lord.

3:22b–23 "Behold, we are coming to you, for you are the Lord our God. Truly the hills and the multitude—or, *strength*—**of the mountains were liars. Truly the salvation of Israel is in the Lord our God."** Let the repentant person say this, abandoning all pride—the multitude or height of mountains and hills—through which that person acted haughtily toward God. Let that person say, bowed down in humility, "**Truly the salvation of Israel is in the Lord our God.**"

3:24 "Ever since our youth, confusion has devoured what our parents labored for—their flocks and herds, their sons and daughters." All the labors of the heretics, about which it is written, "they have failed in their search"

(Ps 64:6), ever since the youth of those whom they deceived (that is, their sons and daughters who progressed in heresy or, through indulgence, were kept like herd animals) were crushed by confusion. For this reason they say:

3:25 "We shall sleep in our confusion, and our shame shall cover us, since we have sinned against our God, we and our ancestors, from our youth even to this day. And we have not listened to the voice of the Lord our God." Let Israel, who did not listen to its Lord, say this. Let every repentant heretic say this. For confessing and acknowledging one's sins is a part of salvation: "Admit your sins, so that you may be justified" (Isa 43:26). For Israel truly rejected Christ, its Lord and God. It sinned against him not only when he appeared in the flesh but also prior to his coming. For this reason they say: **"We and our ancestors, from our youth even to this day. And we have not listened to the voice of our God** who spoke to our ancestors." "If you believed Moses, you would have believed me, for he wrote about me" (John 5:46).

Chapter Four

A Call to Conversion

4:1a If you return, O Israel, says the Lord, be converted to me. [Jerome:] The Septuagint translates this passage as: "If Israel will return to me, says the Lord, then it will be converted to me." This is the meaning: If Israel returns to me, it will be returned from captivity, or, in other words, when it offers what it has. If someone has something, more will be given to that person, but if someone only seems to have something, even that will be taken away (Matt 13:12; 25:29). This is the meaning in the Hebrew: If you return to me, O Israel, while desiring salvation and admitting that you sinned and did not listen to the voice of the Lord your God, then be completely converted. Believe in the one whom you denied, and then you will have a complete conversion.

4:1b If you remove your stumbling blocks from my sight, you shall not waver. When we waver and say, "My feet almost wavered" (Ps 73:2), we are not enduring this because of weakness of nature but because we are placing our stumbling blocks and idols against the Lord.

4:2 And you will swear, "The Lord lives in truth, and in judgment, and in justice," and nations will bless him, and him they will praise. How is it that the gospel forbids us to swear (Matt 5:33–37)? But here **"you will swear"** is used as a confession and a condemnation of the idols by which Israel had sworn. Finally the stumbling blocks are removed and Israel is swearing by the Lord. Regarding the phrase **"the Lord lives,"** it is used in the Old Testament to swear an oath condemning the dead things by which all idolaters swear. And, at the same time, pay attention to the fact that this oath has these companions: truth, judgment, and justice. If these things are missing, it will not be an oath, but perjury. He says: And when Israel has done this, and when there is "a teacher of the Gentiles" (1 Tim 2:7), then all **nations will bless him,** or will be blessed *in* him, **and him they will praise,** because salvation has come forth out of Israel.

4:3–4 For thus says the Lord to the men of Judah and Jerusalem: Break up your fallow ground again, and do not sow on thorns. Be circumcised to the Lord; remove the foreskins of your hearts, men of Judah and inhabitants of Jerusalem, lest my indignation come forth like fire and burn, and there will be no one to extinguish it, because of the wickedness of your thoughts—or, *plans.* Where we have written, **Be circumcised to the Lord; remove the foreskins of your hearts,** Symmachus rendered it, "Be purified to the Lord; remove the wickedness of your hearts," understanding "circumcision" as "cleansing" and "foreskin" as "vice." Now this is directed to the men of Judah and Jerusalem who follow the true faith and dwell in the church, commanding them not to **sow on thorns.** The gospel message says these thorns signify the things that choke out what is sown by God (Matt 13:22). So first they should work the fallow ground, dig out the thornbushes, and remove the brambles, so that the pure plowed soil may receive pure seeds. This is what is said in another passage: "Do not throw your pearls before swine, and do not give what is holy to dogs" (Matt 7:6). For how is it possible to hear God's word, receive seed, and bear fruit, if one's soul is filled with the cares of the world?

The part that follows, **Be circumcised to the Lord; remove the foreskins of your hearts,** is directed to none other than the men of Judah and inhabitants of Jerusalem, commanding them to forsake the letter that kills and follow the Spirit that gives life (2 Cor 3:6). He says: If you do not do this, **my indignation** will **come forth like fire and burn, and there will be no one to extinguish it.** Therefore, by threatening and announcing it ahead of time, the Lord will not be compelled to do it. We examine what happened to the Ninevites to whom judgment was foretold so that they would turn away the imminent wrath through their repentance. All these evils will come **because of the wickedness of** our **thoughts** or plans. Where are those who say that they have not sinned in their thoughts, since, according to the truth of the gospel, all vices proceed from the heart (Matt 15:19)? [Maurus:] But the Lord, who does not wish the death of sinners (Ezek 18:23), but their conversion, and seeks life, first forbids us to commit sins. The Lord commands us to walk in the way of righteousness and obey his commandments. Then if we sin and transgress his commandments, the Lord exhorts us to be converted from sins to repentance. And so the Lord promises pardon to the person who has failed and then orders us to keep the way of discipline and strive hard to do good works. For this reason, after the prophet admonishes the Israelites to be converted away from error and toward the Lord, and to walk "in truth, and in judgment, and in justice" (4:2), and to cleanse the field of their heart from the impurity of evil deeds, he encourages them to arm themselves with spiritual armor to fight against the fiercest lion (1 Pet 5:8), enter the fortified cities of holy scripture, and lift up the banner of the cross, battling courageously against the most wretched enemy, as it is announced in the opening passage of the following book.[37]

The Invasion of Jerusalem Predicted

4:5–6 Declare it in Judah and make it heard in Jerusalem. Speak out and sound the trumpet in the land. Cry out loudly and say: Assemble yourselves and let us enter fortified cities. Raise the banner in Zion. Take courage and do not remain, for I bring evil and great sorrow from the north. Let Judah hear this, and Jerusalem, where there is the confession of faith, where Christ's peace dwells, and to whom this was said through Isaiah: "Go up to a high mountain, you who bring good news to Zion. Lift up your voice, you who bring good news to Jerusalem" (Isa 40:9). He cries out loudly and thus commands: **Let us enter fortified cities.** When the heretics' wars rise up, let Christ's fortifications defend us. Raise the banner of the cross in the watchtower, in the heights of the church. **Take courage,** you who fear.

---

37. Rabanus Maurus's commentary on Jeremiah was divided into twenty "books," which do not correspond with present-day chapter divisions. Prior to the twelfth century, the biblical books were not yet divided according to the chapter system familiar to us. Frans van Liere (*An Introduction to the Medieval Bible* [New York: Cambridge University Press, 2014], 43) notes that "division into chapters close to the one known today" became common in the thirteenth century. This sentence from Rabanus is the conclusion of book 2.

Do not remain, but run to Christ's protection. **For I bring evil and great sorrow from the north,** namely, Nebuchadnezzar, whom I permit to exist in this world so that your courage and victory may be confirmed.

4:7 The lion has gone up from its den, and the robber of the nations has roused himself. He has gone forth from his place to make your land deserted. Your cities will be destroyed, left without any inhabitants. As we have said, this is Nebuchadnezzar, about whom Peter speaks: "Our adversary the devil prowls around like a roaring lion" (1 Pet 5:8). He has **gone up,** as it were, from the abyss in which he is to be bound, and he asks not to be sent back. The **robber** or destroyer **of the nations has roused himself,** the one about whom it is written: "He shall rule over all his enemies" (Ps 9:26 LXX). And he boasts in the Lord's presence: "I have walked around the entire earth and I have trampled on it" (Job 2:2). For who is there whom the devil's poisons do not touch, apart from the one who alone is able to say, "Behold the ruler of this world is coming, and he has no power over me" (John 14:30)? The devil constantly makes the entire land of the church a wasteland so that those who had departed from the church might fight against the church. The evangelist says about these: "They went out from us, but they did not belong to us, for if they had belonged to us, they would undoubtedly have remained with us" (1 John 2:19). The cities of the land of Judah are destroyed while the assemblies of the heretics flourish. If someone is a patron of the founders of perverse doctrines, this can be said about that person: **The lion has gone up from its den, and the robber of the nations has roused himself,** and so forth.

4:8 Because of this, clothe yourselves with sackcloth. Lament and howl, for the fierce anger of the Lord is not turned away from us. Or, as the Septuagint translates it, *from you.* We are not able to escape the lion and ferocious beast unless we repent and are converted to the Lord, not only in mind but also in deed. As long as the lion ravages the church and the land of Judah, and lays waste to Jerusalem, God's anger is manifest.

4:9 And it will come to pass in that day, says the Lord, that the heart of the king shall fail, and also the heart of the princes. The priests shall be astonished, and the prophets shall be amazed. While the robber destroys the Lord's church, and the Lord's anger remains against us, all help will be useless. **The heart of the king shall fail,** because his heart ought to be in God's hand, **and also the heart of the princes,** who are considered to be wise. For God has made the wisdom of the world foolish because they did

not know God through wisdom (1 Cor 1:21). Furthermore, the priests themselves, who ought to teach the Lord's law and defend the people under their
care against the lion's frenzy, will be struck senseless, gaping with a sort of
stupor. The Septuagint translated this stupor as "going out of their mind."
And the prophets shall be amazed, or, as Aquila translated the Hebrew
word *iethmau,* "they will be senseless." For who would not go insane, whose
heart would not fail, when they see their princes, kings, priests, and prophets
subject to the lion?

4:10 And I said: "Alas, alas, alas, Lord God," which the Septuagint translates
as, *"O Lord God."* **"Have you deceived this people and Jerusalem, saying,
'You shall have peace'? Behold, the sword reaches even to the soul."** Since
God said above, "At that time they will call Jerusalem 'the throne of the
Lord,' and all nations will be gathered to it in Jerusalem in the mountain of
the Lord" (Jer 3:17), and now says, "The heart of the king shall fail, and also
the heart of the princes; the priests shall be astonished, and the prophets
shall be amazed," the prophet is disturbed and thinks God lied to him. He
does not understand that what was first promised would take place much
later, and that the current prophecy is for a time in the near future. As the
Apostle says: "Has God rejected his people? By no means!" (Rom 11:1). Now
the sword reaches even to the soul when no life remains in the soul. At the
same time it shows that peace and promise do not follow unless a sword first
goes forth to eliminate and purge the soul's vices.

**4:11-12a At that time it shall be said to this people and to Jerusalem: A
scorching**—or, *dewy*—**wind is in the highways that are in the desert, but
not to winnow or cleanse the ways of the daughter of my people. A full
wind from these places will come to me.** When the sword reaches all the
way to the soul and the threshing has been completed, then a wind will come
from the desert, not to cleanse and winnow the threshing floor by dispersing
the chaff so that the grain may be gathered into granaries. **A full wind will
not come** to the people but **to me,** so that my wheat may be scattered. The
Hebrews use the same word, *ruha,* for "wind" and "spirit," and we need to
understand the word as either "wind" or "spirit" based on the context of the
passage. Others explain this passage in the following way—that after the
threshing floor has been cleansed, the remnants shall be saved, so that it is
written, "The spirit of fullness will come to me."[38] As the evangelist says: "We

---

38. This is the Septuagint translation of Jer 4:12a.

all have received from his fullness" (John 1:16). And we shall receive the grace of the Holy Spirit. Understood in the historical sense, the scorching wind is Nebuchadnezzar, who devastated the entire world. Tropologically, it refers to the enemy power that comes from the desert and wasteland where there is no divine shelter, and it tries to destroy the church of God.

4:12b And now I—I will speak my judgments on them. This is an example of *aposiopesis,* like this passage from Virgil: "Whom I—but it is better to calm the turbulent waves."[39] God is about to say favorable things but then interrupts himself and adds harsh things to the harsh things previously spoken. For God speaks these judgments on his own people so that they may know that it is just for them to endure what they are enduring.

4:13 Look! He will go up like a cloud, and his chariots like a whirlwind. His horses are swifter than eagles. Woe to us, for we are destroyed. Seeing the things that are about to occur, he describes the Babylonian army. The thunderous noise of their chariot wheels is compared to an extremely ferocious whirlwind. The speed of the horses matches that of eagles. Though the prophet had spoken these things and virtually pointed out the coming enemies with his own finger, the people do not groan over these things when they are about to occur. They only do so when they notice that the events have already taken place, saying: **Woe to us, for we are destroyed.** This same passage also applies to the church, since the army of the true Nebuchadnezzar attacks us each day, and Pharaoh's chariots and his entire cavalry are swifter than attacks by eagles. If a churchman were to understand this passage and believe the statement "When you return and groan, then you will be saved" (Isa 30:15), he would say: **Woe to us, for we are destroyed.**

4:14 Wash your heart from wickedness, O Jerusalem, so that you may be saved. How long will harmful thoughts linger within you? To the people who are saying, "Woe to us, for we are destroyed," the prophet answers—or God answers through the prophet: **Wash your heart from wickedness, O Jerusalem** with the water that Isaiah spoke about, "Wash yourselves, become

---

39. Virgil, *Aeneid* 1.135, trans. H. Rushton Fairclough, revised by G. P. Goold, LCL 63 (Cambridge, MA: Harvard University Press, 1999), 270. *Aposiopesis,* Greek for "becoming silent," is a rhetorical device in which the speaker breaks off or changes direction instead of completing the original discourse; Arthur Quinn and Lyon Rathbun, "Aposiopesis," in *Encyclopedia of Rhetoric and Composition: Communication from Ancient Times to the Information Age,* ed. Theresa Enos (New York: Garland, 1996), 14.

clean" (Isa 1:16) with the water of salvific baptism, the water of repentance. He addresses the Judeans' main city, but it should be understood that, by naming the city, he really means the people. "How long will you be subject to the sinful thoughts that 'proceed from your heart'" (Matt 15:19)? In the holy scriptures, we should understand **heart** to refer to the soul and the mind.

4:15 For a voice of one declaring from Dan and giving notice of the idol—or, *affliction*—from Mount Ephraim. A divine message now speaks regarding a location in the land of Judah. For Dan, a tribe near Mount Lebanon and the city now called Paneas, looks toward the north, the direction Nebuchadnezzar is about to come from. He describes the **idol** Bel, or "affliction," or "iniquity," as coming from Mount Ephraim. After the tribe of Dan, one passes through Ephraim next when approaching Jerusalem. **Dan** is interpreted as "judgment." **Ephraim** means "abundance." Therefore the Lord's judgment will come to wrongdoers, with all abundance of punishment.

4:16–17 Say to the nations: Behold, it is heard in Jerusalem that guards are coming from a faraway land and have raised their voice against Judah. They are set around her like watchers over fields, because she has provoked me to wrath, says the Lord. He wishes all the surrounding nations to know God's judgment and that, after Jerusalem has been scourged, all of them will be disciplined. He is saying: In conversation that is widespread throughout Jerusalem, it is reported that enemies **are coming from a faraway land** and the noise of a howling army is rising up against the city. They will blockade the city and barricade it with fortifications so effectively that you would think they were less like enemy soldiers and more like **watchers over fields** and vineyards. This has not taken place because of the powerfulness of the enemies but because of the guilt of Jerusalem that **provoked** God **to wrath.** For if the adversarial powers do not even have authority over swine (Matt 8:28–32), how much less do they have authority over humans—and especially humans who once belonged to God's city?

4:18 Your ways and your thoughts have brought these things upon you. This is your wickedness. Because it is bitter, it has touched your heart. He makes an *apostrophe* to the city of Jerusalem,[40] saying that its ways and thoughts,

---

40. An *apostrophe,* from the Greek *apostrophein* (to turn away), is a digression, interruption, or an aside directed to an audience different from the one previously being addressed; Arthur Quinn and Lyon Rathbun, "Apostrophe," in Enos, *Encyclopedia of Rhetoric and Composition,* 14.

with which it sinned in word and deed, have caused all these things to come upon the city, and that its wickedness has caused a bitterness that touched the city's heart and penetrated to the inmost parts of its soul. Therefore whatever happens to us occurs on account of our vice, through which we turn a sweet God bitter and we compel God—who does not wish it—to act furiously.

God's Lament for the Destruction of the People

4:19-20 My belly, my belly. I am in pain. The feelings of my heart are troubled. I will not keep silent, because my soul has heard the sound of the trumpet, the cry of battle. Destruction upon destruction is called for, and all the land is laid waste. My tents are immediately destroyed, my curtains in a moment. Where we followed Symmachus and wrote "**are troubled,**" and the Hebrew says *homae,* the Septuagint and Theodotion rendered it *maimassei.* I still do not know, even at this time, what this word means.[41] Aquila used *ochlazei,* a word that means "tumult." Let this be enough discussion regarding the word, about which I know there is great contention among most readers. Here the voice of the prophet is introduced—and through the prophet the voice of God, who says that he suffers pain because of the destruction of his people, and that, just like a human, his internal organs are being torn apart. In the same way, the Savior suffered anguish over the death of Lazarus (John 11:33-35), lamented over Jerusalem (Luke 19:41-44), and did not want to conceal his pain with silence. [Gregory:] The word "womb" is rightly interpreted as "mind," since thought is generated in the mind the way an offspring is conceived in the womb; and thoughts are contained in the mind the way food is contained in the belly.[42] [Jerome:] All the blasting **of the trumpet** and roaring of the battles disturbs his emotions, while disasters are piled upon disasters, and the entire land of the two tribes is laid waste. God says, "Before I knew it, what was once **my tent** and **curtains** were demolished by raging Babylon. What was once my lodging turned into plunder for the enemies." God says this very thing when witnessing the turmoil and discord of sedition in the church, when the shouting in its assemblies each day turns God's peace into war. So he continues:

41. The Hebrew word *hmh* means "be in an uproar." See the discussion of this verb in Holladay, *Jeremiah 1,* 161.
42. Gregory the Great, *Moralia on Job* 12.55.64, ed. Marcus Adriaen, CCCM 143A (Turnhout: Brepols, 1979), 668.

4:21 How long shall I see people fleeing? How long shall I hear the sound of the trumpet? Either they are fleeing from the Babylonian king, or else "they are fleeing from me and retreating from my service."

4:22 For my foolish people have not known me. They are foolish and senseless children. They are wise about how to do evil but ignorant about how to do good. The cause of the destruction, the devastation, the fleeing, and the trumpet is that the people became stupid, not by nature, but by deliberate effort. This foolishness is demonstrated by the fact that they do not know God. Instead of being wise children they have become foolish and **senseless children.** For what could be greater foolishness—when the ox knows its owner and the donkey its master's crib (Isa 1:3)—than the fact that Israel did not know the Lord, and when the Lord was present with them they despised the very one they always longed to see. When it continues, **They are wise about how to do evil but ignorant about how to do good,** we should understand "wisdom" as a bad quality, as it is used in the phrase, "the children of this age are wiser than the children of light." The wicked steward is reported to have done certain things wisely (Luke 16:8). And the serpent in paradise is described as shrewder than all the other animals (Gen 3:1). Therefore true wisdom is that which is joined to the fear of God. In general, where there are plots and subterfuges, it should not be called "wisdom" but "cunning" and "craftiness." Where we have rendered it, **For my foolish people have not known me,** the Septuagint translates it, "Because the leaders of my people did not know me," indicating that the teachers are guiltier than are the people who lack knowledge of God.

Jeremiah Foresees the Destruction of Judah

4:23-26 I looked at the earth, and lo, it was a waste and void; and to the heavens, and there was no light in them. I looked upon the mountains, and lo, they were quaking, and all the hills were troubled. I looked, and there were no humans, and all the birds of the air were gone. I looked, and lo, Carmel was a wilderness, and all its cities were destroyed in the presence of the Lord and in the presence of his raging anger. Through the Spirit, the prophet sees the things that are about to occur so that the people listening will become frightened and, by repenting, avoid enduring the things that they dread. The land is waste, because its inhabitants are wiped out. The heavens have no light since the people are unable to see, as a result of their enormous fear. The mountains themselves, and the hills, do not have safe hiding places. Through *hyperbole,* they are seen as quaking and troubled.[43] He looked, gazing all around from one place to another, and he was not able to spot any birds. For the unspeaking elements sense God's anger, and irrational animals become terrified. The entire world now shows this to be true, for when the multitude of humans has been slaughtered, the winged creatures that normally accompany human inhabitants also depart and perish. Even Carmel, which is near the Great Sea [the Mediterranean], and is planted with olives and densely covered with woodlands and vineyards, will come to such desolation that it will be as empty as a desert. All the cities will become deserted. The cause of all these terrible things is that God's anger was stirred up by the sin of an erring people. Everything we have said about Jerusalem and Judah according to the historical sense we can apply to God's church when it offends God. Where there once was an entire choir of virtues and gladness, there now dwells a multitude of sins and sorrows.

4:27–28 For thus says the Lord: The entire land shall be desolate, but I will not destroy it completely. Earth shall mourn, and the heavens shall lament from above, because I have spoken. I have resolved, and I have not repented. Nor am I turned back from it. God's compassion is intermingled with anger. The entire land is desolate but not brought to a complete end, so there may be some who recognize God's mercy. Heaven above will also seem to be mournful. The land itself will lament because God's judgment endures to the end and because God will not repent from the things he has planned and spoken. Now it speaks of God's repentance when a judgment announced by God is removed and the raging anger does not endure to the end. God made a threat through Jonah, but the multitude of tears and lamentations overcame the impending sword (Jonah 3:1–10).

4:29a At the voice of the horseman and archer—or, *stretcher of the bow*—**the entire city**—or, *region*—**flees. They enter thickets and climb up the rocks.** The part that follows, *And they entered mountain passes* (or, *caves*), was added by the Septuagint.

---

43. *Hyperbole,* from the Greek word for "overshooting," is a rhetorical device "using self-conscious exaggeration"; Elizabeth Patnoe, "Hyperbole," in Enos, *Encyclopedia of Rhetoric and Composition,* 334.

4:29b All the cities are abandoned, and no humans dwell in them. This divine message describes the raging Babylonian army and how all the people abandon the city because of their fear of the army. All of them climb up into the thickets but yet are not able to deflect the Lord's wrath. Now, as we said above, whatever is interpreted in the historical sense as referring to Jerusalem can also be applied to the church when it has offended God and has been handed over to enemies, whether during times of persecution or when it is handed over to vices and sins.[44]

4:30a But when you are made desolate, what will you do? Instead of **desolate,** which in Hebrew is *sadud,* and which Aquila alone translated this way, the others translated "unhappy" and "pitiable," because of the city's guilt, which offended the merciful God so that it was handed over to enemies. Then it continues:

4:30b When you dress yourself in scarlet, when you adorn yourself with gold ornaments and paint your eyes with cosmetics, you are arranging your appearance in vain. Your lovers have despised you. They will seek your life. Using the metaphor of an adulterous woman, he says: Once you have offended God and abandoned the Creator who is like your husband, you are looking for your ornaments **in vain. Your** demon **lovers have despised you.** They definitely do not seek the filth of wantonness. Instead they seek the ruin of your life. This same thing should be understood spiritually as speaking against those who have destroyed the marital affection and chastity of the true faith. He says: If **you dress yourself in scarlet,** by accepting the faith of the blood of Christ; if **you adorn yourself with gold ornaments,** by meditating on the meaning and understanding of what is spiritual; if you **paint your eyes with cosmetics,** by having eagerness for mysteries and knowing the secrets of God, **you are arranging your appearance in vain,** for you had also prepared these things for your lovers. Since a narrow bed does not have room for both [God and your lovers], God does not accept the ornaments with which you previously pleased your lovers.

4:31 For I have heard the voice like that of a woman in labor, the anguishes—or, *groans*—**like that of a woman giving birth. The voice of the daughter of Zion dying away and stretching out her hands: "Woe is me, for my soul has fainted because of those who were killed."** Using the image

---

44. Note that this is an example of the allegorical sense of Scripture.

of a woman giving birth, specifically one who is bringing forth her first child, he describes the city of Jerusalem wailing and crying out. It is like a woman giving birth who has never before experienced labor pains. She passes out and is scarcely able to breathe as she endures the **anguishes.** She collapses with her hands outspread. In the same way, the daughter of Zion—when she sees her children killed—breaks forth into these words and says: **"Woe is me, for my soul has fainted because of those who were killed."** For in one passage two examples are used as a comparison—giving birth or mourning children. What a woman suffers in pregnancy or the death of her children is just like what Jerusalem suffers for her people.

HUGH OF ST. CHER

On Jeremiah

Jeremiah 7–8

Chapter Seven

Introduction to Chapter Seven

7:1 The word of the Lord that came [to Jeremiah]. Here the Lord shows the prophet how he would make him the examiner of the Lord's people, for Jeremiah was sent to warn the Lord's people, who did not listen to him. Instead, they despised him. For this reason, Jeremiah found sufficient proof of their wickedness. Now this chapter is divided into four parts. In the first part (7:1-3), Jeremiah is ordered to stand in the gate through which the multitude of people entered in order to pray, so that in this way, at least, they would hear his preaching. The second part (7:4-16) shows what evils would come upon the Judeans if they refused to listen to the prophets sent to them, despising them instead. For this reason the prophets were ordered not to pray for them. The third part (7:17-28) shows that the Judeans' burnt offerings and sacrifices, in which they placed their trust, were not pleasing to God. It also shows that they had been commanded not to perform [the sacrifices] that were being offered. Indeed, they were committing even greater idolatry through the sacrifices, so that God was scarcely honored at all. In the fourth part (7:29-34), God warns the people to make lamentation for the sins they had committed and warns them of the miseries that would be coming upon them.

Jeremiah Is Commanded to Preach in the Gate

7:2 According to the literal sense, the Lord ordered Jeremiah to stand in the gate of the house of the Lord, so that those who refused to listen to the word of the Lord would at least hear Jeremiah preaching in the gate while they entered through the gate. The Lord himself did this often, for we read that he preached in synagogues on the Sabbath when the people assembled. This teaches us to do the same thing at certain times and places. For this reason 2 Tim 4:2 states: "[Preach the word.] Be persistent in favorable times and unfavorable times." So this means: **Stand in the gate** where everyone comes together so they can hear you whether they want to or not. First he warns them gently, so they will pay closer attention. For their hearts were hard and obstinate; and thus they were softened by many summons and attentive encouragements.

Understood according to the moral sense, standing **in the gate of the house of the Lord** means that the preacher carefully contemplates his own entrance into and departure from this life, and he announces the same thing to others.[1] In Gen 16:8, the angel said to Hagar when she fled: "Hagar, servant of Sarah, where are you coming from and where are you going?" Genesis 49:14-15: "Issachar shall be a strong donkey lying down between the boundaries. He saw that rest was good and that the land was excellent, and he bowed his shoulders for carrying." The two boundaries are the beginning and the end of life. Or else, standing **in the gate** is to consider oneself to be constantly at the beginning point of good, as in Ecclus 18:7: "When someone has finished, that person will begin again." And in Ps 76 [77:10]: "I said, 'Now I have begun.'" And in Ps 37 [38:6]: "I have walked sorrowfully all day long."[2] Or else, preaching **in the gate of the house of the Lord** means to exhort people to enter into the house of the Lord. Isaiah 2:3: "Come, let us go up to the mountain of the Lord, and to the house of the God of Jacob." **You who enter**, either the temple or Jerusalem. Psalm 9:13-14: "You lift me up from the gates of death so that I may proclaim all your praises in the gates of the daughter of Zion."

1. Though there were cases of women preaching in the Middle Ages, I have used the pronoun "he" to designate the preacher throughout this translation, since Hugh and his Dominican colleagues almost certainly had in mind a male preacher. For information about female preachers in the Middle Ages, see part 2 of Beverly Mayne Kienzle and Pamela J. Walker, eds., *Women Preachers and Prophets through Two Millennia of Christianity* (Berkeley: University of California Press, 1998), 99-195.

2. Psalm 38, a psalm of contrition, supports Hugh's point about human fallibility.

7:3 Make your ways good. Make your wills good. Make them straight because they are perverse and evil, since they aim not to the right but to the left [*ad sinistram*]. Proverbs 4:27: "The Lord knows the ways that are on the right, but the ways that are on the left are perverse." The same passage says: "He makes straight the paths for your feet, and all your ways will be made secure" (Prov 4:26). **And your pursuits;** that is, your doings. **And I will dwell with you in this place,** in your homeland. Another literal interpretation is: I will confirm you in this place and make your dwelling place endure so that no enemy will be about to harm it. **I will dwell with you,** because as Matt 18:20 states, "Where two or three are gathered together in my name, I am there in the midst of them."

False Confidence in the Temple of the Lord

7:4 Do not trust in lying words, in the words of false prophets, **saying: "The temple of the Lord. The temple of the Lord** is with us, so we cannot be captured." He says **temple** three times because they went up into the temple to worship three times a year. When the true prophets said to them that Nebuchadnezzar was coming, they said, "It is not true, since the Lord will not abandon his temple, which is too beautiful, and too precious and holy, to be destroyed and trampled underfoot, and especially since we offer worship and honor there three times a year." But the Lord does not regard the temple made with hands—or paneled, glittering, gold-covered buildings—to be his own temple. Instead, the Lord considers his temple to be the soul in which the elegance of morals, virtues, and sanctity dwells. Or else he says [**temple**] three times because of the three powers of the soul.[3] For this reason Matt 24:2 says: "You see all these buildings? Truly I tell you, there will not remain a stone upon a stone that shall not be pulled down."

This is also spoken against some people who put too much trust in their own religious practices and in the holy places where they are, since there are many relics there. Or else he says **temple** three times because they boast or brag, since they uttered the three religious vows [poverty, chastity, and obedience] there. They claim that this passage from 1 Cor 3:17 addresses them: "God's temple—which you are—is holy." So also, certain people presumptuously say, "Because of this we are God's temple. God made us and

---

3. The three powers of the soul are memory, intellect, and will. See Augustine, *On the Trinity* 15.7.12, ed. W. J. Mountain and Fr. Glorie, CCSL 50A (Turnhout: Brepols, 1968), 475.

will not condemn us, because God would not have made us if we deserved to be condemned." Against those who boast about a place and say that, because of its holiness, it is not possible for the place to be destroyed even if its inhabitants sin, 2 Macc 5:19–20 states: "The Lord did not choose the people because of the place but chose the place because of the people, and for that reason the place itself was made a participant in the people's evils." And in the same passage: "On account of the sins of the people dwelling there, the Lord became angry with the city, and so contempt for the place arose" (2 Macc 5:17).

7:5 Therefore you should not place confidence in your temple. Instead, you will be able to have confidence **if you order your ways well,** if you do such things as shunning evil and doing good, so that you may receive well-deserved blessings. **[If you order your] ways** or deeds **and cares** or thoughts. So that you may not go after idols or sins in either deed or thought you should keep yourselves inwardly pure in your mind and externally pure in body and deed, as the psalmist says: "Bless the Lord all my soul, and all that is within me bless his holy name" (Ps 103:1). For this reason it is possible to explain the term **"if you bless"** to mean: **If you bless** the Lord in mind and deed.[4] **If you execute judgment,** etc. This means: If you seek honest judgment and impartiality in all matters regarding your neighbor, as in Ezek 18:8–9: "If he has executed true judgment between one man and another, and has kept my judgments in order to do what is true, he is righteous and shall live."

7:6 And if you do not make false charges against the foreigner, the orphan, and the widow, because such people are especially unable to defend themselves. Leviticus 19:13: "You shall not make false charges against your neighbors or oppress them by violence." Exodus 23:9: "You shall not trouble a foreigner. You know the hearts of foreigners, because you yourselves were foreigners in the land of Egypt." **If you do not shed innocent blood in this place,** literally, through homicide, since Gen 9:6 says: "Whoever sheds human blood, that person's blood shall be shed." Or **[if you do not] shed [innocent blood],** as the *Gloss* says on this passage: "By placing a stumbling block before the neighbor."[5] The argument for this interpretation is that

    4. The text of 7:5 in Hugh's commentary reads, "If you bless [*benedixeritis*] your ways," one of the variant readings of the Vulgate. Another reading is, "If you order your ways well [*bene direxeritis*]." See *Biblia Sacra iuxta Vulgatam Versionem*, ed. Bonifatio Fischer et al. (Stuttgart: Deutsche Bibelgesellschaft, 1983), 1176 n10.
    5. *Glossa interlinearea* on Jer 7:6.

when someone draws others into sin through bad example, that person is striking them dead. Leviticus 19:16: "You shall not stand against the blood of your neighbor." Therefore, addressing the wicked prelates who are obligated to provide a good example, Ezek 3:18 says: "I will require their blood at your hand." Genesis 4:23: "I have killed a man in my injury," that is, "as an *example* of my injury." Romans 14:15: "Do not destroy with food the one for whom Christ died." Or else, [**if you do not**] shed [**innocent blood**] through fraternal hatred, because whoever hates one's brother or sister is a murderer (1 John 3:15). Or by seizing their goods, as Ecclus 34:25 states: "The bread of the needy is the life of the poor. Whoever defrauds them is bloodthirsty." Likewise, someone who does not give to those who are in need deprives them of life and kills them. As Jerome says: "Feed those dying of hunger," etc.[6] And in Prov 28:24: "Whoever takes anything from one's father and mother and says, 'This is not a sin,' partakes in homicide." This refers to taking things that are necessities. Ambrose says: "When you have possessions and do not give to those in need, this is not a smaller transgression than taking away the things that belong to a person."[7] **And if you do not walk after foreign gods to your own detriment,** because it leads you to punishment and guilt. Following **foreign gods** refers to worshipping idols, or following perverse doctrines, or desiring worldly things, which leads to wretchedness, which is slavery to idols.

7:7 I will dwell with you in this place, etc. At that time you will securely possess your place and the temple. For just as God holds the place they possess in dishonor because of the sins of its inhabitants, so also God would have honored their site if they had been good. For this reason 2 Macc 5:20 states: "The place itself was made a participant in the people's evils, but afterward it shall be made a partaker of good things. And just as it was forsaken in the Almighty God's wrath, it will be exalted again most gloriously when reconciled with the Lord who is great." This can also be addressed to the foolish virgins who have lamps with no oil (Matt 25:1–13), those who have bodily chastity without purity or self-control of mind. Such people boast about the temple with respect to its exterior appearance, when it is filled inside with all sorts

---

6. The full quotation, frequently repeated in medieval literature, is "Feed those dying of hunger. If you do not feed them, you have killed them." It is not from Jerome, but it is found in a sermon attributed to Leo the Great. See Ermenegildo Lio, "Finalmente rintracciata la fonte del famoso testo patristico 'Pasce fame morientem,'" *Antonianum* 27 (1952): 356.

7. I have not found this precise quotation in Ambrose, but this sentiment is expressed in his treatise "On Naboth," PL 14:765–92.

of filth. For this reason, in 1 Cor 7:34, the Apostle says that the virgin alone is "the one who is chaste in body and spirit." And so he says in 2 Cor 7:1: "Since we have these promises, let us cleanse ourselves from all defilement of the flesh and spirit, making sanctification perfect in the fear of the Lord."

7:8–9 Behold, you put your trust in lying words, etc. In other words: In vain you put your trust in your temple and boast in your land's buildings, believing that God dwells in them, when you have expelled God from your hearts, which ought to be your temples, because you pollute them with thefts, lies, murders, and other things of this sort. So **you put your trust in lying words,** in the false words of false prophets who promise you peace. Or: **You put your trust in lying words** so you can lie without punishment and commit other evils that are listed here. Or, after the phrase **in lying words,** add the words: "saying it is good **to steal, to kill.**" Or here, when the prophet says, **to steal, to kill,** it is an ancient grammatical usage, employing the infinitive for the indicative so that he says, "you are stealing," and "you are killing." Or the infinitive is used as the imperative so that he says, "Kill! Steal!" and you should supply the words: "You are saying this to your neighbors and to you yourselves. These are lying words because these things should not be committed." These things are also spoken against those who pray aloud and kneel in the temple, but nevertheless conceal all these evil deeds, just as the Jews did when Christ was crucified. The person who makes offerings to Baalim is the one who serves one's belly, since the word "Baalim" means "devourer." The god of such people is the belly. **And to go after false gods,** etc., after idols, or lust for earthly things.

7:10 And you stood before me, etc., in the temple where faithful people worship me. But Isa 1:15 says: "When you stretch out your hands, I will turn my eyes away from you, and when you multiply prayer, I will not hear you, because your hands are full of blood." **And you have said, "We are delivered from this [eo],** etc." The word *eo* is ablative, so that it means: "**We are delivered** from this sin, which we have committed by performing these abominations." Or, they believe they are literally delivered because they serve idols, which is to commit an abomination. Or: **You have said** that you did this since you thought you would be delivered from Nebuchadnezzar's persecution on this account, because you are doing these things that are abominations at a time when you are strong. For many still do this even now. They are so blinded by worldly happiness and prosperity that they think either that they can commit sin with impunity, or that God does not see their sins. This is because God waits patiently for sinners and does not punish them immediately. As Ecclus 8:11 says: "Because sentences are not speedily pronounced against evils, the children of humanity commit evils without any fear." And since they see things going well for them, they sin all the more because of their lying conscience. Therefore Ecclus 5:4 reads: "Do not say, 'I have sinned, and what harm has befallen me?' For the Most High is a patient rewarder," which is like saying, "God is merciful but nonetheless just."

Judgment on Shiloh, Jerusalem, and Wicked Church Leaders

7:11 Has [this house] become a den of robbers? It is as though you are entering into it stealthily or after committing theft, since it seems that you regard it as a den of robbers, because you congregate there while you are robbers. This also refers to churches that receive goods such as alms given by moneylenders or thieves, for robbers divide up their spoils in dens. Or, it is because, as Augustine says, "Seizing something belonging to another, against God's wishes, is theft."[8] For all souls belong to God, as in Ezek 18:4: "Behold, all souls are mine. As the soul of the parent is mine, so also is the soul of the child." Therefore wicked prelates commit theft by taking souls away from the Lord through their bad example or teaching. Hosea 6:8–9: "Gilead is a city of idolaters, overthrown through blood. Like the jaws of bandits, they conspire with the priests who murder on the road the people who are departing from Shechem." This passage refers to the church whose children perpetrate idolatry by choosing a wicked prelate. That is why Zech 11:17 says: "O shepherd and idol!" The church is overthrown through blood because such a prelate overthrows it through blood, defrauding the church "through blood" by promoting his own family members and building up the church with blood relatives. And those who conspire with the priests—namely the vicars and subordinates of the greater prelates—are "jaws of bandits," since they take charge of churches for no other reason than to steal the goods of poor people whom they despoil, or they are "jaws of bandits" when they receive the offerings of moneylenders. And they kill those who are departing from Shechem when, through their bad example, they destroy those who wish to depart from sin. For the word "Shechem" means "toil" since sin entails great toil. The

---

8. This common saying, here attributed to Augustine, is found in many medieval writings. See, for instance, Bonaventure, *On the Ten Commandments,* Sermon 6, in *Opera Omnia,* ed. A. C. Peltier (Paris: Ludovicus Vives, 1868), 12:251.

following verse from Matt 21:13 is taken from this passage: "My house shall be called a house of prayer, but you have made it a den of robbers." Only the last part comes from this passage (Jer 7:11). The first part is taken from Isa 56:7: "My house shall be called a house of prayer for all peoples." But nowadays it is more like a house of commerce, as in John 2:14, for in that place are sellers of doves, which refer to sellers of the sacraments that are the vessels of the Holy Spirit's gifts; and sellers of sheep and oxen, referring to worldly possessions received by the church at the present time, or when churches or prebends are appraised; and in that place are moneychangers, because churches and ecclesiastical orders are acquired with money through simony.[9]

I, I am, because I am able to do all things. **I have seen, says the Lord,** all the things that you think are hidden from me, and therefore you say that I will not punish you for something that I am not aware of. Using the verb "being" ["I am"], God says that he himself is the judge. By using the verb "seeing," God says that he himself will be a witness. So God says below: "I am judge and witness, says the Lord" (Jer 29:23). Malachi 3:5: "I will come to you in judgment and will be swift to bear witness."

7:12 Go to my place in Shiloh, where my name dwelled from the beginning, since the beginning of the time they inhabited the promised land until the time of David because the Lord's tabernacle was first placed there. First Samuel 3:21 states that the Lord appeared in Shiloh, and the ark of the covenant was there. **And see what I did,** etc., so you do not place confidence in your temple, since it will be destroyed on account of your sins. In the same way I destroyed the tabernacle that was in Shiloh because of the sins of Eli's sons, and I permitted the ark of God to be captured and the priests Phinehas and Hophni to be killed, as in 1 Sam 4:17, so also I will destroy the Jerusalem temple because of your sins. For this reason Ps 77 [78:60] states: "He rejected his tabernacle at Shiloh." Interpreted spiritually, this means that just as the destruction of Shiloh was an example of the destruction of Jerusalem or the temple, so the destruction of the temple is an example of the destruction of the church. Romans 11:21: "If God did not spare the natural branches, we should be afraid, lest God spare us even less."

7:13 And now, because you have done all these things, the evil things previously mentioned. **And I spoke to you, rising up early,** speaking through

---

9. A "prebend," from the word *praebere*, "to supply [a living]," was a monetary benefit held by certain clerics, including canons associated with a cathedral.

the prophets who literally rose up early to preach to you—especially Jeremiah, who did not remain in the city, signifying by this that the Lord wanted to free them from the darkness of sins and captivity, warning them to do the things that would cause them to be delivered, if they were willing. This is also spoken against sluggish people who do not want to rise up early for prayer or work, when the soul is more alert and freer to be more discerning and more capable of meditating, and the human frame of mind is less occupied with exterior matters and is more easily diverted from preoccupation with food and luxury, as Jerome says.[10] Psalm 5:3b: "Early in the morning I will stand before you and I will see." And in another place: "Early in the morning you shall hear my voice" (Ps 5:3a). For manna was collected only early in the morning, according to Exod 16:21. Isaiah 26:9: "My soul yearned for you in the night, and with my spirit within me I have kept watch for you ever since early morning." Ecclesiastes 11:6: "Sow your seed early in the morning." When Jacob rose up early in the morning, he took the stone that had been under his head and he set it up as a monument (Gen 28:18), because there is leisure time in the morning for prayers and vigils in the early morning. So also, in Exod 19:16–20, Moses went up the mountain in the morning to receive the law. If you use this as an excuse to say there should not be preaching after breakfast, I disagree; yet it is better for there to be preaching early in the morning. Psalm 54 [55:17]: "Evening [and morning] and at noon I will speak" the works of the Lord. **And speaking, but you did not listen.** Proverbs 1:24: "Because I called and you refused." **And I called you and you did not answer** by obeying my precepts or counsels. Proverbs 1:25: "You have despised all my counsel and ignored my reproofs."

7:14–15 I will do to this house in which my name is called on, the temple in which you have placed your trust and have boasted, **and to the place,** etc., namely, Jerusalem. **Just as I did to Shiloh,** by destroying the place, driving out the tabernacle, so I will also destroy the temple. And just as the ten tribes were banished, so I will also banish the two tribes. For this reason, **I will cast you away from my face, just as I cast away all your brothers and sisters,** the ten tribes. For this reason he says: **The entire offspring of Ephraim.** God calls the ten tribes "Ephraim," because their first king, Jeroboam, was from Ephraim.

---

10. Jerome, *On Jeremiah* 7:13–15, ed. Sigofredus Reiter, CCSL 74 (Turnhout: Brepols, 1960), 78.

7:16 Therefore do not pray for this people. God speaks this quite frankly. It is just like someone who truly wishes to do something because it is clearly an advantageous thing to do, but, on the other hand, it is unable to be accomplished. So the individual says to a friend: "Do not ask me about this, requesting that I do otherwise, because I am completely unable to do this. Therefore I am telling you this because I do not wish to upset you with a forceful rebuff." Thus God says the same thing to the prophet, so that, by not accomplishing what Jeremiah was pleading for, the Lord would not be seen as offending or despising the one who was earnestly pleading. It is right and just that someone praying for a sinning people should not be heeded. **Do not pray** for your volition unless those who intend to repent ask you to do this. **Do not offer praise on their behalf.** Do not display their good works before me, or the good works of their ancestors, believing that you can persuade me by doing this. **Or prayer** to take away evil things or provide good things. Or, God says, [**do not offer**] **praise,** meaning: Do not use *captatio benevolentiae,* which you might do because you believe I would be more likely to listen to you when you are interceding.[11] For instance, in the following prayer, the attempt to gain goodwill occurs first when it says: "God whose property is always to have mercy and to forgive." And the request follows afterward: "Receive our humble petition," etc.[12] **And do not resist me.** As Jerome says, "The prayers of the saints often restrain God's wrath."[13] For instance, the prayers of Moses restrained the rage of the Lord who wanted to destroy the people. His prayers kept the Lord's rage in check, as in Exod 32:11–19. And in Wis 18:21–25, regarding Aaron: "A blameless man making haste to pray for the peoples, bringing forth prayers as the shield of his ministry, and making supplication with incense, he withstood the wrath." As Num 16:47–48 says: "When Aaron ran into the midst of the multitude that the fire was now destroying, he offered incense. Standing between the dead and the living, he prayed for the people, and the plague ceased." Psalm 105 [106:30]: "And Phinehas stood up and made appeasement, and the affliction ceased." On the other hand, if God is deeply aggrieved, there is no religious leader who can restrain him, since Isa 64:7 claims: "There is no one calling on your name who can stand up and take hold of you." And Ezek 13:5: "You have not gone up to face the enemy, nor

11. *Captatio benevolentiae* is the term for the rhetorical device of attempting to gain the audience's goodwill through praise or some other means.

12. This quotation is from a frequently used collect for forgiveness. Gregory the Great, *Liber sacramentorum* no. 195, PL 78:197.

13. Jerome, *On Jeremiah* 7:16, CCSL 74:79.

have you set up a wall for the house of Israel so it can stand in battle on the day of the Lord." So how can someone turn back God's anger, since Job 9:13 says, "God, whose anger no one can turn back"? The solution: You should understand it to mean: God, whose anger no one can turn back—except that a holy person can do this effectively. Or you should say that anger can be understood two ways. First, as a fixed verdict, such as one pronounced on those who are damned. No one can actually stop this. We should understand Job 9:13 as referring to this kind of anger. And [second] there is a conditional anger, with which the Lord is angered at enemies so that he punishes them if they do not repent. We can understand it in this way: some people, such as Pilate and Judas, are utterly damned; other people are damned conditionally—that is, damned unless they are prayed for, as was the case with Trajan.[14] Holy people who turn back the Lord's anger through their prayers are called "repairers of fences, turning away the paths of wickedness." Where we have the phrase "repairer of fences" in Isa 58:12, another version says, "setting up a wall for those who are walking along."[15] Where we have "turning away the paths of wickedness," it says there, "turning the paths into rest."[16] Regarding this passage, Jerome says that two things prevent prayers from being heard by the Lord. The first is stubborn faithlessness.[17] That sort of thing, according to Jerome, does not deserve pardon because it destroys the foundation for meriting pardon, which is faith. Therefore you should explain it this way so that it does not contradict this passage from 1 Tim 1:13: "I received mercy because I had acted ignorantly." For, granted that Paul had been ignorant, he nevertheless did not err with a stubborn or ongoing mistake. In fact, he does not say this about every sort of error, but only errors in the matter of faith—infidelity, where truth is stubbornly declared to be false or inverted. A second example is an unrepentant heart—unrepentant because of desperation or presumptuousness, having the intention not to repent. For such impenitence is the sin against

14. A treatise spuriously attributed to John of Damascus relates the story of Gregory the Great successfully praying for the emperor Trajan to be delivered from hell. John of Damascus, *De his qui in fide dormierunt*, PG 95:264.

15. This is Symmachus's translation of Isa 58:12, reported in Jerome, *Commentary on Isaiah* 58:12, ed. Marcus Adriaen, CCSL 73A (Turnhout: Brepols, 1963), 674.

16. Jerome, *Commentary on Isaiah* 58:12, CCSL 73A:672. For details on the Vulgate's textual variants of Isa 58:12, see *The New Testament in Scots, Being Purvey's Revision of Wycliff's Version Turned into Scots by Murdoch Nisbet c. 1520*, ed. Thomas Graves Law, Scottish Text Society 52 (Edinburgh: William Blackwood & Sons, 1905), 3:293n12.

17. Jerome, *On Jeremiah* 7:16, CCSL 74:79.

the Holy Spirit, which, as Jerome says, is blasphemy in words or in one's heart when one knowingly, from intentional wickedness, impugns God's goodness.[18] Matthew 12:31–32 says that this sin is eternally unforgivable. Therefore we can understand this passage from 1 John 5:16: "There is a sin unto death. I do not say that someone should pray about this." This verse is explained in a fourfold way. First, why is it "the sin unto death"? This is because it persists all the way up to and including death, into death itself. No one praying for such a person receives a favorable response, since in this case there is final impenitence, which causes the sin against the Holy Spirit to be unforgivable. Or it can be understood this way: "There is a sin unto death. I do not say that someone—other than a great person—should pray about this." Or: "I do not say that someone should pray *publicly* the way one prays for other sins." Or: "I do not say" means "I do not command." In the case of the last three reasons, the sin against the Holy Spirit is unforgivable, not inherently, but because it precludes the opportunity for forgiveness, and therefore it is inexcusable and deserves no forgiveness. By committing this sin, a human impugns fraternal love and the goodness of God. Likewise it is because a person committing this sort of sin is unable to humble oneself in repentance. For this reason Augustine says that the fault in this sin is so great that it is not possible to humble oneself in prayer.[19]

Literal Interpretation of Making Cakes for the Queen of Heaven

7:17 Do you not see? You should not consider me cruel because I will not listen to you praying for them. Instead, you should blame this on them, for I would gladly listen if they wished to repent, but they do not wish to do so. Instead they persist in sins. For this reason: **Do you not see what they are doing in the cities of Judah and in the streets of Jerusalem?** They are committing the following evils both inside and outside the city. Or: They are committing the evils secretly as well as openly. Lamentations 1:20: "Outdoors the sword destroys, and at home it is like death." The secret sin is signified by the death of the girl raised from the dead at home (Matt 9:18–26). The open sin is signified by the death of the young man raised from the dead in the

18. Jerome, *Commentary on Matthew,* book 2, 12:32, CCSL 77 (Turnhout: Brepols, 1969), 94–95.

19. Augustine, *On the Lord's Sermon on the Mount* 22.74, ed. Almut Mutzenbecher, CCSL 35 (Turnhout: Brepols, 1967), 84. See Thomas Aquinas, *Summa Theologiae* 3a, q. 86.

gate (Luke 7:11–17). Isaiah 3:9: "They have proclaimed their sin like Sodom and have not hidden it."

7:18 The children gather wood. They are as tough as oak, because a human is strong during youth. **And the fathers kindle the fire.** They are more mature, and so they better understand how to arrange the pile of wood to make fire. **And the women sprinkle the fat,** so the fire would burn better. In other words, all these people work together to show that, regardless of age and regardless of sex, everyone is consenting to idolatry. Understood literally, the children, who were more vigorous, gathered wood for the fire of the idols' sacrifice; the fathers, who were more discerning, made the fire, kindling the pile of wood over the coals; and the women put fat on the fire, immolating as a sacrifice to idols something that belonged to God alone. Leviticus 3:16–17: "All the fat shall be the Lord's, by a perpetual law." **To make cakes** [*placentas*], offerings with which they could please [*placerent*] an idol; though, properly speaking, *placenta* is a bread, made from wheat flour, that is called *foisse* in French.[20] **For the Queen of Heaven,** the moon, which is called by this name because it provides light at night, and therefore they worship it. Or, **Queen of Heaven** refers to the heavenly army, namely, all the stars.[21] **And offer libations to foreign gods.** They lift up libations to idols, which they call gods even though they are not. **And thus they provoke me to anger.**

7:19 Not that I am affected mentally by anger that causes me turmoil. Therefore: **Is it I whom they provoke to anger, says the Lord?** It is as if the Lord were saying: Can anger, which troubles, occur in me? In other words: No. **Is it not they themselves that they provoke, to their own detriment?** This means that, instead, they are provoking themselves, because they are causing themselves to be punished with eternal turmoil, since they do not trouble God through their own sins, but they are preparing for themselves eternal ruin, "storing up wrath for themselves on the day of wrath," as it says in Rom 2:5. It is written everywhere that sinners provoke God to wrath, especially in Hos 12:14: "Ephraim has provoked me to wrath with his bitterness," because

20. *Foisse,* also known as *fougasse,* is flat, latticed focaccia bread cooked in a hearth.
21. Jeremiah was referring to the Assyro-Babylonian astral goddess Astarte, also called Ishtar. Instead of "Queen" of heaven, the LXX has "army" or "host" (*stratia*) of heaven. See William L. Holladay, *Jeremiah 1: A Commentary on the Book of the Prophet Jeremiah Chapters 1–25,* Hermeneia (Philadelphia: Fortress, 1986), 251; and J. A. Thompson, *The Book of Jeremiah,* New International Commentary on the Old Testament (Grand Rapids: Eerdmans, 1980), 284–85.

they are doing something that causes God to exercise vengeance against them; for God sometimes resembles a human who is angry with someone else.

Moral Interpretation of Making Cakes for the Queen of Heaven

7:18-19 The children gather wood. Wood signifies wicked desires with which the devil's fire is kindled in the hearts of sinners united to him, and their deeds are revealed by these desires. Isaiah 30:33: "Its nourishment is fire and much kindling." Numbers 15:32-36 says that a person who collected wood on the Sabbath was stoned. For sinners collect this sort of "wood" especially on festival days, and therefore the Lord says in Isa 1:14: "My soul hates their Sabbaths and solemnities." Lamentations 1:7: "Enemies (that is, demons) have seen her and have mocked her Sabbaths." **And the fathers kindle the fire,** because they do not correct their children but instead give them clothing, money, and other opportunities for them to collect this wood—that is, harmful desires—more easily. First Samuel 3:13-14: "I have sworn to the house of Eli that the wickedness of his house will not be expiated by sacrifices and offerings forever, because he knew his sons acted wickedly and he did not correct them." **And the women sprinkle the fat,** by raising their children indulgently, giving them frivolous adornments, and pampering them too much. Lamentations 4:10: "The hands of compassionate women have cooked their own children." That is, they are too compassionate toward their children, and so they are kindling in them the fire of harmful desires. **To make cakes for the Queen of Heaven,** sacrificing their body to the moon through the sin of extravagance, by constantly attending celebrations, so that there is no place untouched by their extravagance. **Is it I whom they provoke to anger?** It is as if God were saying: No. Wisdom 12:18 says: "For you, the master of power, judge with tranquility, and you deal with us with great restraint."

God's Burning Rage

7:20 Behold my rage, which I have devised and planned against them, the means by which I will vindicate myself against them. **And my indignation,** with which I carry out the acts of rage that I devised and planned, by completing acts of punishment. **Is kindled against this place,** or according to another literal translation, "trickled down."[22] God does not say, "poured out," but "trickled down," or **kindled.** It is as though God were saying: I will inflict punishment moderately, less than is deserved. As Jerome says: "For if there is so much harshness in a trickle of rage, how much would there be if it were poured out completely?"[23] Similarly, Job 26:14 reads: "Since we have endured barely a little trickle of his word, who shall be able to endure the thunder of his greatness?" Or: It **is kindled,** for I waited patiently for your repentance for a long time, since I did not wish to do what I am now compelled to do because of the multitude and duration of your sins. So now, when I am angry, you might pay attention to me—the one whom you refused to acknowledge when I was kind. For this reason, it is not I who make myself angry toward you, for I am gentle by nature. Instead, you yourselves turned me to cruelty." Job 30:21: "You have turned cruel toward me." Lamentations 3:33: "For he has not willingly afflicted and cast off the children of humanity." **Upon men, upon livestock, upon the trees of the region, and upon the fruits of the land,** so that they are destroyed—the owners themselves and their possessions. Thus humans and the things with which they sinned will experience a similar wrath, as it says in Ecclus 14:19: "Every work that is corruptible shall fail, and the one who made the work will go with it." Therefore the king of Nineveh decreed a fast for both humans and livestock in Jonah 3:7–9, and, for that reason, God chose mercy. **And it,** my rage and indignation against them, **will burn and not be quenched.** And **it will not be quenched** because they are not doing, or will not do, what can cause it to be quenched, namely penance. Isaiah 1:31: "Your strength will be like cinders of flax, and your work will be like a spark. Both will burn together and there will be no one to quench them."

God Desires Obedience rather than Sacrifices

7:21 Add your burnt offerings. This is spoken ironically, as if to say: All these sacrifices will benefit you not at all. For just as God rejected their temple, so also God does not care for their sacrifices, with which they actually drive God away from themselves. Burnt offerings are offered to God in their entirety; with sacrifices, the priests receive a portion for themselves and offer another portion [to God]. **And eat meat** from your sacrifices. In other

---

22. Jerome, *On Jeremiah* 7:20, CCSL 74:80.
23. Jerome, *On Jeremiah* 7:20, CCSL 74:80–81.

words: You do not sacrifice because of reverence for me but, rather, because of an appetite for food.

7:22 For I did not speak with your ancestors, etc., regarding the matter of burnt offerings and sacrifices. On the other hand, Ezek 20:11 says: "I gave them statutes."[24] The *Gloss* says these statutes were "manifold ceremonies of the law."[25] Therefore God did give commands. The solution: God did not give them these commands on the day in which he led them out of Egypt but afterward. And this is what is meant here in the text and in the *Gloss*. Therefore, **I did not command them [on the day I led them out of the land of Egypt, regarding the matter of burnt offerings and sacrifices]** means: First, I certainly gave them the Decalogue of commandments, as stated in Exod 20:1–17. But God did not give them a commandment regarding ceremonies or performing sacrifices until after their sin of idolatry that they committed with the calf (Exod 32). But, because of this event, God commands them regarding sacrifices, preferring that the sacrifices be offered to himself rather than to idols. So it is possible to explain it this way: **I did not command them,** voluntarily or because I wished it, but I was forced to do it so they would not do worse things. Or, **I did not command** sacrifices for their own sake, but as a mystery and a sign. Or, **I did not command** means: I did not give this to them as a command, but as a heavy burden for people who exalt themselves.

7:23 Instead, this is what I commanded them, saying. This refers to the statement: **Listen to my voice,** to the commandments that I gave them on the stone tablets. These are the commandments that I chiefly wanted them to observe. In these commandments was true devotion—if you had done these things. **And I will be your God,** protecting you, caring for you, and keeping you safe. **And you will be my people,** serving and obeying only me. **And walk in all the way [that I have commanded you],** by advancing more and more in keeping the commandments, and in love. **So that it may be well with you,** through grace in the present time and through glory in the future. For this reason blessings are pronounced over those who obey the Lord's commandments in Deut 28:1–14. It is as if God were saying: I have given you commands only for your own benefit, not for mine, because I am not in need

---

24. Hugh notes a possible contradiction between Jer 7:22 and Ezek 20:10–11a: "Therefore, I brought them out from the land of Egypt and brought them into the desert. And I gave them my statutes." The contradiction is heightened when Ezekiel is read in light of the gloss.

25. *Glossa ordinaria* on Ezek 20:25.

of your goods or your service. Therefore I have wished that these commandments be observed more than I have wished that sacrifices be offered to me.

7:24-25 Yet they did not listen or incline their ear. That is: **They did not
listen** attentively, with mindful hearts or obedient deeds. Joshua 22:5: "That
you may attentively observe the commandment and the law, and fulfill them
in your deeds." Deuteronomy 8:1: "Take care to observe diligently every commandment that I have commanded you, so that you may live and be multiplied." **But they departed into their own pleasures,** voluntarily, and by
persisting in these deeds, contrary to this statement from Ecclus 18:30: "Do
not follow your own lusts, but turn away from your own will." **And into the
depravity of their wicked heart,** through the faithlessness of errors. **And
they went backward and not forward.** They are worse than they were earlier, as though they fell back even more, by lapsing into their former sins or
perpetrating deeds that are even worse than before, rather than advancing
from where they were earlier by moving forward to better things, contrary
to what Phil 3:13 says: "Forgetting the things that are behind me, by strain-
ing forward to the things that are ahead." Similarly, as it says below: "I said:
Listen to my voice, but they did not hear, nor did they incline their ear. But
each and every one of them departed in the perverseness of their own wicked
hearts. They returned to the earlier iniquities of their ancestors, and they
have gone after foreign gods to serve them" (Jer 11:7-8, 10). And above: "They
have turned their back to me and not their face" (Jer 2:27). Judges 2:17: "They
soon forsook the way in which their ancestors had walked, and, hearing all
the Lord's commands, they did everything opposed to them." And this: **From
the day their parents came out of the land of Egypt all the way up to this
day.** In other words: During that entire time they did not advance but always
became worse. I say this about most of them, not about the good people who
were among them. And so that the Judeans could not vehemently defend
themselves by saying there was a lack of preaching or admonition, God adds:
And I sent you all my servants the prophets, through whom I spoke to you,
rising up early in the morning, day after day. In other words: I warned
you assiduously and unceasingly. Jeremiah says the same above (Jer 7:13).
Or these words are directed against flatterers, whose children are beginning
to admire the words spoken by their elders and the sin that the women are
committing (Jer 7:18).

7:26 Nor did they incline their ear, as noted above. **Instead they stiffened
their neck** through stubbornness and contempt for my commandments,"

as it says in above in 5:3: "They have made their faces harder than rock, and they have refused to return." Deuteronomy 31:27: "I know your inflexible stubbornness." "Indeed, the entire house of Israel has a stubborn forehead and a hard heart," as it says in Ezek 3:7. **And they have done worse than their ancestors.** Therefore the Lord's wrath against them is justified, as is the kindling of the Lord's rage and indignation, because, as Ezek 18:4 says, the very soul that commits a sin will die.

7:27 And you shall speak all these words to them, and they will not listen to you, so that they are less free from blame, and God will be shown as being compelled to punish them rather than wishing to do so voluntarily: "Since I have not voluntarily rejected the children of humanity, you should warn them to repent, speaking all these words to them. But again and again they will not listen to you when you speak." Therefore the preacher should not cease preaching even if the listeners are disobedient. Nor should the preacher take offense if they do not heed him, or if they regard the preacher as unworthy. For the Lord regards the offense to be committed against himself rather than against the preacher. As it says in Ezek 3:7: "The house of Israel refuses to listen to you, because they refuse to listen to me." And in 1 Sam 8:6–7: "The Lord said to Samuel, who was displeased because the people asked for a king: 'Listen to the voice of the people in all that they say to you, for they have not rejected you but me, that I should not reign over them.'" **And you shall call them** to repentance, **but they will not answer you** with their obedience. Or: Even when you call them to listen to you, their arrogance is so great that they will not deign to answer you. Thus the prophet could wonder why the Lord is sending him, when the Lord himself says to him that his own message will not benefit them. But the prophet wished to comply with the divine counsel rather than follow human opinion by rejecting the Lord's command. So also, when the Lord told Moses that he should go to Pharaoh and say to him, "Let my people go," the Lord himself said the same thing to Moses: "I know, however, that he will not let you go or listen to you" (Exod 3:19). Nevertheless Moses went, because he believed that even if Pharaoh did not let them go immediately, he would nonetheless be frequently urged to let them go. Thus, even when it is not possible that frequent preaching will convert others, at least there is benefit in the fact that the preacher frees himself and causes those under his authority to be without excuse.

7:28 This is a nation that lives as though it were of Gentile stock, persisting in sins. Thus it is not the people of God. **That has not listened to the voice**

of those commanding them, **and has not accepted discipline** of counselors. Or: **That has not listened to the voice** telling them they should do what the Lord commanded, **and has not accepted discipline** teaching them not to do what the Lord prohibited. **Faith is lost** from their hearts, since believing in one's heart is reckoned as righteousness (Rom 4:3; 10:9). **And it is taken away from their mouth,** since confessing with the mouth leads to salvation (Rom 10:9). "For all have turned aside and have become worthless together" (Ps 14:3; Rom 3:12). The Hebrew reads "faithfulness," which has vanished among many people today. Proverbs 20:6: "Many men are merciful, but who will find a faithful man?" Luke 18:8: "When the Son of Man comes, do you think he will find faith on earth?"

Literal Interpretation of Jeremiah Shaving His Hair

7:29 Shave off your hair and cast it away, because the prophet warned them with words but they did not listen. Therefore he is ordered to warn them with a deed, because they were uncultured and simple. So the Lord ordered the prophet to shave himself and throw away his hair, to suggest that they previously clung to the Lord through love, and worship, and they were the Lord's adornment like hair on the head, but now the Lord had cast them away. **And raise a lamentation.** In other words: **Cast away** the sheared hair **in that direction,** in front of you, and weep **in that direction** of the shaved hair. Therefore shaving the hair and casting it away signifies the Lord's casting away the Judeans, so that they would no longer cling to him like hair on the head. And just as, at a funeral in our own time, the mourners turn their gaze in the direction of the corpse, so the prophet is told to look in the direction of the cast-off hair as though he were mourning it, suggesting that even though the Lord had cast off the Judeans, nevertheless the Lord was weeping for them. The Lord rejected them for their guilt and abandoned them as punishment. Thus: **For the Lord has rejected and abandoned the generation of his wrath.** The Lord rages or extends his wrath somewhat. Furthermore, because it was the custom for ancient people to shave their hair when they were in mourning, and bow their shaved head to the ground, just as Job did when he heard about the violent death of his children in Job 1:20, so also the haircut itself signifies grief.

7:30 For the children of Judah have done evil in my eyes, says the Lord, since they are unable to hide it. Hence: "Against you alone have I sinned"

(Ps 51:4). Or: **In my eyes** means "in my temple," where God's glory appeared. **They have set their abominations in the house in which my name is invoked, so that they defiled it.** This refers to the idols that were the cause of their ruin.

7:31 And they built the high places of Topheth. Topheth is a place near Jerusalem that is very pleasant, shady, and watered by the springs of Siloam, so there are delightful gardens there. **Which is in the valley of the son of Hinnom,** which was named for a certain person who had that name. In this place were *tophi,* or *cophi,* which are porous, hollow stones in which there is said to be perpetual fire.[26] For this reason the very name is interpreted by the Hebrews to signify eternal fire. Hence Isa 30:33 says: "Topheth has been prepared since yesterday." Thus it is also said to be Gehenna, from the word *ge,* which means "land," and Hinnom.[27] For the people who offended God perished there. But since it is a valley, this seems to contradict the meaning of this text, that **they built high places** in the valley. The solution: They are called **high places** not because of the height of the location but because of the height of the trees that were there. Or **they built high places** means that they built there in the valley what they usually built in elevated places. For ancient people usually built these sorts of shrines in the mountains, and in pleasant, shady locations. From this custom, the idols themselves were called "high," because people frequently made sacrifices to idols in the high places. **So that they were burning their sons and their daughters in the fire,** making them pass through fire—not burning them up completely. As in 2 Kgs 17:14: "They did not listen, but they stiffened their necks, just like the necks of their ancestors who refused to obey the Lord their God." And later: "They made for themselves two cast images of calves, and groves, and they worshipped the entire host of heaven. And they served Baal and consecrated their sons and their daughters through fire" (2 Kgs 17:16–17). In the same way that children are now passed through water at baptism, at that time idolaters passed their children through fire. Psalm 105 [106:37]: "They sacrificed their sons and their daughters to demons." **Which I did not command, nor did I plan this in my heart,** for this is not in accordance with God's law. But didn't Jephthah offer or sacrifice his daughter to the Lord, as in Judg 11:29–40? So

---

26. *Tophus* is a kind of volcanic rock.

27. A discussion of the etymology of the Hebrew names can be found in Jerome, *Commentary on Jeremiah,* trans. Michael Graves, ed. Christopher A. Hall, Ancient Christian Texts (Downers Grove, IL: IVP Academic, 2011), 54nn154–58.

this was not idolatry, was it? Jerome resolves this by saying that it was not. Nevertheless the offering still did not please God, as Jerome says: "For it is not the sacrifice that pleases God, but the soul of the one making the offering. For if a dog or some unclean animal had been the first to meet Jephthah, he would have been required *not* to offer it."[28] Doing this would have made him a transgressor of the law found in Lev 11. But if his soul was pleasing to God, his intent was good, and so his consequences were good, which is proved through Augustine who said, regarding Heb 11:32, that Jephthah is praised for the sacrifice of his daughter, which is clear because Judg 11:29 says: "The Spirit of the Lord was poured into Jephthah." Therefore it seems that this proceeded from the Holy Spirit. On the other hand, Mic 6:7 says: "Shall I really give my firstborn for my wickedness, the fruit of my body for the sin of my soul?" In other words: No. The solution: There was a threefold will in Jephthah. The first was the making of a vow in exchange for victory. The second was making the vow to sacrifice whatever met him. The third was the fulfilling of the vow. The first was good, because the soul of the one making the vow was generally pleasing to God, the soul that trusted that the Lord would help him conquer his enemies. The other two were wicked.

Spiritual and Moral Interpretations of Jeremiah Shaving His Hair

7:29 Interpreting the passage spiritually: **Shave off your hair and cast it away** contradicts Lev 21:5, "They shall not shave their hair and beard." This order is given to priests, yet it is certain that Jeremiah was a priest, as noted above in the first chapter (Jer 1:1). God is Lord over the law and the commandment, so God was able to order someone to keep the law and to order something contrary to the law, except that God would not bring about something disgraceful such as fornication or that sort of thing, because God would not be able to order anything he regarded as prohibited. As others say, you should assert that the only things God could order are those that are not inherently wicked.

Interpreted morally, shaving hair refers to giving away temporal things. In Luke 7:37–38, Mary bathed the Lord's feet with her tears; that is, she had compassion on the poor. And she wiped his feet with her hair; that is, she provided relief to the poor from her own abundance.[29] Isaiah 58:10: "When

28. Jerome, *On Jeremiah* 7:30–31, CCSL 74:84.
29. In the western Christian tradition, the unnamed woman of Luke 7 was conflated

you pour out your soul to the hungry and satisfy the afflicted soul." Note the two things mentioned earlier: compassion and relief offered with temporal things. Regarding this matter, Num 8:7 says: "Let the Levites shave all the hairs of their flesh." This is directed against those who do not give up all temporal things but give up only a few things when they enter religious life, or it is directed against those who give very little to the poor. The more one's hair is shaved, the more it multiplies. So also with temporal things, as it says in Luke 6:38: "Give and it will be given to you." Proverbs 3:9-10: "Honor the Lord with your substance, and give to the poor from your first fruits, and your barns will be filled with plenty." It does not say "tear out" your hair but "shave." For shaving does not entail pain. Second Corinthians 9:7: "Not with sadness or under compulsion, for God loves a cheerful giver." Ecclesiasticus 25:11: "With every gift, show a cheerful face, and consecrate your tithes with joy." Ecclesiasticus 4:8: "Incline your ear to the poor cheerfully, and pay what you owe." One says "hair," not "hairs," even when one has shaved *hairs,* because when people donate something, it should seem to them that what they are giving is nothing at all. For what they give *is* nothing compared to what the Lord promises to those doing the giving.

Cast it away. In other words: Disburse it widely, not only to neighbors or relatives. For many people **cast it away** so closely that it is as though it is simply passing from one hand to another. They do not give unless they believe they will receive something from them, either temporal goods, or praise, or some sort of temporal benefit. Therefore Matt 6:3 states: "Do not let your left hand know what your right hand is doing." Psalm 25 [26:10]: "Their right hand is filled with bribes." Ecclesiasticus 29:10: "Lose your money for your brother and your friend." **And raise a lamentation in that direction.** In other words: Lament in secret for God alone, not for human favor. Isaiah 15:5: "They go up weeping through the ascent of Luhith," which means "cheeks" or "lower face," where tears visibly trail down. So Ecclus 35:18-19 reads: "Do not the tears of a widow run down the cheek? And from the cheek they go up all the way to heaven." Isaiah 15:2: "Dibon has gone all the way up to the high places to weep." Dibon is translated as "able to understand difficulty," or "fully aware of the armed bandit." **For the Lord has rejected** because of their

---

with Mary Magdalene and Mary of Bethany. See Katherine Ludwig Jansen, *The Making of the Magdalen: Preaching and Popular Devotion in the Later Middle Ages* (Princeton: Princeton University Press, 2000), 32-33. In most of the scriptural accounts of the foot washing or anointing, the woman is reproached by the disciples for *not* using her resources for the poor (Matt 26:6-13; Mark 14:3-9; John 12:1-8). However, in Hugh's moral interpretation, the foot washing represents use of resources for precisely this sort of care of the poor.

guilt **and abandoned** to punishment **the generation of his wrath,** namely the scribes and Pharisees, or the clergy, who are called "a wicked and perverse generation" in Matt 12:39. Regarding these people, Isa 1:2 says: "I have raised children and brought them up, but they despised me."

7:30 For the children of Judah have done evil in my eyes. Below, 11:15 says: "What does it mean that my beloved has committed many wicked deeds in my house?" This also refers to the evil of the clerics in the Lord's eyes, because they administer the sacraments all day, even touching the Lord himself with their hand and mouth. **They have set their abominations in the house in which my name is invoked, so that they defiled it.** These are prelates' sins, which are a stumbling block to others in the Lord's house, the church, when they follow their example. For prelates are "a snare to those they watch over and a net spread upon Tabor" (Hos 5:1). Tabor is translated as "coming light." Light ought to come from them into the church, but, instead, night comes from them. Or **abominations in the house** are the prelates in the church. Hosea 6:10: "In the house of Israel I have seen a horrible thing. The fornications of Ephraim are there."

7:31 And they built the high places of Topheth. That is, they obtained eternal death because of their sins. Wisdom 1:16 says that unrighteousness is the acquisition of death: "With their hands and words they have summoned it." On the other hand, Isa 30:33 says: "Topheth has been prepared since yesterday, prepared by the king." Again, in the same verse: "The breath of the Lord is like a torrent of brimstone kindling it" (Isa 30:33c). The solution: In fact, the Lord had foreknowledge of, and even prepared, this Gehenna. However, the Lord would not have made it if sins had not preceded it. Thus, properly speaking, humans made Gehenna. In the same way, people say to a child behaving badly: "You are making a rod with which you will be beaten." "Hinnom" is translated as "fountain of sadness" or "fountain of grief." There evil people will be made to pass through fire, that is, through various fiery punishments. The ideas [of both God and humans "making" Gehenna] are compatible.

The Slaughter of the People

7:32 Therefore, behold the days are coming, etc. **Therefore,** because of these evils, **behold the days** of the siege **are coming,** which the Judeans endured from the ninth year of King Zedekiah until the eleventh year, as it says in 2 Kgs 25:1–2. **And they shall no longer say "Topheth" and "the valley of the son of Hinnom."** In other words: It will no longer be called by that name, **but "the valley of slaughter."** That is, the former name will be changed to this one because of the slaughter of many people, which will be committed by the Chaldeans. For this reason the Chaldeans **will bury in Topheth** the corpses of the Judeans slaughtered there so they would not be infected by the stinking decay. Or the people who remain in the city after its destruction, certain lowborn and poor people, the vinedressers and farmers, **will bury** them **in Topheth,** in the place that was honored by them as a religious place. **Because there shall be no place** available for burial. Since they had been killed there, it would be very difficult to carry them somewhere else. Or, as it is said, this place was deep and did not have a bottom. Therefore the Hebrews pass down the tradition that a certain pit there was called "the mouth of Hell" because it could never be filled up, and they hurled bodies into it, for they were too exhausted to make a multitude of graves.[30] Or, **because there shall be no place** means that the cemeteries could not hold the multitude of the slaughtered. It is said that when Nebuchadnezzar wished to come to destroy Jerusalem, the Judeans entered into an alliance with Pharaoh, king of Egypt, who came to them with a multitude to provide aid. When the Chaldeans came, the Egyptians went out against them to fight. There a great multitude of Judeans and Egyptians were slaughtered.[31] And this was in Topheth, but Pharaoh fled to Egypt. So Nebuchadnezzar led part of his army with him to destroy Egypt, and he sent the other part with Nabuzaradan to besiege the city. They buried the slaughtered Judeans and Egyptians in Topheth so that the armies would not be infected by the stinking decay, and the birds and beasts devoured those they were not able to bury due to the small size of the place. For this reason:

7:33–34 And the carcasses of this people will be [food for the birds of the air and the beasts of the earth, and there will be no one to drive them away. And I will silence,] from the cities of Judah and the streets of Jerusalem, that is, the streets that were in that city as well as the streets that were near that city, **the voice of joy and the voice of gladness.** That is: I will

---

30. See *Jeremiah: A New English Translation*, translation of text, Rashi, and commentary by A. J. Rosenberg (New York: Judaica Press, 1985), 1:73.

31. Josephus, *Jewish Antiquities* 10.7.3, ed. and trans. Ralph Marcus, LCL 326 (Cambridge, MA: Harvard University Press, 1995), 216–18.

remove all gladness from that place, and will remove all the familiar songs normally sung at weddings. Their pleasant place where they committed their sins will be turned into a grave so that they would be punished in the same place where they sinned.

Spiritual and Moral Interpretation of the Slaughter of the People

7:32–33 According to the spiritual sense, **Topheth,** which is translated "fountain of sadness," signifies sin, because evil people will have no more power, or enough "space" to commit sins, but they will be in the valley of slaughter, since they will endure so much punishment and no delight in sin. And there their corpses will be devoured by demons.

Or, interpreted morally, the birds represent certain clerics rushing from church to church to acquire benefices.[32] Beasts represent resident clerics who "consume" everything through their bad example. These clerics eat the people's **carcasses**—the offerings and the revenues that were given to the church on behalf of the dead. Psalm 78 [79:2]: "They have given the corpses of your servants as food to the birds of the air, the flesh of your saints to the beasts of the earth." Hosea 4:8: "They shall eat the sins of my people."

7:34 [I will silence] the voice of spiritual, interior **joy, and the voice of gladness,** which is the voice of happiness or external exultation, expressed through good behavior, **and the voice of the bridegroom.** In other words, the song of spiritual marriage will disappear because spiritual marriages will disappear from Jerusalem, that is, from the church. Regarding these marriages, 2 Cor 11:2 says: "I have espoused you to one husband, in order to present you as a chaste virgin to Christ," etc. For spiritual marriage, which takes place through penitence, contains spiritual joy. However, this is not found in many people because of the bitterness of penitence. But actually, though penitence seems bitter at first, afterward it is pleasant. Thus Prov 4:11–12 says: "I will lead you through the paths of uprightness. When you enter, your steps will not be hampered." So also, in John 2:1–11, at the wedding attended by the Lord, Mary said: "They have no wine," and there the water was changed into wine.

---

32. A benefice was an ecclesiastical office, usually held for a lifetime, which provided revenues to the person holding it.

Chapter Eight

Introduction to Chapter Eight

At that time, says the Lord, etc. (Jer 8:1). He continues by dealing with their punishment, first by describing how the bones of the kings, the princes, the prophets, the priests, and the entire people will be cast out of their graves. Second, after a prediction of their confusion, he calls them to repentance where he says, "Shall the one who falls not rise again?" (8:4). In the same place, he enumerates their sins from which they ought to be converted. Third, the chapter compares their ignorance and obtuseness with irrational animals. He even prefers the animals to the people where he says, "The kite in heaven" (8:7). Fourth, he reproves their prelates for deceitful teaching and for the root of all their crimes, which is greed; and he imposes destruction on them and on the people who imitate them, where he says, "How can you say, 'We are wise'?" (8:8). Fifth, what had been threatened earlier, he now explains in particular detail by describing the way they will be afflicted and their downfall, where he says, "Gathering, I will gather them together" (8:13). Sixth, he introduces the voice of the repentant people, and nonetheless, in the same place, he continues to discuss the punishment of unrepentant people, and he mentions the fact that God pities them and expresses amazement at such great destruction of the people, when he says, "Why do we sit still?" (8:14). Therefore the Judeans would not be able to say, "We do not care," and so forth.

The Bones of the People and Their Leaders: Literal Interpretation

8:1 They shall cast out the bones. According to Jerome, this took place during the Babylonian and Roman captivities.[33] **At that time.** Since it could have been possible for the Judeans to say, "We do not care whether we are destroyed since, after death, we will rest in our tombs, beyond the reach of hardship," the Lord responds that this is not the case. Instead, the Chaldeans would dig up their graves and fling out their bones. Just as some say regarding [Jesus's burial narrated in] John 19:39–40, the Judeans buried their dead with very expensive clothing, and gold and silver jewelry. Thus the Chaldeans dug them up in order to get these things.[34] **They shall**

33. Jerome, *On Jeremiah* 8:1–3, CCSL 74:85.
34. Jerome, *On Jeremiah* 8:1–3, CCSL 74:85.

cast out the bones of the king of Judah. On the other hand, Zedekiah himself was led into Babylon and was buried there with royal honor. The *solution: This should not be understood as pertaining to Zedekiah but to the kings that preceded him.* **And the bones of princes, and the bones of the priests,** etc., so that all who were similar in guilt would receive a similar punishment.

8:2 And they shall scatter them, etc. Note that—parallel to what he said earlier regarding those who were buried at Topheth where they offered sacrifices, so that they would be punished in the same place where they had committed their crimes—he says here that these people's corpses would be laid out in the sight of the sun, moon, and stars, **whom they served** when they abandoned God. Thus, abandoned and cast off by God, they would be exposed to the view [of the sun, moon and stars]. **And to the whole host of heaven,** that is, the stars. Thus they would be displayed here in sight of the stars that they had worshipped, so everyone would see that the very things they had worshipped were unable to provide them any help; therefore they would recoil from the sin of idolatry. Or it was a sign indicating that these others had not served God while they were alive. **Whom they adored,** etc. They served them by surrendering their minds in worship. **And after whom they walked,** seeking answers from them, obeying them, and trusting in them. **And whom they have sought,** by going from city to city, with a sort of diligence and solicitude, seeking new forms of idolatry. **And worshipped,** offering to them what should belong only to God. **They will not be gathered,** etc. In other words, they will remain unburied, just like those who are excommunicated from Christian fellowship. Just as it is said regarding Nebuchadnezzar in Isa 14:19–20: "But you are cast out of your grave like a useless branch, defiled, and covered with those who were killed with the sword and descended to the bottom of the pit. Like a putrid corpse you will not have any fellowship with them, even in burial." **They will be as dung,** etc. They will be like putrid, stinking dung because they will have been thrown in a heap.

8:3 And death will be chosen rather than life, etc. In other words, if those who had been able to flee to a place where the enemy armies could not reach, in that place they would endure so many evils—sickness, famine, and trouble—that they would prefer death to such a life. **By all who remain from this evil family, [those who are left,] in all the places,** etc. That is, in all the places left for them to flee.

The Bones of the Leaders: A Moral Interpretation

8:1–3 The king and secular princes represent teachers and preachers. Prophets and priests represent the church's prelates. The inhabitants of Jerusalem represent members of religious orders. **They shall cast [their bones] from their graves.** Their dry bones remain on the ground with rotting flesh. Thus, after the death of prelates, sins endure in others because of the prelates' sinful example. For the devil tries to dig up these dead just like a hyena who mauls dead things. The devil does this through detractors who, through their disparagement, uncover the rotting stench of the sins of others. As it says below in 12:9: "Is my inheritance like a speckled bird to me?" In that place, another literal translation says: "Is my inheritance like a hyena's den to me?"[35] Therefore, following the example of Tobit, when we are in danger of slander and receive hatred from neighbors who shun us, we ought all the more to "bury the dead," and even, for this reason, we ought to send away our meals and expose ourselves to mortal danger, as it says in Tob 2:1–9. To "bury the dead" is to conceal the sins of our neighbors so that we do not urge others toward these sins by our disparagement. Ecclesiasticus 19:10: "Have you heard a word against your neighbor? Let it die within you, trusting that it will not burst you." So also Moses "hid the slain Egyptian in the sand," as it says in Exod 2:12. Because of this [the act of disparaging], practically the entire tribe of Benjamin was wiped out in one day, because the Levite did not hide or bury his dead wife who was killed by the Benjamites, but instead "in futility he divided her corpse along with her bones and sent the pieces to all the borders of Israel," as Judg 19:29 says.

As dung, etc., because, when it is collected together it stinks and rots, but when it is scattered on the cultivated earth, it fertilizes the earth and makes it fruitful. Confessing these sins with contrition greatly nourishes the cultivated earth of free choice to produce good works. But sins that have accumulated, and are piled high **on the surface of the earth,** rot because they provide a bad example. Job 20:6–9 says: "If their pride ascends all the way to heaven and they touch the clouds (through pride and worldly arrogance), they will finally perish like dung. All who see them will say, 'Where are they?' Like a dream that flies away, they shall not be found. They shall pass away like a night vision. The eyes that had seen them will see them no longer. Nor will their place (that is, God, in whom alone is rest) behold them any more," because, in the end, such people will not be remembered, either by God or by humans.

35. Jerome, *On Jeremiah* 12:9, CCSL 74:123.

And death will be chosen rather than life. This will be in hell, for there people will wish for the very thing that they fear and hate here. As Rev 9:6 states: "In those days people shall seek death, but they shall not find it. They shall desire to die, but death will escape them." Likewise, digging up the bones of the dead, and the rulers, and the teachers, and casting them out of the tombs that are "outwardly whitewashed" but inwardly stinking (Matt 23:27) is to consider the strength and vanity of the eminent people of this world to be something rotten; or it is to contemplate one's own weakness and the inevitability of death. Therefore someone "digs up tombs" by looking at others who are dying and pondering one's own weakness in them, seeing that what seems to be quite strong in humans—their bones—rot and are reduced to nothingness. Job 3:21–22: "Those who long for death and it does not come are like those who dig for treasure. And they rejoice exceedingly when they have found the grave." The one who "digs up the grave" finds the "treasure" of fear. Ecclesiastes 7:2: "It is better to go to the house of mourning than to the house of feasting, for in the former we are reminded of the final end of all humans," etc. Ecclesiasticus 28:6: "Remember your last days," etc. And when the prophet says, "They shall cast out the bones of kings and princes and priests" (8:1), there are no exceptions, because death is common to all. For it takes all people without distinction. As Ecclus 9:13 holds: "You may be sure it is communion with death." Ecclesiastes 2:16: "The learned person dies just like the unlearned person."

And they shall scatter them to the sun, and to the moon, which happens when, with bright perception, we disperse the deeds and behaviors of the wicked. Or people do this when they glory in their own good works or in evil works. For "glory" is "brightness." As Job 31:26–27 says: "If I looked at the sun when it shined and the moon advancing brightly, and my heart rejoiced secretly, [and I kissed my hand with my mouth,] which is a great wickedness," etc. And these are the sort of bones they scatter to the sun. People scatter the bones of others to the sun when they examine their vanity and convert it to self-criticism. **They will not be gathered,** as something worthy of imitation. **And they will not be buried.** That is, despite attempts to completely obliterate the memory [of the wicked deeds], they will not be concealed. **They will be as dung,** etc. Let us fertilize the field of our mind. As Prov 21:11 says: "When a pestilent person is punished, [a simple person becomes wiser]." Psalm 82 [83:10]: "They perished at Endor and became like dung for the earth." These are indulgent things. Regard for these leads the mind to great suffering.

The Judeans Refuse to Repent

8:4 Shall not the one who falls? After such evils, he provokes to repentance those who had been able to remain behind, saying: **Shall not the one who falls** by sinning and turning oneself toward lesser creatures **rise again** by repenting? **And shall the one who is turned away** from me by having contempt **not turn back again** to me? In other words, it is human to fall and sin, but it is diabolic to persist in sin. Psalm 40 [41:8]: "Shall the one who sleeps rise again no more?" Where he says **"falls,"** and **"turning away"** from God, and **"turned away,"** this is because, as Augustine says, sin is "rejection of the immutable good," etc.[36] Where our text reads, **"Shall the one who is turned away not turn back again?"** the Hebrew reads, "The one who has turned away will not be turned away." This means that, indeed, the one who has been turned away from guilt will be turned away from suffering the wrath of God. Or: "The one who has turned away will not turn away" means that the person who has turned away from guilt through repentance will, in fact, turn God's wrath away from oneself. For God is saying: Is it not remarkable? Is it not astonishing that I called you in this way so often, but you are not coming to me? Or God is saying: I am certain that scarcely anyone will repent, since I call them in this way so often. It is just like when someone calls often to another person who is running away. That person hardly ever turns back. But Amos 5:2 says: "The house of Israel has fallen, and there is no help so that it may rise again." Or it is possible to read this as a question: "Will it not rise again?"

8:5 Why then has this people in Jerusalem turned away with a stubborn revolt? They turned away **with a stubborn revolt** by refusing to return to God after being called so many times. In other words: They stubbornly turned away from me, for the more I called them to repentance, the more they retreated from me, by engaging in sin and especially by mocking and showing contempt for me. But, as Isa 30:21 says: "Your ears will hear the voice of one admonishing you behind your back." **They have held fast to falsehood.** That is: They revolted stubbornly because **they have held fast to falsehood** or other sorts of sin. In other words: They quickly clung to sin and held on to it firmly, because they are prone to sin and find it difficult to do good. **Falsehood** is the worthlessness of temporal things. Psalm 4:2: "Why do you love what is worthless and seek falsehood?" Ecclesiasticus

---

36. Augustine, *On Free Choice* 2.20.54, PL 32:1269.

34:1–2: "The hope of a senseless man is empty and false, and dreams lift up fools. The one who gives heed to a lying vision is like one who grasps a shadow and follows the wind." **And they have refused to return.** It does not say that they were unable to return, but **they have refused.** In other words, they embraced wickedness with great eagerness, as it says above: "They have made their faces harder than rock, and they have refused to return" (Jer 5:3).

8:6 I have listened. In other words: Because they despise me and refuse to listen to me, but I myself do not despise them, I have certainly listened to their heart, to discern whether I could find contrition in their hearts. **And I have paid attention** to their words, to hear whether there was a confession of sin. **No one speaks what is good,** and so confession has disappeared from them. **There is no one who does penance,** and so contrition has disappeared, because, among them, there is no repentance or work of making amends. There is no one among them who would seek to do penance, despite the fact that the benefit of penance and contrition is so very great. As 2 Cor 7:11 says: "For see this very thing—that you have received a godly sorrow that is producing a great earnestness in you," to seek, for your salvation, "defense" of the truth—even against you yourselves—through true confession; and "indignation" against sin; and "fearful caution" against falling again; and the "desire" to do well and to make progress in doing better; and "zeal" to imitate good things; and "vengeance" against what should be punished in yourselves; what you began to do in making rightful amends.[37] **Saying, "What have I done?" Saying,** with one's mouth or with one's heart, **"What have I done** by committing a fault that is so vile and disgraceful?" For this reason Lam 1:6 reads: "All her beauty has departed from the daughter of Zion." This refers to the image of God, which, through sin, was replaced in her soul by the image of the devil. Again, how momentary this is! For the things that delight are momentary, and the things that torture are eternal. First John 2:17: "The world and its desire are passing away," for it is useless. On the contrary, how harmful and destructive the world is. By abandoning God, one rushes to Gehenna, losing body and soul. Therefore God is saying that there are no people who ponder their sins with sorrow and contrition, since they act against their own interests by speaking disloyally, arguing, and throwing away the good things they received from God, exchanging them for evil things. **All are turned [to their own course].** In other words, everyone follows the evil to which they are prone. Not only do they walk

---

37. This sentence is an interpretive elaboration of 2 Cor 7:11.

after their own desires, but they even run after them, in opposition to what appears in Ecclus 18:30: "Do not go after your desires." Genesis 8:21: "For human perception and thought, from youth on, are prone to evil." **Like a horse rushing [to battle],** without judgment or awareness, because they follow their desires with as much swiftness and fervor as a horse exhibits when running to battle. Job 15:26–27: "He has raced against God with an outstretched neck, and he is armed with a fat neck." An "outstretched neck" refers to an audacious and arrogant mind. A "fat neck" is eagerness for temporal abundance, or haughtiness because of wealth. This is directed to the sinner in Acts 9:5: "It is hard for you to kick against the goad."[38] For a sinner voluntarily dashes into sin just as a horse dashes into battle against those who are armed. Gregory says: "One runs against God with a raised neck by boldly doing things that displease the Creator."[39] Ecclesiasticus 6:2 speaks against this: "Do not extol yourself in the thoughts of your soul like a bull, lest your strength be crushed through foolishness." And Jeremiah says that **all [are turned to their own course]** because, according to Ps 13[14:3], "All have gone astray. They have become useless together," etc. **All,** that is, nearly **all.** Psalm 11 [12:1]: "Save me, Lord, for no one is holy."

God's People Are Less Prudent than the Birds of the Air

8:7 The kite [in heaven has recognized its time]. Here he declares that their foolishness is greater than the foolishness of birds. For birds know the difference between the favorable weather and the stormy so that, during the cold and tempestuous season, they depart and cross over to other regions. But humans who are utterly fallen do not consider the judgment of God, and they fail to take heed for their future. For this reason he says: **The kite,** which is **in heaven**—that is, in the air—**has recognized its time** for mating, reproducing, migrating to other regions, and avoiding stormy weather. Ecclesiastes 3:1: "All things have their time." **The turtle dove, and the swallow, and the stork have observed the time of their coming.** They come in their own times to suitable regions, and they depart. Now there are two kinds of turtle doves. One variety is present all the time. The other variety arrives and

---

38. This sentence, which derives from Acts 26:14, is present in Acts 9:5 in the Vulgate but not in the most ancient versions of the New Testament.

39. Gregory the Great, *Moralia on Job* 12.43.48, ed. Marcus Adriaen, CCSL 143A (Turnhout: Brepols, 1979), 658.

departs with the change of seasons. So also, fish are found in certain waters at one time and in different waters at another time. **But my people have not recognized** (that is, they have scornfully refused to understand or reflect on) **the** coming **judgment of the Lord,** the **judgment** of condemnation or death. In other words, they refused to recognize anything regarding the coming judgment or death, which comes unexpectedly. Ecclesiasticus 7:36: "My child, remember [your final end in all you do, and you shall never sin]." Or **the judgment** of discernment; that is, they did not wish to do penance or examine their consciences. Or **the judgment of the Lord** refers to the law of the Lord, which ought to be observed, or the will of the Lord, which ought to be done. Isaiah 1:3: "The ox knows its owner, and the donkey its master's crib. But Israel does not recognize me, and my people do not understand." Job 12:7–8: "Ask the beasts, and they shall teach you, and the birds of the air, and they shall tell you. Speak to the earth, and it shall answer you, and the fish of the sea will declare." Where our text has **"kite,"** another text reads "heron." Where we have **"swallow,"** the Septuagint reads "sparrows of the field." **The judgment of the Lord** could also refer to the time of their oppression by Nebuchadnezzar that would arrive due to the judgment of God.

The Leaders Will Perish Together with the People

8:8 How do you say, "We are wise"? After denouncing the people's obtuseness, here God denounces their teachers' and prelates' false teaching and tenacious greed that leads people astray. This is also addressed to the pseudo-prophets, scribes, Pharisees, priests, and prelates of our own time. **"And the law of the Lord."** That is: You are boasting about your knowledge. **"Is with us,"** by keeping [the law]. In other words: How can you boast about your knowledge and your way of life when you do not have knowledge of the law or observe its works? For the birds are wiser than you and are more diligent in taking precautions for themselves and looking after their needs. **Truly [the lying pen of the scribes] has worked falsehood.** It wrote and set forth a deceitful law and a lying statute. In other words: You boast about your knowledge of the law and yet you are writing wickedness and lies. In this way you subvert the people through your interpretations and teachings, and you oppress the poor through your statutes. As Isa 10:1–2 says: "Woe to those who make wicked laws and, when they write, they write injustice in order to oppress the poor in judgment and do violence to the cause of the humble of my people, so that widows might be their prey and so that they might rob orphans." Matthew 15:3: "Why do you break the commandment for the sake of your traditions?"

8:9 The wise are confounded. Their teachers and priests—whose responsibility it is to know and teach the Lord's law—will be confounded at the time of captivity. Therefore they are called **wise,** not because they actually were wise but because they ought to have been wise or because they considered themselves to be wise. Or **wise** means they were shrewd in wickedness or in creating traditions and statutes. For their wisdom is correctly proved to be foolishness, as Jerome says: "For they condemn themselves with their own 'knowledge' and their own 'judgment,' because the very ones who command others not to steal are thieves. About them Rom 2:21 says: 'You who teach others do not teach yourselves.'"[40] **They are terrified and taken captive.** That is, they will be terrified when the enemies arrive and the city is besieged, and they will eventually be taken captive when the city is destroyed. And this is because **they have cast away the word of the Lord** by not observing it in their deeds. **And there is no wisdom in them** because they do not reflect on the Lord's law in their minds. So they have falsely said that they are wise and that the law of the Lord is with them. Thus, as Jerome says: "It is in vain that they boast of their knowledge of the law when they ruin their teaching through their works."[41] As Ecclus 34:28 says: "When one builds up and another destroys" by their example or manner of life, "what do they gain but trouble," the torment of Gehenna? Augustine says: "To speak well but do evil is nothing other than to condemn oneself with one's own voice."[42] It says rightly that **there is no wisdom in them,** since they teach others but not themselves. So they do not know for themselves what they teach to others. Hosea 4:6: "Because you have rejected knowledge, I will banish you from serving as priest for me." Therefore it says that **they have cast away [the word of the Lord],** because they pour it out for others but do not retain it for themselves. As Isa 47:10 says: "Your wisdom and your knowledge have led you astray."

8:10 Therefore I will give their women to outsiders. I will give their wives to foreigners. This means: I will hand over their wives, or their daughters,

40. Jerome, *On Jeremiah* 8:9a, CCSL 74:88.

41. Jerome, *On Jeremiah* 8:9b, CCSL 74:88.

42. Prosper of Aquitaine, *The Book of Sentences* 6, ed. P. Callens, CCSL 68A (Turnhout: Brepols, 1972), 258. Prosper of Aquitaine (ca. 390–ca. 463), an admirer of Augustine, compiled a collection of 392 sayings, taken primarily from Augustine.

to their enemies to be violated, which, for men, is the worst disaster.[43] **And their fields,** which refers to all sorts of possessions, **as an inheritance** to strangers, who will hold on to their possessions permanently, as though they possess them as a rightful inheritance and not just temporarily. In the same way the churches and souls of their subjects will be handed over to demons because of the laziness and greed of prelates. **Because from the least to the greatest, all are following greed,** and, as a result, all other evils. First Timothy 6:10: "Desire [for money] is the root of all evils," etc. All people—from the lesser person to the greater—are dedicated to greed. Amos 9:1: "Strike the hinge, and the lintels will be shaken; for there is greed in the head of all of them. And I will slay the last of them with the sword." Isaiah 1:5b–6a: "The whole head is weak," referring to the prelates and princes, "and the whole heart mourns," referring to the prophets and the wise people, "from the sole of the foot to the top of head, there is no health in it." Therefore: **From the prophet to the priest, [all work falsehood].** This means that they fashion lies and deceitfully invent slanders, or they cheat others by deceptively stealing things that are not their own. Jerome says: "Those who ought to be preventing others from sinning are the first ones entangled in crimes."[44] Or, **all work falsehood** means that they commit sins, especially by worshipping idols, which are nothing other than lies and false images.

8:11 And they healed the grief. This means that they softened the prophets' and the law's threats that were made against transgressions in Jerusalem. Thus **they healed the grief.** That is, they said it would be healed, or they preached that pardon would be obtained for them easily, saying, "Do not be sad. The Lord is merciful." **Of the daughter of my people,** Jerusalem, saying that it will not be crushed by enemies and thus was healed or would be healed. They said, "But there is healing, or promise of healing." **Causing disgrace,** that is, causing the deception or confounding of those who trust in such words, or the words of those who say, "They are healed; I declare it." **Saying, "Peace, peace. Peace is certain."** The repetition expresses its certainty. **When there is no peace.** On the contrary, the war with the Chaldeans was imminent. Or, **peace** in the present and **peace** in the future; or

---

43. Many medieval commentators regarded sexual violation of women to be chiefly an offense against their husbands and fathers. See Joy A. Schroeder, *Dinah's Lament: the Biblical Legacy of Sexual Violence in Christian Interpretation* (Minneapolis: Fortress, 2007), 5.

44. Jerome, *On Jeremiah* 8:10–11, CCSL 74:88.

peace of mind and **peace** of body. Or, according to Jerome, "**They healed their grief,** after the previously mentioned wickedness, as if they were good physicians," as if they were saintly men, "and tried to heal the wounds of others with their words, when these very words were the cause of all the crimes."[45] But Gregory says: "The person who tries to reform others ought to be free of filth."[46] For it causes **disgrace,** either the disgrace of those who mislead others or the disgrace of those misled by them. Such people say, **"Peace, peace,"** although they do not have peace with God or their neighbor. Hosea 4:8: "They will eat the sins of my people," that is, they will obliterate [their sins] and will say they do not exist, and thus "they shall lift up their souls to wickedness," making them prone to even greater sins. So this is how they heal, **causing disgrace.** They say that they will heal their wounds through prayers, but they are not healed. On this topic, 41:1–8 below says that Ishmael, who promised them peace, killed the eighty men with shaved beards who came to Gedaliah. In the same way, priests grant license to usurers and self-indulgent people to commit usury and fornication in exchange for anniversaries, tricenaries, and other offerings, which they impose on them, indulging their vices, pretending they do not exist, which is to give license to commit sin.[47] They do this, **causing disgrace** because of their greed, and they say, **"Peace, peace."** In other words, "Give this to me, and God will be well-disposed toward you." First Maccabees 7:12, 14–16, 18, says: "A company of the scribes, who wished to require the things that are just, assembled before Alcimus (who wished to become high priest), and they sought peace from him. For they said, 'A person who is a priest from the offspring of Aaron has come. He will not deceive us.' And he spoke peaceful words with them, saying, 'We will not do harm to you or your friends.' And they believed him. And he seized sixty men from among them and killed them. For this reason fear and trembling fell on all the people, for they said: 'There is no truth or justice among them, for they have broken the covenant and the oath that they swore.'" "Alcimus" is interpreted to mean "leaven of useless counsel." These individuals "pardon the guilty in exchange for gifts," as it says in Isa 5:23. "For a handful of barley, they preserve the life of souls that should die," as it says in Ezek 13:19.

45. Jerome, *On Jeremiah* 8:10–11, CCSL 74:88.

46. Gregory the Great, *Moralia on Job* 7.36.56, ed. Marcus Adriaen, CCSL 143 (Turnhout: Brepols, 1979), 377.

47. Tricenaries were Masses said for thirty successive days on behalf of someone who was deceased. Nicholas Coureas, *The Latin Church in Cyprus, 1195–1312* (Brookfield, VT: Ashgate, 1997), 101n175.

8:12 Are they confounded because they have committed abomination?
According to Jerome: "This is read as a question."[48] In other words: Were
they ashamed of their crimes? Did they recognize the abominations that they
committed? It is as if he were saying: No. Instead they had broken out into
such great insanity that distress did not cause them to reform their faults.
Nor did hope for forgiveness cause them to confess their crimes.[49] Therefore
he continues: **On the contrary, they are not confounded with distress** that
beneficially leads to repentance. **And they do not know how to blush.** They
refuse to blush. As it says above: "You had a prostitute's forehead, you refused
to blush" (Jer 3:3) with "the shame that leads to glory" mentioned in Ecclus
4:25. **Therefore they will fall among those who topple.** This means that they
will perish among the people who die. **In the time of their visitation.** That is,
when they are visited with the captivity that they deserve. **They will topple.**
The greater people will fall together with the lesser people, and vice versa.
This means that absolutely all of them will fall. Look! Since they misused
their status, these great people will be united with lower-ranked people in
punishment. In fact, the more they descend from higher status, the worse
their punishment will be. For this reason it was said to the prince of the angels in Isa 14:15: "But you are dragged down into hell, into the depth of the
pit." For, since they are similar in crime, all of them will have similar torment.
All of them, from the least to the greatest, occupy themselves with greed,
and so they will all **topple** together. The arrival of Nebuchadnezzar is called
a "visitation." Just as the pope "visits" provinces using his legates as agents,
and he uses his legates to elevate some people and to depose and humble
others, so also the Lord visited the Judeans through Nebuchadnezzar, who
overthrew some people and even elevated others.

The Babylonians Will Seize the Land's Produce

8:13 Gathering. Here, after reproving them for sins and threatening them
with captivity, the Lord specifies the manner in which their downfall and
affliction will occur. **I will gather them together** in Jerusalem, in order for
them to be besieged there for a long time by the Chaldeans. For when the
siege was imminent, they gathered themselves together so they could defend

---

48. Jerome, *On Jeremiah* 8:12a, CCSL 74:89. In the Latin text, this phrase can be read
either as a statement or as a question.
49. Jerome, *On Jeremiah* 8:12a, CCSL 74:89.

the city. But there they would endure scarcity and hunger because **there is no grape on the vines, and there are no [figs on the fig tree]** for you rather than your enemies. In other words: You will not collect the fruits of your grapevines and other trees, but your enemies will take them at the time of harvest and grape-gathering. **The leaf has fallen.** In other words: Time will pass, and autumn will follow summer, and, when winter arrives, the leaves will fall, and you will know that they collected the fruits of your land, and you will not receive any of it as food for yourselves. Therefore: **I have granted them [the things that have passed away].** That is: I have granted that the Judeans would see the things that passed away from them. I granted that they would see how these things would pass away from them and be given to their enemies, which was a source of terrible sorrow for them—to know that they could not risk collecting their own goods and that these things would pass into their enemies' hands. Isaiah 1:7: "In your presence, foreigners devour your territory"—as if to say, "This will pass in front of your eyes, or nose, and you will not taste it." Or, **I have granted them** means: In their land **I have granted them** an abundance of good things, which, nevertheless, **have passed away.** These things passed away from them and went to their enemies. Or, **I have granted them the things that have passed away** means: In other years I gave them things that have now passed away, because they have eaten and used up all the things that I had previously given them, so that during the siege they will have nothing to eat—either from past years or from the coming year, because enemies will harvest their fields and vineyards, which were very fruitful then, so that the Judeans would be even more sorrowful when they saw the enemies seizing all of their things.

Moral Interpretation of Grapes and Figs

8:13 There is no grape. There is no remembrance of sin, from which the wine of remorse is pressed. Psalm 59 [60:3]: "You have made us drink the wine of remorse." **On the vines.** That is, among people who are repenting. **And no figs.** That is, sweetness of soul and pleasantness of spirit; or a sweet and cheerful will to do good. **On the fig trees.** That is, among the proficient, or the perfect, or the religious, or the contemplatives.[50] For today, among each of these, one finds the thorn of avarice and greed, and the thistle of carnal

50. The terms "proficient" and "perfect" refer to degrees of progress in monastic or mendicant religious life. See Thomas Aquinas, *Summa Theologiae*, 2-2, q. 183, a. 4.

desire. So they have no grape or fig—no bitter repentance or sweet delight of soul. Matthew 7:16: "Do people gather grapes from thorns or figs from thistles?" **The leaf has fallen.** Since it is worthless and dry—lacking the fluid of grace—their word drops down. That is, it flows downward since it lacks devotion and usefulness, and it strives only for emptiness. But 1 Sam 3:19 says: "And Samuel grew, and the Lord was with him, and not one of his words fell to the ground." Proverbs 11:28: "Those who trust in their riches shall fall, but those who are just will spring up like a green leaf." Below, in 17:8: "They will not fear when summer heat comes, and their leaf will be green." And Ecclus 21:25b: "The words of the just will be weighed in the balance." **I have granted them the things that have passed away.** This means: I have given them these transitory temporal things that ought to be considered things that are "passed away" rather than "present." This is the reason why spiritual leaves have fallen, because priority was given to temporal things, which pass away since fortunes change.

The Judean People Speak

8:14 Why do we sit still? This is the voice of the people encouraging one another to enter the walled cities—or just one city, Jerusalem, since all the other cities except for that one were now captured. So it says: **Assemble yourselves, and let** all of us **enter. Why do we sit still** in our homes outside places of fortification, in country houses, as though we are safe, when the arrival of enemies is so imminent? The people who say this are those who remained outside the city. **And let us be silent there.** Let us endure the siege and the hunger inside the city without grumbling. Or: **Let us be silent,** since people besieged in cities are silent during the day so they can hear where part [of the city] might have an incursion, so they can rush there; but at night they make a clamor to keep from sleeping and so they appear not to fear the enemies. Or, **Let us be silent there** means: Let us not presume to pray to God with an outward voice, but let us ponder our sins there silently in our heart. **For our Lord [has made us become silent].** The Lord has scourged us so much that we do not have confidence in prayer or knowledge of the law to know what to utter. Another translation says, "Let us be cast away," or, "Let us be thrown away."[51] We are like dung, because the Lord has cast

---

51. This is the Septuagint's translation, information derived from Jerome, *On Jeremiah* 8:14–15, CCSL 74:90.

us away from himself **and has given us the water of bitterness to drink.** During the siege, the Lord gave us bitter, putrid waters. Or: The Lord gave us the bitterest tribulation. In other words: Our life was tribulation because we have lived in misery. And why is this? **For we have sinned before the Lord**—either in the Lord's sight, or against the Lord.

8:15 We waited for peace. We, who did nothing good, waited for a time of tranquility. **And there was nothing good** to wait for. Or, "**there was nothing good**" means: The good that we waited for did not come as we expected. We waited **for a time of healing, but, behold, terror,** at the arrival of their enemies, because the Judeans had been stricken at the time of Sennacherib, but afterward they had peace. Since they had been at peace at this time under Hezekiah, they considered it a time of healing. They believed that peace would continue and that they would have an abundance of temporal things that would be a sort of healing in comparison with the previous evils. Or one could say that, at the time that Nebuchadnezzar left Judea to go to Egypt, the Judeans said that he would not return, and they promised themselves a time of peace and healing from their prior affliction. But once again, with the arrival of his army in Judea, fear suddenly came upon them and the good that they had hoped for was absent.

Moral Interpretation of the Words of the Judeans: A Call to Religious Life

8:14 Why do we sit still? Why do we remain silent due to our habit of sinning? In other words, as it says in Wis 5:8: "In the end, what benefit will we gain from haughtiness, and what will boasting about riches grant to us?" Romans 6:23: "For the wages of sin is death." **Assemble yourselves.** In other words: Come to a monastery or the religious life. **And let us enter into the fortified city,** into the religious life where it is safe, like a fortified city. **And let us be silent there.** According to the literal sense, we ought to maintain silence there. As Ps 140 [141:3]: "Set a watch before my mouth," etc. Isaiah 32:17: "The service of justice will be silence." In Isa 30:15: "In silence and in hope will be your strength." **For our Lord has made us become silent.** In other words: The Lord gave us an opportunity to be silent and not grumble. This refers to remembrance of sin, which ought to make a person keep peace and not talk or grumble in the midst of scourges. It says rightly, "In silence and in hope will be your strength" (Isa 30:15), since hope of the eternal banquet provides strength to humans, fortifying them for everything they endure from within and from without—for fasting and other bodily mortifications. Silence fortifies them for the things they endure from others, so they do not grumble about obedience to prelates, or about criticism and reproaches inflicted on them by others. Or it is possible to direct this statement to theologians at Paris who study so much all day.

8:14 Why do we sit still? Assemble yourselves, and let us enter into the city to preach. Psalm 126 [127:2]: "Rise up after you were seated, you who eat the bread of sorrow," which is sacred scripture, since it is entirely filled with sorrow, suffused with Christ's passion. Genesis 3:19: "In the sweat of your face [you will eat your bread]." Isaiah 21:5: "Prepare a table. See in the watchtower those who are eating and drinking. Rise up, princes, and take up the shield," the word that is a "shield tried by fire," as in Prov 30:5. But Gen 38:14 says that Tamar, who was a widow without a husband, sat in the fork in the road, because Shelah had grown up and she had not received him as a husband. So there, as a consequence, she committed fornication, even though Judah said to her: "Remain a widow in your father's house until my son Shelah grows up" (Gen 38:11).[52] **And he has given us the water of bitterness to drink.** We are reminded of the pure, delicious water, so that we might have bitterness of mind. Or, the water that offers refreshment signifies that benefices given to members of religious orders and clerics ought to be accepted with sorrow and bitterness. As it says in Ps 79 [80:5]: "You will feed us with the bread of tears, and you will give us tears for our drink in full measure." Or the water of bitterness is the delight of a spiritual heart, which is accompanied by bitterness and mortification of the flesh. And this is to eat lamb with wild lettuce.[53] Or the water of bitterness is repentance, which is sweet to the healthy soul but dreadful to the soul that is sick, even though a human ought to take delight in this drink. As Ps 101 [102:9] says: "For I ate ashes like bread," which is dreadful for a sinner. Thus, Ecclus 1:25: "To the sinner, devotion to God is an abomination." **For we have sinned before the Lord.** Luke 15:18: "Father, I have sinned against heaven and before you." Psalm 50 [51:4]: "Against you alone have I sinned, and I have done evil in your sight."

52. The point of mentioning the story of Judah and Tamar (Gen 38) seems to be to highlight the contrast between being inside the (symbolic) fortified city, or the house, of religious life, where one is safer from temptations on the one hand and, on the other hand, the dangers of the outdoor byways where fornication can take place.
53. This is a reference to the Passover meal of lamb and wild lettuce (bitter herbs) in Exod 12:8.

8:15 We waited for peace, for a time of mercy, or for eternal peace. **And there was nothing good** with respect to worldly prosperity, for expectation of eternal goods and deprivation of present things ought to be joined together. For "blessed are the poor in spirit," etc. (Matt 5:3). **For a time of healing,** in the future, when "God will wipe away all tears from the eyes" of his saints, as it says in Rev 21:4, and when "the Lord shall bind up the wound of his people and shall heal the injuries inflicted by his blows," as it says in Isa 30:26. **But, behold, terror,** namely, fear in the present time, during which people fear the punishment in Gehenna. For hope of reward and fear of suffering ought to be joined together. Psalm 85 [86:11b]: "Let my heart rejoice, that it might fear your name."

Literal Interpretation of the Attack from the North

8:16 From Dan was heard the snorting, etc. The tribe of Dan had territory in the north, and Nebuchadnezzar's army crossed through it to Jerusalem. Or, Dan was the name of a certain fort that was in the territory of Dan. In this place, as Jerome says, the river Jordan arises.[54] But, on the other hand, Matt 16:13 states: "Jesus came into the district of Caesarea Philippi." There the *Gloss* says that the Jordan arises at the base of Mount Lebanon.[55] The solution: there is no contradiction, because the town of Dan is next to this mountain. **The snorting of his,** Nebuchadnezzar's, **horses.** As it says above in 4:15: "A voice of one declaring from Dan and giving notice of the idol from Mount Ephraim." **At the sound of the neighing of his warriors.** That is, the sound of the exultant cry of his warriors, or the neighing of the horses used or ridden by the riders who were fighting. **The whole land quaked.** This is hyperbole. It means there was such a great multitude of warriors who shouted exultantly, or whose horses neighed, that the earth seemed to be moved. Or, **the whole land quaked** means that all the inhabitants of Judea—whoever heard this noise—would be terrified. The word *hyperbole* derives from *hyper,* which means "over," and *bole* or *bolus,* which means "thrown." Or [**the whole land quaked**] is a figure of speech, because it means less than it seems to say. **And** warriors **came, and they devoured the land.** Or, rather: They will come and devour **the land and all its plenitude,** that is, all that fills the land—namely, its humans, or produce, or other territory. And not only will

54. Jerome, *On Jeremiah* 8:16, CCSL 74:91.
55. *Glossa ordinaria* on Matt 16:13.

they lay waste to the land surrounding the city and reduce it to wasteland, but they will even destroy **the city and its inhabitants,** namely, Jerusalem.

Moral Interpretation of the Attack from the North

8:16 Interpreted according to the moral sense: **From Dan,** which means "judgment," **was heard** their **snorting,** which is the prompting of the devil's minions. For judgment, or fear of judgment, opens ears so they understand the promptings and temptations of the devil. **At the sound of the neighing of his warriors,** which is the prompting of demons, **the whole land quaked,** earthly beings trembled to commit sin. Below, 11:16 says: "At the sound of the utterance, a great fire was kindled in it."

Literal Interpretation of God Sending Serpents

8:17 For behold, I will send you terrible serpents—or, according to the Septuagint, deadly serpents; or basilisks, as Aquila translated it.[56] That is: [I **will send**] the Chaldeans who will strike you ferociously, and nothing will be able to convince them to have peace. Hence it says: **Against which there is no charm,** since they will not listen to persuasion or supplication. For this reason, 5:15 states, "a nation whose language you will not know." This indicates their brutality. **And they will bite you,** etc. They will destroy and kill you. For the bite of serpents causes dread and danger of death; the same was true of the coming of the Chaldeans. Deuteronomy 32:24: "I will send the teeth of beasts against them, with the fury of creatures that trail on the ground and serpents." Or, interpreted according to the literal sense: I will send serpents that will drive you out of the caves, so you will not be able to hide; but we do not read about this.

Moral Interpretation of the Coming of Serpents

8:16-17 And they came; demons will come. **And they devoured,** they shall devour, **the land,** etc., that is, whatever is in it, **the city and its inhabi-**

---

56. Jerome, *On Jeremiah* 8:17, CCSL 74:91.

tants. They pollute the soul, corrupt the natural good qualities, and destroy the virtues in it. It calls the tempters—that is, the demons—**terrible serpents,** that is, basilisks, who slay flying birds with a single deadly breath of temptation.[57] For, with the breath of temptation, demons slay contemplatives who, with the wings of virtues, go in search of higher things; or they slay prelates who, with the wings of vices, ascend to positions and dignities. **Against which there is no charm,** for the devil is brutal since he will have no compassion. Or the serpents who kill with their breath are detractors **against which there is no charm.** In all their conversations, these members of religious orders speak disparagingly to others about all the good men around them, or they belittle them to others, or destroy them through disparagement and jealousy. Ecclesiasticus 12:13 says: "Who will pity a charmer—a preacher—struck by a serpent?" For detraction especially oppresses preachers.

Literal and Moral Interpretations of Sorrow above Sorrow

8:18 My sorrow. Here it deals with the Lord's great mercy, the destruction of Jerusalem, and the Lord's distress due to unbearable compassion, so that he is said to have not only **sorrow** but also **sorrow above sorrow** for them. Thus Isa 1:24: "I will console myself regarding my enemies." Or these are the words of the prophet lamenting the captivity of the Judeans: **My sorrow** about the destruction of the two tribes [Judah] is increased **above** the **sorrow** for the destruction of the ten tribes [Israel]. **My heart mourns within me.** That is: My mind is sorrowful because of the destruction of my people. For this reason the Septuagint says: "They will bite you incurably, says the Lord, with the sorrow of your fainting heart" (8:17b–8:18a).[58]

Interpreted according to the moral sense: Any righteous soul placed in exile ought to have **sorrow above sorrow,** sorrow that is piled up, or sorrow coming from above and sorrow coming from below, so that one says: **My heart mourns within me.** I have inward sorrow for my sins, which I do not exhibit outwardly like the boastful hypocrites who make a show of displaying their penitence and their tears. Or, the one who has "a heart

---

57. A basilisk is a mythical reptile with deadly breath. According to Isidore of Seville (*Etymologies* 12.4.6, PL 82:443): "Indeed, no flying bird goes past its face unharmed, but no matter how far away, the bird is burned up and devoured by the basilisk's mouth."

58. Jerome, *On Jeremiah* 8:17–18, CCSL 74:91.

mourning within oneself" rather than outside of oneself is the person who grieves because of an inward lack of virtues rather than an outward lack of temporal things. Psalm 142 [143:4]: "*My spirit is in anguish within me; my heart is troubled within me.*" Genesis 6:6–7: "Touched inwardly by sorrow of heart, [God] said, 'I will blot out humanity.'" For the Lord feels sorrow for what we lack inwardly, not what we lack outwardly.

The Cry of Jerusalem

8:19 Behold, the voice of the cry [of the daughter of my people]. In other words: I feel the deepest sorrow for my people because **the voice of the cry [of the daughter of my people]**—that is, the personification of my people in Jerusalem—has been heard. **From a faraway land.** This means that the cry is so loud that it can be heard from a land that is far from the place where the weeping is, namely, Jerusalem. Or, **from a faraway land** refers to the arrival of the Chaldeans who are coming **from a faraway land,** because those [Chaldeans] who cry out with joy thinking about their future victory are far away from Jerusalem. Or, **the voice of the cry of the daughter of my people from a faraway land** means that the cause or occasion for **the cry,** or the reason for their weeping, was that the Chaldeans were coming **from a faraway land. Is not the Lord in Zion,** etc.? In other words: They do not have the Lord their leader or defender against the enemies. The Lord departed from them, and therefore in vain they believe they will be liberated when they are not able to defend themselves without me. Micah 4:9: "Is there no king in you, or has your counselor disappeared? For sorrow overwhelms you like a woman in labor." Therefore they cry out because there is no one to defend them. **The Lord** is the Father. **Her king** is the Son. **Why, then, [have they provoked me to wrath with their statues],** with their idols, **and with their foreign, worthless things,** with Gentile rites and ceremonies? For they had received idols and the worship of idols from the foreign nations. He says: **Why, then,** as if he were saying: Indeed, it is because they had worshipped idols that this has befallen them, or come to pass, that it is said, "**The Lord is not** among them and has ceased being their help." For the Lord says: Through their worship of idols, they provoked me—the one who was their **King**—to wrath. Or: "**Why, then,** has the Lord withdrawn from them?" It is because **they have provoked me to wrath,** etc.

Literal and Moral Interpretations of the Summer and Autumn Seasons

8:20 [The harvest] is passed, etc. This is spoken by the people who are enclosed in Jerusalem during the lengthy siege. **The harvest is passed, the summer is ended.** In other words: The seasons have changed. The yearly cycle has turned. **And we are not saved.** We are not saved as the false prophets promised, but, instead, our hope is in vain.

The harvest is passed. Interpreted, morally, this refers to Lent, when the soul ought to gather the harvest and replenish its storehouses—the soul's reserves of strength—with good fruits. **The summer is ended.** This refers to the season of the warmth of grace, or the season of this present life, in which we ought to harvest what we shall eat in the future life, just as the ant does, "who, though it has no commander, or leader, or ruler, provides food for itself in the summer," etc., Prov 6:7-8. **And we are not saved,** because we did not seek salvation at the time of salvation, "For now is the acceptable time, now is the day of salvation," as it says in 2 Cor 6:2. It is possible for those condemned in hell to say this.

Literal Interpretation of Balm in Gilead

8:21-22 Because of the affliction, etc. This is *anthropopathos.*[59] For the prophet presents God as sorrowful, because of **the affliction of the daughter of** his **people,** and presents God as astonished because they are incurable. For this reason **I am afflicted,** etc., because of the wounds of my people, because they are not healed even when they have physicians and many medicines. Hence: **Is there no balm [*resina*],** etc. He mentions two things that are needed by someone who is sick: medicine and a physician. For one is of little use without the other. These two things were **in Gilead,** among the Judeans, to whom the medicine chest of the prophets' testimonies was entrusted. For they had "balm," which is the law, or legal purifications, especially circumcision and repentance. And they had "physicians," who were the prophets and priests. For this reason it says: **Is there no [balm],** etc.? In other words: Certainly the Judeans have the law as medicine if they wish! But, according to Jerome, **balm in Gilead** signifies "repentance" or "opportunity for repentance."[60] Understood literally, it is a medicinal balm flowing from terebinth

---

59. The literary device of attributing human emotions to the deity.
60. Jerome, *On Jeremiah* 8:22, CCSL 74:92.

trees, which abound in Gilead. We should understand "Gilead" as referring to Jerusalem. **Or is there no physician there?** This refers to the prophet or priest *whose prayers or sermons are able to heal the people,* as in Luke 16:29: "They have Moses and the prophets. They should listen to them." **Why then [is not the wound of the daughter of my people closed],** that is, cured? **[Why then is not] the wound**—the injury from sin, or from a scourge—**of the daughter of my people closed,** just as skin is closed when a wound is cured? For then the wound is covered over with skin and it is closed up.

Moral Interpretation of Balm in Gilead

Balm is the medicine of penance, which is **in Gilead,** in the church, where there is the medicine chest of testimonies, namely, the Old and New Testaments; and the medicine chest of witnesses, namely, the apostles, martyrs, confessors, and virgins. Hebrews 12:1–2: "Therefore, having a cloud of witnesses over our head, laying aside every weight and sin that surrounds us, let us run with patience," etc. Or, **balm** refers to the sacraments that flowed forth from the terebinth, which is Christ. Ecclesiasticus 24:16: "I have stretched out my branches like a terebinth tree, and my branches are glorious and graceful." For the word *resina* [balm], which is more commonly called "gum," is said to come from the word *reein,* which means "to flow." The balm from the terebinth is the most precious, especially the balm that flows spontaneously.[61] Now the terebinth under which Jacob buried the idols in Gen 35:4 signifies the cross, under whose shade and protection we ought to bury our sins. And the balm flows spontaneously from this tree when we undertake voluntary penance in imitation of the cross of Christ, and this is extremely precious. But just as balm is nothing in comparison with the terebinth from which it flows, so the penance that we undertake is nothing in comparison to the Lord's passion. For all our righteousness is like a rag of a menstruating woman, as Isa 64:6 states. And Gregory says that all our righteousness, compared to God's righteousness, is unrighteousness.[62] For this reason the Apostle does not say that when Abraham believed, it was righteousness, but that it was reckoned to him as righteousness, as it says in Rom 4:3. It is only because of great divine mercy that God permits any human work to be called "righteousness."

61. Isidore, *Etymologies* 17.7.70–71, PL 82:619.
62. Gregory, *Moralia on Job* 11.1.1, CCSL 143A:586.

Or is there no physician there? In other words: There certainly is. For the church has teachers and priests who administer healing to the wounds of sinners. But, alas, this verse could also resemble Isa 3:7: "I am no physician, and there is no bread or clothing in my house." For how can those who are sick heal others? For they are directed: "Physician, cure yourself," as Luke 4:23 says.

THOMAS AQUINAS

On Jeremiah

Jeremiah 9, 11, 14, 15, 17, 18, 20

Chapter Nine

The Prophet's Sorrow for the People

9:1-6 This passage shows the people's obstinacy in sins directed toward their neighbors. First the prophet describes how painful his sympathy is: **Who will give [water to my head and a fountain of tears to my eyes]?** (9:1a). It is as though he were saying: Because of my sadness and sympathy, my bodily fluid [*humor*], which is the substance that tears are made of, does not provide enough **water** for the never-ending **fountain** [of tears]. Lamentations 3:48: "My eye has flowed with streams of water because of the grief of the daughter of my people." And regarding the degree of their guilt: **Who will give me [a traveler's lodging] in the wilderness?** (9:2a). In other words: I would rather live in the wilderness than see their sins. **A traveler's lodging** [*diversorum*] is a place where no one resides, through which various [*diversi*] people pass; or, in the wilderness, none or very few of these various travelers pass through it. Below, 12:7: "I have forsaken my house. I have abandoned my inheritance."

Second, this passage describes the condition of the people: **Because they are all adulterers** (9:2b). First, he describes how great their guilt is and, second, how great their punishment, where he says: "Therefore, thus says the Lord of Hosts" (9:7a). Regarding the first part, there are two points. First, he presents the sin that comes from violating another person's bed: **They are adulterers** (9:2b). Jeremiah 5:8 above states: "Each and every one of them neighed after his neighbor's wife." Because of the transgression of the human—or divine—covenant: [**They are**] **an assembly of transgressors** (9:2c). It is as though he were saying: They transgressed their sworn oath. Isaiah 24:16: "The transgressors have transgressed, and they have transgressed with the transgression of treachery." Because of their lies, he asserts: **They have bent their tongue like a bow** from which the arrow of deceitful speech goes forth (9:3a). Hosea 7:16: "They returned so they would be without a yoke. They became like a deceitful bow." Second, he amplifies this. First, because of the increase of their guilt: **They have strengthened themselves in the earth** (9:3b), in earthly sins, or stripped of heavenly goods because of their earthly goods. Psalm 72 [73:3]: "I was zealous on account of the wicked when I saw the sinners' prosperity." **They have proceeded from evil to evil** (9:3c), adding sin to sin. Hosea 4:2: "Cursing, lying, murder, theft, and adultery have overflowed, and bloodshed has followed bloodshed."

The second part deals with the circumstances of the sinning, because it occurred among close associates, those to whom loving deeds are usually directed. So first he counsels caution: **Let everyone take heed for their neighbor,** who is associated with you in any civil or spiritual relationship. [**And let no one put trust in any**] **brother,** who is joined to you by a natural pact (9:4a). Micah 7:5: "Do not believe a friend, and do not put trust in a leader." Regarding the second, he assigns blame to fraudulence. First he mentions the sin of fraud: **For every brother who supplants** by unjustly seizing someone else's things (9:4b). Genesis 27:36: "Look! He has supplanted me a second time. First he took my birthright, and now this second time he stole my blessing." Then he shows how fraud is committed in actions, because **every friend goes around fraudulently** (9:4c). Isaiah 32:7: "The devices of the fraudulent are the most wicked." And how the fraud is committed in words: **And a man will mock his brother** (9:5a). Job 12:4: "Those who are mocked by their friends, as I am, shall call on the Lord, who will hear them." The future tense [**will mock**] indicates their persistence. Second, he indicates the reason, because people familiar with lies **taught** [**their tongue to tell lies**] through their habits, and people devoted to wicked deeds **labored** [**to commit iniquity**] (9:5b). Proverbs 4:16: "For they cannot sleep unless they act wickedly, and they obtain no sleep unless they have supplanted someone." Wisdom 5:7: "We have wearied ourselves in the way of wickedness and destruction, and we have walked difficult ways, but we have not known the way of the Lord." Third, he concludes: **Your habitation,** O Jeremiah, or O Jerusalem, **is in the midst of deceit,** in the midst of a deceitful people (9:6a). Ezekiel 2:6: "Unbelievers and destroyers are with you, and you dwell with scorpions."

9:7-9 This passage presents the pitiable condition of the people and the extent of their punishment. First he pronounces the sentence, and, second, he prescribes the punishment, where he states: "I will begin weeping and lamentation for the mountains" (9:10a). Regarding the first of the two, first he pronounces the sentence, saying: **I will melt [and test them]** (9:7b) like gold in fire, so that in this way, at least, they would be purified. Ecclesiasticus 27:5: "The furnace tests the potter's vessels, and the trial of affliction tests just people." Second, he shows the justice of the sentence; first by closing off the way of mercy: **For what else shall I do in the presence of the daughter of my people?** (9:7c). It is as if the Lord were saying: Since no other way remains, nothing is left except for me to punish them. Isaiah 5:4: "What more is there that I ought to do for my vineyard that I have not already done to it?" Second, he pronounces guilt: **[Their tongue is a piercing] arrow,** which pierces from afar and penetrates all the way to someone's innermost parts (9:8a). Proverbs 26:22: "The words of a talebearer seem simple, but they reach to the innermost parts of the belly." And Prov 25:18: "A person who bears false witness against a neighbor is like a dart, and a sword, and a sharp arrow." Psalm 63 [64:7]: "The arrows of children have become their wounds." Psalm 27 [28:3b]: "They speak peace with their neighbor, but mischief is in their hearts." Third, he concludes the discussion of the punishment, **Shall I not visit them for these things?** (9:9a), just as he does in 5:9 above.

The Destruction of Jerusalem Foretold

9:10-14 The prophet here focuses on pronouncing the punishment. First, he pronounces the punishment, and, second, he excludes the false trust that they will escape it, where he states: "Thus says the Lord: Let not the wise person boast in wisdom" (9:23a). Regarding the first part there are three points. First he presents the devastation of the lands. Second, he presents the affliction of humans where he states: "Therefore, thus says the Lord: [Behold I will feed this people with wormwood]" (9:15a). Third, he presents the discarding of corpses, where he says: "Speak: Thus says the Lord, [even human carcasses shall fall like dung in the open country]" (9:22a).

Regarding the first of the two: first he makes a pronouncement about the destruction of the land, specifying that the things occupying the land will be destroyed by fire: **Because they are burned up** (9:10b). Joel 1:19: "To you, O Lord, I will cry, because fire has consumed the beautiful places of the wilderness, and flames have consumed all the trees of the country." **There is not a man who passes through** (9:10c). Above, 4:25: "I looked, and there were no humans, and all the birds of the air were gone." **And they have not heard the voice of the owner** (9:10d), because the owner is no longer able to go there. And with respect to the cities: **And I will cause Jerusalem to become heaps of sand** (9:11a). Isaiah 17:1: "Behold, Damascus will cease to be a city, and it will be in ruins, as a pile of stones." Second, he provides the reason. First, he asks a question: **Who is the man who can understand this** on his own, **and to whom the word of the mouth of the Lord may come,** so he can understand it through revelation? (9:12a). Isaiah 42:23: "Who is there among you to hear and pay attention to this, and listen in the future?" Second, he offers the response: **And the Lord said,** regarding their turning away, **Because they have forsaken [my law],** they were not persistent in meditating on it. **They did not listen;** they were not quick to obey it. **They have not walked [in it];** they were not effective in fulfilling it (9:13). First Maccabees 1:62–63: "Many of the people of Israel determined with themselves that they would not eat unclean things, and they chose to die rather than to be defiled with unclean foods, and they would not break God's holy law, and they were put to death." And with respect to their conversion (9:14): They refused. They followed their own depraved wishes and followed **Baalim,** which is plural in number and masculine in gender. Ecclesiasticus 18:30: "Do not go after your lusts, but turn away from your own will."

9:15–22 This section threatens punishment inflicted on the people themselves. First, he specifies the extent of affliction that is their punishment: **I will feed them with wormwood** (9:15b), with the tribulations that they endured from the Chaldeans; **[and give them gall] as drink** (9:15c), because the Egyptians' aid would be changed into bitterness for them—the aid with which they believed they would escape tribulations—just as food is easily spoiled by drink. Lamentations 3:15: "He has filled me with bitterness. He has inebriated me with wormwood." And regarding their captivity: **I will scatter them** (9:16a). And regarding their slaughter: **And first I will send [the sword]** (9:16b). Ezekiel 5:2: "You shall scatter a third part into the wind, and you shall unsheathe the sword after them."

Second, he invites sorrow for mourning: **Thus says the Lord** (9:17a). And first he calls for mourning women, according to the custom of the Judeans, so they might provoke weeping: **Call for the mourning women** (9:17b). This custom is mentioned below in 22:18: "They will not lament for him, saying: 'Alas, my lord,' or, 'Alas, your majesty.'" And in Luke 23:28:

"Daughters of Jerusalem, do not weep for me, but for yourselves and for your children." Second, he presents the command to weep, first by ordering the people present to mourn: **Let our eyes shed tears** (9:18b). Lamentations 2:18: "Let tears run down like a torrent day and night, and give yourself no rest, and do not let your eyes have respite." And foretelling the future, as though the event were already occurring: **For a voice [of wailing] was heard** (9:19a) through the prophetic spirit. Or he uses the past tense for the future. And he assigns the reason in the voice of the mourners in Zion: **How are we destroyed** (9:19b), due to the devastation of the region, **and greatly confounded,** due to slavery? **We have forsaken [the land]** due to captivity (9:19c). Above in 4:13: "Woe to us, for we are destroyed." Second, he orders the mourning women themselves to mourn: **Therefore, women, listen to the word of the Lord** (9:20a). Isaiah 32:9: "Rise up, you wealthy women, and listen to my voice," etc. And he specifies the reason: **For death has come up [through our windows, it has entered into our houses]** (9:21a). That is, the Chaldeans are bringing death. This verse indicates the speed and strength of those who were not satisfied to enter through the doors, so they climbed up through the roof and windows. Joel 2:9: "They shall climb up the houses and enter through the windows like a thief."

9:22 This passage presents the punishment against the corpses themselves, which remained unburied, **like grass** that is despised by the person mowing it, like something worthless.

The Uselessness of Boasting in Human Strength

9:23-26 This passage excludes the false trust in escape: **Let not [the wise person] boast,** believing that one can thus free oneself, **in wisdom,** which, among humans, is the soul's highest good; **in strength,** which, among humans, is the body's highest good; or **in riches,** which are the most important goods in external things (9:23). First Samuel 2:3: "Do not continue to speak of lofty things, boasting." And he shows what true faith is: **Let the one who boasts, boast in this—in understanding,** through intellectual cognition, **and knowing [me]** through the experience of sweetness in emotions (9:24a). Psalm 61 [62:7]: "In God is my salvation and my glory, and my hope is in God." Second Corinthians 10:17: "Let the one who boasts, boast in the Lord." And he indicates the reason: **For I am the Lord, who works mercy,** so I might liberate you; **and judgment,** so I might vanquish your enemies; **and justice,** so that there might be fairness. **[These things]** among you **are pleas-**

ing [to me] (9:24). Micah 6:8: "I will show you, O human, what is good, and what the Lord requires of you: truly, to do justice, and to love mercy, and to walk humbly with your God."

Second, he excludes trust in ceremonial laws, especially circumcision, which is the most important and, indeed, originates with their ancestors; for it is imperfect, since it is only in the flesh and not in their heart. For this reason they are punished together with the uncircumcised: **Behold the days are coming, [says the Lord, that I will visit upon everyone whose foreskin is circumcised]** (9:25). Acts 7:51: "You stiff-necked people, uncircumcised in ears and hearts, you have always resisted the Holy Spirit."

Collations on Boasting in Human Wisdom, Strength, and Riches

Note that a human should not boast in wisdom, because it is transitory. Isaiah 29:14: "The wisdom of their wise people will perish, and the discernment of the discerning will be hidden" because it is imperfect. Ecclesiastes 8:17: "I understood that no one can discover knowledge of all the works of God that are done under the sun," because it is harmful. First Corinthians 8:1: "Knowledge puffs up, but love builds up." For knowledge is laborious. Ecclesiastes 1:18: "In much wisdom there is much vexation, and the one who adds knowledge also adds labor."

Likewise, one ought not to boast in strength, because it is weak. Job 6:12: "My strength is not the strength of stones, nor is my flesh bronze," for it is often helpless. Ecclesiastes 9:11: "I saw that, under the sun, the race is not to the swift, nor the battle to the strong, nor bread to the wise, nor riches to the learned, nor favor to the skillful, but in all things it happens according to time and chance," because strength is not acceptable to God. Psalm 146 [147:10]: "[God] shall not take delight in the strength of a horse nor take pleasure in the legs of a man," because strength is an occasion for sin. Wisdom 2:11: "But let our strength be the law of justice, for what is weak proves to be useless."

Likewise one ought not to boast in riches, because they are transitory. James 5:2: "Your riches are rotted, and your clothing is moth-eaten." For riches are inadequate. Proverbs 17:16: "What does it profit a fool to have riches, since it is not possible to purchase wisdom?" For [riches] hinder God's word. Matthew 13:22: "The deceitfulness of riches chokes the word, and it is rendered fruitless," because riches are harmful. Ecclesiastes 5:13: "Riches are gathered, to the harm of their owner."

Chapter Eleven

God Charges the People with Breaking the Covenant

11:1-6 This section shows the people's dignity, since they were joined with God by entering into the covenant. First he presents the covenant and threatens punishment for transgressors. Second, he makes an argument regarding the justice of one taking vengeance, in 12:1: "You indeed are just, O Lord." Regarding the first of the two: first, he sets forth the covenant; second, the transgression of the covenant, where he states: "Summoning, I appealed to your ancestors" (11:7).

Regarding the first of the two: first the prophet is brought in to make an announcement: **Hear [the words of this covenant],** you and those with you, who are noble and privileged (11:2a). **And you shall say to them** (11:4a). Regarding this covenant, Ezek 16:8: "I covered your disgrace, and I swore an oath to you, and I entered into a covenant with you, says the Lord God, and you became mine." Second, the people are brought in to observe. First he sets forth two arguments. The first argument deals with the punishment of transgressors: **Cursed is the man [who will not listen to the words of this covenant]** (11:3b). Deuteronomy 27:26a: "Cursed be the man who will not abide in the words of this law or fulfill them in deeds." And then he points out justice: **On the day that I led them from the land of Egypt,** as if to say, It is just to punish those who acted ungratefully after so many blessings; **from the furnace,** referring to their affliction, **made of iron** (11:4b), because the tyranny was so inflexible. Deuteronomy 4:20: "For the Lord took you and brought you out of the iron furnace of Egypt to make you a people of inheritance, as it is to this present day." And he sets forth the covenant's format: **Saying** that God seeks something, namely, obedience. **Listen [to my voice and do all I command you]** (11:4c), and God promises something, namely, the glory of divine familiarity. **You will be my people, and I will be your God** (11:4d). Above, Jer 7:23: "This I commanded them saying, 'Listen to my voice, and I will be your God, and you will be my people.'"

Second, he offers an argument based on the reward for those who observe [the covenant]: **That I may accomplish [the oath that I swore to your ancestors],** because it has practically disappeared due to imminent captivity, **[to give them a land flowing with] milk,** because of the abundance of animals, **[and] honey,** because of the abundance of produce from the earth (11:5a). Or [milk and honey] indicate hyperbolically the abundance of all good things. Deuteronomy 6:3: "You shall be multiplied greatly, just as the Lord God of your ancestors promised you a land flowing with milk and honey."

Then it presents the prophet's assent: **I answered [and said], "Amen"** (11:5b). That is: "Indeed, I will do what I promised." Or: "Let the things that you are promising be done." Deuteronomy 27:26: "And let all the people say, 'Amen.'" Third, he concludes that they should observe [the covenant]: **And the Lord said [to me: Proclaim aloud all these words in the cities of Judah, and the streets of Jerusalem, saying: "Hear the words of the covenant, and do them"]** (11:6). Isaiah 40:9: "Lift up your voice with strength."

11:7-10 This section shows how they transgressed the covenant: first, by sinning against God; second, by sinning against the prophet, where he asserts: "But you, O Lord, have shown me, and I have known" (11:18). Regarding the first of the two: first, he presents their guilt; second, he threatens punishment: "For this reason, thus says the Lord, [I will bring evils upon them]" (11:11). Regarding the first matter, there are three points.

First, he extends a loving admonition. First because of the oath: **Summoning** (11:7a), as though adjuring them; then because of the length of time: **On the day that I brought [them out of the land of Egypt]** (11:7b). Then because of the timely opportunity: **Rising early in the morning** (11:7c) when a person is more prepared to understand. Jeremiah 7:13, above: "And I spoke to you, rising up early and speaking."

Second, he presents the transgression of the disobedient people: **And they did not listen** (11:8a). Isaiah 56:11: "All have turned aside into their own way. Each and every one of them has turned aside to their own gain, from the greatest of them to the least."

Third, he presents the stubbornness that aggravates their guilt: **And I brought upon them [all the word of this covenant]** (11:8b), because they were corrected through neither the punishments nor the blessings contained in the covenant of the law declared to them. Proverbs 1:24-26: "Because I called but you refused, and I stretched out my hand but no one paid attention, and you despised all my counsels and ignored my rebukes, therefore I too will laugh at your destruction and mock when the thing you feared will come upon you." Since there was a conspiracy: **A conspiracy is found [among the men of Judah]** (11:9b). In other words, they all sinned together, as though they conspired to do this, for a conspiracy is an agreement to do something, confirmed by an oath. Isaiah 8:12: "All that this people speaks is a conspiracy." Since it was their habit: **They turned back [to their ancestors'**

former iniquities] (11:10a). Hosea 7:16: "They turned back so that they could be without a yoke. They became like a crooked bow."

Fourth, he concludes: **They made [my covenant] void** (11:10b). Hosea 6:7: "But they, like Adam, have transgressed the covenant. They dealt treacherously with me." Proverbs 2:17: "She forsakes the guide of her youth, and she has forgotten the covenant of her God."

11:11–17 This passage speaks against their incorrigible guilt and warns that punishment is inescapable. First he presents the punishment: **Behold, I [will bring evils upon them]** (11:11a). Isaiah 24:18: "The one who extracts oneself from the pit will be captured in the snare." Second, he closes off the possibility of escape; first, because their own prayers poured out to God will not aid them: **They shall cry to me, but I will not listen to them** (11:11b). Proverbs 1:28: "They will call upon me, but I will not listen. Nor will prayers poured out to idols aid them: **And the cities of Judah [and inhabitants of Jerusalem] will go [and cry to the gods to whom they offer sacrifice, and they shall not save them in the time of their affliction]** (11:12). Isaiah 45:20: "They have no knowledge—those who set up the wood of the sculpture and pray to a lord who cannot save them." And they add a multitude of idols: **For according to the number of your cities were your gods, O Judah** (11:12a). Ezekiel 16:24–25: "You made for yourself a brothel house on every street. At the head of every road, you built a sign of your prostitution." He states the same thing above in 2:28. Nor shall the prayers of someone else aid them: **As for you, do not pray for this people, and do not offer praise for them** (11:14) in order that you might call forth my mercy by praising me as merciful. First Samuel 16:1: "How long will you mourn over Saul, since I have rejected him from reigning over Israel?" Jeremiah 7:16 states the same thing.

Second, he claims that the offering of sacrifices will not aid them and explains the reason for the disapproval: **What does it mean that my beloved,** the people of Judah, **[has done so much wickedness] in my house,** by worshipping idols there in the temple? (11:15a). Ezekiel 8:6: "Son of man, what do you think when you see what these people are doing, the great abominations that the house of Israel is committing, to make me depart far away from my sanctuary?" And he mentions the disapproval of their sacrifices: **Shall holy flesh** of sacrificed animals **[take away your crimes]?** (11:15b). Hebrews 10:4: "It is impossible for sins to be taken away by the blood of bulls and goats."

Third, he shows that their own strength will not aid them, and on this matter there are two points. First he recalls their former glory: **An olive tree, plentiful,** with an abundance of branches in which the multitude of people are sealed; **fair,** green in color, blooming with prosperity, flourishing with the soul's virtues; **fruitful,** with a great quantity of fruit and an abundance of good and great works; **beautiful,** with its parts gracefully arranged, indicating the orderliness required of the people. [The Lord] **called [you by this name],** so that such a great reputation would come forth from you (11:16a). Hosea 14:6: "His glory will be like the olive tree, and his fragrance like that of Lebanon."

Second, he announces future punishment; first by mentioning the punishment itself: **At the sound of a [great] voice,** at Nebuchadnezzar's command, **a fire was kindled in it,** in the vineyard that is the house of Israel. **[Its] branches [are burned]** (11:16b). Understood according to the literal sense, this refers to humans and their belongings. Or **a great voice** means: "I expected lofty things from you because of your distinguished calling, and therefore you have deserved punishment." Isaiah 27:4: "I will march against [the vineyard] in battle. I will burn it together." Second, he mentions the power of the one inflicting punishment: **The Lord of Hosts** (11:17a). First Samuel 2:6: "The Lord puts to death and brings to life. He casts down to hell and brings back again," etc. Third, he mentions the cause: **Because of the evils [of the house of Israel and the house of Judah]** (11:17b). Deuteronomy 32:21: "They provoked me with something that was no god, and they vexed me with their vanities, and so I will provoke them with that which is no people, and I will vex them with a foolish nation."

Jeremiah's Persecution Prefigures Christ's Suffering

11:18-23 This passage shows how they transgressed by sinning against the prophet himself. According to the literal sense, this pertains to Jeremiah who drew the people's hatred because of the evil events he foretold. But Jeremiah's persecution prefigures Christ's passion, as the *Gloss* on this passage asserts.[1] Now when the *Gloss* claims we should regard this as applying to the person of Christ rather than Jeremiah, it seems to contradict the earlier statement, etc. However, all the prophets prefigure Christ to a great extent, so something that is fulfilled in Jeremiah during his time was also prophesied regarding Christ in the future. Regarding this, there are three points.

First, the prophet makes a statement about his enemies' guilt, and, first of all, the revelation about their shared guilt: **[You, O Lord,] have**

1. *Glossa ordinaria* on Jer 11:13, PL 114:27.

shown me, through an interior revelation, **[and then] you displayed,** through external signs, **their doings,** their plots against me (11:18). Isaiah 8:11–12: "With a strong arm, he taught me that I should not walk in the way of this people [and he said: Do not say, 'A conspiracy,' for all that this people speaks is a conspiracy]." And then he states why the revelation is needed, since he was not able to know this on his own by thinking about it, nor did he suspect it, because he was innocent and did not deserve such things: **And I was like a lamb, and I did not know** (11:19a). Christ also, according to his earthly humanity, received this knowledge from God—all the things that he knew through the grace of union,[2] just as others receive the things they know through the grace of revelation. Isaiah 53:7: "Like a lamb silent before its shearers, he shall not open his mouth." First Corinthians 2:11: "For who knows a person's affairs except the spirit of the person within?" Psalm 93 [94:11]: "The Lord knows a human's thoughts, that they are empty." **Let us throw wood [on his bread],** that is, yew, so that he might die of poisoning. **Let us erase him [from the land of the living],** so that no memory of him remains, just like a writing tablet whose previous writing was erased (11:19b). Interpreted spiritually, **Let us throw wood [on his bread]** refers to the body of Christ on the wood of the cross. Or, **wood on bread** means: Let us set up a stumbling block for his teaching, which is bread, by means of the wood of the cross. Isaiah 53:8: "Because he is cut off from the land [of the living]."

Second, the prophet asks for vengeance, naming the authority and power through which God can do this: **But you, Lord of Sabaoth,** that is, of hosts (11:20a). The prophet mentions justice, through which the one **who judges justly** exercises his will; and knowledge with which God knows: **And you test the kidneys,** that is, the affections, **and the hearts,** that is, the thoughts; **let me see your revenge on them** (11:20b). This is spoken in the person of Christ, who prayed for others, even when they were obstinate. Luke 23:34: "Father, forgive them, for they do not know what they do." Lamentations 3:59: "O Lord, you have seen their wickedness against me. Judge my cause." And he provides the reason: **I have revealed it to you** (11:20c), not as if you do not already know, but I am entrusting my entire cause to you. Psalm 54 [55:22]: "Cast your concerns on the Lord, and he will take care of you."

2. The divine and human natures united in one person, the Son; or the Son's union with God the Father. For a discussion of the grace of union, see Thomas Aquinas, *Summa theologiae* 3, q. 2, a. 12.

Third, the Lord threatens punishment, and first he returns to the topic of their wickedness. **Therefore, thus says the Lord to the men of Anathoth who seek your life** in order to kill you (11:21a). Psalm 37 [38:12]: "Those who sought my soul used violence." And he adds the cause of this wickedness: **And they said, "You will not prophesy"** (11:21b). In other words: "You will be able to escape death only if you stop prophesying." Isaiah 30:10: "They say to the seers, 'Do not see.'" Second, he threatens punishment; first by foretelling the visitation: **Therefore, thus says the Lord: [I will visit upon them]** (11:22a). Psalm 88 [89:32]: "I will visit their iniquities with a rod, and their sins with scourges." Second, he presents the outcome of the punishment: **Their young men [shall die by the sword]** (11:22b). Jeremiah 15:2 below asserts: "Those destined for the sword shall go to the sword; those destined for famine shall go to famine." Third, he states the power of the one punishing: **For I**, the one who has the power to do this, **will bring evil [upon the men of Anathoth]** (11:23b). Below, 17:18: "Bring upon them the day of affliction, and destroy them with a double destruction." Understood according to the spiritual sense, the men of Anathoth, which is translated as "obedience," signify the men of Jerusalem who once were obedient to the Lord and later persecuted Christ.

Collation on How Holy People May Be Compared to Olive Trees

Note that a holy person is called an olive tree. The olive's richness is the holy person's devotion. Romans 11:17: "You are made partakers in the rich root of the olive tree." The luster from its oil is contemplation. Zechariah 4:14: "These are the two anointed ones [literally, 'children of oil'] who stand before the Lord of the whole earth." First Kings 6:23: "In the inner sanctuary he made two cherubim from olivewood, ten cubits high." The greenness of its leaves is mental virtue. Genesis 8:11: "The dove returned in the evening carrying in its mouth an olive branch with green leaves." Its fruitfulness is the abundance of good works. Psalm 51 [52:8]: "But I, like a fruitful olive tree in the house of God, have hoped in God's mercy forever and ever." Its beauty is the glory of the saints. Ecclesiasticus 24:14: "I was lifted up like a beautiful olive tree in the fields, and like a plane tree by the water." Hosea 14:6: "His glory will be like the olive tree, and his fragrance like that of Lebanon."

Chapter Fourteen

Jeremiah's Prayer for the People during the Drought

14:1-5 Here the prophet begins to intervene with his prayer to God on their behalf, that, after some punishments, they might at least obtain some mercy. This section is divided into two parts. The first part presents the prophet's argument with God, asking God to accomplish something. Eventually, the second part presents the final answer. Jeremiah 15:1: "And the Lord said to me," etc. Regarding the first point, there are two parts. The first presents the affliction of the people, which is the occasion for the prayer. The second presents the prophet's argument with God, where it states: "If our iniquities have testified against us" (14:7).

Regarding the first part, there are two points. The first presents the term used for prophecy, which is the **word [*verbum*]** of interior revelation **that came regarding the messages [*sermonibus*],** the external announcements, **of the drought** that was coming upon them when their captivity was imminent (14:1). Or, **regarding the messages of the drought** means: with messages appropriate for the occasion of the drought. The second describes the great difficulty caused by the drought: first, with respect to human affliction—how the scarcity of drink brought about sorrow. **Judah has mourned, afflicted with thirst** (14:2a). Isaiah 24:7: "The grape harvest has mourned, the vine has withered, and all the merry-hearted have sighed." **The gates**—the judges who sat in the gates—**have fallen** from their earlier joy, and **they are obscured,** covered by the shadow of tribulation (14:2b). Lamentations 2:9: "Her gates have sunk into the ground. He has destroyed and broken her bars." Or, the city wall was crumbling because it was too dried out, so the gates were falling down, since they were not able to be repaired due to the water shortage. **The outcry** of complaint and lament **[is going up]** (14:2c). Isaiah 24:11: "There will be an outcry for wine in the streets. All rejoicing is abandoned. The earth's joy is taken away." And [the prophet] explains the reason for the sadness: **Nobles sent their inferiors to the water; [they came to draw water and, finding none, they carried their vessels back empty]** (14:3a). Isaiah 41:17: "The needy and the poor search for water, and there is none. Their tongues became dry with thirst." And because of the earth's barrenness, which is an attack against their possessions: **They were dismayed and afflicted, and they covered their heads,** as a sign of their dismay (14:3b). Jeremiah 12:13 asserts: "You shall be dismayed about your fruits, because of the fierce wrath of the Lord." And regarding those who cultivate the land:

Because no rain came [the farmers were dismayed] (14:4b). Joel 1:11: "The farmers were dismayed, the vinedressers howled over the wheat and barley, because the field's harvest has perished, the vineyard is ruined, and the fig tree has withered."

Second, he mentions the affliction of the woodland animals. Regarding the deer: **For even the doe,** which is extremely solicitous in taking care of her offspring, **gave birth in the field and abandoned it [because there was no grass]** (14:5). Job 39:1: "Do you know the time when the mountain goats give birth among the rocks, or have you observed deer when they fawn?" And regarding the wild donkeys: **And the wild donkeys,** which are able to endure thirst for a long time (as Psalm 103 [104:11] states, "the wild donkeys shall wait in their thirst"), **on the rocks,** where there is more wind, **inhaled [the wind]** to cool their thirst **like dragons,** who inhale wind because they are thirsty (14:6). Jeremiah 2:24 above says: "A wild donkey accustomed to the wilderness in her soul's desire, inhaled the wind of her lover."

14:7-12 Here the prophet begins to pray to God for the people. First he introduces an argument for mercy based on the divine disposition; second, an argument based on the pronouncement of the prophets, where he says: "And I said: Ah, ah, ah!" (14:13); third, an argument based on God's former love for the people, where it says: "Have you cast Judah away utterly?" (14:19). Regarding the first part, there are two points.

First it presents the prophet's prayer, in which he states three things. He acknowledges God's mercy: **If our iniquities have testified against us,** saying we should be punished, **[act for your name's sake]** (14:7). Isaiah 59:12: "Our iniquities are multiplied before you, and our sins have testified against us," etc. Psalm 45 [46:1]: "A helper in troubles, which are great." Then he mentions God's constancy: **Why will you be like a tenant in the land?** (14:8b). In other words: It is not worthy of your constancy that you abandon your vineyard like a tenant abandoning someone else's field; **like a traveler** treating your own home as though you were a traveler spending the night in lodgings. **Why will you be like a wandering man,** treating your own inheritance as though you were a vagrant, treating your own home like temporary lodgings? **(14:8c-9a).** Jeremiah 12:7 above states: "I have forsaken my house, I have abandoned my inheritance." Jeremiah also mentions God's power: **And like a mighty person who cannot save** (14:9b). In other words: It is unworthy of your power that you do not save those whom you once took into your protection. Numbers 14:16: "The Egyptians might say, 'He could not bring the people into the land that he swore to them, so he killed them in the wilderness.'" And Jeremiah asserts that God has an obligation to care for them: **But you are among us,** your inheritance, **and your name [is called upon],** just as subjects are protected under the name of the king (14:9c). Second Corinthians 6:16: "I will dwell in them, and I will walk among them, and I will be their God, and they shall be my people." And he concludes: **Do not forsake us,** lest your constancy and power be blasphemed (14:9d). Psalm 26 [27:9]: "Do not forsake me, and do not despise me, O God my salvation."

Second, he presents God's response: **Thus says the Lord** (14:10a). First he acknowledges their guilt: **Those who loved to move their feet** (14:10b). This refers to their inclinations, because they do not remain in what is good, and they go from evil to evil. Proverbs 7:11: "A wandering woman, refusing to be quiet, unable to keep her feet at home." Or he refers to their sending to Egypt for help. Isaiah 30:7: "Egypt shall help in vain, and to no purpose. Therefore I have cried out about this: 'It is only pride. Sit still.'" Second, he threatens punishment: **Then he will remember [their iniquities]** (14:10c), implying punishment. Psalm 88 [89:32]: "I will visit their iniquities with a rod, and their sins with scourges." Third, he excludes the possibility of a remedy. First he excludes the remedy of prayers: **And the Lord said: Do not pray for this people for their good** (14:11). Jeremiah 7:16 states: "Therefore, do not pray for this people, do not offer praise on their behalf, or prayer. And do not resist me, because I will not hear you." Second, he excludes the remedy of fasting: **When they fast [I will not hear their prayers]** (14:12a). Isaiah 58:3: "Why have we fasted and you have not paid attention? And why have we humbled our souls and you have not noticed?" Third, he excludes the remedy of sacrifice: **If they offer [burnt offerings and sacrifices, I will not receive them]** (14:12b). Malachi 1:10: "I take no pleasure in you, says the Lord of Hosts, and I will not accept a gift from your hand."

14:13-18 Here the text presents an argument based on the pronouncement from the prophets. First it presents the prophet's cry, "**Ah, ah, ah,**" because of the threefold punishment that was just discussed. **The prophets** falsely **[say to them, "God will give you] true peace** that is lasting and not feigned by your enemies" (14:13a). Jeremiah 4:10 above says: "Have you deceived this people and Jerusalem, saying, 'You shall have peace'? Behold, the sword reaches even to the soul." Then Jeremiah presents the Lord's response: **And the Lord said** (14:14a). First, he shows the falsehood of the prophets, regarding the action that they were undertaking: **I did not send them** to relate this; **I did not command them** to take up this duty; **nor did I speak,** inspiring them with the gift of prophecy (14:14b). Below, in 23:21: "I did not send

179

prophets, yet they ran. I have not spoken to them, yet they prophesied." And regarding the peace that they predicted: **A lying vision, a seduction of the heart,** words contrived to lead them astray (14:14c). Ezekiel 13:6: "They see vain things, and they foretell lies, saying, 'The Lord says,' when the Lord has not sent them."

Second, he threatens punishment—both against the prophets making the proclamations as well as the people who believe them: "Therefore, thus says the Lord" (15:1a). Isaiah 9:16: "Those who called the people blessed, causing them to err, and those who are called blessed are cast down headlong."

Third, the prophet announces compassion for the people: **And you shall say to them: Let my eyes**—or, *your* **eyes—shed tears** (14:17a).[3] And thus he mentions penitential lamentation. Lamentations 2:18: "Let tears stream down like a torrent." He then provides the reason for this: **Because [the virgin daughter of my people is afflicted with a great] affliction,** on account of the multitude of people slaughtered, **with [a misfortune] that is exceedingly grievous,** because it is unalterable and ongoing (14:17b). Isaiah 30:14: "With a mighty affliction, I will smash them like a potter's vessel." And he indicates the type of affliction—punishment of slaughter. **If I go forth,** abroad, **[behold, those slaughtered with the sword]. And if I enter [the city]** to look, **[behold, those consumed with famine]** (14:18a). Lamentations 1:20: "Abroad the sword will destroy, and at home there is terror, for the young man together with the maiden, the nursing child together with the elderly person."[4] And regarding the captivity: **The prophet also [and the priest have gone into a land that they did not know]** (14:18b). Jeremiah 9:16 above states: "I will scatter them into nations that they and their parents did not know."

14:19-22 Here the prophet presents an argument based on God's former love for the people. Regarding this there are three points. First, he is astonished at the rejection of the beloved people, and he is surprised at the hatred: **Have you really cast away Judah?** (14:19a). It is as though he were saying: This seems astonishing. The conclusion of Lamentations (5:22): "But you have utterly rejected us. You are exceedingly angry against us." **[Why have**

---

3. The Vulgate, following the Hebrew text, reads "my eyes." Probably drawing from Jerome's commentary, Aquinas provides an alternative reading "your eyes," which follows the Septuagint. See Jerome, *Commentary on Jeremiah*, trans. Michael Graves, ed. Christopher A. Hall, Ancient Christian Texts (Downers Grove, IL: IVP Academic, 2011), 92n132.

4. The first portion of the quotation ("Abroad the sword will destroy") comes from Lam 1:20. The remainder is from Deut 32:25.

you struck us,] so that there is no healing? (14:19b). Isaiah 14:6: "With an incurable wound, subjecting nations in fury." Second, he recognizes the punishment: **We waited [for peace, and there is no good]** (14:19c). Above, 8:15: "We waited for peace, and there was nothing good; for a time of healing, but, behold, terror." And he recognizes guilt: **We have acknowledged [O Lord, our wickedness]** (14:20a). Psalm 50 [51:3]: "I recognize my wickedness, and my sin is always before me." Third, he presents a petition. **Do not make us [a reproach]** (14:21a). Psalm 43 [44:13]: "You have made us a reproach to our neighbors, a laughingstock and source of derision among those around us." Fourth, he gives the reason for the petition as the temple's holiness: [**Do not disgrace] the throne of your glory,** that is, the mercy seat, and the ark, in which you showed that you are glorious through miracles and revelations (14:21b). Below in 17:12: "O glorious throne, exalted from the beginning, the place of our sanctification, the hope of Israel." And an argument based on the powerlessness of idols: **Are there any of the carvings that can send rain? Or can the heavens provide rain showers,** by themselves as the primary cause? (14:22a). Job 5:10: "Who is the father of the rain, or who gives birth to the drops of dew?" And an argument based on God's power: **Are you not our God? You have made these things**—the rains, and all things of this sort (14:22b). Above, in 10:13: "At his voice there is a multitude of waters in the heavens, and he makes the mists to rise from the ends of the earth."

Collation on True and False Peace

We should note that there is such a thing as "false peace." Wisdom 14:22: "Since they live in a war of great ignorance, they call so many and such great evils 'peace.'" And a "treacherous peace," as Ps 27 [28:3] asserts: "They speak peace with their neighbor but have evil in their hearts." And a "transitory peace," as in the last chapter of 1 Thessalonians (5:3): "For when they say, 'Peace and security,' then unexpected destruction will come upon them."

Collation on the Spiritual Meanings of the Word "Throne"

Also note that, interpreted spiritually, the meaning of "throne" (14:21b) is threefold. There is a "throne of glory," so called for four reasons. Because of its natural loftiness, as Isa 6:1–3 asserts: "Behold the Lord, seated on the throne high and lifted up, and the entire earth was full of his majesty." Because of its peaceful tranquility, as above in 3:17: "They will call Jerusalem 'the throne of the Lord,' and all nations will be gathered to it in Jerusalem in the name of the Lord," etc. Because of its profound knowledge, as Ezek 10:1 states: "And I looked, and, behold, in the firmament over the heads of the cherubim, there was something like a sapphire stone, and over them appeared something resembling a throne." Because of its eternal duration, as in the final chapter of Lamentations (5:19): "But you, O Lord, will remain forever, and your throne from generation to generation."

Another throne is the "throne of mercy," of someone prepared for obedience to God, as Isa 22:23–24 says: "And I will fasten him like a peg in a secure place, and he will be as a throne of glory for the house of his father. And on him I will hang all of his father's glory." And of someone prepared to render justice, as in Prov 16:12: "The king's throne is established by justice." And of someone prepared for compassion toward neighbors, as Isa 16:5 says: "And a throne will be prepared in mercy, and one shall sit upon it in truth in the tent of David." And of someone prepared for the grace of humility, as Ezek 43:7 says: "The place of my throne, and the place of my footprints, where I dwell in the midst of the children of Israel forever."

And, in fact, there is a "throne of justice" of someone prepared for arbitration, as in Job 23:3: "Who will grant me the ability to know and find him, and come even to his throne?" And for the correction of evil, as Prov 20:8 says: "The king who sits on the throne of justice scatters away all evil with his gaze." And for condemning those who refuse to be corrected, as 1 Kgs 22:19 says: "I saw the Lord sitting on his throne, and all the army of heaven standing beside him, to the right and to the left." And for defending good things, as Isa 9:7 says: "He shall sit upon the throne of David and upon his kingdom, to establish it and strengthen it in judgment and justice, from this time onward and forevermore."

Chapter Fifteen

God Refuses to Have Pity on the People

15:1–4 Here the text presents the definitive rejection of the prophet's prayer for the people. First, it presents the rejection of the prayer; second, it presents the people's stubbornness, which is the cause of this rejection, as 17:1 states: "Judah's sin is written with an iron pen, with a diamond point." Regarding the first, there are two points. First, the Lord forbids the prophet to pray for the people. Second, the Lord orders him to shun their company, as though they were excommunicated, in 16:1–2: "And the word of the Lord came to me, saying: [You shall not take a wife, nor shall you have sons and daughters in this place]." Regarding the first point, there are two parts: first, it presents the rejection of prayer of the prophet who was praying for the people; second, as though despairing of the people's salvation, he pours out a prayer for himself, where he says: "Woe is me, my mother" (15:10).

Regarding the first part, there are two points. First, the prayer is rejected. Second the prophet gives the reason for the rejection: "For who will have pity on you, O Jerusalem?" (15:5). Regarding the first point, there are two parts: first, he presents the rejection of the prayer: **If Moses and Samuel** (who were efficacious in praying because they were solicitous about the people and made entreaties on account of enemies) **stood [before me]** (15:1b). He says this about Moses in Exod 32:11–14 and about Samuel in 1 Sam 12:19–25. **[My] soul,** my affection, **[is not toward this people]** (15:1c). It is as if he were saying: The reason the prayer is not heard is not because of the failure of the person doing the praying but because of the failure of the people for whom the prayer is offered. Ezekiel 14:14: "And even if these three men—Noah, Daniel, and Job—were in their midst, they would rescue only their own lives by their justice." And later in the same passage: "And if these three men were in their midst, they would not rescue sons or daughters, but only they themselves would be rescued" (Ezek 14:18).

Second, he presents the rejection of the people for whom the prayer was offered; and first, the starting point: **Cast them away,** show that they are cast away, **from my face,** so that they may not see me, and so they are not protected by my presence (15:1d). Genesis 4:14: "Behold, today you are casting me away from the face of the earth, and I shall be hidden from your face," etc. Second, at the conclusion, he presents a fourfold punishment: **And if they say to you: "Where shall we go?" you shall say to them: Those destined for death, to death** by disease; **[and those destined for the sword, to the sword; and those destined for famine, to famine; and those destined for captivity, to captivity]** (15:2). It is as though God were saying: Different people will be subjected to different punishments. Ezekiel 5:12: "One-third of you will die of disease and will be consumed by famine in your midst; one-third of you will fall by the sword around you; and one-third of you I will scatter into every wind, and I will unsheathe the sword after them." And, regarding the dead, God precludes the relief of the consolation of the grave: **I will visit you with four kinds** previously mentioned: death, sword, famine, and captivity; and, in addition to these, I will add dogs (15:3a). Jeremiah

7:33 above: "The carcasses of this people will be food for the birds of the air and the beasts of the earth, and there will be no one to drive them away." And regarding mercy for the captives: **And I will give them up to the rage,** that is, the raging hatred, **[of all the kingdoms of the earth] on account of Manasseh,** who did many evil things, (15:4), as we read in 2 Kgs 21:1-18. For this reason 2 Kgs 23:26 says the same thing: "But yet the Lord did not turn away from the fierceness of his great indignation, with which his anger was kindled against Judah because of the provocations with which Manasseh provoked him." Now people are punished for a king's sins in cases where a bad person is permitted to reign due to the people's sins. Job 34:12: "Who makes a hypocritical person reign due to the people's sins?" This refers to times when the people follow after the sins of the king. Ecclesiasticus 10:2: "As the ruler of a city is, so are its inhabitants." Proverbs 29:12: "If a prince gladly listens to lying words, all his officials will be wicked."

15:5-9 This section points out the reason for the rejection. In the first part, the prophet poses a question expressing astonishment. First, he precludes the judge's mercy: **Who will have pity?** (15:5a). Second, he precludes the encouragement of someone with compassion: **Or who will lament?** (15:5b). Third, he precludes the prayer of any sort of mediator: **Or who will go to pray,** since God rejected you and you have so much sin? (15:5c). Hosea 1:6: "Call her name 'No Mercy,' for I will no longer have mercy on the house of Israel, but I will utterly forget them."

Second, he points out the reason for the rejection. First, he places blame on their ingratitude: **You have forsaken [me]** (15:6a). Isaiah 1:4: "They have forsaken the Lord, they have blasphemed the Holy One of Israel, they have backslid and estranged themselves." And he mentions their punishment: **And I will stretch out my hand against you** (15:6b). Isaiah 9:12: "Despite all these things, his anger is not turned away, but his hand is stretched out still." Second, he blames their stubbornness, first because they are not persuaded by entreaties: **I am weary of begging** (15:6c). It is as if God were saying: I have begged you so many times to return to me that I would have been worn out if that were possible. Isaiah 43:24: "You have burdened me with your sins, you have wearied me with your iniquities." And he mentions their punishment: **And I will scatter them with a winnowing fan,** using the Chaldean army, as though the people were chaff from a threshing floor, **into the gates of the land** (15:7a); that is, to the outermost parts of the land, for a gate is the outermost part of a house or city. Luke 3:17: "His winnowing fan is in his hand, and he will clear his threshing floor, and he will gather the wheat into his barn but burn the chaff with unquenchable fire." Second, because they are not corrected by lashings.

First, he mentions the harshness, mentioning the lashings in a general way: **I have killed and destroyed [my people],** by giving them into captivity (15:7b). Jeremiah 2:30 above: "In vain I struck your children. They accepted no correction." And, in particular, he mentions how it affects the women, who are very miserable and pitiable when they lose their husbands: **Their widows are multiplied unto me, more than the sand [of the sea]** (15:8a). This is meant hyperbolically. In other words, they are innumerable. Isaiah 9:17: "Nor shall he have compassion on their orphans and widows." And when she loses her only child: **I have brought a destroyer,** the murderer of her child, **at noonday** (15:8b). This shows the power of the enemies who are fighting openly rather than ambushing them. **Suddenly** (15:8c). This shows their powerlessness to defend themselves because they were not on guard. Isaiah 30:13: "Destruction shall come suddenly, when it is unexpected," etc. And he even speaks of the death of many children at the same time, mentioning the death of offspring: **She is made weak,** deprived of her children who are a mother's strength (15:9a). And he mentions the sorrow of a mother: **Her soul has fainted away** because she is in shock. **The sun** of rejoicing **goes down for her,** because of the pain of her sorrow, which casts a shadow over her heart. **She is** inwardly **confounded** and outwardly **shamed,** for what she had boasted about has been taken away (15:9b). Amos 8:9: "Let the sun go down at midday, and I will darken the land in broad daylight." Second, he threatens punishment: **And those who remain** after the aforementioned lashings **[I will give to the sword]** (15:9c). Deuteronomy 28:25: "The Lord will hand you over defeated to your enemies, and you will go out against them by one road and you will flee from them by seven roads, and you will be scattered throughout all the kingdoms of the earth."

Jeremiah's Prayer for Himself

15:10-14 Here the prophet, as though despairing about the people, prays for himself. And first he presents his complaint, mentioning the discord of his enemies. **Woe is me, [my mother].** It is a shame that I was born! **[A man] of strife;** that is, a man on whose account there is strife since I am making pronouncements about crimes and evils. **[A man] of discord,** because some people are attacking me and others are defending me (15:10a). This was also fulfilled by Christ. Job 10:18: "Why did you bring me forth from the womb?

If only I had died before any eye had seen me." Discord especially arises from business contracts, and he has nothing to do with this cause of discord: **I have not lent money for interest, yet all people curse me** (15:10b). Psalm 108 [109:28]: "Let them curse, but you will bless. Let those who rise up against me be put to shame, but let your servant rejoice." Second, he presents the Lord's consolation: **The Lord says** (15:11a). First, he speaks of his own well-being, an increase in good things for himself and those belonging to him: **If your remnant,** those who adhere to you—for he did not have children, as noted above in chapter 16—will not be **well** (15:11b). This is *aposiopesis*.[5] You should supply the phrase: "Far be it from me." And regarding his rescue from evils: **If I do not hasten [to you]** ready to help (15:11c). Second Corinthians 1:3–4: "Blessed be the God and Father of our Lord Jesus Christ, the Father of mercies and the God of all consolation, who consoles us in all our afflictions."

Second, he deals with his adversaries' affliction, threatening them with an implacable enemy. And first, he removes the possibility of a peace agreement with the enemies, since they wanted to make peace with the prophet: **Shall** the Judean people, who are **iron** because of their hardness, **and brass** because of their impatience, **be allied with the iron from the north,** the Chaldeans? (15:12). In other words: No. Jeremiah 6:28–29 says: "Brass and iron, they are all corrupted. The bellows have failed; the lead is consumed in the fire." Or: "You [Jeremiah] are iron, preaching hard things. You are not able to be allied with those who are iron and brass." John 15:18: "Do not be surprised if the world hates you. For you should know that it hated me before hating you." Second, he removes the possibility of trust in an alliance secured by their gifts of tribute: **I will give away your riches and your treasures as plunder for nothing** (15:13). In other words: They will do you no good. **In all [your sins],** that is, because of all your sins. Nahum 2:9: "Plunder the silver. Plunder the gold. For there is an endless amount of riches, from all the precious vessels." Or [he removes the possibility of trust in an alliance] on account of their entreaties: **And I will bring [your enemies out of a land which you do not know]** (15:14a). It is as if he were saying: You will not be able to entreat them, because they will not understand. Isaiah 5:26: "He will raise a signal to the nations far away and whistle to the one that is at the ends of the earth." Third, he points out the reason: **For a fire is kindled** (15:14b). Deuteronomy 32:22: "A fire is kindled in my wrath, and it will burn even to the lowest hell, and it will devour the earth with its yield, and it will burn up the foundations of the mountains."

5. *Aposiopesis,* a rhetorical device, is an interruption or breaking-off in a speech.

15:15-18 Here the text presents the prophet's petition. First, it presents his own prayer, and second, the Lord's response, where it says: **Therefore, thus says the Lord** (15:19). Regarding the first part, there are three points. First, the prophet provides the solace of divine consolation, mentioning the divine knowledge: **You know** what I am enduring and what I have done. **Remember,** through your mercy (15:15a). Lamentations 3:19: "Remember my poverty and transgression, the wormwood and the gall." He asks for consolation: **And visit me** to console me (15:15b). Job 10:12: "Your visitation has preserved my spirit." And he rejects a delay: **Do not be patient [in supporting me]** (15:15c). Ecclesiasticus 5:4: "The Most High is a patient rewarder."

Second, he asserts his own merit, mentioning the hatred that he patiently sustained on God's account, as well as the bad treatment he endured: **Know**—show through your response that you know—**[that I endured reproach] on your account,** while I obeyed your commands and announced difficult things to the people (15:15d). Psalm 68 [69:7]: "Since for your sake I have suffered reproach. Shame has covered my face." And he mentions the spiritual delight of suffering: **[Your words] were found;** your deeds were fulfilled; **and I ate,** taking delight in them (15:16a). Psalm 118 [119:103]: "How sweet are your words to my taste, sweeter than honey to my mouth." He also provides the reason: **For your name is invoked upon me,** when I am called "the prophet of the Lord" (15:16b). Above, 14:9 says: "Your name is invoked upon us." He also speaks of the company that he wisely avoided, mentioning his solitude: **I did not sit in the company of merrymakers**—much less the company of evildoers—so that I would not depart from seriousness and so that I could devote my time to your commands (15:17a). Tobit 3:17: "I have never joined in with merrymakers, nor have I been a partaker with those who are frivolous." He mentions interior exaltation: **And I boasted because of the presence of your hand** that corrected me (15:17b).[6] Second Corinthians 12:9: "I will gladly boast about my weaknesses." Or it is the **hand** of the one who consoles him with spiritual gifts. He also provides the reason for his solitude: **I sat alone, because you filled me with threats** (15:17c). In other words: I was weighed down with so much bitterness that I did not have an opportunity to be merry. Lamentations 3:15: "He has filled me with bitterness."

6. The Latin text reads: *Non sedi in concilio ludentium, et gloriatus sum a facie manus tuae.* Aquinas chooses to read the second half of the sentence as an affirmation that Jeremiah boasted in God's presence. An alternative translation, the interpretation chosen by the Douay-Rheims translators, could be: "I did not sit in the company of merrymakers or boast in the presence of your hand."

Third, surprised at the sting of the sorrow that was inflicted, he mentions the sorrow: **Why has my sorrow become perpetual?** (15:18a). It is as if he were saying: After offering so many prayers and experiencing so much tribulation, why has my sorrow not gone away? Below, 30:12 says: "Your bruise is incurable, your wound is very grievous." According to the Jews, this is spoken in the *persona* of Jerusalem.[7] And he adds the consolation: **It became to me as the falsehood of treacherous waters** (15:18b). It is as if he were saying: Nevertheless, I take consolation in this, that eventually these tribulations will go away, just like treacherous waters that accumulate from rain showers. Psalm 68 [69:1]: "The waters have come in, all the way to my soul." Or he says this because of the treachery of his adversaries.

God's Response to Jeremiah's Prayer

15:19-21 Here he provides the response of the Lord who was understanding. First, the Lord promises success to those who are blessed, in proportion to the uprightness of their life: **If you turn** others **away** from their sins, toward me, **I will turn you away** from tribulations; **you will stand [before my face]** through uprightness of life or prominence in contemplation (15:19a). First Kings 17:1: "As the Lord lives, in whose sight I stand." The conclusion of James (5:20): "Those who cause sinners to be converted from the error of their way will rescue their own souls from death and shall cover a multitude of sins." And regarding the authority of preaching: **And if you separate the precious from the vile,** by distinguishing bad works from good works, **[you will be like] my mouth,** because I will speak through you (15:19b). Matthew 10:20: "For it is not you who speak, but the Spirit of your Father who is speaking in you."

Second, regarding rescue from wickedness: first, the Lord mentions rescue from the evils of guilt: **They themselves will be turned toward you [and you will not be turned to them]** (15:19c). In other words: They will imitate you, you will not imitate them. First Corinthians 4:16: "I beg you, be imitators of me, just as I am an imitator of Christ." Second, rescue from the evils of punishment: **And I will make you to be a strong wall of bronze for this people** (15:20a). Above, in 1:18-19: "I have made you a fortified city, and a pillar of iron, and a wall of bronze over all the land, to the kings of Judah

7. Jerome, *On Jeremiah* 15:17-18, ed. Sigofredus Reiter, CCSL 74 (Turnhout: Brepols, 1960), 152.

and its princes, to the priests and people of the land. And they will fight against you, and they will not prevail, for I am with you, says the Lord, to rescue you." Second, the Lord promises defense: **And they will fight against you [and they will not prevail]** (15:20b). Psalm 22 [23:4]: "Even though I walk in the midst of the shadow of death, I will fear no evils, for you are with me." Third, the Lord promises rescue: **I will rescue you [from the hand of the wicked]** (15:21a). Isaiah 43:1: "Do not fear, for I have redeemed you, and I have called you by your name."

Collation on How the Saints May Properly Boast

We should note that the saints boast in the good of virtue. They boast in the tribulation of suffering, as in Rom 5:3: "Not only this, but we also boast in tribulations." And they boast in the association with those who are close, as in 2 Cor 7:4: "I have great confidence in you, and I boast about you often." And in purity of conscience, as in 2 Cor 1:12: "This is our boast, the testimony of our conscience." Saints also boast in God, in the divine love shown through the passion, as in the final chapter of Galatians (6:14): "May I never boast, other than in the cross of our Lord Jesus Christ." And they boast in divine knowledge, as above in 9:24: "Let the one who boasts boast in this—in understanding and knowing me." And they boast in divine imitation, as in Ecclus 23:28: "For it is a great glory to follow the Lord, for length of days will be received from him."

Chapter Seventeen

Judah's Sin Written in Stone

17:1–10 Here the prophet clearly shows the stubbornness of the people, which is the cause of their rejection. So first, he shows their stubborn malice; second, the punishment brought to completion in 19:1: "Thus says the Lord," etc. Regarding the first point, there are two parts. In the first, he mentions the causes of the stubbornness. In the second, he proves with evidence the stubbornness itself, as it says in 18:1: "The word that came to Jeremiah from the Lord." The first point has two parts. In the first, he presents the reasons for the stubbornness; in the second, he calls them back to pure religious worship, where he says: "Thus says the Lord," etc. (17:5).

Regarding the first of the two: first he mentions one cause, their wicked disposition, and places the blame, offering an example: **The sin of Judah,** the two tribes, **is written.** That is, the imprint of their disposition is so deep, especially with respect to their idolatry, that it is like something written **with an iron pen, with a [diamond] point;** that is, written with diamond, which is a stone polished into the shape of a point (17:1a). Zechariah 7:12: "They made their heart like diamond stone so they would not listen to the law and the words that the Lord of Hosts sent in his Spirit by the hand of the earlier prophets." Or **sin** refers to the sentence of punishment for their sin. And he explains their disposition toward sin: **It is engraved,** that is, poured out, **upon the expanse [of their heart, and in the horns of their altars];** that is, upon a heart that has been stretched out by disposition toward sin (17:1b). So a heart that has been stretched out this way is parallel to "diamond" [in the preceding phrase], and the horns **of the altars** of the idols are parallel to "iron pens." For God ordered that four horns should proceed from the altar, from which a grate would hang down, as in Exod 27:5. And they constructed the same sort of thing on the altars of the idols. Hosea 8:11: "Ephraim multiplied for himself altars for sinning. Altars have become a cause of offense for him." It also serves as a sign, pointing out their character to the descendents who follow them: **When their children shall remember,** by maintaining devotion, in various places, to **altars** which were constructed in the cities (17:2a). Jeremiah 2:20 above: "Under every leafy tree you were prostrated on the ground like a prostitute."

And next he mentions the punishment, the plundering of their possessions needed to sustain life: **[I will give away your] strength,** that is, the possessions that you think make you strong, such as arenas and fortresses (17:3a). Jeremiah 15:13 above: "I will give away your riches and all your treasures as plunder for nothing, because of all your sins, throughout your territories." That is: When your wickedness has been so thoroughly accomplished that children imitate their parents by worshipping idols in every location, then **I will give your strength and your treasures as plunder** (17:3b). And also the possessions that pertain to idolatrous worship: **Your high places,** where they worshipped idols (17:3). Ezekiel 6:3-4: "Behold, I will bring a sword upon you and I will destroy your high places, and I will demolish your altars, and your statues will be broken into pieces, and I will throw down your slain in front of your idols." He also threatens captivity: **You will be stripped,** O Jerusalem, **of your inheritance,** stripped of your people when they are conquered (17:4a). Or: O nation, you will be stripped of the land when you go into captivity. Lamentations 1:1: "How lonely sits the city that once was full of people. She who ruled nations has become like a widow; the prince of the provinces has been made a vassal." He also threatens slavery: **And I will make you serve your enemies** (17:4b). Deuteronomy 28:48: "And you will serve your enemy, whom the Lord will send upon you, in hunger and thirst, and in nakedness, and in lack of everything. And he will put an iron yoke on your neck until he has destroyed you." And he mentions the proximate cause of the punishment, namely, divine anger, which is the inclination to inflict punishment: **Because you have kindled a fire [in my wrath]** (17:4:c). Deuteronomy 32:22: "A fire is kindled in my wrath, and it will burn even to the lowest hell." Second, he mentions another cause: trust that there will be escape from punishment: **Cursed be the person who trusts in humans** (17:5a).

Now they promised themselves that they would be free of punishment for three reasons. First, because of the power of their friends the Egyptians, and he deals with this first. Second, because of their vast riches; he deals with this where he says: **The partridge hatched eggs that she did not lay** (17:11a). Third, because of their disbelief in the divine warnings; he deals with this where he says: "Behold, they say to me, 'Where is the word of the Lord?'" (17:15a). Regarding the first, there are two points. First, he distinguishes between those who trust in the Lord and those who trust in humans. Second, he mentions the source of this distinction where it says: **The human heart is perverse** (17:9a). Regarding the first point, there are two parts.

First he places a curse on those who place their confidence in human help, where he presents the curse: **Cursed [be the person who trusts in humans],** beholden to someone who is wicked, **and makes flesh one's arm,** that is, one's strength (17:5a). It is irrational to place hope in this because human weakness is signified by flesh. **And [whose heart] departs from the Lord** (17:5b). Here he gives the reason for the curse: for it is permissible to place trust in humans as well as God, but not so much that God is forsaken. And he says this regarding the Judeans who despised God and placed their hope in the Egyptians. Isaiah 31:1: "Woe to those who go down to Egypt for help, trusting in horses and placing their faith in chariots because they are many, and in horsemen, because they are very strong; and they have not trusted in the Holy One of Israel and have not sought after the Lord." Psalm 145 [146:3]: "Do not trust in princes, in the children of humans, in whom there is no help." And he presents something resembling a curse: **That person will be like tamarisks,** which are considered worthless (17:6a). Symmachus translates it: "Like an unfruitful tree in the wilderness."[8] **That person will not see**

---

8. Jerome, *On Jeremiah* 17:5–6, CCSL 74:164.

[good arrive] (17:6b), because before the liberation from captivity, almost all of them will have died. **But that person will dwell** (17:6c). This part shows the horror of the place of captivity, not because the place itself was innately bad, but it was bad for those who were oppressed in slavery. **In dryness, in the desert,** because it was uncultivated and had dry air, which made the trees unfruitful, **in a salt [land]** (17:6d), which refers to the dryness of the land, caused by the sun's burning heat drying up the moisture. Psalm 106 [107:33]: "He turned rivers into a desert and springs of water into thirsty ground."

Second, he blesses those who trust in divine aid. First, the blessing: **Blessed is the man who trusts in the Lord and the Lord will be his confidence** (17:7), which means that in every situation where one has confidence, the reason for the confidence is God. Psalm 2:12: "When [the Lord's] anger is quickly kindled, blessed are all who trust in him." Isaiah 30:18: "Blessed are all who wait for him." Second, he uses a tree as an image for comparison. First, with respect to the strength of its roots: **He shall be like a tree [that is planted by the waters, that spreads out its roots toward moisture]** (17:8a), which symbolizes the strength of divine protection. Psalm 1:3: "He shall be like a tree that is planted by the running waters, which will bring forth its fruit in due season." Second, with respect to the greenness of its leaves: **And its leaf [will be green]** (17:8b). This signifies temporal prosperity and spiritual verdure. Proverbs 11:28: "The righteous will spring up like a green leaf." Third, with respect to abundance of fruits: **Nor shall it ever cease to bear fruit** (17:8c). Revelation 22:2: "Producing its fruit each month."

The Judeans might deny the possibility of people receiving distinctly different rewards based on the differences in their inward thoughts. This passage suitably articulates the source of this distinction. First, the prophet poses a question: **[The heart] is perverse,** caught up in many evils, **[and unsearchable; who can know it?]** (17:9). Proverbs 20:5: "The counsel in the heart of a man is like deep water, but a wise person will draw it out." Second, he responds, naming two things that provide sufficient discretion in judgment, namely, knowledge: **I am the Lord, searching hearts** (17:10a). This refers to inward thoughts. **And kidneys** (17:10b). This refers to emotions. Romans 8:27: "The one who searches hearts knows what the Spirit desires, for the Spirit intercedes for the saints according to God's will." And the second thing is justice: **The one who gives to all people according to their ways,** according to the disposition of their heart; **[and according to] the fruit [of their plans],** according to their outward works (17:10c). Isaiah 3:10: "Tell the righteous people that it is well for them, for they shall eat the fruit of their labors."

False Confidence in Riches

17:11-14 This passage deals with the second matter—where their hope of impunity originated, namely, their abundance of riches. First, it deals with wicked people's source of confidence—their confidence in riches—by comparing these people to a partridge, which steals other birds' eggs, broods over them, and eventually is abandoned by the chicks. Mentioning the unrighteous flock, the prophet says, **The partridge has hatched eggs [which she did not lay]** (17:11a). And he explains: **The one who has amassed riches, and not justly** (17:11b). Habakkuk 2:6: "Woe to those who accumulate what is not their own. How long will they burden themselves with heavy sorrow?" And he mentions the loss of these things: **In midlife, that person will abandon these things,** by dying at a young age or losing them while still alive when the Chaldeans plunder them. **In the end,** during divine judgment or at death when one finds that riches do no good at all, **that person will be**—will be shown to be—**a fool** (17:11c). As in Psalm 48 [49:10-11]: "They will leave their riches to strangers and graves will be their houses forever." Job 12:16: "[The Lord] has known both the cheater and the one who is cheated."

Second, he presents righteous people's hope, which is in divine worship: **A glorious throne** (17:12a). This means that the hope and trust of the people of Israel was the temple, the ark, and sacrifices; they believed that divine worship consisted of these things, because he says: **A high and glorious throne** (17:12a). For there the Lord's glory was made known through revelations when the law was first given. **The place of sanctification,** where I [Jeremiah] am sanctified, or the place that you have sanctified in our presence or on our behalf (17:12b). Jeremiah 14:21 above says: "[Do not dishonor your] throne of glory. Remember, lest you break your covenant with us." And next he mentions the penalty for those departing from this faith, referring to the punishment: **Lord, all who forsake you will be put to shame; those who depart from you will be recorded in the land [*terra*]** of captivity, continually remaining there like residents; or with those who are wise in earthly things; or they have descended into earthly corruption (17:13a).[9] Psalm 48 [49:11] speaks about this: "They have called their lands by their names."[10]

9. Since *terra* can mean "land" or "earth," Aquinas allows for a reading of the text that refers to Babylon as the land of captivity, or a reading in which *terra* refers to earthly, terrestrial things.

10. The entire verse, which would be familiar to members of religious orders who regularly recited the Psalms, reads: "And their graves will be their houses forever, their dwelling places to all generations; they have called their lands by their names" (Ps 49:11).

And it designates the reason: **Because they have forsaken the fountain of living water** (17:13b). In 2:13 above: "They have forsaken me [the fountain of living water]." Third, he offers his own petition to the one who is his own hope: **Heal me** from the weakness of sin and the trials that overwhelm me; **make me safe,** by preserving me in the good; **[for you are] my praise,** the one whom I praise, or the one in whom I am praised (17:14). Psalm 40 [41:4]: "I said, 'O Lord, be merciful to me, for I have sinned against you.'"

17:15–18 This is the third time he mentions their confidence that they would not be punished, since they did not believe the divine threats. Regarding this there are three points. First, he quotes the insult from unbelievers: **Where is the word [of the Lord? Let it come]** (17:15a). In other words: These things will not come to pass. Isaiah 5:19: "You who say, 'Let him make haste, and let his work come quickly, that we may see it; and let the counsel of the Holy One of Israel approach and come, that we may know it.'" Amos 5:18: "Woe to you who desire the day of the Lord! Why do you want it?"

Second, the text presents the prophet's explanation regarding his steadiness of mind: **And I am not troubled** by their opposition, **since I follow [you as my shepherd],** fulfilling what you commanded me. **[I have not desired a human] day,** this present life, because I am prepared for death; or, [I have not desired] present prosperity and glory (17:16a). First Corinthians 4:3: "But, to me, it is a very small thing to be judged by you or by a human day." And he explains the truthfulness of his preaching: **You know [what went forth from my lips] has been right in your sight,** even if it was not right in their sight (17:16b). Job 16:19: "My witness is in heaven."

Third, he offers his own petition, and first he asks for salvation: **Do not be [a terror] to me** (17:17a). In other words: The only thing I fear is your indignation. Job 9:34: "Let him take his rod away from me, and let dread of him not terrify me." Matthew 10:28: "Do not fear those who kill the body but are not able to kill the soul; but rather fear the one who can destroy both soul and body in hell." Second, he asks that the unbelievers be afflicted with shame in their hearts because of their guilt: **Let them be put to shame** (17:18a). Psalm 39 [40:14]: "Let those who seek after my soul, to take it away, be confounded and put to shame." And he asks that they receive fear of punishment: **Let them be afraid** (17:18b). Proverbs 10:29: "Fear to those who work evil." Wisdom 17:11: "Since wickedness is cowardly, it is handed over into total condemnation." And he asks that they receive bodily punishment: **Bring upon them the day of affliction,** in life; **destroy them** through death **with a double [destruction],** with sword and famine, or in body and soul.

Acceptable Worship and Sabbath Observance

17:19-27 Here the Lord tries to call them back to their former religious devotion, to the command regarding Sabbath observance. Since this is not difficult at all, their stubbornness is revealed all the more. Two points are made regarding this matter: first, the Lord designates the place for preaching, **in the gate** (17:19a), so that unwilling people would be compelled to listen. The final chapter of 2 Timothy (4:2): "Be persistent whether the time is favorable or unfavorable: reprove, entreat, rebuke." **Of the children [of the people]**, for they are my people; but they are also the people's children. **Through which [the kings of Judah] enter** (17:19b). Now this was a special gate next to the royal house, through which kings entered into the city. Jeremiah 7:2 above says: "Stand in the gate of the Lord's house and preach this word there," etc. Second, the Lord provides the wording of the proclamation: **And you shall say to them** (17:20a). And regarding this, he makes three points.

First, he gives the command, asking for their attention: **Listen** (17:20b). Psalm 2:10: "And now, you kings, understand. Receive instruction, you who judge the earth." Jeremiah is told to promulgate the command: **Thus says the Lord: Guard** against sin. **[Do not] transport heavy loads** of merchandise outside the city or perform servile **work** (17:21b, 22b). This refers either to the servitude of guilt or the servitude of punishment; for they were required to abstain even from things that were not sins. We are not required to abstain from all of these things, but only from the things commanded by the church when it makes orders about this. **Sanctify [the Sabbath day]**, so you have free time to do good works (17:22b). Exodus 20:8: "Remember the Sabbath day to keep it holy." The final chapter of Nehemiah (13:15-16): "In Judah I saw people treading [the winepresses] on the Sabbath, carrying sheaves, and loading donkeys with wine, grapes, figs, and all sorts of burdens, and bringing them into Jerusalem on the Sabbath day. And I warned them," etc. And he mentions their contempt of the command: **And they did not listen** (17:23a). Above, 7:24: "They did not listen or incline their ear, but they departed into their own pleasures, and into the depravity of their wicked heart," etc.

Second, he promises a reward to those who are obedient: **And it will come to pass, if you listen** (17:24a). He mentions three ways the city will be glorious. One is in its royal dignity, where he says: **[Kings and princes] will enter in [through the gates of the city]** (17:25a). Isaiah 1:26: "I will restore your judges as they were before, and your counselors just as they were in former times." Another [way it will be glorious] is in the multitude of the people, where he says: **And [this city] will be inhabited** (17:25b). Isaiah 62:4: "You will no longer be called 'Forsaken,' and your land will no longer be called 'Desolate.'" Another [way it will be glorious] is in the worship at the temple: **And they will come from the cities of Judah and the places surrounding Jerusalem, and from the land of Benjamin, and from the plains, and from the mountains, and from the south,** even from Egypt, **[bringing burnt offerings, sacrificial animals, sacrifices, and incense, and they will bring an offering into the house of the Lord]** (17:26). Isaiah 60:7: "They will be offered on my acceptable altar, and I will glorify the house of my majesty."

Third, he threatens the scorners with fire: **But if you do not listen . . . I will kindle a fire in the gates** (17:27). For the Chaldeans entering through the gates hurled fire into the city. Isaiah 1:31: "And both will burn together, and there will be no one to extinguish it."

Collation on Bearing Spiritual Fruit

Note that the saints bear fruit through the contemplation of wisdom, as Ecclus 6:19 says: "Draw near to [wisdom] as one who plows and sows, and wait for her good fruits." And through the fervor of charity, as in Song 4:16: "Let my beloved come into his garden and eat the fruit of his apple trees." Through the confession of praise, as in Heb 13:15: "Through him let us always offer the sacrifice of praise to God, which is the fruit of lips confessing God's name." Through meritorious activity, as in Ps 84 [85:12]: "For the Lord will give goodness, and our land will yield its fruit." Through the conversion of neighbors, as in John 15:16: "You should go and bear fruit, and your fruit should remain."

Collation on Various Ways to Follow Christ

Again it should be noted that some people follow Christ through integrity of the flesh, as Rev 14:4 states: "For they are virgins, and they follow the Lamb wherever he goes." Through intention of heart, as in Phil 3:12: "I follow after, to reach my goal by any means." Through the suffering of trials, as in 1 Pet 2:21: "Christ suffered for us, leaving you an example, that you should follow in his steps." Through observance of the commandments, as in Job 23:11: "My foot has followed his steps. I have kept his way and I have not turned aside from it." Through the receiving of glory, as in Ecclus 23:28: "For it is a great glory to follow the Lord, for length of days will be received from him."

Chapter Eighteen

The Potter and the Clay

18:1-6 Here he shows the stubbornness of this people, providing evidence: first, they despise the preaching; second, they persecute the preacher, where it says: "Come let us devise plots against Jeremiah" (18:18a). Regarding the first part, there are two points. First, he describes the preacher calling them to repentance; second, he describes the hopelessness of the despisers, where it says: "They said, 'We have no hope. We will follow our plans'" (18:12a). Regarding the first point, there are two parts. First, the Lord designates the place for the prophet's revelation: [**Go down**] **into the potter's house** (18:2b), so that, with this action, the prophecy would be received through an object lesson.[11] This signifies that the Lord's words are revealed to the one who descends into reflection about one's own weakness. Proverbs 3:32: "The Lord's communication is with the simple." **I went down** (18:3a). I went into the lower part of the city, where these sorts of artisans were staying. Second, he provides the word that was revealed. First, he presents the object lesson; second, he presents an argument derived from the object lesson, where he says: "I will suddenly speak against a nation" (18:7a).

Regarding the first part there are two points. First, he describes the potter's action in destroying the vessel, which is used as an object lesson: **Behold, he was crafting a work on the wheel** (18:3b). Ecclesiasticus 38:29: "So the potter sits for his work, turning the wheel with his feet, always carefully positioned to do his work, and all his products are innumerable." And he describes the restoration of the destroyed vessel: **And turning it, he made another vessel** (18:4b). Wisdom 15:7: "The potter works the soft earth and laboriously fashions each kind of vessel for our use, and from the same clay makes vessels for clean uses as well as those used for the opposite purpose." Second, he applies the object lesson: **Then the word of the Lord came to me** (18:5). First, a question is posed: **Can I not do with you as this potter has done, O house of Israel?** (18:6a). Isaiah 64:8: "And now, O Lord, you are our Father, and we are clay; and you are our maker, and we are all the works of your hands." Second, the answer: **Behold, just like clay [is in the hand of the potter, so you are in my hand, O house of Israel]** (18:6b). Wisdom 7:16: "For both we and our words are in his hand, and all wisdom, and the knowledge and skill of crafts."

11. Here I have translated *similitudo* (similitude) as "object lesson."

18:7–11 Here he draws an argument from the aforementioned object lesson. Now someone might make an objection against what it says here, based on Num 23:19: "God is not a human, that he should lie, nor is God like a child of a human, that he should change his mind." But it seems false if someone foretells a future that does not come to pass; and there is a change of mind if they repent. Therefore [there seems to be a contradiction].

In response, one should say that there are two kinds of prophecy, as Jerome says in the *Gloss* on Matthew chapter 1.[12] There is prophecy regarding things that are predestined, which are not governed by free will, but only by God's disposition, which is unchangeable. Therefore this necessarily comes to pass in every way. Another is prophecy about things that are foreknown; it concerns things that likewise are not subject to free will but proceed from God since God foreknows the final outcome of every single thing. And thus the divine decree is not changed; a change occurs in the human, but not in God. Therefore repentance is accepted [by God] not because of a change in the divine disposition, but the divine decree is deferred because of lesser causes. Therefore the text says, **[I will speak] suddenly** (18:7a) and **[I will speak] unexpectedly** (18:9a), talking about God in comparison with a human. For it is said that if someone speaks "suddenly," that person speaks without forethought; but this applies when someone has concern only for the present moment, leaving aside consideration of the future.

Regarding this passage, there are two points. First he mentions the revocability of the divine sentence against the evil ones, providing the pronouncement of the decree: **That I may root out,** by removing all weakness (18:7b). Jeremiah 1:10 above says: "See, I have set you over nations and kingdoms, so that you shall root up and you shall destroy, and you shall scatter and you shall disperse, and you shall build up and you shall plant." And he provides the revocation of the decree: **If that nation repents of its evil . . . I also will repent of the evil [that I planned to do to them]** (18:8). Hosea 11:8: "My heart is turned within me; at the same time, my repentance is stirred up." And, regarding those who are good, he provides for the promulgation of this decree: **And I will suddenly [speak of a nation and of a kingdom to build up and plant it]** (18:9). Job 22:23: "If you will return to the Almighty, you will be built up, and you will cause wickedness to be far from your tent." And he speaks about the revocation of the decree, if they do evil. Ezekiel 18:24: "But if just people turn away from their justice and act

---

12. *Glossa Ordinaria* on Matt 1:22, PL 114:71–72. See Jerome, *Commentary on Ephesians* 1.1.2, PL 26:445–46.

wickedly, following the abominations which the impious are accustomed to doing, shall such people live? All the just acts that they did will not be remembered. They will die in the treachery that they performed and in the sin that they committed."

Second, he mentions knowledge; first, by treating the topic of the punishment that is planned: **Now, therefore, tell the men of Judah: Thus says the Lord: Behold I,** like a potter, **am shaping evil** of punishment [**against you**] (18:11a). Isaiah 45:7: "I the Lord make peace and create evil." Second, he explains what repentance is: **Let each and every one of you turn from your evil ways, and direct**—make straight—**your ways and your efforts,** that is, your deeds and thoughts (18:11b). Ezekiel 33:11: "Turn yourselves back from your evil ways."

Jerusalem's Idolatry

18:12–17 Here the prophet deals with the hopelessness of the despisers, and first he mentions the hopelessness: **We have no hope** (18:12a). He says in 2:25 above: "You said, 'I have lost hope. I will not do it. For I have loved strangers and I will walk after them.'" Second, he mentions the condemnation of those who have lost hope: **Therefore thus says the Lord** (18:13a). First he asserts that their guilt is horrible in comparison with that of the Gentiles: **Ask among the nations, ["Who has heard such horrible things?"]** (18:13b). In 2:10–11 it says: "Cross to the islands of Chettim and look. Or send to Kedar and examine diligently. See if such a thing has ever been done. See if a nation has ever changed its gods—though certainly these are not gods." Ezekiel 5:6: "And Jerusalem has despised my judgments, so that she is more wicked than the Gentiles, and she despised my commandments more than the countries surrounding her." He uses the example of nonsentient things, which hold fast to the arrangement established for them by God: **Will the snow of Lebanon withdraw from the rock of the field?** (18:14a). Note that Lebanon is a great mountain, and it is very broad in its summit; on it are fields and rocky caves where the sun's rays do not reach, so snow is constantly preserved there. **Or can the cold waters that gush out be removed,** so that they do not flow down from Lebanon and other high mountains (18:14b)? In other words: No. Ecclesiastes 3:14: "I have learned that all the things that God has made continue forever. We cannot add anything to them, or take anything away from what God has made, so that God may be feared." Because of the condition of their works, which are useless, he says: **In vain they sacrifice** to idols (18:15a). Romans 6:21: "What advantage did you then gain from those things, about which you are now ashamed?" For these things were harmful: **[My people] were stumbling,** that is, giving offense (18:15b). Isaiah 59:10: "We stumbled at noonday as in the darkness, in dark places as though we were dead people." And these things were shameful: **In worldly footpaths** of idolatry, which the entire world follows after (15:15c). Job 22 [22:15-16; 21:14]: "Do you desire to keep to worldly footpaths which wicked men have trodden? They were taken away before their time, and a flood has washed away the foundation of those who said to God, 'Depart from us, and we refuse to know your ways.'" And these things were difficult: **[They forsook ancient paths] to walk their journey on ways not trodden** by their holy ancestors (18:15d). Or it is because they plotted useless sins. Wisdom 5:7: "We walked difficult ways, but the way of the Lord we have not known." Numbers 20:19: "We will walk the beaten path."

Second, he threatens a terrifying punishment. First, regarding the desolation of the earth: **Their land will be given up to desolation, [and to a perpetual hissing; all who pass by it will be astonished and shake their head]** (18:16). Shortly after this, Lam 1:12 says: "O, all you who pass by the way, look and see if there is any sorrow like my sorrow." Second, regarding the destruction of the nation: **Like a [burning] wind** that dries out the crops, **[I will scatter them before] the enemy,** Babylon (18:17a). Jeremiah 4:11 above reads: "A scorching wind in the desert highways [buffets] the journey of the child of my people, but not to winnow or cleanse." Third, regarding the cessation of divine aid: **[I will show them] my back,** in the manner of an angry human (18:17b). Deuteronomy 32:20: "I will hide my face from them, and I will consider what their final end will be." Psalm 73 [74:1]: "Why, Lord, have you cast us off forever? Is your wrath kindled against the sheep of your pasture?"

Jeremiah's Enemies Plot against Him

18:18-23 Here the text shows their stubbornness that caused them to persecute their preachers, prefiguring the persecution of Christ. First, it presents the persecution by the enemies, describing the counsel of those persecuting: **Come, [let us devise plots against Jeremiah]** (18:18a). Wisdom 2:1: "The impious spoke, reasoning with themselves, but not correctly." And, below, in the same place (Wis 2:12), it says: "Let us lie in wait for the just person, for this person is useless to us and is opposed to our actions," etc. It presents the reason for the persecution: **For** administration of **the law will not per-ish [from the priest], nor the counsel** of divine revelation **[from the wise]** (18:18b). In other words: Jeremiah falsely predicted this future. And their statement is contrary to Ezek 7:26: "The law will perish from the priest, and counsel will perish from the elders." And it describes the means of persecution: **[Let us strike him] with the tongue,** by disparaging him and making accusations. **And let us pay no attention [to any of his words]** (18:18c). In other words: Let us not fear his warnings. Psalm 63 [64:3, 5]: "They sharpened their tongues like a sword. They held fast to their evil purpose." Ecclesiasticus 28:17: "The blow from a whip makes a bruise, but the blow from a tongue will break bones."

Second, it presents the prophet's prayer; and first he asks for a hearing: **Lord, give heed to me,** to my merits (18:19a). Lamentations 3:61: "You have heard their reproach, O Lord, and all their plots against me." Second, he discusses the guilt of ingratitude, describing this ingratitude: **Shall evil be given in return for good?** (18:20a). In other words: It is not fitting. It is not just. **[They have dug] a pit** of deceit in order to take my life (18:20b). Psalm 108 [109:5]: "They repaid me evil for good, and hatred for my love." And he presents evidence of their ingratitude: **Remember [how I stood before you to speak on their behalf and turn your wrath away from them]** (18:20c). The final chapter of 2 Maccabees (15:14): "Here is one who loves his siblings and the people of Israel. This is the one who prays fervently for the people and for all of the Holy City, Jeremiah, the prophet of God."

Third, he calls down punishment and first asks for punishment to be inflicted on their children: **Deliver their children [to famine]** (18:21a). Jeremiah 15:2 says: "Those destined for the sword shall go to the sword; those destined for famine shall go to famine; those destined for captivity shall go to captivity." Regarding the enjoyment of marriage he says: **Let their wives be childless** (18:21b). Hosea 9:14: "Give them a womb without children, and dry breasts." And regarding their men of war: **Let their young men be stabbed by the sword in battle. Let a cry** of lament **be heard (18:21c–22a).** Isaiah 15:5: "They will raise a cry of destruction." Second, he mentions concealment of the punishment, so they would not be able to take precautions: **You will bring the robber,** Nebuchadnezzar, who will come upon them suddenly (18:22b). Obadiah 5: "If thieves had gone unto you, if robbers entered at night, how would you have held your peace?" And he provides the reason: **They have dug a pit** (18:20b). In other words: It is just for those who wished to deceive me to be deceived. Psalm 56 [57:6]: "They prepared a snare for my feet, and they bowed down my soul." And he introduces the proof: **But**

you, O Lord, you know (18:23a). Lamentations 3:59: "O Lord, you have seen their wickedness against me. Judge my cause."

Second, he precludes a revocation of the sentence, by precluding mercy: **Do not forgive [their wickedness]** by cleansing them from guilt. **Do not let [their sin] be blotted out,** freeing them from punishment (18:23b). Psalm 108 [109:14]: "May the wickedness of his fathers be remembered in the sight of the Lord, and do not let the sin of his mother be blotted out." And the prophet prays for punishment: **Let them be overthrown. Abuse them** (18:23c). That is: Give them over to evil.

Collation on Good and Bad Hissing

It should be noted that there is a certain good *sibilus* [hissing, whistling] (18:16) of divine inspiration, as in Zech 10:8: "I will whistle for them, and I will gather them together, because I have redeemed them." And a whistling of humble strength, as in 1 Kgs 19:12: "After the fire, a whistling of gentle air." And a hissing of compassion, as in 49:17 below: "All who pass by [that country] will be astonished and will hiss at all its disasters." But there is also a bad *sibilus* of wicked persuasion, as in Wis 17:9: "Terrified by the hissing of serpents, they died of fright." And a hiss of insult, as in Lam 2:15: "All who pass along the way have hissed, and they wagged their heads at daughter Jerusalem, saying, 'Is this really the city of perfect beauty, the joy of the entire earth?'" And a hiss of astonishment, as in 24:9 below: "I will make them an object of astonishment, and hissing, and perpetual desolation."

Collation on "Speaking on Their Behalf"

Also, regarding the phrase, **To speak on their behalf** (18:20c), note that Christ speaks on our behalf in order to obtain forgiveness. Luke 23:34: "Father, forgive them, for they do not know what they are doing." And [Christ speaks on our behalf] in order to free us from guilt, as in 1 John 2:1-2: "We have an advocate with the Father, Jesus Christ the just, and he himself is the propitiation for our sins." And to obtain glory, as in John 17:24: "I desire that where I am, they also may be with me, in order to see my glory that you have given me."

Chapter Twenty

A Warning to the Religious Leaders

20:1-6 After finishing warning the people, the text begins to warn the leaders. First, it presents the prophet's threat against the leaders; second, it presents the leaders' conspiracy against the prophet, in 26:1 below: "In the beginning of the reign of Jehoiakim, son of Josiah, king of Judah." Regarding the first part, there are two points. First, the Lord threatens the leaders of the Judean people; second, the Lord threatens these and leaders of other nations in 25:1 below: "The word that came to Jeremiah from the Lord." The first point has two parts. In the first part, the Lord threatens the highest-ranking leaders; in the second part, the Lord threatens all of them, in 23:1 below: "Woe to the shepherds who scatter my flock and tear it to pieces." Regarding the first part, there are two points. First, the Lord threatens the highest spiritual authority, namely, the high priest. Second, the Lord threatens the highest temporal authority, namely, the king, as below in 21:1: "The word that came to Jeremiah from the Lord." Regarding the first point, there are two parts. First, the text presents the threat against the high priest; second, because of the dangers present to the prophet, it presents his complaint: "You have seduced me, O Lord" (20:7a).

Regarding the first part, there are two points. First, the text explains that the occasion for the threat [against the leaders] was the prophet's persecution, and it gives the reason for the persecution: [**Now the priest Pashhur, son of Immer, who was appointed chief officer in the house of the Lord, heard Jeremiah**] **prophesying these words** against the city (20:1). For it was the duty of the high priest to reprove those who prophesied falsely, as we read in 29:26 below: "The Lord made you priest instead of Jehoiada the priest, so that you would be ruler in the house of the Lord, over every man who raves and prophesies, to put them into stocks and into prison," etc. It describes the persecution of the prophet: **And [Pashhur] struck the prophet and put him** into prison, **into stocks,** a kind of instrument of torture used to detain captives, **[that were in the upper gate] of Benjamin,** which led toward the tribe of Benjamin (20:2a). For the city was situated at the boundary of the two tribes. **The upper [gate],** for there were many gates leading into this land, **in the house of the Lord** (20:2b). Judicial decisions regarding prophets and temple ministers were rendered in this gate, and there they were confined in prison. Lamentations 3:7: "He has walled me in so I cannot get out; he has made my chains heavy." And it describes the liberation of the prophet:

And at daylight the next day, Pashhur released Jeremiah from the stocks (20:3a). Acts 4:5: "And it came to pass on the next day that their leaders, elders, and scribes were assembled in Jerusalem."[13] Psalm 67 [68:6]: "He leads out those who were strongly bound." Second, it presents the threat; and first, it indicates the punishment by a name change: **And Jeremiah said to him, ["The Lord has not named you 'Pashhur,' but 'Terror All Around'"]** (20:3b). He is speaking about the tendency of a fearful human to look around everywhere. Proverbs 10:29: "[The way of the Lord is strength for the upright, and] terror to those who work evil."

Second, he presents the threat of punishment: **For thus says the Lord: [Behold, I will deliver you up to fear]** (20:4a). And first, regarding his friends: **You and all your friends** (20:4b). Psalm 77 [78:64]: "Their priests fell by the sword." Second, regarding their subjects, it mentions the captivity of the people: **And all Judah** (20:4c). Lamentations 1:3: "Judah has changed her dwelling place because of her affliction and hard servitude. She dwelled among the nations and found no rest." And it speaks of the plunder of their goods: **And I will give away all the wealth of this city** (20:5a). Isaiah 39:6: "All that is in your house, and all that your ancestors stored up until this day, will be carried away into Babylon. Nothing will be left, says the Lord." Third, regarding those in his household: **But you, Pashhur, and all who dwell in your house, will go into captivity . . . and all your friends, to whom you prophesied a lie,** promising favorable things (20:6). Isaiah 22:18: "The Lord will toss you like a ball into a large and spacious land. There you will die," etc. Amos 7:17: "Your sons and your daughters will fall by the sword, and your land will be parceled out with measuring lines; and you yourself will die in an unclean land, and captive Israel will migrate from its land."

Jeremiah's Complaint to the Lord

20:7-13 Here the text presents the prophet's complaint. First, he laments the duty pressed on him; second, he laments the occasion of his birth. Regarding the first point there are two parts. He laments the duty pressed on him first because of the mockery that resulted and second because of the per-

---

13. Here Aquinas notes the parallel between Jeremiah and Peter and John, who were imprisoned overnight, questioned by the priests and other religious leaders the next day, and released in Acts 4:1-21.

secution, where it says: **For I heard the reproaches of many people [and terror on every side: "Persecute him!"]** (20:10a). Regarding the first part, there are three points. First, in a sort of complaint, he describes the way the duty was pressed on him: **You have seduced me.** Your words deceived me. I believed that I would prophesy against the Gentiles, and not against the Judeans from whom I suffer persecution (20:7a). For he did not wish to lodge an accusation of deception against God, since he would be blaspheming. **You have prevailed** by imposing this duty on me when I resisted (20:7b), as it says in 1:6 above. This is chiefly because he did not see the results of his preaching. Isaiah 49:4: "I have labored in vain. I have used up my strength for nothing and in vain." Second, he describes what happened when he preached, and he mentions the mockery: **I have become a laughingstock. Everyone mocks me** by wrinkling their noses and displaying their derision (20:7c). Lamentations 3:14: "I have become a laughingstock to all my people, their taunting song all day long." And he provides the reason, mentioning the message of the preaching, in which he openly charged them with guilt and threatened punishment: **For I am already speaking for a long time, crying out against their wickedness, and [I announce] devastation** that nevertheless has not yet come (20:8a). Isaiah 16:7: "To those who rejoice on brick walls, tell them about their wounds." And he talks about the resulting disgrace: **And the word of the Lord became a disgrace for me** (20:8b); that is, the cause of disgrace. Acts 26:24: "Festus said to Paul, 'Too much learning drove you to insanity!'" Third, he renounces the duty that was pressed on him: **Then I said** (20:9a). First he abandons his duty: **I will not remember.** I will no longer ponder how to speak to the people (20:9b). For he did not want to cast pearls before swine, as in Matt 7:6: "Do not give what is holy to the dogs."

Second, he resumes the duty that he had abandoned: **And it became like fire** (20:9c). This is because the more a person avoids speaking outwardly, the more that person feels burning love inwardly. Psalm 38 [39:3]: "My heart grew hot within me, and in my meditation a fire blazed up." **In my bones,** in my inmost thoughts. **And I was wearied,** for the reasons already mentioned. **I was not able to endure** the interior fire, **for I heard the reproaches of many people** (20:9d–10a).

Here he complains about the duty that he accepted, which caused him to endure persecutions. First, he mentions the persecution from enemies, dealing first with the great number of persecutors: **Many people** whom he was unable to withstand (20:10a). **"Persecute him!"** (20:10b); this refers to their conspiracy. He also mentions that they had been his friends: **From all the men who were peaceable toward me** (20:10c). This shows the threatening peril. Obadiah 7: "All the men who were your allies have deceived you. The men who were peaceful toward you have prevailed against you."

Second, the text discusses the encouragement the prophet received, and it mentions divine assistance: **But the Lord is with me** to defend me (20:11a). Isaiah 50:7: "The Lord is my helper. Therefore I am not put to shame." And it speaks about the service God rendered: **And therefore they will fall,** because they persecute me (20:11b). Isaiah 40:30: "Children will faint from exertion, and youth will fall down with exhaustion." **They will thoroughly be put to shame** because they said disgraceful things, **because they did not understand**—that is, they refused to understand—**the [everlasting] disgrace** of eternal damnation, or of their future captivity (20:11c). Psalm 39 [40:14]: "Let those who seek my life, to take it away, be put to shame and be filled with fear."

Third, he offers a prayer, in which he seeks to gain God's good will by commending God's justice: **Tester [of the righteous]** (20:12a); that is, approver or inquisitor and examiner. And by commending God's knowledge: **Who sees the kidneys,** which refers to emotions; **and the hearts,** which refers to thoughts (20:12b). In 17:10 above: "I am the Lord, searching the heart and examining the kidneys, the one who gives to all people according to their ways," etc. The prophet asks for vengeance: **I beg you, let me see your retribution on them** (20:12c). He provides the reason: **For I have shown you,** not that you were unaware but because I entrusted **my** entire **cause** to you (20:12d).

Fourth, he is thankful: **Sing to the Lord** (21:13a). Psalm 71 [72:12]: "For he will rescue the poor from the mighty, and the needy who had no helper."

Jeremiah Laments His Birth

20:14-18 Here he laments the occasion of his birth. Now one could object to what this passage says. For holy people should boast in their tribulations as Rom 5:3 indicates. Therefore it seems that Jeremiah should not have broken into cursing because of his tribulations. Furthermore, a day is God's creation; it is a sin to curse something created by God. Therefore [Jeremiah sinned by doing this]. Furthermore, a day is something that is transitory, and so it is stupid to apply the punishment of a curse to it. Therefore [Jeremiah sinned by doing this]. Furthermore, no one ought to curse someone who is innocent, and the person who did not kill Jeremiah was innocent.[14] Therefore Jeremiah sinned by cursing that person.[15]

To the first objection, one should answer that the tribulations themselves are considered to be evils inasmuch as they are opposed to natural good, as Augustine says.[16] Thus it is not a sin to abhor them with a natural hatred. However, if, on account of these tribulations, people were led away from their own upright conduct, it would be a sin. But tribulations can be viewed as something that brings about good—so that holy people boast in them—just as when someone who is ill undergoes surgery that causes healing. To the second and third objections we should answer that Jeremiah does not curse the day considered according to its own nature, since that would be foolishness and a sin; rather, he curses it to the extent that it is evil, to the degree that something evil occurred on that day, just as, conversely, a festival day is observed because something good occurred on that day; and that is what this curse means. However, Gregory, giving consideration to the character of this day, says that it is not possible to interpret this curse literally.[17] And similarly we should respond to the final objection by saying that he did not curse these people, except for their connection to his own delivery. So, in order to express his own sense of revulsion, he speaks hyperbolically about the misery of his life due to the afflictions that he suffered.

Therefore he makes two points about this. First, he places a curse on the time of his birth: **Cursed be the day [that I was born]** (20:14a). Job 3:3: "Let the day perish on which I was born, and the night on which it was said, 'A human is conceived.'" And [he places a curse] on the one who announced the birth: **Cursed be the man who brought news to my father, saying, "A male child is born to you," and made him rejoice greatly** (20:15). Genesis 21:6: "The Lord brought me joy, and everyone who hears about it will laugh with me." And he explains what form the curse takes: **Let that person be like the cities that the Lord overthrew** (20:16a). Isaiah 25:2: "You have reduced the city to rubble, the fortified city to ruin." And a curse against his birth attendant for preserving his life: **Let that person hear a cry** of death, [**the**

14. Here Aquinas refers to the curse of the person who brought news of Jeremiah's birth to his father and who did not kill Jeremiah in his mother's womb (20:15–17).

15. Note that this section takes the form of a scholastic question, offering several objections and responses to them.

16. Augustine, *City of God* 14.9, 19.4, and 22.22, ed. Bernard Dombart and Alphonsus Kalb, CCSL 48 (Turnhout: Brepols, 1955), 425–30, 664–69, 842–45.

17. Gregory the Great, *Moralia on Job* 4.1–4, ed. Marcus Adriaen, CCSL 143 (Turnhout: Brepols, 1979), 158–63.

one who did not kill me in the womb] **so that my mother would be my grave (20:16b–17a),** so Jeremiah would not have been counted among the living. **An everlasting conception** (20:17b); so he would not have had to be born. Job 3:11: "Why did I not die in the womb? Why did I not perish as soon as I came out of the womb?"

Second, he presents the reason for the curse: **Why did I come forth from the womb?** (20:18a). Jeremiah 15:10 above says: "Woe is me, my mother. Why did you give birth to me, a man of strife, a man of contention to the whole land?" First Maccabees 2:7: "Woe is me that I was born to see the ruin of my people, and the ruin of the Holy City, to dwell there when it is given into the hands of the enemies."

Collation on How God Seduces and Overpowers

Take note, regarding the phrase, **You have seduced me, O Lord, and I was seduced; you were stronger than me and you have prevailed** (20:7a). It is because the Lord seduces by using persuasion. The end of 2 Corinthians (12:16): "Since I was crafty, I captured you by guile." And the Lord seduces by luring people with things that are soothing, as above in 10:10: "[In my mouth the book was as sweet as honey, but] when I ate it, my stomach was made bitter." And by comforting with promises, as in 4:10 above: "Have you deceived this people and Jerusalem, saying, 'You shall have peace'? Behold, the sword reaches even to the soul." Now the Lord prevails by administering correction, as in Isa 8:11: "He taught me with a strong arm that I should not walk in the way of this people." And by diverting people from harm, as in Hos 2:6: "I will hedge up her way with thorns, and I will fence her in with a wall." And by restraining them through love, as in Hos 11:4: "I will lead them with the cords of Adam, with the bands of love."

NICHOLAS OF LYRA

Literal Postill on Jeremiah

Jeremiah 23, 28–31

Chapter Twenty-Three

Introduction to the Chapter

The text continues here with Jeremiah prophesying against the priests and false prophets, whom he calls "shepherds" because they had the responsibility to tend the people through their example of a good life and through sound teaching; but they did the opposite. Therefore this present chapter is divided into three parts, because Jeremiah first briefly accuses them of wickedness. Second, he proclaims the coming of a good shepherd, Christ, where it says: "And I [will gather together the remnant of my flock]" (23:3a). Third, he returns to the matter of the wickedness of the shepherds, dealing with this more fully, where he says: "To the prophets" (23:9a), so that, by providing this contrast, the things stated would shine forth all the more clearly.

God Reproaches the Religious Leaders

23:1 Woe [to the shepherds], the false prophets and priests, **who scatter my flock and tear it to pieces,** through the example of a bad life and false teaching. Therefore he continues by mentioning punishments when he says:

23:2 Behold, I will visit you, by punishing you harshly, **for the wickedness**

that you were eager to commit. From this it is clear that they knowingly and intentionally did such things.

The Coming of the Good Shepherd

23:3a And I [will gather together the remnant of my flock]. Here he continues by announcing the coming of the good shepherd, Christ, who is the main focus of this prophecy and other prophecies, as we stated in the beginning of this book.[1] However, some of our [Christian] interpreters explain that this entire section up to "To the prophets" (23:9) is about the return from Babylonian captivity, and that when it continues, "I will raise up shepherds over them" (23:4a), this refers to Joshua son of Jehozadak (Hag 1:1), Ezra, Nehemiah, Haggai, and Zechariah. And later, when he says, "I will raise up for David a righteous branch" (23:5), they explain that this is about Zerubbabel, who was descended from David, as is clear in Matt 1:13.[2] Zerubbabel was the leader of the people when they returned from captivity, as they mention later.[3] "And this is the name they will call him: 'Righteous Lord'" (23:6), since, as these same interpreters assert, in ancient times Jews gave their children God's names.[4] But this explanation [of Jer 23:3–6] does not seem to be true, since, first, it says: "They will no longer be afraid, and they will not tremble with fear" (23:4b). For when they returned from Babylonian captivity they often experienced great affliction and dejection, as it says in Neh 1. And they were so afraid of the surrounding nations that they performed acts of force and sometimes took up the sword. Second, [this interpretation does not seem accurate] since the passage continues: "And none from their number will be sought," that is, lacking (23:4c). For not all of the Judeans returned from Babylon; instead, many remained because of love for the wives that they took, and because of love for the offspring that they produced, as it says in Ezra 1.[5] When they interpret the phrase "I will raise up for David a righteous

---

1. "Preface" in Nicholas of Lyra, *Postill on Jeremiah*, in *Postilla super Totam Bibliam* (Strassburg, 1492; repr., Frankfurt am Main: Minerva, 1971), vol. 2, unpaginated.
2. Hugh of St. Cher, *On Jeremiah* 23:3–5, in *Opera Omnia in Universum Vetus & Novum Testamentum: Tomi Octo In Libros Prophetarum, Isaiae, Ieremiae, & eiusdem Threnorum, Baruch* (Lyon: Ioannes Antonius Huguetan and Guillielmus Barbier, 1669), 4:233r.
3. Hugh of St. Cher, *On Jeremiah* 23:5, in *Opera Omnia* 4:233r.
4. Hugh of St. Cher, *On Jeremiah* 23:6, in *Opera Omnia* 4:233r.
5. Though Ezra 1 does not specifically say that some Judeans stayed in Babylon out of love for Babylonian wives and offspring, Ezra 1:5 does indicate that not all Judeans left Babylon.

branch" (23:5a) as dealing with Zerubbabel, this is not correct, because it adds, "And a king will reign" (23:5b); for Zerubbabel was not a king. "And this is the name" (23:6b). Where our translation says "Lord," the Hebrew text uses the Tetragrammaton name of the Lord, which, according to Hebrew [i.e., Jewish] scholars, is appropriate to use only for the Most High Creator, and therefore it could not fittingly be used for any mere human.[6] Therefore what these interpreters later say—that Jews gave the names of God to their children—is fictitious and baseless with respect to the Tetragrammaton name of the Lord; for, because of the holiness of this name, no one other than the priests dared to utter this name, and they did not utter this name everywhere, but only in the temple. Therefore these interpreters Judaize more than the Jews, who say that, interpreted literally, this should be understood as being about the Christ.[7] And the Chaldean translation that the Hebrews have is accurate; in the place where our translation says, "I will raise up for David a righteous branch" (23:5a), their Targum says: "I will raise up for David a righteous Messiah," because this word is explained as referring to Christ.[8]

Now this passage is divided into three parts. First, it predicts the gathering together of the faithful. Second, it continues with the establishment of the one gathering them together, where it says, "Behold, the days are coming" (23:5a). Third, it mentions the recognition of much great blessing, where it says, "Therefore, on this account, behold the days to come" (23:7a). The first part is spoken in the *persona* of the Lord: **And I will gather together [the remnant of my flock]** (23:3a). This gathering should not be understood as something that comes about through moving to a place, but through unity in faith and the bond of love, as it says in John 11:51–52, that Christ was going to die for the nation, so that, drawing them from the different Gentile and

6. The Tetragrammaton ("four letters") refers to the Hebrew letters *yod, he, vav, he* (YHWH or YHVH), which are the consonants for the proper name for God used in numerous passages of Hebrew scripture. For many centuries, observant Jews have abstained from vocalizing this divine name. See Louis F. Hartman and S. David Sperling, "God, Names of," in *Encyclopaedia Judaica*, ed. Fred Skolnik and Michael Berenbaum, 2nd ed. (Detroit: Thomson Gale, 2007), 7:672–76.

7. See, for instance, the comments on Jer 23:5 on this passage by David Kimhi (ca. 1160–1235), also known by the acronym RaDaK (Rabbi David Kimhi), translated in *Jeremiah: A New English Translation*, translation of text, Rashi, and commentary by A. J. Rosenberg (New York: Judaica Press, 1985), 1:186.

8. *The Targum of Jeremiah*, trans. and introduced by Robert Hayward, The Aramaic Bible 12 (Wilmington, DE: Michael Glazier, 1987), 111. *The Targum of Jeremiah* is an Aramaic paraphrase that may date as early as the fourth or fifth century CE. See Hayward's introduction to *The Targum of Jeremiah*, 34–35.

Jewish sects where they were dispersed, he might gather together the children of God, who were scattered, into one observance of the Christian faith.

23:3b And I will make them return [to their own farms], for the Lord's field is the church. Now just as it is "one field" because of the unity of the universal church, so also it is possible to speak in the plural about "fields," because of the different territories where the worship of Christ flourishes, and because different sites are consecrated to this worship to which the faithful assemble. And here they are called **farms,** but the Hebrew text reads, "To their own manors," which signifies more clearly that they are sites consecrated to God.

And they will increase and multiply. It is clear that this was fulfilled by the multiplication of faithful people.

23:4 And I will raise up shepherds, namely, Christ—who is the leader of the shepherds—and the apostles and their successors.

And they will no longer be afraid. This refers to the state of the church triumphant, which proceeds at the same time together with the church militant, beginning at the time of Christ's passion through which the heavenly door was opened. In this state fear has no place, but there is only steadfast and eternal safety.

And none from their number of those who are predestined **will be sought.** No one belonging to the retinue of the heavenly homeland will be lacking.

The Coming of the Branch of David

23:5 Behold, the days are coming. Here he continues by describing the establishment of the one who gathers them together, Christ who is true God and true human, whose true humanity is revealed in this passage.

And I will raise up [a righteous branch] for David, since he was made king, from the offspring of David, according to the flesh, as it says in Rom 1:3.

And a king will reign, for, as he says at the end of Matthew: "All power in heaven and on earth has been given to me" (Matt 28:18).

And he will be wise, with both uncreated and created wisdom.

And he will execute judgment of discernment at the present time, by separating the faithful from the unfaithful, by calling some to faith, and sending others away through his righteous judgment, though it is hidden to us. And he will execute judgment by handing down verdicts at the end of the world.

And justice, by giving the evangelical law that contains perfect justice and, at the end of the world, by handing down just verdicts to reward those who are good and to punish those who are evil, as we read in Matt 25:31–46.

23:6 In those days Judah will be saved, all who acknowledge the name of the Lord in their heart and with their mouth. The fact that this should be understood this way is made clear not only through Latin interpreters but even by Hebrew interpreters, for a certain Hebrew gloss on Gen 41 says, "Will it not be possible for there to be a redeemer lifting up his face?"—as someone who accepts people. The text continues: "He will be absent, but he will save all people who acknowledge him in their heart and mouth, and through their deeds, as it is written in Jer 23."[9] **In those days** he will save those who acknowledge him, as it says in this gloss.

And Israel will dwell confidently. This refers to the state of the church triumphant, where there is the greatest security.

And this is the name they will call him. The Hebrew text uses the Tetragrammaton name of the Lord, which is not able to be uttered except regarding the true God. In *The Guide for the Perplexed,* Rabbi Moses says that this name is given to God to signify the bare divine essence, according to itself, apart from any reference to what is created, and for this reason it is completely inexpressible.[10] Other names express something in a certain way, just as the name "lord" [*dominus*] means "a great person who has subjects." Someone who causes something to exist is called its "creator," and those whom one brings into existence are commonly called that person's "creations." Similarly the name God [*Deus*] is used because judges are called "gods" [*dii*] in Exod 22:9, where it says: "The judicial case of both parties will come before the gods." And through this [Tetragrammaton name], the true divinity of Christ himself is revealed. For among the Hebrews this name is considered ineffable, and therefore, in place of this, the translator commonly used an epithet,[11] and this name is translated in this way wherever it is found in the Old Testament.

---

9. I have not found this specific quotation in rabbinic sources, but a similar sentiment is expressed in the comments on Gen 41:16 in *The Zohar,* a medieval kabbalistic text. See *The Zohar* (*Miqez,* 195a), trans. Harry Sperling and Maurice Simon, vol. 2 (London: Soncino, 1956), 241–42.

10. Moses Maimonides, *The Guide for the Perplexed* 1.61, trans. M. Friedländer, 2nd ed. (New York: Dover, 1956), 89. Moses Maimonides (1135–1204) was a Spanish-born scholar, philosopher, and commentator. See Alexander Broadie, "Maimonides and Aquinas on the Names of God," *Religious Studies* 23 (1987): 157–70.

11. Jerome translated YHWH as *Dominus* (Lord).

Some people say that this Tetragrammaton name of the Lord is not used only for God but also for others. For instance, as it says at the end of Ezekiel: "The name of the city is 'the Lord'" (Ezek 48:35). And where we have "the Lord," in Hebrew the Tetragrammaton is used. Therefore this Tetragrammaton name that is used here for the city is not said to be used regarding God. Again, in Gen 22:14, "Abraham called the name of that place, 'The Lord sees.'" And where we have "the Lord," in Hebrew the Tetragrammaton name of the Lord is used. Again in Judg 6:24 it is written: "Therefore he built an altar to the Lord, and he called it, 'The Lord's Peace.'" There, in the Hebrew, the Tetragrammaton name of the Lord is used. Again, in Exod 17:15: "Moses built an altar to the Lord and he named it 'The Lord, my exaltation.'" Where we have "Lord," the Hebrew text uses the Tetragrammaton name of the Lord. But these things do not detract from what Rabbi Moses says, because none of the aforementioned things are given the name of God in an unqualified sense as their own proper name, but they are given the name on account of some accomplishment of God. Therefore no human being is called "God" as one's own proper name in an unqualified way, but with a certain connotation and because of some accomplishment of God, just as many people have been named "Deodatus," which means "the Lord gave." And similarly, this occurs just as often with the names of humans as with place names, such as the places mentioned above, as it is clear to someone who examines this closely. Nevertheless, when the first quotation says, "And the name of the city" (Ezek 48:35), the word "Lord" [*Dominus*] ought to be used there. For this reason the Chaldean translation says: "They explain the name of the city as being about the day in which the Lord will make his divinity descend there."[12] And so it is clear what should be said with respect to the other things, for there is always a certain qualification when this name is used for something other than for the true God.

Our just one, the one who justifies us. This wording also shows the divinity of the one whose character is to justify the impious. Now you should understand that the Hebrews whom we cited as authorities for this passage do not confess the divinity of the Christ, who they expect will come as someone who is purely human—though holier than Moses. They say that the literal Hebrew meaning is this: "And this is his name because he [the Messiah] will call him [God], 'the Lord, our just one.'" And they say that the Tetragrammaton name of the Lord is appropriate only for God alone,

12. See the translation of Ezek 48:35 in *The Targum of Ezekiel*, trans. and introduced by Samson H. Levey, The Aramaic Bible 13 (Wilmington, Del.: Michael Glazier, 1987), 129.

and according to them this verse does not refer to the Messiah, but it refers to the God who will call him to redeem the Jews. And they are able to change the literal meaning easily because the Hebrew word used here, *asser,* can be used for either the word "who" or the word "what."[13] In addition, the phrases "they will call him" and "he will call him" are written in just the same way using Hebrew letters, but they are pointed differently, so it is quite easy for this pointing ["*he* will call him"] to be used.[14] The fact that Jews could commit such an error in this passage is made clear because the seventy interpreters, who were extremely learned Jews, translated this passage as follows: "And this is the name that they will call him, 'the Lord our just one.'" However, they did not reveal Christ's divinity, which they intended to conceal, to King Ptolemy, as Jerome says in many places.[15] For when they translated the Tetragrammaton name of the Lord, they used the Greek noun *kyrios,* which means "lord," just as the noun "lord" [*dominus*] is used in Latin translation. This noun is not only used for God but also for any great person. The aforementioned error is also apparent when we look at the Chaldean translation which says in this passage: "And this is the name that they will call him."[16]

13. A literal translation of Jer 23:6 reads: "The name by which ['*ăšer*] he shall be called."
14. Biblical Hebrew was originally written with consonants only. In order to facilitate vocalization, later interpreters added vowel pointing. Regarding this passage, Michael Graves explains: "[The Hebrew] *yqr'w,* which is vocalized in the MT [Masoretic text] as a singular verb with an objective suffix (i.e., 'he will call him'), as translated by the LXX. In contrast, Jerome takes the final *waw* as a sign of the plural verb (i.e., 'they will call'—with 'him' being assumed), as does the [Targum]"; in Jerome, *Commentary on Jeremiah,* trans. Michael Graves, ed. Christopher A. Hall, Ancient Christian Texts (Downers Grove, IL: IVP Academic, 2011), 138n205.
15. According to early Jewish legends, the Septuagint (LXX), a Greek version of the Old Testament, was created when the Egyptian ruler Ptolemy II (ca. 288–247) commissioned seventy-two Jewish scholars to translate Hebrew scripture into Greek. Legends report that each scholar worked in solitude, but miraculously each translation was found to be identical to the others, which was taken to be affirmation of divine guidance given to the translators. Christians often referred to the translators as "the Seventy." Early and medieval Christian traditions reported that the Seventy obscured a number of direct references to Christ so as not to confuse Ptolemy, who had become a monotheistic worshipper of the God of Israel, since references to Christ's divinity or the Trinity might be interpreted as polytheism. See Abraham Wasserstein and David J. Wasserstein, *The Legend of the Septuagint: From Classical Antiquity to Today* (New York: Cambridge University Press, 2006), 130. Lyra's point is that the Jews responsible for the LXX and the Chaldean translation, which he quotes later in this paragraph, correctly allowed for a Christian interpretation of Jer 23:6, while the Jews who were Lyra's contemporaries were in error.
16. *Targum of Jeremiah,* trans. Hayward, 111.

23:7 Therefore [behold the days are coming]. Here the prophet continues with a review of the great blessings when he says: **And they shall say no more, "The Lord lives [who brought the children of Israel out of the land of Egypt]."** For just as a lesser light is obscured in the presence of a greater light, so also the coming blessing of the incarnation of Jesus Christ, and our redemption through him, obscured all other blessings, as though the things in the old law were consigned to oblivion like things that, in comparison, were little or nothing.

23:8 But the Lord lives who brought out and has led to this place [the off-spring of the house of Israel from the land of the north, and out of the lands to which I had cast them out]. It is not possible to interpret this as a reference to the return from Babylonian captivity, since this blessing was substantially inferior to the time the children of Israel were brought out of Egypt with such great signs and divine miracles, and such a great multitude, because there were six hundred thousand, not counting women and children (Exod 12:37). Therefore this ingathering is understood as the call to faith in Christ. For various people were called from all parts of the earth, and this calling is incomparably greater and more excellent than all the blessings in the Old Testament.

And they will dwell in their own land, in the church militant, and afterward in the church triumphant, which is the land of the living, promised as a reward to the faithful, as I have frequently asserted above.[17]

The Wickedness of the Bad Shepherds

23:9 To the prophets. Next he returns to a more extensive discussion of the worthlessness of the bad shepherds. First, he denounces their lifestyle, and second, he denounces their teaching, where it says: "Thus says the Lord" (23:16). Now the first part is divided into two parts: first, their wicked lifestyle is denounced; second, their punishment is discussed where he says: "Therefore [their way will be like a slippery path in the dark]" (23:12). Regarding the first part, Jeremiah says:

My heart is broken (23:9b) because he felt sorrow on account of the wicked lifestyle of the priests and false prophets. For he still felt compassion

---

17. Nicholas makes this point a number of times in his Jeremiah commentary. See, for instance, his comments on Jer 3:14 in Nicholas of Lyra, *Postilla super Totam Bibliam—Liber Hieremiae* (Strasburg, 1492; repr., Frankfurt am Main: Minerva, 1971), 2:n.p.

for them because of the evil things that he saw were at hand for them, even though he hated their guilt.

I have become like a drunken man (23:9c). He is stunned by their wickedness and their resulting punishment, and so he adds: **In the presence of the Lord** who is preparing vengeance.

23:10 Because the land is full of adulterers, as he said above in 5:8: "Each and every one of them neighed after his neighbor's wife."

For, due to cursing, that is, because of their blasphemies against God and their other wickedness, **the land has mourned, [the pastures in the wilderness have] dried up,** due to excessive drought, which was discussed extensively in chapter 14 above. For just as a meadow can metaphorically be described as "laughing" when it flourishes, so also the land can be said to mourn when it is parched.

And their course has become evil, for they were racing to evils without the bridle of reason and divine law.

And their strength is different from that of their ancient ancestors.

23:11 For the prophet and the priest are defiled by indulgence and greed. **And in my house,** in the temple dedicated to my name, **I have found their wickedness,** the idols that they worshipped, as it says in 2 Kgs 21:1-9.

23:12 Next comes a discussion of the punishment when he says: **Therefore their way will be like a slippery path [in the dark].** In other words: I will inflict even more evils on them.

23:13 And [I saw foolishness] in the prophets of Samaria, who were led into captivity in the sixth year of Hezekiah's reign, as it says in 2 Kgs 18:10-12. Where our text says "foolishness," the Hebrew text says "blasphemy." Therefore he continues: **And they prophesied by Baal,** by seeking a response not from God but from an idol—or, rather, from the demon in the idol. Thus it was a form of blasphemy, because they showed that they esteemed Baal more than God.

23:14 And in the prophets of Jerusalem I saw resemblance to the prophets of Samaria **in the commission of adultery,** that is, idolatry; **and the way of lying.** The prophets of Jerusalem deceived the people of Judah in the same way that the prophets of Samaria deceived the people of Samaria. The Hebrew text reads: "I saw the foulness of adultery and the way of lying." For there is foulness of adultery when an adulteress welcomes an adulterer into the same bed alongside her husband, and so these prophets did the same thing when they placed an idol in the Lord's temple.

And, by their bad example and false words, **they strengthened the hands of the wicked** so that they would persist in sin. **And to me they became like Sodom,** abominable like the people of Sodom. Therefore he continues by speaking about the infliction of the punishment.

23:15 Behold I will feed them with wormwood; I will fill them with the bitterest punishment, **for from the prophets of Jerusalem the pollution** of idolatry and other evils **has gone forth into all the land** of Judah, since the people imitated them.

God Denounces the Teachings of the False Prophets

23:16 Thus says the Lord. Next he denounces the teaching of the false prophets and priests; first, by condemning their falsehood, and second, by mocking them with the truth, where it says: "Therefore, if [this people or the prophet or the priest asks you]" (23:33). The first part is divided into two parts, because first God condemns their falsehood, and second he condemns the way they embellish their message, where he says: "I have heard [what the prophets who prophesy lies in my name have said]" (23:25). Regarding the first point he says:
Do not listen to the words of the prophets who prophesy falsehood in order to deceive you (23:16b).
[They speak] a vision of their own heart, counterfeited by them (23:16c).

23:17 They say to those who blaspheme me with their lips and their deeds, **"You will have peace."** They make them feel secure and encourage them in their evil deeds.

23:18 For who has stood in the council of the Lord? Who among the prophets has spoken this way? In other words: No one, for the opposite will occur. Therefore he continues:

23:19 Behold the whirlwind of the Lord's indignation, an attack of divine vengeance **upon the head of the wicked,** whether they are priests or common people.

23:20 The Lord's wrath will not turn away. It will not be impeded; rather, there is no doubt that it will come. **In the latter days,** in the time of the destruction of the city (which here is called "last" because this was the end of the Judean kingdom) **you will understand my counsel.** In other words: Through the outcome you will see the punishment I have planned to inflict.

23:22 If they had stood in my council by believing the words of my prophets, **and if they had made my words known to the people,** which was their responsibility, **I would have turned all of them from their evil way,** by conferring on them the spirit of true repentance.

23:23 Do you really think I am a God nearby, says the Lord, and not a God far off, knowing only the things that are near me and not the things that are far away? This is not mentioned in order to deny God's presence everywhere but to deny the false teaching of certain priests who said that God paid attention only to higher matters and not to these lesser things. This error began at the time of holy Job. For this reason, Job 22:14 says, in the voice of someone committing this error: "He walks around the corners of heaven and does not pay attention to our matters." But since God's care, though hidden, pertains to all things, whatever they may be, he continues:

23:24 If a man can be hidden in secret places [and I will not see him]. In other words: He cannot be hidden. This is proved because God's presence is everywhere, as it says: **Do I not fill heaven and earth?** In other words: Yes, I do.

23:25 I have heard the things. Next he condemns the way the prophets embellish their message. **I have heard the things that the** false **prophets have said,** for their words are known to me, **those who prophesy lies in my name.** They preface their false prophecies with the words, "Thus says the Lord," just as genuine prophets do. They say: **"I have dreamed.** I received a vision from God in a dream." Since, as he said, they did this in order to deceive the people more easily, he continues:

23:27 They seek to make my people forget my name, through their own false teaching. Therefore he continues:

23:28 Let the prophet who has a meaningless **dream tell the dream.** In other words, that person should refer to it as a dream and not preface it with the words, "Thus says the Lord."

And let the one who has my word, as Jeremiah and other genuine prophets do, **speak my word,** prefacing it with the phrase, "Thus says the Lord."

What does straw have in common with wheat? Just as straw should not be mixed together with wheat, or vice versa, neither should the Lord's name be attached to the false teaching of prophets.

23:29 Are my words not like fire [and like a hammer that breaks the rock to pieces]? It is as if he were saying: Yes, they are. For this reason Jeremiah said above in 20:9: "The word of the Lord came into my heart as something like a burning fire." In other words: Just as fire consumes straw and a hammer breaks rocks, so the power of my name by which they embellish their falsehoods will be the means by which they are crushed and consumed. Therefore he continues:

23:30 Behold I—supply the words "am set"—**against the prophets,** to punish the false prophets, **who steal my words** from the genuine prophets. They carefully observed the genuine prophets' manner of speaking, and they used this in their false prophecies. So, at the beginning of Zedekiah's reign, Hananiah heard Jeremiah saying, "Thus says the Lord of Hosts: Behold, I will break the bow of Elam," in Jer 49:35 below. And, imitating this, Hananiah said in the fourth year of Zedekiah's reign, "Thus says the Lord: I will break the yoke of Nebuchadnezzar," etc. in 28:2. Therefore he continues:

23:31 Those who use their tongues, who use the Lord's prophets' manner of speaking, **and say, "The Lord says,"** in their false prophecies.

23:32 Behold I [am set] against the prophets. This should be explained the same way that it was explained above (23:30).

Who have lying dreams, saying they had a vision from God in their dreams, **and led my people astray through their lies** that they had fabricated, **and through their wonders.** The Hebrew text reads, "through their ecstasies." Sometimes they pretended that they were rapt in a trance, losing awareness of their senses, in order to falsely convey the magnitude of the revelation that came to them. Such things can be called "wonders," because they cause naive people to marvel.

God Denounces Those Who Mock True Prophecy

23:33 Therefore if this people asks. Here he condemns their wickedness when they mock the truth. Regarding this point, you should understand that the priests and the false prophets derisively referred to the prophecy of Jeremiah and the other prophets of the Lord as a "burden." And they caused the people to speak in this fashion for two reasons. The first reason is that the prophets of the Lord, when condemning people's faults, threatened them with heavy punishments, which the false prophets called "burdens." The other reason is that these punishments were announced by the Lord's prophets a very long time before they actually occurred, and therefore the false prophets derisively said, "a burden, a burden," insinuating by this that these prophecies were laughable, something frivolous and ineffectual. For this reason, the Lord threatens the mockers with punishment. Here, when this is said to Jeremiah, acting as the Lord's representative, a detailed discussion is presented.

Therefore if this people [or the prophet or the priest] question you, saying, "What is the burden of the Lord?" derisively calling your prophecy a "burden," **you shall say to them, "You are the burden,** unable to be held up, because of the weight of your sins." Therefore he continues: **Indeed, I will cast you away** into captivity, **says the Lord,** just as a burden that is unable to be supported is cast down.

23:34 As for the prophet and priest and people who say, "The burden of the Lord," mocking genuine prophecy, **I will visit that man and his household.** I will severely punish him directly, and I will punish him through his relatives. Consequently he instructs them to speak respectfully about the prophet of the Lord whenever he is discussed.

23:35 Every one of you will say to your neighbor and to your relative; you should speak this way about the Lord's prophecy: "**What has the Lord answered** when Jeremiah is asked for prophecies? **And what has the Lord said** by inspiring prophets?"

23:36 And the burden of the Lord will be mentioned no more. You will no longer call the Lord's prophecy "a burden." Every person's own word will be called a "burden." Those who spoke this way about the Lord's prophecy, calling it a burden, will be severely punished for talking in such a way. **For you have perverted the words of the living God, [of the Lord of Hosts, our**

God]. You have referred to the prophecy in a twisted way, derisively calling it a "burden." The Hebrew text reads, "And you have perverted the words of the living *Gods*," through which the plurality of the divine persons is shown; and the unity of essence is shown when it adds, in the singular, "of the Lord of Hosts, our *God*."

23:37 Thus you shall say to the prophet, ["What has the Lord answered you? And what has the Lord spoken?"] One ought to speak with the Lord's prophet in a respectful way. This is made apparent from the fact that the words are repeated, identical to what was said in the earlier assertion (23:35). Since they had contempt for this warning from God, the punishment follows where he says:

23:39 Therefore, behold I will take you away from your land, **carrying you** to a foreign land, which was fulfilled, in part, through the deportation of Jehoiachin, king of Judah, and it was completed through the Babylonian captivity in the time of Zedekiah.

Paul of Burgos's Addition to Lyra's Comments on Jeremiah 23:6[18]

In chapter 23, regarding the part where the postill says, "Now you should understand that the Hebrews [whom we cited as authorities for this passage do not confess the divinity of the Christ]":

Here the Hebrews not only endeavor to evade the truth of this authoritative passage that makes Christ's divinity abundantly clear, when they have a different understanding of the literal meaning, just as the author of the postill says when he correctly refutes this different understanding in the postill. But they also say that the Tetragrammaton name of the Lord is, in its essence, not appropriate for any sort of creature whatsoever. In Scripture, the aforementioned creature is named because of something accomplished by God himself. To address this point, they cite Exod 17:15, where it says: "Moses built an altar and named it 'The Lord, my exaltation.'" And where we have "Lord" [*Dominus*], in Hebrew the Tetragrammaton name is used, which is not appropriately applied to the altar in its essence [as an altar], but it receives this

---

18. Paul of Burgos (né Solomon ha-Levi, d. 1435) was a learned Spanish rabbi who converted to Christianity and eventually became archbishop of Burgos. He wrote additions to Lyra's postill, which were frequently included in early printed editions.

name because of the accomplishment of the Lord himself, who exalted the people of Israel. Hence, in the same place the postill offers this explanation, that when they assert that when God's proper name is used—namely, **the Lord, our just one**—regarding this righteous branch raised up from David, it is not used to refer to its essence, but because of what was accomplished by God himself who did the justifying. But this splitting of hairs does not hold up, for just as it says in the Talmud, in the book *Bababata,* also called *Babalbatra,* in the section that begins "The one who sells a ship," it expressly says that the Messiah is called by the Tetragrammaton name of God. On this matter, they invoke this passage from Jeremiah as support: **This is the name they will call him, "The Lord, our just one"** (23:6).[19] And thus it is clear that the name of God is understood to refer to God's essence in this source, for there they are speaking about the name of God, understood essentially, as it is apparent in that very passage.

Paul of Burgos's Addition to Lyra's Comments on Jeremiah 23:33

In the same chapter, regarding the part where the postill says: "Regarding this point, you should understand that the priests and the false prophets derisively referred to the prophecy as a 'burden.'" In this passage, where we have "burden," the Hebrew text uses the term *masa,* which can be understood in one sense as "burden." In another sense it means "taking up," namely, the message *taken up* by the prophet.[20] For this reason, in Num 23:7 and 24:3, where it says regarding Balaam, "taking up the oracle, he said," in Hebrew it uses the term *masa,* understood in this sense. For it means "taking up" the word or oracle of God, and it has the same meaning in other similar passages. Therefore, when what was prophesied was serious or weighty, scoffers called this prophecy a "burden," understanding the term according to the first meaning. Since the prophets were accustomed to announcing harsh things to sinners in order to call them back to repentance, the fact that God often mercifully delayed these punishments caused the people who were misled by the false prophets to suppose that the things that the Lord threatened

19. Baba Batra 75b, in *The Babylonian Talmud, Seder Nezikin, Baba Bathra,* ed. I. Epstein, trans. Israel W. Slotki (London: Soncino, 1935), 1:289.

20. The Hebrew word is *maśśā'*. Michael Graves explains: "The word derives from *nś'* ('to carry, lift up') and commonly refers to a 'load' or 'burden.' . . . It is also occasionally used in prophetic literature to introduce oracles, perhaps with the sense 'to raise one's voice'"; in Jerome, *Commentary on Jeremiah,* 146n276.

them with would not come to pass. For this reason, they turned genuine and serious prophecy into a joke, and they spoke to the genuine prophets with derision, saying, "These men declare the heavy weight or burden of the Lord." So it was said that they no longer had prophecies or visions, but only the burden or heavy weight of the Lord. Thus the Lord said to Jeremiah: **Therefore if this people [or the prophet or the priest question you, saying, "What is the burden of the Lord?" you shall say to them, "You are the burden"]** (23:33). This interpretation is held in greater honor.

Chapter 28

Introduction to the Chapter

28:1 And it came to pass. Next Jeremiah prophesies against the false prophet Hananiah. And this is divided into two sections, because first Hananiah's prophecy is presented, and second, the prophecy is condemned by the Lord where it says: "The word of the Lord came to Jeremiah" (28:12). The first section is divided into two parts, because first Hananiah prophesies with words, and second, he prophesies with a visible sign where it says: "And Hananiah took [the chain]" (28:10). Furthermore, this first part is divided into two, because first Hananiah's prophecy is presented, and second Jeremiah's response is provided where it says: "And Jeremiah said [to the prophet Hananiah]" (28:5).

Hananiah's Prophecy

28:1 [And it came to pass in that year, at the beginning of the reign of Zedekiah, king of Judah, in the fourth year, in the fifth month, that Hananiah son of Azzur, a prophet from Gideon, spoke to me in the house of the Lord before the priests and all the people, saying.]
Regarding the first section, the time is indicated when it says: **And it came to pass.** It is in the fourth year of Zedekiah, when the king's messengers had come to him, according to what is added afterward (37:1–3). **In the fourth year.** But, contrary to this, it seems that this takes place in the beginning of Zedekiah's reign, since it is not possible to properly refer to the fourth year of his reign as its "beginning." For this reason, Rabbi Solomon says that here the beginning of his reign is understood as referring to the time in which Nebu-

chadnezzar placed him in command of five kings, as previously mentioned in the preceding chapter (27:3), and this was the fourth year of Zedekiah's reign.[21]

Hananiah spoke to me, by addressing a message to me when I was asserting the opposite.

28:2 "Thus says the Lord of Hosts, the God of Israel: I have broken the yoke of the king of Babylon." For Hananiah had heard Jeremiah speaking during the first year of Hezekiah's reign when Jeremiah said, "Thus says the Lord of Hosts: Behold, I will break the bow of Elam" (49:35). Then, after this, in the fourth year of Zedekiah's reign, Hananiah imitated Jeremiah's words when he said, **"Thus said the Lord,"** because false prophets make use of the Lord's prophets' manner of speaking, just as says above in chapter 23.[22] The literal meaning of the rest of this part is clear.

28:5–6 And Jeremiah said. Next the text presents the response of Jeremiah who said: **Amen! May the Lord do so. [May the Lord fulfill your words that you prophesied, that the vessels may be brought again into the house of the Lord, and that all of the exiles may return from Babylon to this place.]** For Jeremiah desired the return of the exiles and the vessels that had been carried away when Jeconiah was exiled; however, divine will took precedence over this wish. Since he knew these things were not going to come to pass, he added the following:

28:7 Nevertheless, listen to this message, through which it will become clear whether your prophecy is true or not.

28:9 The prophet who prophesied future **peace** for the people, **when that one's word comes**—when it comes to pass—**that prophet will be known.** In other words, this will cause people to recognize that this is a true prophet sent by God. The Jews have used this passage as an occasion for going astray, since they said that God's promises for future good are absolute and are not retractable, while warnings about bad things are conditional, coming to pass

---

21. See Rashi's comments on Jer 28:1 translated in *Jeremiah: A New English Translation*, translation of text, Rashi, and commentary by A. J. Rosenberg (New York: Judaica Press, 1989), 2:223–24. Rabbi Solomon ben Isaac of Troyes (1040–1105), commonly known by the acronym Rashi, established an academy in Troyes and commented extensively on the Bible and the Talmud. For a discussion of the five kings said to be placed under Zedekiah's command, see Rashi's comments on Jer 27:3, in *Jeremiah*, trans. Rosenberg, 2:218.

22. See Nicholas of Lyra's comments on Jer 23:30 above.

if they do not repent and are retracted if they undertake repentance, just like the prophecy of Jonah regarding the downfall of Nineveh and the repentance of the Ninevites (Jon 3:1–10).[23] So they explain that when it says here, **The prophet who prophesied peace,** Jeremiah means: "Hananiah, you prophesy good to the people and I prophesy evil to the people. So let it be known that you are a prophet of the Lord if your prophecy is fulfilled, because such a prophecy is not alterable, but if the bad punishments that I prophesy do not occur, I cannot be denounced for falsehood, because sometimes such prophecy is not fulfilled because the people's repentance supersedes it." But this saying appears false when one considers the words of Jeremiah in chapter 18 above, where a promise of something good is deemed retractable since sin supersedes it, just as a warning about something bad is superseded on account of repentance: "I will suddenly speak against a nation and against a kingdom, to root out, to pull down, and destroy it. If that nation, against which I have spoken, repents of its evil, I also will repent of the evil that I planned to do to it" (Jer 18:7–8). And right away, in that same place, this is added regarding a promise of good: "And I will suddenly speak of a nation and of a kingdom to build up and plant it. And if it does evil in my eyes, I will repent of the good that I said I would do to it" (Jer 18:9–10). From this it is clear that just as a threat of something evil is not carried out by God due to repentance, so also a good promise is taken away when sin is committed. On this point, one could also mention many other passages in the holy writings of the Old Testament, but I will omit them for the sake of brevity. However, you should understand that God is more prone to mercy than to condemnation. Consequently, it is more likely that God will not carry out an evil threat than that God will take away a good promise, even a conditional promise and threat, and Jeremiah's message is understood this way: "Let the truth of the prophet who announces something good be known when it comes to pass, since God is not prone to taking away a good promise."

28:10 And Hananiah took [the chain from the neck of Jeremiah the prophet and he broke it]. Next Hananiah confirms his words with a visible sign, by taking the chain from Jeremiah's neck and breaking it, to show by a deed and a visible sign that the king of Babylon's domination would be completely taken away.

---

23. See Rashi's comments on Jer 28:7–8, in *Jeremiah*, trans. Rosenberg, 2:225. Here Rosenberg explains that Rashi and Maimonides shared the view that a favorable prophecy would not be renounced but God could renounce an evil prophecy.

God Reproves Hananiah

28:12 And Jeremiah went away, refusing to contend against Hananiah. **And the word of the Lord came to Jeremiah.** Next the passage deals with the condemnation of Hananiah, first with respect to his false prophecy, which was spoken in the name of the Lord.

28:13 You have broken chains of wood, presumptuously signifying something that was false. **And you will make iron chains for them.** Due to your lies, you will make them rebel against the king of Babylon. Because of this they will incur incomparably more evil than before. The rest of the literal meaning is clear until the point where it says:

28:15 And Jeremiah said [to Hananiah: "Hear now, Hananiah. The Lord has not sent you, and you made this people trust in a lie"]. Here he presents the condemnation of Hananiah himself when he says:

28:16 "Behold I will send you away from the face of the earth," through death, through which humans are removed from the surface of the earth and are buried in the ground.

28:17 And Hananiah the prophet died in that year, so Jeremiah's truthfulness would be proved, **in the seventh month.** Thus, from the time Jeremiah had said this until Hananiah's death, two months had passed, since he had foretold this in the fifth month, as it is clear at the beginning of this chapter (28:1).

Chapter Twenty-Nine

Jeremiah's Letter to the Exiles in Babylon

29:1 Now these are the words of the letter. Next, in this passage, he prophesies against Jeconiah, who had already been taken to Babylon with his mother, as well as the nobility, the priests, and many prophets, but he hoped and longed to return to Judea—as did those who had been transported with him, since they were misled by the false prophets present among them. But by writing to them, Jeremiah was trying to dispel that false confidence. Now this passage is divided into two parts. First, it provides an introduction to Jeremiah's letter; then the letter's contents, where it says: "Thus says the Lord" (29:4).

The introduction first mentions the person who sent the letter when it says: **which the prophet Jeremiah sent** (29:1b). And it mentions the place from which he sent the letter when it says: **from Jerusalem** (29:1c).

Second, the introduction mentions the people to whom Jeremiah sent the letter when it adds: **to remnant of the elders,** etc. (29:1d). The literal meaning is clear until it says:

29:2 And the lady [*domina*], the mother of the king; **and the eunuchs,** the attendants of the king and queen, who are called "eunuchs" not because they had been castrated but because of their honorable chastity. In ancient times such attendants had positions in royal homes, especially to render humble service to the ladies. The Savior uses this expression to refer to such people in Matt 19:12: "There are eunuchs who have made themselves eunuchs for the kingdom of heaven." **And the artisans and metal workers.** These words are explained in chapter 24 above.[24] Third, it explains who carried the letter, when it says:

29:3 By the hand of Elasah son of Shaphan [and Gemariah son of Hilkiah], whom Zedekiah, king of Judah, sent to carry the tribute that he owed to the king of Babylon, or they were sent there for some other matter.

29:4 Thus says the Lord. Next, the text provides the contents of the letter, in which Jeremiah first dispels the false confidence of those who had been deported. Second, it mentions the punishment of those who were being deceptive, where it says: "Thus says the Lord" (29:8). The first section has two parts. First, he dispels their false confidence; second, he declares what is true, where he says: "For thus says the Lord" (29:10). Regarding the first point, Jeremiah speaks in the *persona* of the Lord.

29:5-6 Build houses [and dwell in them; and plant orchards, and eat their fruit. Take wives and have sons and daughters; and take wives for your sons, and give your daughters to husbands, and let them bear sons and daughters. Be multiplied there, and do not be few in number]. In other words: Prepare yourselves to stay in Babylon for a long time by providing yourselves with homes, fruits of the land, and a large number of offspring. Do not place false hope in returning quickly. Therefore he adds:

24. See Nicholas of Lyra, *Postill on Jeremiah* 24:1, where he explains vocabulary that might be unfamiliar to his students and readers: *faber*, which he defines as an artisan able to do intricate work, and *inclusor*, a metalworker who puts gemstones into precious metals such as gold and silver.

29:8 Do not let your false **prophets mislead you** when they announce a return that is close at hand.

29:10a For thus says the Lord. Here he announces to them the promise that is true. First, he makes an announcement to those who were deported into Babylon. Second, he announces the opposite to those dwelling in Jerusalem, where it reads: "For thus says the Lord [to the king who sits on the throne of David and to all those who dwell in this city]" (29:16). Regarding the first part, he says: **For thus says the Lord** (29:10a). In other words: Do not believe the false prophets, for this is the Lord's judgment regarding your return.

29:10b When the seventy years in Babylon begin to be completed. According to the Hebrews, this is the total number of years that passed from the deportation of Jehoiachin until the first year of Cyrus.[25] According to others, the computation of these years begins later, from the destruction of the city under Zedekiah, as we wrote above in chapter 25.[26]

I **will visit you** just as a compassionate father does for his children. The rest is clear until it says: **So that I may bring you back** to Jerusalem. It is not the case that all of them returned in person, since by that time many of them had died, especially those who were already advanced in years.

29:11 So that I may give you an end of your captivity **and patience** in the meantime, until the aforementioned end.

29:12 And you will call on me, and I will listen, and you will go to your land. The rest is clear until it says:

29:14 [And I will gather you] out of all nations, because, in the Babylonian Empire, there were various nations to which the Judeans were deported in the time of Joachim and Zedekiah, and they returned from those places when Zerubbabel led them.

29:15 Because you have said, "The Lord has raised up prophets for us [in Babylon]," since you believed the false prophets who deceived you and said they were speaking in the Lord's name, I have announced to you the time

---

25. See the comments of David Kimḥi on Jer 25:12 in *Jeremiah*, trans. Rosenberg, 1:204.
26. Nicholas of Lyra, *Postill on Jeremiah* 25:1.

when you will return to Judea, so that you will not believe those who say to you that you ought to return right away.

29:16 For thus says the Lord. Here he withdraws this promise from King Zedekiah and his people, those who did not immigrate to Babylon, by announcing that they would suffer things that were much harsher, and so he adds:

29:17 Thus says the Lord of Hosts, that is, of angels.

Behold, I will send upon them the sword, and famine, and pestilence. All these things came upon them when they were besieged in Jerusalem, as it says in 2 Kgs 25.

And I will cause them to be like bad figs that cannot be eaten, abominable to God and humans, just as it says above in chapter 24 in the parable of the figs.

29:18 I will give them over into affliction, through harsh and servile work, **to all the kingdoms of the earth.** This expression is used because there were a number of kingdoms under the king of Babylon.

To be a curse. This refers to the harsh words that were spoken to them.

And a bewilderment, because of astonishment at their misery.

And a hissing of derision. The literal meaning of the rest is clear.

29:21 Thus says the Lord. Here he presents the punishment of the false prophets in Babylon who deceived the exiled people. First, he mentions the punishment of two people at the same time. These two were not only false prophets but also adulterers. Second, he mentions the punishment of a third person who was not only a speaker of falsehood but also a persecutor of the truth where he says: "And to Shemaiah" (29:24). Now the names of the first two are given when it says:

29:21b To Ahab son of Kolaiah and to Zedekiah son of Maaseiah. Then he adds their punishment when he says: **Behold, I will deliver you into the hand of Nebuchadnezzar.** Our interpreters commonly say that these were the two old men whom Daniel convicted for their false testimony against Susannah, and for this reason they were condemned to death, as we read in Dan 13.[27] However, since the Judeans in Babylon were slaves, they did not

---

27. Hugh of St. Cher, *On Jeremiah* 29:21, in *Opera Omnia* 4:243v. Daniel 13, which contains the story of Susannah, is a Greek addition to the book of Daniel.

have any justice system, nor did they have the authority to condemn anyone to death. So it adds here that they were delivered into Nebuchadnezzar's hands, since the Judeans made an accusation against them, because of their false testimony, in the presence of the king or someone acting on the king's behalf. This person sentenced them to death, and the Judeans carried out the execution. Therefore when Dan 13 says that the people put them to death, you should understand that they were only carrying out the execution. The rest is clear until it says:

29:22 [May the Lord make you like Zedekiah and Ahab,] whom the king of Babylon roasted in the fire. But, contrary to this, Dan 13 says that they were stoned to death.[28] In response, one should say that this is because sometimes Scripture refers to capital punishment as "fire," or else because first they were stoned and afterward they were burned up, just as Josh 7:25 says regarding Achan. What is called punishment of "fire" refers to punishment by stoning in Daniel. However, what is said concerning them is not authentic because it is not from the canonical scriptures.[29] The rest is clear until it says:

29:23 I am the judge. This means: No one can escape my justice.

29:24 And to Shemaiah. Here the Lord presents the punishment of the third person, who was not only a false prophet for those who were in Babylon but also persecuted Jeremiah by writing from Babylon to the high priest who was in Jerusalem, telling him to imprison Jeremiah for writing to say that their hope of a quick return from exile was false. This is why he says:

29:25-26 Because you sent books, that is, letters, **in your name,** as though you did it in the name of a true prophet, saying to Zephaniah, **"The Lord made you** high **priest in place of the priest Jehoiada."** Even though Jehoiada

28. In fact, Dan 13:61–62 does not specify the mode of execution for the elders, but since it says that they experienced the fate they intended for Susannah (whose mode of execution is not specified in Dan 13:45), Nicholas presumes that the Judean people at the time of Daniel followed the practice of stoning mentioned in John 8:1–11.

29. Daniel 13 is part of the Greek additions to the book of Daniel. Nicholas, like most medieval commentators, was familiar with Jerome's distinction between "canonical books" (*libri canonici*), which were available to him in Hebrew or Aramaic, and "books of the church" (*libri ecclesiastici*), available only in Greek. See Jan Willem van Henten, "2 Maccabees," in *The Oxford Encyclopedia of the Books of the Bible*, ed. Michael D. Coogan (New York: Oxford University Press, 2011), 2:16.

had lived long before that time, he nevertheless was mentioned by name because he was a person of great authority and sanctity, in order to flatter this person, Zephaniah, as though Shemaiah were saying: "You are as holy and authoritative as Jehoiada was."[30]

"**That you should be ruler,** that is, leader of the priests, **over every man who raves,** who prophesies by the power of a demon inspiring his phantasm, **in order to put him into the stocks,** into a dungeon, so that he may not be able to spread such ideas among the people."

29:27 "And now why have you not rebuked Jeremiah, who is prophesying in that manner in Jerusalem, and not only verbally in Jerusalem but also through his writings in Babylon?" Therefore he adds:

29:28 "For he has also sent a letter **to us in Babylon,** as it says in the beginning of this chapter, **saying,** in the same letter: **It**—the time of your lingering in Babylon—**is long; build houses;** prepare yourselves for a long stay," just as we explained above (29:5–6).

29:29 So Zephaniah the priest read this letter in order to reprove Jeremiah for the letter that he had sent. The rest is clear until it says:

29:32 Behold. Here the Lord mentions Shemaiah's punishment when he says: **I will visit upon Shemaiah the Nehelamite,** punishing Shemaiah himself. **And upon his offspring,** punishing him through his relatives. **He will not have a man sitting**—living—**in the midst of this people** when they return to Jerusalem. **And he will not see the good that I will do to my people** when I liberate them from captivity, **because he has spoken against the Lord,** by accusing Jeremiah of falsehood when he was speaking from the mouth of the Lord.

Chapter Thirty

Introduction to the Chapter

30:1 This is the word [that came to Jeremiah]. Earlier Jeremiah had prophesied harsh things to the people. Here he prophesies favorable things. Now

---

30. Jehoiada, who is mentioned in 2 Chr 22–24, lived during the ninth century BCE.

the most favorable thing he prophesied was the coming of Christ as savior of the world. This was figured by the people's salvation from Babylonian captivity, which he mentioned in the preceding chapter in the midst of the harsh things that he declared (Jer 29:10) so that, by contrast, these favorable things would shine forth all the more brightly. Therefore, after using a figure, it is appropriate to announce the thing that is being figured, namely, general salvation through Christ.[31] Jeremiah does this in this chapter and the next. It is not possible to interpret this passage suitably in any other way than to apply it to the time of Christ, as it will become clearer in the discussion that follows. Now, regarding the sequence of this prophecy, you must understand that when prophets write, they do not always adhere to strict chronological order. Often they write first about things that are done later, and vice versa. As Hebrew [Jewish] scholars say: "There is no earlier and later in the law," by which they mean that, in the Old Testament, the sequence in which things are described does not follow chronological order.[32] Latin [Christian] scholars say the same thing, that often holy scripture says things in anticipation, mentioning later things ahead of time, and mentioning earlier things afterward in recapitulation. In this book, Jeremiah proceeds this way in many places, as it is clear in earlier chapters and will become clear in the following chapters. Jeremiah proceeds in this way in this passage, because first he announces Christ's reign. Second, in the next chapter, he announces Christ's coming. Regarding the first point, you should understand that when Christ became human at the moment of his incarnation, he had dominion over all created things in an authoritative sense though not in an administrative sense, but he received this [administrative] mode of dominion at his resurrection, as it says in Matt 28:18: "All power in heaven and earth is given to me." And he will have it more perfectly at the final judgment. For this reason, the Apostle says in Hebrews 2:8: "At this time we do not yet see all things subjected to him." Moreover, the antichrist's persecution precedes the final judgment. And first, in this passage, the persecution by the antichrist is announced. Second, Christ's dominion is announced where it says: "It will come to pass [in that

31. In this passage, a figure (*figura*) refers to a symbol or image that prefigures another individual or event.

32. A commonly repeated rabbinic maxim, derived from the Babylonian Talmud, states: "There is no earlier and later in the Torah." Pesaḥim 6b, in *The Babylonian Talmud, Seder Moʻed*, ed. I. Epstein, trans. H. Freedman (London: Soncino, 1938), 25. See Tal Goldfain, *Word Order and Time in Biblical Hebrew Narrative* (New York: Oxford University Press, 2004), 7.

day, says the Lord of Hosts, that I will break his yoke from off your neck and strangers will no longer ruler over him]" (30:8). Third, God responds to an unspoken question where it says: "But [I will not utterly consume] you" (30:11).

God Promises Restoration

30:2 Regarding the first matter, Jeremiah is told: **Write down all these things for yourself.** These things will occur in the distant future, and they are worthy of being remembered. Therefore they should be written down.

30:3 Behold the days are coming, says the Lord, that I will restore the captivity of my people Israel and Judah. This cannot be understood as referring to the return from Babylonian captivity, nor any other subsequent temporal deliverance, since, according to the scholars among the Hebrews, and in accordance with actual fact, the people of Israel are still divided from the people of Judah.[33] The Israelite people did not return from captivity, nor do the Jews expect them to return until the coming of the Messiah himself, whom the Jews await. And therefore, for us who confess that his coming has already occurred, it is appropriate to understand the literal sense of this in a different way. And some say that this should be understood as pertaining to the Jews' spiritual return to the preaching of Christ and the apostles. Some of these Jews were from the kingdom of Israel, because, when Shalmanesar captured this kingdom, some people fled and escaped. Afterward they lived in the kingdom of Judah, at the time of Hezekiah (2 Chr 30:6). They were together with those who were brought from the kingdom of Judah into Babylon, and they returned together with the returnees, just as it is written about more fully in 2 Kgs 18. For this reason he continues:

And I will return them to the land [that I gave to their ancestors]. This is understood as pertaining to the Land of the Living, which was the principal meaning of the promise made to Abraham, just as it is written about more fully in Gen 15 and many other places. But since the number of Judeans who believed the preaching of Christ and the apostles was relatively small, therefore the statement, "**I will restore the captivity of my people Israel and Judah,**" is better understood as referring to the general conversion of the Jews to Christ when the falsity of the antichrist is revealed

---

33. See the comments on Jer 30:3 by Kimḥi, in *Jeremiah*, trans. Rosenberg, 2:237.

by Elijah and Enoch.[34] Therefore the text continues with a discussion of the antichrist's persecution.

The Church's Tribulations during the Time of the Antichrist

30:5 For thus says the Lord: We have heard a voice of terror. Now the Lord Christ numbers himself among his faithful who will be suffering at that time, in the same way that he said in Acts 9:4: "Saul, why do you persecute me?"

30:6 Ask now, and see: Can a male produce [*generat*] children? Here you should understand the word "produce" [*generare*] to mean "give birth" [*parere*], for the Hebrew text reads: "Can a male give birth?" This passage refers to the future distress and difficulties that Christ's faithful ones will experience at that time. Therefore he continues:

Why, then, have I seen every man—every Christian, no matter how brave and steadfast—**with his hands on his loins like someone giving birth?** That is, in the manner of a woman giving birth, when she places her hands on her loins. **And all faces have turned pale.** Their complexion is altered because of distress and fear.

30:7 Alas, for that day is great. That day will be "great" because of the intensity of tribulation. **Nothing is like it.** For this reason Matt 24:21 says: "For there will be great tribulation, such as there has never been from the beginning of the world until now, and never will be."

[And it is the time of tribulation for Jacob,] and he will be saved out of it. The name Jacob, which means "one who supplants," here refers to everyone predestined to life eternal.

30:8 And it will come to pass. Here the text mentions the dominion of Christ, who will kill the antichrist "with the breath of his mouth," as it says

---

34. Many medieval Christians believed that at the end times Enoch and Elijah would return to earth, preach against the antichrist, and convert a large number of Jews to Christianity. Enoch and Elijah were identified as the "two witnesses" sent to prophesy in Rev 11:3. See Richard Kenneth Emmerson, *Antichrist in the Middle Ages: A Study of Medieval Apocalypticism, Art, and Literature* (Seattle: University of Washington Press, 1981), 95–101. For a discussion of the "two witnesses" (Rev 11:3) in the thought of Nicholas of Lyra, see Philip D. W. Krey, "The Apocalypse Commentary of 1329: Problems in Church History," in *Nicholas of Lyra: The Senses of Scripture*, ed. Philip D. W. Krey and Lesley Smith, Studies in the History of Christian Thought 90 (Boston: Brill, 2000), 278–88.

in 2 Thess 2:8, as well as a large portion of those who follow the antichrist. Therefore he continues:

I will break his yoke from your neck, the neck of the church militant.

And I will burst his chains, his machinations and deceptions.

And those who are strangers to God will no longer rule over him.

30:9 But they will serve the Lord their God, that is, God the Father, **and David their king,** the incarnate Son of God. Thus, as I have frequently stated, the Chaldean translation that the Hebrews have is accurate: "And they will obey the Messiah, the son of David their king."[35] So according to the learned Hebrews, this is understood, in the literal sense, as pertaining to the Christ.

Whom I will raise up for them. In other words: I will cause salvation to appear to them. And also, understood literally, it means that God the Father raised Jesus from the dead.

30:10 Therefore, do not fear. This is to fortify them against the coming tribulation of the antichrist.

I will save you from a faraway country. At that time the Judeans who were about to be saved were dispersed in faraway countries of the world, and they were captives there.

And Jacob will return to Christ. This should not be understood only about the Jews who would be converted at that time but also about Christians returning from the antichrist—those who will be deceived and will repent afterwards.

And he will be at rest from tribulation when the antichrist is destroyed, **and he will have an abundance of all good things, [and there will be none whom he might fear].** This refers to the state of the church triumphant, where it is kept in infinite goodness and perfect security.

30:11 For I will make a consummation among all the nations, since all the nations will abandon their various religions in order to have faith in Christ.

But I will not make [a consummation among you]. Here there is an answer to a two-part implied question. The second part is treated where it says, "Therefore [all who devour you will be devoured]" (30:16). Regarding the first part, one could ask: "Why does the Lord permit his faithful ones to experience tribulation at the time of the antichrist?" And here the answer is that this occurs so that they may be purged of the sins that will be numerous

---

35. *Targum of Jeremiah*, trans. Hayward, 129.

at that time, as it says in Matt 24:12: "And because lawlessness will increase, [the love of many will grow cold]." Therefore he continues: **But I will chastise you in judgment, that you may not consider yourself innocent.**

30:12 Your wound is incurable, because the persecution of the antichrist will be unable to be alleviated by human means

30:13 There is no one to judge your judgment, because, at that time, no one will dare to stand up in support of the righteous ones, in order to acquit them.

30:14 All your lovers have forgotten you, because the earthly rulers who currently defend the church will not dare to show any friendship.

I have struck you with the wound of an enemy. In other words: At that time I will seem like the church's enemy, just as a father punishing his child harshly seems like an enemy in his outward appearance.

Because of the multitude of your iniquities, which will be far more numerous than they are at this time, as we said.

For your sins are hardened. They became hardened due to lack of correction.

30:15 Why do you cry out over your affliction? In other words: It is imposed upon you justly.

Your sorrow is unable to be cured through human means. For this reason Christ will supply the cure by destroying the antichrist, as we previously mentioned.

30:16 Therefore. Here he provides the answer to the second question, for someone could ask: "What will Christ do about the antichrist who is the persecutor and those who adhere to him?" The answer is that they will not escape divine vengeance. And this is what he says: **Therefore all who devour you will be devoured,** not only with temporal death but also with eternal death. **And all your enemies will be led into captivity** by demons.

30:17 For I will close up your scar. I will give a spirit of repentance to you who have been led astray by the antichrist and his retinue. **For they have called you "outcast," O Zion.** That is: You, O church, called by the name "Zion" in Ps 2:6 and Heb 12:22, will be called "outcast" while enduring the antichrist's persecution.

God's Restoration of the Church

30:18 For I will return the captivity of the tents of Jacob, that is, the congregations of the faithful led astray by the antichrist, because a time for repentance will be granted to them.

And the city, that is, the church, which is the unity of Christ's citizens, **will be built in its high place,** in great honor, because at that time everyone will flee there for refuge.

And the temple will be built properly. The worship of Christ, which had been in a state of decline, will be reformed.

30:19 And out of them shall come divine **praise, and the voice of those who frolic,** not dissolutely but devoutly, just as David said about himself in 2 Sam 6:21–22, "I will frolic before the Lord."

30:20 And their children will be as they were in the beginning, as they were prior to the antichrist's persecution.

30:21 And their leader will be one of their own. This refers to Christ, who became truly human.

And I will bring him near, because the human Christ has access to the Father before all others. Therefore he continues: **Who is this,** because of his great eminence, **who sets his heart,** for the will of the human Christ is, in all respects, conformed to the divine will, **to approach me** willingly? For he is the Son of the Father.

30:22 And you will be my people, that is, the people of God the Father, through the Son. And he continues by speaking of the punishment of the wicked.

30:23 Behold the whirlwind of the Lord, on the day of judgment. **It will rest upon the head [*in capite*] of the wicked,** on the antichrist, who, at the time when he is struck, will be the head [*caput*] of those who are wicked. Or: **In the judgment [*in capite*],** referring in a general way to the final sentencing, when they are told, "Depart, cursed ones into the eternal fire," etc. in Matt 25:41.[36]

30:24 In the latter days you will understand these things. By saying this,

---

36. The word *caput,* normally meaning "head," can also refer to a summary judgment or judicial sentence.

Jeremiah intimates that he is speaking about things that will occur in the end times. Since, at that time, all people will be turned to the one God, as previously mentioned, he continues: **At that time, says the Lord, I will be the God of all the families of Israel** (31:1).[37] This is true, whether understood as pertaining to Israel according to the flesh, since at that time all Jews will be converted to Christ, as it has been said, or whether it is understood as pertaining to Israel according to the spirit, since all the faithful are called by the name Israel, as it says in Isa 54.[38]

Paul of Burgos's Addition to Lyra's Comments on Jeremiah 30:21

In chapter 30, where the postill discusses the passage, **I will bring him near, and he will come to me** (30:21b), this is understood prophetically to pertain to the human Christ, who has a twofold connection or access to God. One is through grace, and the other is through personal union. And, because no one else has a comparable twofold access, he adds: **Who is this who sets his heart to approach me?** (30:21c). In other words, there is no one who has a twofold access or attachment to God in the aforementioned way. Now when it says in the postill, "The will of the human Christ is, in all respects, conformed to the divine will," this is true; however, this could also be stated truly regarding the will of the saints. Thus this is not the reason why the phrase, **"Who is this,"** should be spoken exclusively about Christ. For this reason, the preceding explanation seems more appropriate, etc.[39]

Chapter Thirty-One

Introduction to Chapter Thirty-One

31:2a Thus says the Lord. In the Hebrew, the chapter begins here, with a blank space between this verse and the one immediately preceding, which

---

37. As Nicholas explains in his comments on Jer 31:2, the Hebrew text he consulted includes this verse as part of chapter 30.

38. In his comments on Isa 54:2, Nicholas argues that the admonition "Enlarge the site of your tent" refers to inclusion of those who enter the church from Gentile nations; Nicholas of Lyra, *Literal Postill on Isaiah* 54:2, in *Postilla super Totam Bibliam*, vol. 2.

39. That is, Christ's preeminent access to the Father, mentioned in Nicholas's comments on Jer 30:21.

is joined to the previous chapter as part of the same literary passage.[40] For this reason, I have arranged it this way. This chapter deals with things that pertain to Christ's coming. It is divided into three parts. The first part deals with things pertaining to the prediction of Christ. The second part deals with his incarnation, where it says: "Thus says the Lord" (31:15). The third part deals with things pertaining to the consolation of the evangelical law, where it says: "Behold, the days will come" (31:31).

The Lord Will Restore the People to the Land of Promise

The first part is divided into two sections, since the first section presents a figure and the second section presents the thing that is figured, where it reads: "From afar" (31:3). Regarding the first section, you should understand that the salvation of the Israelite people from Egypt was a figure of the salvation accomplished through Christ, who led the faithful through the desert of repentance to the land of the living, just as Moses, in a physical way, caused the children of Israel to cross through the desert in order to possess the land of promise. Regarding this he says:

31:2b The people who survived the sword found grace in the desert. For all who departed from Egypt, aged twenty years or older, died in the desert as it says in Num 14:28-33. And a great many of them were killed by the sword, as is clear in the books of Exodus (17:8-16) and Numbers (14:39-45). Therefore the people who **found grace** were their children who entered into the land of promise. Therefore he continues:

31:2c Israel will go to his rest. And Jeremiah says **"will go,"** speaking about the future. The fact that he had not mentioned that this was entrance into the land of promise was to signify that this was a figure symbolizing entrance into heavenly rest, which was still to come, as the Apostle speaks about at length in Heb 3 and 4.

31:3 From afar the Lord appeared to me. Here, in turn, the thing symbolized in the figure is revealed. Salvation through Christ, which occurred

---

40. The verse numbered in Christian Bibles as Jer 31:1 is numbered as 30:25 in many Jewish Bibles. See *The Jewish Study Bible*, ed. Adele Berlin and Marc Zvi Brettler (New York: Oxford University Press, 2004), 988.

through the establishment of the church, is symbolized by what occurred previously. And because this time [of salvation] was still a long way off, Jeremiah says: **From afar the Lord appeared to me.** And the text continues in the form of a dialogue, with the *persona* of God responding.

I have loved you with an everlasting love. Granted that the Lord had loved all the elect by predestining them from eternity, nevertheless he loved the elect from among the Israelite people in a special way inasmuch as he was going to take on flesh from them. For this reason he granted spiritual gifts to this people. Therefore he continues:

Therefore I have drawn you, with special benefits by giving the law and similar things. For this reason, Ps 147:20 reads: "He has not dealt in such a manner to every other nation, and he has not made his judgments manifest to them." Nevertheless, since they misused these benefits, they fell from honor. Therefore he continues:

31:4 And I will build you again. Rabbi Solomon explains that the city of Jerusalem and the temple built by Solomon, Zerubbabel, and Nehemiah were toppled because they had been made by humans, but what Jeremiah is speaking about here will be created through divine power; therefore it will stand forever.[41] In this matter he speaks truly, but what he adds is false, that, at the coming of the Messiah whom the Jews await, God will build a new Jerusalem—incomparably more magnificent than the former one—in which the Messiah will reign temporally, and all the nations will be subjected to the dominion of the Jews.[42] But what he falsely says *will* be fulfilled has already been fulfilled; for Christ, the true God, built the church, which is called "Jerusalem" in Isa 2:1–3, Heb 12:22, and Rev 21:2: "I saw the holy city Jerusalem," etc., where Christ reigns, and "his kingdom will stand forever" (Dan 2:44).

And you will be built, O virgin Israel. This refers to the faithful people who are designated by the name "Israel." Isaiah 44:5 says: "They will receive the surname 'Israel.'" This is what it says in the Hebrew text, but our translation [of Isa 44:5] reads, "They will be represented [by the name Israel]."

You will be furnished again with your tambourines. According to the literal sense, this means that the faithful will gather in the church

41. See Rashi's comments on Jer 31:4 [31:3] in *Jeremiah,* trans. Rosenberg, 2:244.

42. Nicholas seems to be overinterpreting Rashi at this point. In his comments on Jer 31, Rashi speaks of the exiles returning from the nations to a rebuilt Jerusalem, but not of Jewish dominion over the Gentile nations. See *Jeremiah,* trans. Rosenberg, 2:243–57.

at the sound of church bells in order to give praise to God. Therefore he continues:

And you will go forth in the chorus of those who make merry, not dissolutely, but devoutly, just as when one choir cheerfully sings counterpoint to another choir.

31:5 And you will yet plant vineyards on the mountains of Samaria. This is not able to be interpreted in the literal sense as dealing with those returning from Babylonian captivity, because they never recovered that territory; instead, peoples from elsewhere, who were called Samaritans, were brought there and occupied that land. Therefore it should be interpreted as dealing with the Samaritans who believed Christ's preaching, as it says in John 4:39–42, and the preaching of the apostles as it says in Acts 8:4–25. For the faithful are designated by the name "vineyards," as is clear in many parts of holy scripture. Furthermore, though the entire church may be called "one vineyard" because of the unity of faith, nevertheless it is sometimes called by the plural ["vineyards"] because of the diversity of nations, places and peoples.

And they will not gather the vintage [*vindemiabunt*] before the time has arrived. *Vindemiare* means "to collect the fruit of the vine," for the final fruit of this vine is perfect blessedness, which is not possessed in the present life, but in the future life.

31:6 For there will be a day when the watchmen, the preachers, **will cry out on Mount Ephraim,** in the church. For Ephraim is interpreted as "increasing" or "fruitful." And, still interpreting it literally, it means that Christ and also the apostles preached in these regions.

Arise, let us go up, by advancing from what is good into what is better, **to Zion,** into the church militant and triumphant, which is called "Zion" in Isa 2:3 and Heb 12:22.

31:7 Rejoice in the joy of Jacob. The Christian people are named in this way because Christ, the apostles, and virtually all of the first faithful ones were descended from Jacob.

And neigh against the head of the nations, against the devil, who held the nations subject to himself through idolatry, which the apostles destroyed—to a great extent—through their preaching. Nevertheless, since it is still the case that not all people believe in Christ, he continues:

O Lord, save the remnant of your people Israel. Here **"remnant of Israel"** refers in a general way to all who would come to believe and, in a special way, to the Jews who will convert around the time of the end of the world.[43] Therefore God's response follows:

31:8 Behold, I will bring them from the north country, and I will gather them from the ends of the earth, etc. For some were brought to faith in Christ from every region of the world, and, at the time of the end of world, this will occur even more fully.

And among them will be the blind, the lame, and the pregnant woman, and the woman who is giving birth, together, a great company of those returning here, that is, those who have impediments keeping them from faith in Christ—impediments that will be removed. It is also possible to interpret this according to the literal sense, because many people were enlightened in body and mind, were made to stand upright, and were healed from similar infirmities—not only bodily infirmities but also spiritual infirmities—by Christ, the apostles, and their successors.

31:9 They will come with weeping, from true contrition.

And I will bring them back in mercy, which is not denied to those who are truly contrite.

And I will bring them through the streams, through the sacraments of the church, in which the waters of grace are offered. As it says in John 4:14: "Those who drink of the water which I give them will never thirst," etc.

In a straight path, in the catholic faith.

For I have become a father to Israel, to the catholic people in a general way, and, in particular, to the converts from Judaism.

And Ephraim is my firstborn, since the first ones called to the catholic faith—such as Andrew, Peter, Philip and Nathanael, as it says in John 1:35–51—were from the kingdom of the ten tribes, which in Scripture is frequently called "Ephraim," because its first king, Jeroboam, was from the tribe of Ephraim, as it says in 1 Kgs 11:26. And because after the calling of the Jews who first believed, though they were relatively few in number, the Gentiles were called, he continues:

31:10 Hear [the word of the Lord, O nations, and declare it in the islands that are far off, and say]: The one who scattered Israel, the one who permitted Israel to be scattered by means of various sects and errors, **will gather**

---

43. For a discussion of the Christian belief that there would be a mass conversion of Jews in the end times, see Emmerson, *Antichrist in the Middle Ages,* 101.

him, into the unity of the catholic faith. The name Israel is understood to refer to any nation predestined to faith, as it says above.[44]

31:11 For the Lord has redeemed Jacob with his own blood.

And delivered him out of the power of the one who was mightier, that is, delivered him from demons, about which it is written in Job 41:33: "There is no power on earth that is its equal."

31:12 And they will come and offer praise on Mount Zion, in the church militant and triumphant, which is called by this name, as we wrote above.

[And they will stream together to the good things of the Lord,] to the grain, the wine, and oil. This should be understood as a figure of speech referring to spiritual benefits that can be understood by humans only by comparison with something physical. The scriptures of the Old and New Testaments frequently use such figures of speech, in which the literal sense is not directly signified through statements but is conveyed through symbolic things, just as it says in Judg 9:8, 14: "The trees went to the bramble," etc. The literal sense does not deal with trees but with humans—Abimelech and the Shechemites. And so, in this passage, "grain" and "wine" are understood as the sacrament of the Eucharist, which is confected under the species of bread and wine. And "oil" refers to the grace that is conveyed in this sacrament and the others.

And to the increase of flocks and herds, the multiplication of the faithful, as it says in Ps 94 [95:7]: "And we are the people of his pasture and the sheep of his hand." And here the smaller ones are called "flocks" and the larger ones are called "herds."

And their soul will be watered like a garden, from the sacraments of the new law, from which waters of grace flow into the soul.

And they will hunger no more. Properly speaking, this refers to the condition of the church triumphant, where hunger is completely satisfied.

31:13 Then the virgin, that is, virgins, **will rejoice in the chorus** of angels, into whose company humans are received.

And I will turn their mourning into perfect and eternal **joy.**

31:14 And I will inebriate, that is, I will fill, **the soul of the priests with fatness,** with fullness of glory, because they are not glorying only in their own glory, but they are also glorying in those who were saved through their

---

44. See Lyra's comments on Jer 31:4.

teaching. For this reason it is said that they have a crown beyond that of ordinary saints (1 Pet 5:1–4).

Rachel Weeps for Her Children

31:15a Thus says the Lord. Here it continues by mentioning things pertaining to Christ's incarnation. First, it deals with his birth. Second, it deals with his conception, where it says: "Set up for yourself a watchtower" (31:21). Third, it deals with what is accomplished by his passion, where it says: "In those days" (31:29). The first part is divided into two sections—a principal section and a supplementary section, where it says: "And there is hope" (31:17). Regarding the first, you should understand that Herod, when he heard about Christ's birth, wished to kill him, as it says in the second chapter of Matthew. Since Herod did not know specifically who Christ was, he killed all the children two years and younger who were in Bethlehem and the vicinity, as it says in the same place (Matt 2:16). And at that time this scripture was fulfilled, as Saint Matthew, illumined by the Holy Spirit, expressly says (Matt 2:17–18). For this reason Catholics who interpret it otherwise Judaize too much, interpreting it in a twisted way. I omit these expositions because of their lengthiness and uselessness.[45] Therefore this is the meaning:

31:15b A voice was heard in the height. The Hebrew text reads, "A voice is heard in Ramah," just as Matthew (2:18) asserts. But you should understand that "Ramah" is an ambiguous name, because, taken one way, it is the proper name of a place that is near Gibeah. Taken in another way, it is a noun describing an attribute, and thus it means "height." Now it is not possible to interpret this as the proper name of a place, because Ramah is not near Bethlehem but is quite a distance away, and Jerusalem is between them. Therefore Jerome translated it as a noun describing an attribute, saying, "**in the height,**" to indicate the magnitude of the cry of the women whose children were slaughtered.

Rachel weeping for her children. For Rachel was buried near Bethlehem, as it says in Gen 35:19. For that reason she was called "mother" of the city of Bethlehem and the entire region, just as, among us, saints whose bod-

---

45. Lyra may be referring to the Dominican postill of Hugh of St. Cher, which says the literal interpretation pertains to the destruction of most of the tribe of Benjamin following the rape of the Levite's concubine in Judg 19–21; Hugh of St. Cher, *On Jeremiah* 31:15, in *Opera Omnia* 4:248r.

ies rest in churches are called patrons not only of these churches but also of the cities and adjacent territories. And so Rachel is said to weep through her daughters—the children's mothers—just as saints are said to suffer together with the afflicted people for whom they are patrons. Now some Jews say that when the Judeans were led captive into Babylon and passed by Rachel's tomb, a voice was heard miraculously coming forth from the tomb, begging God for compassion on those who were led captive.[46] I have provided a discussion of this in my comments on Gen 48, not to affirm this interpretation but only for reference, since this seems to be fictitious—not only because it contradicts the writing of the evangelist but also because it is not probable, for such a great miracle would have been described at the end of 2 Kings, the end of 2 Chronicles, or the end of this book [Jeremiah], in the places where it describes these captives being led off, because the Judeans were very careful to write down the things that gave them honor.[47]

And refusing to be consoled with human consolation.

Because they are not. They are no longer alive in the present age. For this reason it continues with divine consolation.

31:16 Let your voice cease [from weeping, and your eyes from tears], for there is a reward for your work, that is, a reward for your children who are called—and are—the works of their parents, for through this death they have obtained the martyr's prize. Though they died, since they were righteous they descended to hell's limbo.[48] Therefore he adds:

And they will return out of the land of the enemy. This return took place at Christ's resurrection, because at that time Christ led the saints from hell; and at his ascension, when he led them to heaven.

31:17 And there is hope. In the Hebrew text, the stanza begins here, and it is a supplementary section.[49] For [the previous section] dealt with Ra-

---

46. See the comments of the RaDaK (Kimḥi) on Jer 31:14, in *Jeremiah*, trans. Rosenberg, 2:248.

47. See Nicholas of Lyra, *Postill on Genesis* 48:7.

48. Medieval Christians believed that there was a "limbo of the patriarchs," a portion of hell where there was no torment. There faithful people (including the innocent babies slaughtered by Herod) who died before the time of Christ's death and resurrection waited for Christ's descent into hell when he would lead them to blessedness. See Helen Foxhall Forbes, "Diuiduntur in Quattuor: The Interim and Judgement in Anglo-Saxon England," *Journal of Theological Studies* 61 (2010): 680.

49. In the Masoretic text, the letter *samek* before this verse indicates the beginning of a new stanza or paragraph. In the Vulgate, verses 16 and 17 are treated as one sentence.

chel's consolation for the slaughtered infants who are called her children on account of her burial, as we said.[50] Next, this section deals with the consolation she receives regarding her own children—those who receive this designation on account of their birth; for Ephraim, who is understood as referring to the kingdom of the ten tribes [Israel], as previously mentioned, is descended from Rachel through her son Joseph. And here he makes mention of their conversion to God when he says: **And there is hope** of future blessedness.

For your latest ones, for your remaining children, **and** your **children will return to your borders** [*terminos*] to the church militant, which is the destination [*terminus*] in the present life, and to the church triumphant, which is the destination [*terminus*] in the future.[51] This was fulfilled in part when the apostles and others who were from the kingdom of the ten tribes believed the preaching of Christ and the apostles. And it will be fulfilled at the time of the end of the world in their general conversion.

31:18 Listening, I heard Ephraim when he was deported. Ever since then I have been disposed to call him back to faith at a suitable time. Next it speaks in the *persona* of those who are converts now and those who will be converted at the end of the world.

"You chastised me, through whippings in captivity, **like an untamed youth."** The Hebrew text reads, "Like an untamed calf." The people received this name because they worshipped golden calves, which Jeroboam made in 1 Kgs 12:26–33. As it says in Ps 113:16 [115:8]: "Let all who make [idols] be like them, and all who trust in them."

"Convert me, Lord, and I will be converted," for it is not possible for anyone to come to faith without God's prevenient grace, as it says in John 6:44: "No one can come to me unless drawn by the Father who sent me." Therefore it continues:

31:19 "For after I was converted by your prevenient grace **I did penance,** turning back to you advantageously. **And after you showed yourself to me,** shining light on my errors, **I struck my thigh,** curbing my passions. **I was put to shame,** because I provoked you for such a long time." And it continues with the mercy of God who accepts him, when he says:

---

50. That is, Rachel was "mother" or patron of Bethlehem and the surrounding region, because of her burial site there. See Lyra's comments on Jer 31:15.

51. *Terminus* can mean "border" or "destination."

31:20 Surely Ephraim is my honorable son. Here he says "surely," since anyone who returns to God is truly made honorable in his sight.

Surely he is a tender child. The Hebrew text reads, "consoling," meaning "a cause for consolation." As Luke 15:10 states: "There is joy in heaven with the angels over one sinner who repents."

For since I spoke of him, calling him back to a reward, **I will remember him,** giving him a prize. **Therefore my inward parts are troubled.** That is: My inward parts are moved with pity for him.

Prophecies about Christ's Conception

31:21 Set up for yourself. Here it continues by discussing Christ's conception. It is divided into two parts. The first part describes this conception. The second part continues by discussing the spread of the faith, where it says, "Thus says the Lord" (31:23).

In the first part there is a description of the disposition of the people first sent to Christ. This disposition is true repentance, as his precursor John says in Matt 3:2: "Repent, for the kingdom of heaven is at hand." Dealing with this matter, he says:

Set up for yourself a watchtower, to examine your conscience. **Give yourself bitterness,** the sorrow of contrition. **Direct your heart to the right way** of righteousness **in which you**—those who were righteous among the ancient ancestors—**have walked.** Rabbi Solomon says that the true literal meaning of the Hebrew text is: *Set up for yourself watchtowers. Provide palms for yourself. Direct your heart to the right way in which I have walked.*[52] It is possible to explain the phrase, "**Set up for yourself a watchtower,**" in this way: A watchtower is a high place from which someone can look from far off. And this is the meaning: **Set up for yourself a watchtower.** The mystery of the incarnation is still a long way off. As he says in the first part of this chapter: "From afar the Lord appeared to me" (Jer 31:3). *Provide palms for yourself,* by reflecting on the victories of the innocent ones who obtained the palm of martyrdom due to Christ's birth, as it says in the preceding section. These palms were a sign that Christ's birth had

---

52. See Rashi's comments on Jer 31:20 (31:21) in *Jeremiah*, trans. Rosenberg, 2:251. In rabbinic teaching, the palm trees were to be planted to mark or line the path for the returning exiles. In Christian tradition, the palm leaf represents martyrdom. In his translation of the Hebrew text (presented here in bold italics), Lyra draws on Rashi but interprets it in a way that corresponds to Christian salvation history.

come to pass. ***Direct your heart to the right way,*** to the evangelical law, which suffers no distortion—unlike what the law of Moses endured, since it permitted certificates of divorce, as well as charging interest on loans to foreigners, as it says in Deut 23:19–20 and 24:1–4. ***In which I have walked,*** by assuming human nature, as it is written in Acts 1:1: "Jesus began to do and teach."

Return, O virgin Israel, the people predestined to faith, **to these your cities,** to the church militant and triumphant, which are called cities in the Old and New Testaments, as it says above.

31:22 How long will you be dissolute in pleasures, living carnally, **O daughter who wanders** in various vices? **For the Lord created a new thing,** namely, the mystery of the incarnation. He speaks about the future using the past tense because of the certitude of the prophecy. It is placed here on account of the *redditivus* clause in the preceding sentence.[53] In other words: With the coming of Christ's incarnation, the carnal life ought to be put away and a spiritual life should be begun.

A woman will encompass a man. This was fulfilled in Mary, who enclosed Christ, a man perfect in knowledge and virtue, in her womb at the moment of the incarnation.

31:23 Thus says the Lord of Hosts, the God of Israel. Here follows a discussion of the spread of the Christian faith, which occurred after Christ's conception and birth when it says: **Still they will say this word [in the land of Judah].** The name Judah is understood to refer to everyone who acknowledges God. Even the interpreters among the Hebrews say this is the literal sense, as we asserted above in chapter 23.[54] And so the land of Judah is the land of those who believe in and acknowledge Christ.

When I will reverse their captivity, changing it from the slavery of sin to the freedom of grace.

"May the Lord bless you, the beauty of justice, [the holy mountain]." The faithful pray in this way—that the church, which is the beauty of justice and the holy mountain, may be increased in spiritual and temporal goods. In holy scripture, this increase is frequently called "God's blessing."

53. Here the *redditivus* clause (the consequential clause or apodosis) is the first part of the verse, "How long will you be dissolute in pleasure?," which is conditional on the statement "For the Lord created a new thing."
54. See Nicholas's comments on Jer 23:6 above.

31:24 And they will dwell therein, in the church, which is called "the holy mountain," as it says above in chapter 2.[55]

Judah, the faithful one who acknowledges Christ, as we said.

And all its cities, that is, the faithful ones, for it designates the contents by specifying what contains them, just as a city is often used to designate the people contained in it, such as when one says: "Such a great city did this."

The farmers and those who goad the flocks, the eminent shepherds [*pastores*] of the church, and the lesser laborers in the Lord's field, and those who tend Lord's flock.

For I have inebriated, I have filled with grace, **the weary soul** formerly afflicted by sin.

31:26 Therefore I became like someone awakened from sleep. This is the word of Jeremiah, who was weighed down, as though by sleep, when he saw the tribulations that were coming upon his people, but when he heard about the redemption that would take place through Christ, it was as though he woke up, just as it is said regarding Jacob in Gen 45:26, "awakening as though from a heavy sleep," etc., when he heard that his son Joseph was still alive.

And my sleep was sweet to me. It changed into sweetness because of the consolation coming upon him.

31:27 Behold the days are coming, the time of the New Testament, which is called "day," as it says in Rom 13:12: "The night has passed, and the day is at hand."

And I will sow the house of Israel [and the house of Judah], the church, which is the house of all who believe in and acknowledge Christ.

With the seed of humans and the seed of beasts, those who are wise and those who are simple. Rabbi Solomon also explains it this way.[56] In the house of the church, the simple are intermingled with the wise and are increased. It is possible to understand this as dealing especially with the believers coming from the Jews. Of these, certain ones were wise and educated, even from the outset, such as Nathanael, Paul, and many others, and some were simple, such as Peter, Andrew, and Matthew. Around the time of the end of the world, the believers coming from the Jews—both the simple and the educated—will be increased.

---

55. I have not found this in Nicholas's comments on Jer 2, but, throughout his commentary, he identifies Mount Zion with the church. See, for instance, Nicholas's comments on Jer 30:17, in this volume.

56. See Rashi's comments on Jer 31:27 (31:26) in *Jeremiah*, trans. Rosenberg, 2:253.

31:28 And just as I watched over them, etc., in the Babylonian captivity and the captivity by the Romans, **so I will watch over them, to build and to plant.** This has been fulfilled through those who already believed in Christ, and it will be fulfilled more fully through those who will come to believe prior to the judgment.

31:29 In those days. Here he deals with the effect of Christ's passion. At the time of Jeremiah, this proverb circulated among the Judeans about children punished for the sin of their parents: **The parents have eaten a sour grape [and the children's teeth are set on edge].** This endured from the beginning of the world until Christ's passion, because all people descended into hell for the sin of the first parents, but at Christ's passion, by which the door of heaven was opened, this punishment was removed. Therefore this proverb has no place among those who have been made members of Christ through baptism. Certainly, prior to Christ's passion, boys freed from original sin through circumcision descended to that place, together with all sorts of righteous people. Therefore he says: **In those days.**

31:30 But each and every one of them will die for their own wickedness. They will be damned with eternal punishment due to their own wickedness, though, according to judicial ordinances, sometimes children are punished with temporal punishment for the wickedness of their parents, inasmuch as children are, in a certain respect, the property of or a part of their parents.

The New Covenant

31:31a Behold the days will come. Here he continues by mentioning certain things pertaining to the giving of the evangelical law. Since laws are established for cities, its legislation is mentioned first. Second, he deals with the building up of the city's faithful ones, where it says, "Behold the days" (31:38). Regarding the first part he says:

31:31 Behold the days will come, the time of the New Testament, **and I will make with the house of Israel and the house of Judah** (31:31), speaking generally about the faithful who acknowledge Christ, and speaking in particular about the Jews who believe, as it says in Acts 13:46 regarding the Jews: "It is fitting for us to speak God's word to you first," etc.

A new covenant, a new law, for in the Old Testament the law is frequently called a "covenant" and a "pact."

31:32 Not like the pact that I made with your parents, for that was a law of fear but this is a law of love, on the day, at the time, that I took them by the hand and led them from the land of Egypt. For the law was given on Mount Sinai on the fiftieth day after the exodus from Egypt, as it is clear in Exodus (19:1, 16).

The pact that they made void, by transgressing against it many times, as it is clear in the books of Judges, Kings, and Chronicles.

And I held dominion over them, punishing them for their transgressions. He continues with the condition of the new law when he says:

31:33 But this will be [the pact that I will make with the house of Israel], after those days, after the course of the Old Testament is completed.

I will put my law into their inward parts, and I will write it in their heart, for Christ did not write the evangelical law on parchments or physical tablets, but on human hearts. And this happened most powerfully when he sent the Holy Spirit upon believers on the day of Pentecost. Therefore he continues:

31:34 And no longer will a man teach his neighbor, etc., for all of them were taught directly by God about the things pertaining to the new law, and afterward many other saints had knowledge of God poured into them. When interpreted in a general way, this refers to the state of the church triumphant, where all see the divine essence directly.

31:35 Thus says the Lord, who gives the sun as light for the day, [the order of the moon and of the stars as light for the night], arranging all things in an ordered way.

31:36 If these ordinances, the natural phenomena established by me, should fail, [then also the offspring of Israel will fail]. In other words: Just as these things are firmly established, so shall the faithful stand before me when this is fulfilled in the church triumphant.

31:37 If the heavens above can be measured [and the foundations of the earth can be searched out beneath, I also will cast away all the offspring of Israel]. Just as it is not possible for these things to be measured, neither is it possible for the entire offspring of Israel to be cast away, for certain ones were already called to the faith at the time of Christ, and even more will be called at the end of the world.

31:38a Behold the days are coming. Next, in this passage, it deals with the building of the city. Here, according to what Rabbi Solomon rightly says about this, it is not possible to understand this as dealing with buildings constructed by Solomon and Nehemiah, because they were not as large as what is described here.[57] And also because it says at the end: "The Lord's holy place; it will not [be plucked up, and it will never again be destroyed]" (31:40). Now the city built by Solomon was destroyed by the Chaldeans, along with the temple present there; and the Romans destroyed the city and temple rebuilt by Nehemiah. Therefore [Rabbi Solomon] says that Jeremiah is speaking about the rebuilding of Jerusalem and the temple at the coming of the Messiah, at which time Jews expect Jerusalem and the temple to be rebuilt by God in a material way, much richer and larger than it had ever been.[58] However, this idea is based on an erroneous premise—that Christ's coming is yet to come, when in fact it has already taken place. For this reason Jerome and our other interpreters say that this passage cannot be understood as pertaining to the building of a material Jerusalem.[59] Rather, it is spiritual, built by Christ from living stones (1 Pet 2:5). As it says in Rev 21:2, "I saw the holy city Jerusalem," etc., and here its construction is described metaphorically.

31:38 Behold the days are coming, the time of the New Testament.

And the city will be built, that is, the church, about which it says in Ps 86 [87:3]: "Glorious things are said about you, O city of God."

From the tower of Hananel. Hananel means "God's grace." Therefore the tower of Hananel metaphorically designates the apostles and others who first believed. They were strengthened like a tower by the grace of the Holy Spirit descending on them on the day of Pentecost with a visible sign (Acts 2:3). And these first stones were Jews. But because there later were Gentiles, devoutly coming to the faith, who were joined to them in this building, it continues:

57. See Rashi's comments on Jer 31:40 (31:39) in *Jeremiah*, trans. Rosenberg, 2:257.

58. See the rabbinic comments on Jer 31:38–40 (31:37–39) in *Jeremiah*, trans. Rosenberg, 2:256–57.

59. Jerome, *On Jeremiah* 31:38–40, ed. Sigofredus Reiter, CCSL 74 (Turnhout: Brepols, 1960), 323.

All the way to the Corner Gate. Just as two lines are joined together at a corner angle, so the Jews and Gentiles are joined in Christ. For this reason, he is called the cornerstone (Eph 2:20). Since the church militant contains not only righteous people but also sinners, the following is added, referring to their number, though not their worthiness:

31:39 And the measuring line will go out in his sight, etc., to receive sinners, which is expressed even more particularly when it continues:

Upon the hill Gareb, which means "detestable to the magnificent God." The word "Gareb" is translated as "scab."

And it will encompass Goah, which is translated as "a sinning nation."

31:40 And the whole valley of corpses, which refers to carnal people, **and ashes,** which refers to repentant sinners, as it says in the final chapter of Job (42:6): "I do penance in dust and ashes."

And the entire region of death. This refers, in a general way, to all sinners, who dwell in the region of the shadow of death (Ps 23:4)

As far as the torrent Kidron, which is translated "the darkness," with which sin casts a shadow on the mind. Since many of the sinners return to the light of grace and become more eager to be obedient to God, he continues:

All the way to the corner of the eastern Gate of the Horses. They are called "horses" because they are led by the impulse of the Holy Spirit, as it says in Rom 8:14: "All who are led by the Spirit of God are children of God." The Holy Spirit handles them the way a rider handles a horse.

The Holy of the Lord will not be plucked up [and it will not be destroyed, forever]. The worship of God will not be taken away from the church, but it will remain until the end of the world. At that time, it will not be destroyed but will be made more perfect in the homeland where there will be continual and everlasting praise, as it says in Ps 83 [84:4] "Blessed are those who dwell in your house, O Lord. They will praise you forever and ever."

An Alternative Interpretation of Jeremiah 31:38-40

Now even though this [the preceding interpretation] is stated well, it nevertheless seems to me that it is more sound to interpret this passage as dealing with the rebuilding of Jerusalem by the emperor Hadrian after the destruction that took place under Titus and Vespasian, in which the wall of Jerusalem was expanded so that the site of the Lord's passion and burial is now enclosed, as Hugh of Fleury and other historians say.[60] This site was outside Jerusalem at the time that it was destroyed by the Romans, as it is clear in John 19:20, 41, and Heb 13:12. Aelius Hadrian handed the city over to Christians to live in, prohibiting any Jews from dwelling there.[61] Therefore it is possible to explain the literal sense as follows:

31:38 Behold the days are coming and the city, Jerusalem, **will be built to the Lord,** to the honor of the Lord, because only Christians were permitted to live there, as we said.

From the tower of Hananel, all the way to the Corner Gate. In ancient times there were a certain tower and a certain gate by that name, as it says in Neh 3:1 and 2 Kgs 14:13. The space between the two was, as it were, the length of the city, for the wall was extended on the north side, as we said. Therefore he continues:

31:39 And the measuring line will go out beyond the ancient boundaries of Jerusalem in order to encompass the aforementioned sites. Therefore he continues:

Upon the hill Gareb, Mount Calvary, where Christ suffered. Sometimes a single place is called by multiple names, just as Mount Sinai is also called Mount Horeb and the Mountain of God.

And it will encompass Goah. This seems to be the place that is called Golgotha in John 19:17. The names of places frequently alter in this way over time, just as the same place that is called Shechem in Gen 33:18 is called Sychar in John 4:4.

31:40 And the whole valley of corpses, which received that name because people who were condemned to death were punished there, and their corpses remained there. For the same reason it is called **the region of death** and **ashes,** because different punishments were carried out there; some people were burned there, and their ashes remained.

---

60. Hugh of Fleury, *Chronicon,* ed. Bernhard Rottendorf (Münster: Bernhard Roesfeldt, 1638), 72. The *Chronicon* of Hugh of Fleury (fl. 1100–1110), a Benedictine monk, treated world history, biblical history, and ecclesiastical history.

61. After suppressing the Bar Kokhba revolt (132–136 CE), Emperor Hadrian expelled Jews from the province of Judea, which was renamed Syria-Palestina. See Thorston Opper, *Hadrian: Empire and Conflict* (Cambridge, MA: Harvard University Press, 2008), 89–92.

As far as, but not including, **the torrent Kidron,** for, according to the descriptions of the city made by those who have seen it, the aforementioned extension of the wall continues to a point near the torrent of Kidron.

All the way to the corner of the eastern Gate of the Horses, thus named because horses were led through it in order to be watered in the torrent Kidron. It is called "eastern" to distinguish it from another gate, which was called the Gate of the Horses, which was near the temple and received that name because humans were able to ride horses all the way to that place; leaving their horses there, they proceeded on foot to the temple, as it is says in Neh 3:28. That gate was in the western part of the city, as was the temple. This gate, on the other hand, was in the eastern part.

The Holy of the Lord will not be plucked up [and it will not be destroyed, forever]. This refers to the sepulcher building, which the Saracens did not destroy when they captured the city, but they preserved it honorably up until the present day, as it is related by those who have seen this and left written accounts.[62]

Paul of Burgos's Addition to Lyra's Comments on Jeremiah 31:12

In 31:12, regarding the part where the postill says, "And so, in this passage, 'grain' and 'wine'": Just as grain and wine here are understood to refer to the sacrament, so oil in this passage ought to be understood as the oil that is the matter for the sacraments of confirmation and extreme unction. The idea that "oil" should be understood as "grace" seems to pertain more to the mystical sense.

Paul of Burgos's Addition to Lyra's Comments on Jeremiah 31:13

In the same chapter, regarding the place where the postill says, "**Then the virgin,** that is, virgins, **will rejoice**":

When [the scripture passage] says, **Then the virgin will rejoice,** it is not necessary to put it into the plural by saying "virgins." For it is possible

62. See Oleg Grabar, "Space and Holiness in Medieval Jerusalem," in *Jerusalem: Its Sanctity and Centrality to Judaism, Christianity, and Islam,* ed. Lee I. Levine (New York: Continuum, 1999), 275–99; and Jerome Murphy-O'Connor, *The Holy Land: An Oxford Archaeological Guide,* 5th ed. (New York: Oxford University Press, 2008), 52–59.

to interpret this as referring in particular to the Blessed Virgin, who is given the autonomastic designation "virgin." For in a way that surpasses the other blessed ones, she rejoices in the chorus that is constituted not only of angels but also all of the saints, about whom it adds, **Youths and the elderly together.** The term "youths" should be understood as referring to the New Testament saints, who arrived more recently, and the term "elderly" refers to the Old Testament saints, who rejoice together with them in the church triumphant, which is alluded to here, as the writer of the postill says. Since the aforementioned virgin, together with the holy youths and elderly people under discussion here, experienced the sorrow and mourning of this age before reaching the state of blessedness, it continues: **I will turn their mourning into joy.**

Paul of Burgos's Addition to Lyra's Comments on Jeremiah 31:15–17

In the same chapter, regarding the place where the postill says, "This seems to be fictitious, because it contradicts the writing of the evangelist":

The arguments that the postill writer uses to counter the Jews' false interpretation of this prophecy, "A voice is heard in Ramah," etc., are true, but they are not accepted by them. This is clear with respect to the first argument, since the Jews do not accept the truth of the gospel. Now, regarding the second argument, they say that this is expressed well enough by Jeremiah in this passage; they say that this is sufficient enough publication of this miracle, especially since Jeremiah lived after the captivity of the ten tribes, and this seems to narrate an incident of Rachel's weeping that had occurred previously.[63] But another argument against them is stronger, an argument from the verse that follows: **Thus says the Lord: Let your voice cease from weeping,** etc. (31:16a). This is not the sort of consolation offered to a mother or woman weeping about a current massacre or captivity of a tremendous multitude of children, even if she could be assured that after the course of many years the descendants of those who were captured or killed would return to their own homeland or to their own borders, as they explain regarding what follows: **There is a reward for your work, and they will return out of the land of the enemy** (31:16b). With an empty hope [the

63. Some medieval rabbinic interpreters said that Rachel's refusal to be consoled "because they are not" (Jer 31:15) referred to the exile and dispersion of the northern kingdom Israel. See Kimḥi's comments on Jer 31:15 in *Jeremiah*, trans. Rosenberg, 2:248.

Jews] believe that this will be fulfilled for them at the coming of the Messiah. At that time, according to them, the descendants of the aforementioned captives and slaughtered people will return to the land of promise. For it is laughable, and you have heard it said that it is entirely incompatible with reason, that any woman who was weeping and mourning because of the slaughter or massacre of children presently occurring could be consoled and cease weeping by being assured that descendants of the slaughtered children would be restored after more than two thousand years or so. For according to the Philosopher, in book one, chapter 15 of the *Ethics*, "Regarding the good fortunes and ill fortunes of the living, any impact that these have on the dead is weak and small."[64] Indeed, this unsuitable interpretation does not accord with the Catholics' true exposition, which says that the very children who were slaughtered would return **from the land of the enemy,** who is Herod, **to their own borders** (31:17b), to the kingdom of heaven, which is the final hope: **And there is hope for your last times** (31:17a).[65]

Paul of Burgos's Addition to Lyra's Comments on Jeremiah 31:33

In the same chapter, regarding the place where it says in the postill: **"I will put my law into their inward parts, and I will write it in their heart"** (31:33):

Since the new law is the gospel itself, about which John 20:31 says, "Now these things are written so that you may believe," it seems that the new law is written down rather than imparted. But as it says in 1.2, question 106, article 1, in the response [of the *Summa*], "The new law is principally the very grace of the Holy Spirit, which is given to the faithful," concerning which it says in Rom 8:2: "The law of the Spirit of life in Christ Jesus liberated me from the law of sin and death."[66] Nevertheless, the new law contains certain things that are written down in accordance with the aforementioned grace of the Holy Spirit. These things are contained in the gospel for the purpose of manifesting the divinity or humanity of Christ, or to teach about the re-

---

64. Aristotle, *The Nicomachean Ethics* 1.11, trans. H. Rackham, LCL 73 (Cambridge, MA: Harvard University Press, 2003), 56–57.

65. The Vulgate reads: *Et est spes novissimis tuis,* which can mean, "There is hope for your last times" (i.e., "There is hope for you at the last"), which is how Paul of Burgos reads the verse. Lyra interpreted *novissimis tuis* to mean, "There is hope for your latest ones," Rachel's remaining children.

66. Thomas Aquinas, *Summa theologiae* Ia-IIae, q. 106, a. 1.

jection of the world; these things are present in the new law in a secondary way, since it was necessary to instruct Christ's faithful about these things through words and writings. One must say the same regarding the things that pertain to the use of the aforementioned spiritual grace, such as works of virtue; in many ways the people in the New Testament offer exhortations to do these works. For this reason, one must say that principally the new law is imparted, but in a secondary way the law is written down, etc.

DENIS THE CARTHUSIAN

Exposition on the Prophet Jeremiah

Jeremiah 32–33 and 36–39

Chapter Thirty-Two

Jeremiah Purchases a Field

32:1–5 The word that came to Jeremiah from the Lord in the tenth year of Zedekiah king of Judah, who reigned eleven years; **it was the eighteenth year of Nebuchadnezzar,** who, according to Jerome, began to reign in the fourth year of Jehoiakim.[1] However, it says in Daniel [1:1] that it was in the third year of Jehoiakim that Nebuchadnezzar came against him. Now Jehoiakim had reigned eleven years when King Nebuchadnezzar began the eighth year of his reign and replaced Jehoiakim with Zedekiah (2 Chr 36:5–11). Thus the tenth year of King Zedekiah was the eighteenth year of King Nebuchadnezzar. **At that time the army of the king of Babylon,** the aforementioned Nebuchadnezzar, **was besieging Jerusalem.** So the Chaldeans began to besiege Jerusalem in Zedekiah's ninth year, as it will say below. **And Jeremiah was confined in the hall of the prison, which was in the house of the king of Judah,** inside the palace. **For King Zedekiah had confined him, saying, "Why do you prophesy, saying, 'Thus says the Lord: I will give this city into the hand of the**

---

1. Jerome, *Commentary on Jeremiah* 32:1–3, ed. Sigofredus Reiter, CCSL 74 (Turnhout: Brepols, 1960), 327. Jehoiakim reigned from 608 to 598 BCE. His son Johoiachin, also called Coniah and Jeconiah, reigned in Jerusalem for three months before being deported to Babylon in 597 BCE (2 Kgs 24:8–12). Nebuchadnezzar then placed Zedekiah on the throne.

king of Babylon, etc., **and he will lead Zedekiah into Babylon and he will be there until I visit him,** that is, until he dies? (For indeed death is God's final visitation on a person in this life.) **Now if you fight against the Chaldeans you will have no success;** on the contrary, it will go badly for you, and you will be conquered.'"

32:6-7 And Jeremiah said to those who were present with him in the hall of the prison: **The word of the Lord came to me saying: Behold, your cousin Hanamel, son of Shallum,** that is, the son of your paternal uncle. For Shallum, the father of Hanamel, was the brother of Jeremiah's father Hilkiah. According to Jerome, this Hanamel is spelled differently in Hebrew than Hananel mentioned in the preceding chapter, where it says, "The city will be built, from the tower of Hananel" (31:38).[2] So they do not refer to the same thing. **He will come to you, saying, "Buy my field that is in Anathoth,"** in its suburb. For property surrounding cities was given to priests to pasture their livestock. Hanamel said this through divine inspiration, so that the Judean people's return from Babylonian captivity to their own land would be signified not only by words but also by a deed. **"For it is your right to buy it, because of your close kinship."** According to the law, it was illegal to let property pass from one tribe to another or from one family to another (Num 36:7-8). It was especially the case that no one was able to sell the priests' suburban properties, other than to someone eligible to buy it because of blood kinship (Lev 25:34).

32:8-10 And Hanamel came to me in the hall of the prison and said to me, "Take possession, through purchase, **of my field that is in Anathoth in the land of Benjamin,"** for Anathoth was in the territory belonging to Benjamin (Josh 21:17-18). **"For you have the right of inheritance and you are next of kin to possess it."** I understood that this was the word of the Lord, a message declared to me by my nephew about buying his field, and that there was mystical reason that God prompted him to do this. **And I bought the field and weighed out the money, seven *staters* and seven pieces of silver.** A *stater* is half an ounce. **And I wrote in a book,** in the letter of contract, **and I signed** this letter with a seal or some comparable sign. **Then I called on witnesses,** as is customary when making contracts, **and I weighed the money in the scales,** showing that the money or price of purchase was a fair amount.

2. Jerome, *Commentary on Jeremiah* 31:38-40, CCSL 74:324.

32:11-15 And I took the signed certificate of ownership, the deed of purchase, through which the right of ownership could be asserted, so no one could deny that this had been transacted, **and the stipulations,** which were the questions and responses of the buyer and seller, **and the ratifications,** which were the words of consent from both parties, **and the seals** applied to the **outside**—something like a seal used to close an open letter, as soon will become evident below. It is clear from this that all legal requirements for wills and contracts should be observed and proceed in a methodical way. **And I gave the certificate of ownership to Baruch son of Neriah son of Mahseiah in the sight of Hanamel and the witnesses who signed the certificate of purchase,** the aforementioned letter of contract, **in the sight of all the Judeans who sat in the hall of the prison,** those who came to Jeremiah either to hear the word of the Lord or to visit him while he was confined. **And in their presence I ordered Baruch, saying, "Take these writings,** namely, **this sealed certificate of purchase and this certificate that is open,** the aforementioned letters, one of which was open (the one about which he said, 'and the seals outside'), **and put them in a clay jar, so they may last many days."** It was customary to preserve such letters carefully in this way. Then some sort of seal is applied [to the jar]. **Thus says the Lord: Houses and fields and vineyards shall be possessed again in this land,** after the captives return from Babylon.

Jeremiah Prays for Understanding

32:16-17 After I had handed the certificate of ownership to Baruch, I prayed to the Lord, saying: Alas, alas, alas, Lord God. The reason why he says "alas" three times has often been explained.[3] **Behold, you have made heaven and earth by your great strength**—by your infinite strength, since creating is an act of infinite power. **And you stretched forth your arm;** through your power you extended yourself in this act, not doing everything you were capable of doing, but arranging it through your wisdom. (I recall that these words are carefully explained above.[4]) **No word will be difficult for you;** that is, no word is so difficult that you cannot fulfill it. The angel

3. In his comments on Jer 4:10, Denis explains that Jeremiah says "alas" three times because humans have sinned in three ways, in thought, word, and deed. Denis the Carthusian, *Exposition on the Prophet Jeremiah,* in *Opera Omnia* (Monstrolii: Typis Cartusiae Sanctae Mariae de Pratis, 1900), 9:55.
4. See Denis's comments on Jer 27:5, *Exposition on the Prophet Jeremiah,* 203.

says something similar in the gospel: "For no word will be impossible with God" (Luke 1:37). For when there is infinite power, it is not possible to limit the possibility of doing infinitely more and greater things. Hence it says in Wisdom [12:18]: "For it is in your power to do as you will."

32:18 You show mercy upon thousands. This shows the vastness of divine mercy. **And you return the sins of the parents to the bosom of their children after them,** especially if the children follow their parents in sinfulness. Sometimes children are punished with earthly penalties due to their parents' sin, even if they themselves did not commit the sin their parents did, because, in some sense, the children belong to their parents with respect to the physical body they have. I have explained above at length how this should be understood.[5] These words agree with what Moses said in Exodus [34:6–7]: "Lord God, merciful and gracious, you show mercy on thousands and repay the parents' sins upon their children and grandchildren." Now when God is said to show mercy to thousands, it uses an undefined number rather than a defined number, to imply that God is more prone to mercy than to vengeance, as it says in this verse: "He has compassion over all his works" (Ps 145:9). And James [2:13] said: "Mercy exalts itself over judgment." **O, most mighty,** infinitely mightier than every single thing; **great,** not in size but in majesty and completely immeasurable nobility; **powerful,** both in your existence and in what you are able to do; **the Lord of Hosts is your name,** for you alone command the heavenly angelic armies.

32:19 Great in counsel, in depths of wisdom. I have explained above how it is appropriate to speak of God's taking counsel.[6] For God infinitely surpasses the capacity of every created mind and is not advised by anyone except himself, through his own understanding. Since God is perfectly infinite, his cognoscibility is as vast as his actuality, and God is pure unbounded actuality.[7] As it is written in Job [36:26]: "Behold, God is great, exceeding our knowledge." And again: "Behold, God is lofty in his strength. Who can search out God's ways?" (Job 36:22–23). **Whose eyes are open upon all the ways of the children of Adam,** whose mind and wisdom ob-

---

5. See Denis's comments on Exod 20:5, *Enarratio in Exodum,* in *Opera Omnia,* 2:3.

6. See Denis's comments on Jer 23:18, *Exposition on the Prophet Jeremiah,* 191.

7. In medieval scholastic theology, God is considered *actus purus* (pure act or pure actuality). God was also regarded as cognoscible (knowable) but only through revelation or divine assistance, and created beings remain limited in their ability to understand the infinite fullness of God. See Thomas Aquinas, *Summa theologiae* Ia, q. 12, a. 1.

serve all human actions, thoughts, intentions, emotions, words, and deeds. As it says in Ecclesiasticus [23:19]: "The eyes of the Lord are brighter than the sun, gazing all around at the ways of humans." **To render to each and every one according to their ways and the results of their contrivances,** according to the merits and faults of their conduct and according to the usefulness or injuriousness of the things that they plan. As it is written in Job [34:10–11]: "Let impiety be far from God, and let wickedness be far from the Almighty. For God will render to humans according to their deeds and reward all people according to their ways." From this it is certain that those who refuse to acknowledge God's providence strongly deny God's wisdom and justice.

32:20–23 Who has set signs and wonders, great and wondrous things performed through Moses, **in the land of Egypt,** namely, the ten plagues with which you struck the Egyptians, **even to this day;** from that time until the present day you have continued to repeat your wondrous works through Joshua, Elijah, Elisha, and other holy people, **in Israel and among humans,** among the Israelite people as well as other nations. Just as God wondrously struck down and assailed the Egyptians, God often did this to the Amorites, the Philistines, and the Israelites' other enemies in Old Testament times. **And you have made for yourself a name, as on this day.** You elevated your fame by performing distinguished deeds, so that the eminence of your majesty became known to humans, even as it is known and endures in the present time. **And you brought forth your people Israel from the land of Egypt with signs and wonders, and with great terror** caused by the dreadful Egyptian plagues, especially when their firstborn were killed, and when the Egyptians were drowned in the Red Sea. **And you gave to them,** to the Israelite people, **this land flowing** or fruitful **with milk and honey, which you yourself swore to give them. And they entered and possessed the land, but they did not obey your voice or walk in your law, and all these evil things came upon them.** Though Jeremiah speaks collectively about the entire people of Israel, different things refer to different people, or some things refer only to certain people. Not everything refers to each individual. Certainly those who entered the land of Israel with Joshua obeyed God very well and all these evil things did not come upon them. But their children were wicked, as it is written in the books of Judges and Kings. This way of speaking is common in Scripture, but some people who are not careful think it is appropriate for them to criticize other people's narrations, and they think they themselves speak better when this should not be the case.

32:24-25 Look, siege ramps have been constructed; the Chaldeans have now built siege works in a circle **against the city** of Jerusalem **to capture it.** Ezekiel [4:2] deals more fully and specifically with these implements used for waging an attack. **And the city is given into the hands of the Chaldeans;** it is about to be given into their hands, or, in your wisdom, you have preordained it to be given into their hands. This is a manner of speaking, to say that something has been done when it is about to be done. **From the appearance,** the presence, **of the sword** of the Chaldeans, **and from famine and pestilence** prevailing in that city. **And all that you have spoken** about this city's punishment **has come to pass,** since part of it has already occurred and the other things will soon be fulfilled. **And you, Lord God, say to me: "Buy a field"?** It is as if Jeremiah were saying: At first consideration, this seems astounding!

God Promises Their Return From Captivity

32:27-32 The most merciful God answers this, saying: **Behold, I am the Lord God of all flesh,** the God of all the nations, as it says in the Psalm [65:2]: "All flesh will come to you." And in Isaiah: "And all flesh will see the salvation of our God" (Isa 40:5; 52:10; Luke 3:6). Or, according to Jerome, **all flesh** indicates that irrational creatures are also subject to divine providence.[8] **Shall anything be hard for me?** Certainly not! Indeed, all things are easy for God, because nothing is strong enough to resist God's omnipotence and because God is able to do anything instantly, at will. **Therefore,** because I am the Lord God of all flesh, and in my providence I repay everyone what they deserve, **see, I am delivering this city into the hand of the Chaldeans and they shall set it on fire, along with the houses on whose roofs** (the flat thatched rooftops or other places used to practice idolatry) **you sacrificed to Baal. For the children of Israel and the children of Judah,** the ten tribes and the two tribes, **have continually done evil in my sight from their youth,** either from the youth of each and every person who acted impiously, or from the youth of the entire people, from the time they dwelled in Egypt and their departure from there. It is not the case that absolutely everyone in every time period was wicked, but the majority of people often were. **The children of Israel who even now provoke me;** though I am normally affectionate and kind, they cause me to inflict severe punishments for their disgraceful deeds, so that I have the appearance of someone who has been

---

8. Jerome, *Commentary on Jeremiah* 31:26-29, CCSL 74:339.

provoked. **This city has become for me a source of rage and indignation.** Its residents have deserved my wrath and punishment (in the sense that was previously explained) **from the day on which** its builders **constructed it,** which was either the time of Melchizedek who built this city, or Solomon who expanded it and fortified it with a triple wall, **until this day, in which it is being taken out of my sight,** destroyed by the Chaldeans as I watch, **because of the evil of the children of Israel,** etc.

32:33–35 And they have turned their backs to me and not their faces, they rebelled and refused to hear God's words, **when I taught them at daybreak,** early in the morning, immediately, in a timely way, through the prophets and angelic inspiration, **[and they refused to listen] and accept discipline,** either parental instruction, or punishments and corrections, that I administered to them because of their digressions, refusing to bear this patiently or reform themselves. **And they placed their idols in the house in which my name is called on.** (As I have often said, this refers to the Jerusalem temple.) **And they have built the high places of Baal, which are in the valley of the son of Hinnom.** This is mentioned above and explained there.[9]

32:36–37 Next, after sorrowful things are declared, favorable things are now promised, because God does not withhold divine mercy even in the midst of God's own wrath. After being struck with illness, a person better appreciates health and finds it more pleasant; if opposing things are placed side by side, one can better distinguish between them. **And now because of these things**—because of the things stated about the punishment of sins or, more likely, because of the purchase of the field, since this is God's response to Jeremiah's words—**thus says the Lord to this city, about which you said it would be delivered into the hands of the king of Babylon: Behold, I will gather them,** some of the residents of this city and the other Judean towns, **from all the lands to which I have cast them,** or am about to cast them, **in my rage,** the severity of justice. **And I will bring them back to this place and make them dwell securely.** Some say this was fulfilled in the time of Ezra, but Jerome contradicts this because at that time they often experienced great fear, as it says in the book of Ezra [Neh 5:1–5] and frequently even after that time, as we see in the books of Maccabees and Judith.[10] Nevertheless this

9. See Denis, comments on Jer 7:30–31, *Exposition on the Prophet Jeremiah*, 85.

10. Jerome, *Commentary on Jeremiah* 32:37–41, CCSL 74:345. The books now called Ezra and Nehemiah were called 1–2 Esdras.

was fulfilled in some sense, since afterward they sometimes dwelled safely again in Judah. However, it was fulfilled more fully for the apostles and the other believers at the time of Christ, as it has frequently been explained; this better pertains to them and to the time periods that follow.

32:38-40 And they will be my people and I will be their God. And I will give them one heart, a unity of will in religious devotion, as the Apostle urges: "You should all speak the same thing, and there should be no schisms among you" (1 Cor 1:10). And again: "You should glorify God with one mouth and one heart" (Rom 15:6). **And one soul,** through love of God and Christ, as it says in Acts [4:32]: "The multitude of believers was one heart and one soul." For this reason Christ prayed: "Holy Father, protect in your name those whom you have given me, that they may be one as we also are" (John 17:11). This is what the Apostle teaches: "Taking care to protect the unity of spirit in the bond of peace" (Eph 4:3). **So that they may fear me all their days** with the dutiful fear one has for a parent, about which we sing: "Fear the Lord, all his saints, for those who fear him experience no want" (Ps 34:9). **And that it may be well with them,** that they may live wholesomely and make progress in spiritual gifts, **along with their** spiritual **children after them.** This refers to their disciples and those who follow their example; or it refers to their biological children. **And I will make an everlasting covenant with them.** This is understood to refer especially to the evangelical law, which nothing will supplant. **And I will not cease to do good.** This seems not to have been fulfilled very much for the Judeans who returned from Babylon, except for some people at certain times, but it was fulfilled abundantly for those who converted to Christ. **And I will put my** dutiful, pure, and reverent **fear in their heart, so they may not depart from me.** Regarding this fear, Scripture says: "Whoever fears God neglects nothing" (Eccl 7:18). And again: "Nothing is sweeter than fearing God" (Ecclus 23:27). And also: "The fear of the Lord is holy, enduring forever" (Ps 19:9). It is also possible to interpret this verse as referring to the fear [of the Lord] that is one of the seven gifts of the Spirit (Isa 11:2). Or it refers to the fear that is a certain action or effect of divine love, a fear that contains this love.

32:41-44 And I will rejoice over them, when I shall do them good. Not that the divine mind's delight arises from a created being or depends on an object, but God rejoices inwardly at the favorable progress of God's own elect, inasmuch as God himself is the cause of every good in them, and God innately prefers to bestow benefits rather than vengeance. For this reason it is written in the Psalm [104:31]: "The Lord shall rejoice in his works." And: "The Lord is well pleased with his people" (Ps 149:4). Also in the second book of Ezra, or Nehemiah [8:10]: "The Lord's joy is your strength." For this reason the Apostle writes: "Your sanctification is God's will" (1 Thess 4:3). God himself, who is glorious and worthy of adoration, testifies: "My delight is to be with the children of humanity" (Prov 8:31). **And I will plant them in this land in truth.** "In truth" means "just as I promised," or "in the truth of the faith." For this reason the Septuagint translates it "in faith," which is fulfilled when Christ comes to the chosen remnant of the Judeans. **With my entire heart and with my entire breath;** that is, with all my intellect and with my whole mind. I have often written about how God can be said to have "breath." This sort of promise seems too great to refer to the time and favorable occurrences following the return from Babylon, unless it refers to the time of Christ, when chosen Judeans were given more favors than they had ever received before. Nevertheless, it was fulfilled to a certain extent at that time. For this reason the following is added:

32:42-44 For thus says the Lord: Just as I have brought upon this people all this great evil (siege, hunger, sword, destruction, captivity), **so I will bring upon them all of the good that I speak to them,** which I am announcing that I will give to them. **And fields will be owned again in this land** of Judah, **which you say has become deserted because humans and livestock do not remain** in it. At the time of this prophecy much of Judah had in fact already been devastated, so that, comparatively speaking, practically no one was left, and most of those who did remain were soon going to be destroyed. **Fields shall be purchased for money, and they shall be recorded in books,** in deeds and letters of contract, **and marked with a stamp,** which is the deed's seal. **Witnesses will be called;** witnesses will be present for these purchases of fields **in the land of Benjamin and the area surrounding Jerusalem.** Now at this time the message deals with the land of the two tribes of Judah and Benjamin, for it continues: **And in the cities of Judah, and in the mountainous cities** (cities located in the mountains), **and in the cities in the plains, and in the cities that are toward the south** (the southern towns), **for I will overturn their captivity,** I will return them to this land, **says the Lord.**

268

Spiritual Interpretation of Purchasing Fields

Furthermore, spiritual fields in the land of Judah are purchased with money when we use unrighteous wealth to make for ourselves friends who may receive us into the everlasting dwellings (Luke 16:9). And the names of the buyers are written in the book of the living. They are sealed with the sign of the cross. And all the choirs of the blessed ones are called as witnesses. Then God overturns our captivity by transferring us to the heavenly paradise, as the psalmist says: "You have ascended on high and you have led captivity captive" (Ps 68:18).

I have been using St. Jerome's commentary until now, but it does not offer explanations beyond this point.[11]

Chapter Thirty-Three

God's Promise of Restoration

33:1-2 The chapter we are about to discuss first foretells the "figure," the return of the Judeans from Babylonian captivity; and then it foretells what is "formed," the true and full redemption of the Judeans and all believers through Christ. **And the word of the Lord came to Jeremiah a second time.** It was not the second time ever, since God's word had already come to him frequently, but it was the second time **while he was still closed up in the hall of the prison,** for the reasons mentioned in the preceding chapter. **Thus says the Lord, who will do this, and will form it, and will prepare it;** that is, the one who will fulfill what was revealed to me, or who will do and form the thing signified by these words. What this thing is will soon be mentioned. **The Lord is his name.** For this one alone, with his own authority, has dominion and control over all things, as it says in Job [34:13]: "Whom else has God appointed over the earth? Or whom has God set over the earth that he has made?" Compared to God, all other rulers and lords are like instruments or servants to the first craftsman and highest prince. Aristotle explains this in the twelfth book of *Philosophy* [*Metaphysics*]: "Beings refuse to be ordered badly. A plurality of rulers is bad. Therefore there is one ruler."[12]

---

11. Jerome's commentary ends at chapter 32.

12. Aristotle, *Metaphysics* 12.10., trans. Hugh Tredennick, LCL 287 (Cambridge, MA: Harvard University Press, 1977), 174.

God testifies in Isaiah [45:18]: "I am the Lord, and there is no other." And again through Isaiah [42:8]: "I am the Lord, this is my name. I will not give my glory to another." Regarding this, the psalmist says: "Let them know that the Lord is your name" (Ps 83:18).

33:3 Then God's words to Jeremiah are presented: **Cry to me.** Call on me lovingly, with a cry that comes from your heart rather than your lips. This cry is fervent devotion or burning love for God. **And I will announce to you great and enduring things,** God's magnificent and enduring works, **which you do not know.** For, over time, the prophet received increasing divine illumination. Hereafter, great and enduring things would be told— things found below in this chapter: the mysteries of the Savior, such as his incarnation, salvation, and dominion. Granted, these things had been revealed to Jeremiah to a certain extent prior to this time, but they were not revealed as fully or as clearly as they now were. Nor is any mortal in this life able to understand these mysteries fully and clearly. At that time, the Judeans' return from Babylon was a symbol of a future event; now it is a symbol of what has already been done through Christ. This chapter briefly deals with this symbolic salvation, and then it discusses true redemption through Christ.

33:4–6 For thus says the Lord to the houses of this city and to the houses of the king of Judah that are destroyed. This refers to the houses that were now about to be destroyed; in fact, most of them already had been destroyed. **And to the buildings** where the residents of Jerusalem stored food and weapons in order to secure themselves against the Chaldeans; **and to the sword of those coming to fight alongside the Chaldeans,** namely, the Chaldeans' supporters who hastened there each day to help the army as it blockaded Jerusalem, **to fill** the houses of Jerusalem **with the corpses of the people** (the Judeans now about to be killed) **whom I have struck down** (whom I now will strike down through the Chaldeans) **in my fury,** my righteous severity. For the Chaldeans were like instruments or agents of divine justice against the Judeans; they would not have been committing a sin by doing this if their intentions had been upright. **Hiding my face from this city,** removing the favor of my protection or the appearance of kindness from the residents of Jerusalem as a righteous judgment because of all their wickedness. **Behold, I will close their wounds and give them health, and I will heal them.** I will draw them out of their afflictions, I will purge away their sins, and I will restore the cities and houses that were destroyed. This began to be fulfilled after their return from Babylon, but complete healing from the wound of sin was accomplished through Christ's incarnation and passion.

Not only Catholics but also Hebrew scholars—though only some of them—explain the things in the rest of this chapter as pertaining to the time of Christ.[13] But we ourselves recognize that these things have been accomplished truly and spiritually, while they wait in vain for these things to be **fulfilled** with the coming of the Messiah. **And I will reveal to them the prayer of peace and truth.** I will show or extend to them the inward peace and truth for which they and their parents prayed to me. As it says in John [1:17]: "Grace and truth came through Jesus Christ." And as the Apostle teaches: "Christ, who has made both peoples one, is our peace" (Eph 2:14). For this reason, when Christ was born, the angels suddenly sang, "On earth, peace to people of goodwill." Indeed, Christ fulfilled and confirmed the truth of the prophets' oracles, making peace between God and the human race, as it says in Ephesians [2:14–18]: "In his own flesh, resolving hostilities so that he might make two peoples into one new humanity in himself and, making peace, might reconcile them to God in one body through the cross, putting hostilities to death in himself; and, when he came, he proclaimed peace to those who were far off and peace to those who were near; for through him we have access to the Father through one Spirit."

33:7 And I will restore the fortunes of Judah and the fortunes of Jerusalem. I will rescue the chosen Judeans and a remnant of Jerusalem from the captivity of sin and the yoke of the devil. Isaiah [1:9] says regarding this: "If the Lord of Hosts had not left us offspring, we would be like Sodom." **Judah** and **Jerusalem** refer to all who acknowledge God and to the church militant itself; this is still the literal understanding, as I have frequently made clear, especially in the thirtieth and thirty-first chapters.[14] **And I will build them up** in gifts of grace and virtues, in the sacraments, and with teachings and rules, **as from the beginning,** at the time of Moses when they were led out of Egypt and instructed in the divine law. Just as the upbuilding and instruction from God was strengthened through various miracles, so Christ also built up and strengthened the church through countless miracles, as the Gospels reveal. For this reason it is written in Hebrews [2:3–4]: "How shall we escape

13. Nicholas of Lyra, *Postill on Jeremiah* 33:6.

14. See Denis the Carthusian's comments on Jer 31:6, *Exposition on the Prophet Jeremiah*, 220. Denis believed that Jerusalem is used here as a symbol representing the church. Thus prophecies regarding Jerusalem are understood here in the literal sense to refer to God's plan for the church.

if we neglect so great a salvation that was confirmed in us, with God bearing witness through signs, wonders, deeds of power, and the various distributions of the Holy Spirit?"

33:8 And I will cleanse them from all their wickedness with which they sinned against me, and I will forgive all their wickedness. No one can do this except the Savior, who fully redeemed the human race with his precious blood; he alone has the ability to do this. The ones who do not obtain the benefits of his passion are those who have fallen away. For this reason it is written concerning Christ: "He loved us and washed us from our sins in his own blood" (Rev 1:5). In Isaiah [53:6, 4] it says about him: "The Lord has placed on him the iniquity of us all. Truly he has borne our weaknesses and carried our sorrows." So also God the Father, or the most blessed Trinity, redeemed the human race from their sins through the human Christ. For this reason Zechariah [3:8–9] says about Christ: "Behold, I will bring my servant the Dayspring, and I will take away the wickedness of this land in one day," the Day of Preparation, on which Christ suffered (John 19:14). Regarding the cleansing of sin truly accomplished through Christ, it is clearly written in Daniel [9:24] through the angel speaking to the prophet: "Seventy weeks will be shortened upon your people and upon your Holy City, so that transgressions may be finished, sin may have an end, wickedness may be abolished, everlasting justice may be brought, visions and prophecy may be fulfilled, and the Holy of Holies may be anointed."

33:9 And they will be for me a name, and a joy, and a praise, and a gladness before all the nations of the earth who will hear all the good things that I will do for them. This was fulfilled truly and abundantly after Christ's first coming, for, when they heard about the inexpressible gifts of grace that Christ bestowed on the newly formed church assembled from these chosen Judeans, nations from all lands throughout the earth called on Christ by name, praised him, and joyfully glorified him. For this reason, this was predicted by Isaiah [24:16]: "From the ends of the earth we have heard praises, the glory of the Righteous One." As Isaiah [43:7] says, God is honored by his chosen ones and servants: "Everyone who calls on my name I have created for my glory." And the psalmist says: "Praise the Lord among his saints" (Ps 150:1). **And they shall tremble and be troubled;** they shall be greatly astonished and dumbfounded, **because of all the good things and the peace that I will make for them,** when they contemplate and consider what favors I will give them. Most people were also dumbfounded by the miracles that Christ's disciples performed. This is what the psalmist predicted: "Nations were troubled and kingdoms were bowed down. He uttered his voice, the earth trembled" (Ps 46:6). This trembling arises from gazing at God's mighty deeds. For this reason it is written in the gospel that the crowds were filled with fear when they witnessed Christ's miracles (Matt 9:8). This disturbance was not wicked, but instead it came from their strong feelings of anxiousness. For not every disturbance is bad, especially since it is written of Christ, "He became disturbed" (John 11:33); and in another place, "He was troubled in spirit" (John 13:21). Moreover, it is certain that the things foretold regarding the time following the return from Babylon would not be fulfilled before Christ's coming. Nor did the Judeans at that time have that much eminence, peace, and glory.

33:10–11a Thus says the Lord: There shall be heard again in this place, in Jerusalem and Judah, **which you say is deserted,** destroyed by the Chaldeans, **since there are no humans or livestock in the cities of Judah and the outskirts of Jerusalem, which are deserted by people, inhabitants, or beasts,** lacking the people and livestock that usually inhabit these places. The Lord said these things had occurred because they were soon about to take place, for Jerusalem was besieged at the time that the Lord spoke these words. **The voice of joy and the voice of gladness, the voice of the bridegroom and the voice of the bride, the voice of those who say, "Give praise to the Lord of Hosts, for the Lord is good, for the Lord's mercy is forever."** All of this was abundantly fulfilled at Christ's first coming. It began to be fulfilled when the angel said to the shepherds: "Behold, I bring you good news of great joy" (Luke 2:10). It was also fulfilled by the parents of the Forerunner [John the Baptist], and righteous Simeon, and the holy prophetess Anna (Luke 1:40–45; 1:63–79; 2:25–38). Luke also states that the Judean people "rejoiced because of all the things gloriously done by Christ" (Luke 13:17). And again: "All the people, when they saw it, gave glory to God" (Luke 18:43). This was fulfilled most powerfully after the Holy Spirit was sent from above and the newly formed church passed its time day and night in divine praises, as it says in Acts [2:46–47].

Furthermore, it is possible to understand the bridegroom as signifying Christ, about whom the psalmist says: "He, like a bridegroom, coming out of his bridal chamber" (Ps 19:5). His voice was heard in the temple, and in Jerusalem and Judea when he preached there in person. The bride represents the church. For this reason the Forerunner, speaking about Christ and the church, said: "The one who has the bride is the bridegroom" (John 3:29). He is also mentioned in the Psalm [22:22]: "I will declare your name to my brothers and sisters. In the midst of the church I will praise you." Nonetheless, faithful marriages and undefiled marriage beds were present among the Judeans who converted, so it is also possible to explain this passage as referring to such brides and grooms.

33:11b And [the voice of] those who carry their vows into the house of the Lord, that is, the believers who offer their vows and prayers to God in the church. We know that the newly formed church's children, converted Judaism, did this in the Jerusalem temple, as it says in Acts [5:12]: "And they were all of one accord in the portico of Solomon." The faithful also offer their vows to God every day in his house: "Therefore I will sing a psalm to your name forever and ever, so that I may pay my vows from day to day" (Ps 61:8). And again: "Offer to God a sacrifice of praise, and pay your vows to the Most High" (Ps 50:14). **I will restore the fortunes of the land, as [*sicut*] in the beginning.** I will restore the synagogue's status among those who believe in Christ. These people's eminence in the gifts of the Holy Spirit was greater than that of the Judeans who preceded them. For this reason the word "**as**" designates a certain similarity, not equality.

33:12-13 Thus says the Lord of Hosts: Once again in this place deserted by humans and livestock, and in all its cities, in Judah and its towns, **there will be a habitation for shepherds to rest their flocks.** From Christ's disciples and the assembly of the faithful there would emerge leaders—the apostles and their coworkers—who preached through all Judea, converting and governing a great number of people. It continues: **And in the cities and on the mountains and plains . . . the flocks shall once again pass under the hand that counts them.** One by one, they will be brought to their shepherd for inspection. He is the one who most certainly knows the number of those who are predestined. As he said: "And I know the ones whom I have chosen" (John 13:18). The one who led, guided, fed, and counted his own sheep declared: "I am the good shepherd, and I know my sheep, and my own know me" (John 10:14). And again, speaking about the good shepherd: "He calls his own sheep by name and goes before them, and the sheep follow him" (John 10:3-4). Lyra reports that a certain scholar, preeminent among the Hebrews, understands "sheep, livestock, and herds" as referring to inferior or subjected humans. I am sharing this so that no one supposes that [my own] explanation is merely spiritual rather than literal.[15]

15. Nicholas of Lyra, *Postill on Jeremiah* 33:10. Nicholas says that his source is Rabbi Sol-

God Promises a Shoot of Justice

33:14-16 Furthermore, the words that follow prove that the previously discussed verses should be seen as referring to the time of Christ. **Behold the days are coming,** the time of the evangelical law, **says the Lord, that I will stir up**—that is, I will fulfill—**the good word,** the promise about Christ and his mysteries, **that I have spoken to the house of Israel,** the ten tribes, **and to the house of Judah,** the two tribes. For Christ's coming was promised to the twelve tribes because Christ came down for the redemption of all Jacob's children. For this reason it is clear that this present word about the liberation of the Jews was not accomplished at the time of Ezra and Zerubbabel. Accordingly, the ten tribes remain captive at the present time, as the words supplied [in this verse] make abundantly clear. **In those days, and** (another way of saying the same thing) **at that time, I will make the shoot of justice** (Christ, who is more just than anyone else and who is the son of David according to the [human] nature that he assumed) **spring forth,** or arise, **onto David.** As Isaiah [4:2] says: "In that day the shoot of the Lord will be magnificent and glorious. The fruit of the earth shall be high and a joy to those Israelites who have been saved." **And he will bring judgment and justice in the earth. In those days Judah will be saved, and Israel,** or, Jerusalem,[16] **shall dwell securely. And this is the name that they will call him: "The Lord is our righteous one."** All of this is written about and explained at length above, in chapter 23.

God's Covenant with David Endures

33:17 Next it discusses the stability and continuity of Christ's reign and priesthood. **For thus says the Lord: David will not lack a man to sit upon the throne of the house of Israel.** There will be a man in King David's succession who shall reign continually and govern the patriarchs' chosen children, the Judeans who have been converted and those who will be con-

---

omon (Rashi). See Rashi's comments on Jer 33:13 in *Jeremiah: A New English Translation*, translation of text, Rashi, and commentary by A. J. Rosenberg (New York: Judaica Press, 1989), 2:273. Denis's point is that the Jewish explanation of "sheep" as humans reinforces his identification of sheep with the human followers of Jesus, as part of the literal rather than allegorical sense.

16. "Jerusalem" and "Israel" are textual variants in this verse. See *Biblia Sacra iuxta Vulgatam Versionem*, ed. Bonifatius Fischer et al., 3rd ed. (Stuttgart: Deutsche Bibelgesellschaft, 1969), 1215, note on Jer 33:16.

verted in the future, together with all believers. This man is Christ, about whom it was written earlier, "A woman will encompass a man" (Jer 31:22). Isaiah [9:7] says about him: "He shall be seated upon the throne of David and upon his kingdom, in order to establish it and confirm it in judgment and justice, from this time onward and forevermore." And in the gospel the angel said: "The Lord God will give to him the seat of his ancestor David. He will reign in the house of Jacob forever, and his reign will have no end" (Luke 1:32–33). Now the throne of the house of Israel, on which Christ was seated, was his own royal dignity and judicial power.

33:18 Nor will the priests and Levites, the presbyters and deacons who are ministers of Christ's new law, **fail to have a man in my presence.** These priests will not be absent, or a man from priests of the old covenant will not be lacking. For Christ was priest and king, and he descended from a royal and priestly tribe. His priesthood lasts forever, as it says in the Psalm [110:4]: "You are a priest forever according to the order of Melchizedek." Also, in the letter to the Hebrews [7:24]: "Christ, because he continues forever, has an everlasting priesthood." **To offer burnt offerings, and to burn sacrifices, and to slaughter sacrificial victims continually.** For Christ, by offering himself on the cross to God the Father for us, offered a burnt offering, a sacrifice, and a sacrificial victim, since his offering on the cross contained and still contains—more than abundantly—the power of all the offerings required by the law. His offering is repeated daily, and it will be repeated in the church at the sacrament of the altar until the end of time. It is also possible and appropriate to understand the terms "burnt offerings," "sacrifices," and "sacrificial victims" to refer to other spiritual sacrifices of Christians who, with prayer and obedience, offer themselves and their possessions to God in the fire of holy love. As the Apostle writes to the Romans [12:1]: "Present your bodies as a living sacrifice, holy and pleasing to God." And, speaking about Christ to the Ephesians [5:2], he said: "He loved us and gave himself for us, an offering and sacrifice to God as a sweet fragrance." And also: "A sacrifice to God is an afflicted spirit" (Ps 51:17). And it says in Ecclesiasticus [35:2]: "Heeding God's commandments is a wholesome sacrifice."

33:19–21 Furthermore, this is reinforced by an example of something that is impossible: **And the word of the Lord came to Jeremiah, saying: If my covenant with the day can be made void, and my covenant with the night,** my establishment or ordering of the alternating succession of days and nights, **so that there is not day or night at their appointed times.** [Day and night will alternate] ceaselessly until the end time preestablished by God, when the motion of the heavens will cease and "time will be no longer," as it is written in Revelation [10:6]. **Only then could my covenant with my servant David be made void so that there would not be a son from him,** Christ, who descended from him according to the flesh, **who reigns on his throne,** reigning through grace in the hearts of believers, and governing the flocks of faithful people through his vicars, and, indeed, directing them through angels, **and [the covenant with] the Levites and the priests my ministers,** the ministers of the altar in Christ's kingdom and the church. For this reason Revelation [1:6] says about Christ: "He made us to be a kingdom and priests to his God and Father." And Peter said about this: "You are a chosen race, a royal priesthood, a holy people" (1 Pet 2:9). For this reason, according to all the scholars, David's reign is perpetuated in Christ. As it says in the Psalm [89:35–37]: "I have sworn once and for all by my holiness: I will not lie to David. His offspring will endure forever, and his throne is just like the sun before me and just like the moon is perfect forever, a faithful witness in heaven." In addition, regarding the aforementioned covenant with day and night, which is unable to be changed naturally, it is written in Genesis [8:22]: "Day and night shall not cease."

33:22 Just as the stars of the heaven cannot be counted by a mortal human **and** the vast quantity of **sand of the sea cannot be measured, so also I will multiply the offspring of my servant David,** Christ's spiritual children, **and my ministers the Levites.** Isaiah [53:10] writes about them: "If he lays down his life for sin, he shall see long-lived offspring." Christ's faithful people are countless, just as Christ says in the Psalm [40:5]: "I have declared and I have spoken: they are multiplied beyond numbering." Frequently what is spoken through David should be understood as referring literally to Christ.

33:23–24 And the word of the Lord came to me, saying: Have you not seen; that is, have you not heard or noticed (for seeing is often used to refer to hearing, as in Rev 1:12: "I turned to see the voice that spoke with me") **what this people have spoken, saying: "The two families,** the tribes of Judah and Benjamin, **that the Lord had chosen** (because the divine worship had continued in these tribes when the ten tribes fell into idolatry and were taken captive) **have been cast aside,** abandoned by God"? The Judeans' Chaldean enemies had said this, together with others who saw the city of Jerusalem when it was now about to be captured, or when it had been captured. **And they have despised my people,** these two tribes, **so that it is no longer a**

nation in their sight, because they are no longer regarded as important, or because now, in the eyes of viewers, most of this people of mine have been destroyed.

33:25-26 Thus says the Lord against those enemies of the Judeans: **If my covenant between day and night can be made void,** for it will not be made ineffectual, as it says above, since the sun maintains its accustomed course and, by orbiting, causes day and night. **And if I have not given my laws to heaven and earth,** for indeed, ever since the beginning, I have provided fixed laws, and a natural course, properties, purpose, and order for the greater and lesser [heavenly] bodies, which is clear in Genesis [8:22]. As Boethius says:

> You compel the stars to obey your law. . . .
> As you steer all things within their established limits. . . .
> You, who bind created things together in harmony.[17]

And the psalmist says: "He established them forever and ever. He issued the decree and they will not go beyond it" (Ps 148:6). **Only then will I cast out the offspring of Jacob and my servant David;** I will never reject all of the children of Israel and David's successors. Indeed, many of them have been chosen, and David's reign has been made secure in Christ; **so that I refuse to accept princes from his offspring.** For Christ descended from David's offspring, and some of the apostles, who were priests and princes of the church, became leaders of the entire world and judges of the twelve tribes of Israel, as Christ asserts: "You who have followed me shall be seated on the twelve seats, judging the twelve tribes of Israel" (Matt 19:28). And in the Psalm [45:16] we sing: "You shall make them princes over all the earth."

Chapter Thirty-Six

This and the following chapters show how much the very blessed Jeremiah would suffer because of his integrity and how great was the Judeans' willfulness, as well as how much kindness and patience God showed them.

17. Boethius, *On the Consolation of Philosophy*, book 1, metrum 5.5, 5.25, 5.43; PL 63:634, 637, 639.

Jeremiah Dictates the Scroll to Baruch

36:1-3 And it came to pass in the fourth year of Jehoiakim son of King Josiah of Judah, the fourth year of Jehoiakim's reign, not of his life, **that the word of the Lord came to Jeremiah, saying: Take a scroll and write in it,** not with your own hand but through your secretary Baruch so that it can be written down immediately, **all the words that I have spoken to you against Israel and Judah,** the ten tribes and the two tribes, **from the day that I spoke to you,** that is, from the day that I began to speak to you, **from the days of Josiah until this present day.** For he began to prophesy during Josiah's reign. **If it should happen, after the house of Judah,** the population of the kingdom of Judah, **hears all the evil things,** the torments, **that I plan to do,** to inflict, **on them, that all the people return from their evil path,** that is, life, **I will forgive their iniquities.** Such is the infinite mercy of God, who sends an envoy so they can be reconciled, even if not because of their love of justice, at least because of their dread of punishment. In the same way a physician sends advice to sick people so they might agree to be cured. "The Father of mercies and the God of all consolations" (2 Cor 1:3) does this daily by using his devoted servants to exhort worldly, wicked, irreverent hearts to improvement, and threatens the unrepentant to eternal damnation. Furthermore, by saying, **"If it should happen,"** the Lord indicates that their actions would be from free choice and not from any ignorance about God.

36:4-8 So Jeremiah called Baruch the son of Neriah, and Baruch wrote from the mouth of Jeremiah all the words of the Lord that he spoke to him, to Jeremiah, **in the scroll.** The construction is intransitive.[18] **And Jeremiah commanded Baruch, saying, "I am confined and I cannot enter the house of the Lord,** the temple." For the wicked King Jehoiakim confined Jeremiah so he would not foretell the devastation of Jerusalem or the destruction of the king and the people. **"Therefore you yourself must enter** the temple **and, in the hearing of the people, read the words of the Lord from the scroll, in the house of the Lord on the day of fasting."** This is understood either as a lawfully required fast or one instituted at that time to beg for God's help against the Chaldeans. **"And, in addition, in the hearing of all Judah,** all the Judeans, **who come out of their cities** to the temple. **Read these** words, **if** (that is, *so that*) **their prayer may perhaps arrive in God's sight,"** meaning, "it may be accepted and appear pleasing to God." He speaks

---

18. Denis is referring to the verb construction of *locutus est,* "he spoke."

well when he says, **"perhaps,"** since our hope has certainty regarding one aspect, its object, which is God and his mercy toward the one who relies on him; however, our hope does not have certainty regarding the other aspect, the subject, which is our frailty, since we do not know whether we are putting up an obstacle to God's grace. **"For great is the rage,** that is, the profound distress, **and indignation that the Lord declared against the people."** And Baruch did all the things that Jeremiah commanded him. This shows his great courage and obedience. For Baruch himself was not lacking in special grace when he did these things. On the contrary, he shared in the knowledge of the heavenly mysteries and the divine miracles that surrounded Jeremiah. And he hoped that, through Jeremiah's prayer and worthy deeds, the Chaldeans' rage would be averted.

Baruch Reads the Scroll in the Temple

36:9-10 Now it came to pass in the fifth year of Jehoiakim that the rulers in the kingdom **proclaimed a fast before the Lord to all the people in Jerusalem and to all the crowds that gathered together in Jerusalem from all the cities of Judah,** in order to pray in the temple that they might be rescued from the Chaldeans. **And Baruch read Jeremiah's words from the scroll in the house of the Lord, in the treasury of Gemariah son of Shaphan the secretary, in the upper court, in the entry of the new gate of the Lord's house, in the hearing of all the people.** Baruch stood in the upper court so that everyone could better hear him. This new gate is the one that Jotham king of Judah built, as it says earlier (2 Chr 27:3).

36:11-13 And when Micaiah son of Gemariah heard all the words of the Lord from the book, he went down into the house of the king Jehoiakim, since the palace was near the temple building, which was on a higher part of Mount Zion; **to the treasury,** that is, the chamber, **of the secretary** of some prince, perhaps one of those mentioned where it continues: **and behold, all the princes** of king Jehoiakim **were sitting there, including Elishama, the secretary, [and Delaiah son of Shemaiah, Elnathan son of Achbor, Gemariah son of Shaphan, Zedekiah son of Hananiah, and all the princes].** And Micaiah told them all the words that he had heard Baruch reading; not every single word but the general message and the main points.

Baruch Reads the Scroll to the Princes

36:14–18 Therefore all the princes sent Jehudi son of Nethaniah to Baruch, saying, "O, Baruch, **take the scroll from which you read and come."** Then **Baruch came to them. And they said, "Sit, and read these things in our hearing."** Therefore Baruch read in their hearing. **Now when they heard all the words, they were stunned** with fear and amazement, **and they said to Baruch, "Should we tell these words to the king?"** For they knew the king was cruel and would respond to these words harshly. **So they questioned him,** Baruch, **saying, "Tell us how you wrote all the words from his,** Jeremiah's, **mouth."** They interrogated him so they could determine whether Jeremiah had composed these things from divine revelation or, instead, had fabricated them. **Then Baruch said to them, "He spoke these words,** about the evils about to come upon the Judean people, **as though he were reading them to me.** That is, he dictated these things to me quickly, as though he had been reciting them from a book." This was an indication of heavenly instruction. For there is no difficulty or delay in learning when the mind is illuminated by the Holy Spirit, whose grace knows nothing of slow exertions or lengthy efforts. For that reason many people, when they write, compose, or give explanations while assisted by the Holy Spirit, are able to produce everything very quickly due to their minds being, in some sense, filled. **"And I wrote in ink."**

36:19–20 Then all the princes said to Baruch, "Go and hide, both you and Jeremiah, and let no one know where you are." They said this because they intended to share these things with the king, who they expected would become furious with Jeremiah and Baruch because of their words and would perhaps search for them in order to have them put to death. Now it seems that, at the time of this directive, Jeremiah was not confined. For if this were the case, how could he hide himself? But then why did he not proclaim these things to the people with his own mouth at that time? Perhaps at that time he hid himself because of the rage of his persecutor, just as Christ did when there was a conspiracy of the Judeans to kill him, so he did not walk around openly, as it says in John (11:53–54). **So they went into the court to the king. However, they entrusted the scroll to the treasury of Elishama, the secretary. And they reported all the words** of Baruch **in the king's hearing.**

King Jehoiakim Burns the Scroll

36:21-26 And the king sent Jehudi to get the scroll. Taking it, Jehudi read it in the king's hearing. Now the king was sitting in the winter house. For kings' palaces have separate rooms for various responsibilities, official matters, needs, and changes in season. **And there was a brazier in front of him, filled with burning coals,** because blazing embers are placed in this sort of iron apparatus to produce heat. **And when Jehudi read three or four pages** (some people understand **pages** to mean verses), the king himself, or Jehudi at the king's command, **cut it with a penknife,** that is, a small knife used to scrape the material that someone writes on, **and threw it into the fire. And neither the king nor his servants were frightened, nor did they tear their garments,** when they heard about the destruction about to come upon them, the way this king's father Josiah did when he heard the words of the prophetess—tearing his garments, weeping, and asking for leniency (2 Kgs 22:8-20). **Nevertheless Elnathan and Delaiah and Gemariah urged the king not to burn the book,** for it seemed to them that this would result in a great offense against God and would provoke greater wrath. From this the stubbornness and willfulness of the king are apparent. **But the Lord hid them,** protecting them supernaturally. It does not say how the Lord hid them, but perhaps it was the same way Christ hid himself and departed from the temple (John 8:59). Certainly Christ did not hide himself behind a pillar! Instead he made himself appear invisible to his enemies. Or perhaps the Lord moved Jeremiah and Baruch to a place unknown to everyone, though not far away.

36:27-32 And the word of the Lord came to Jeremiah after the book had been burned: **Take another scroll again, and write in it all the earlier words, and say to Jehoiakim, "You burned this scroll. Therefore the Lord says these things against Jehoiakim: There will be no one descended from him seated upon the throne of David, and his dead body will be cast out, exposed to the heat by day and the frost by night."** Chapter 22 explains how we should understand these words, where it says: "Write this man barren, a man who shall not prosper in his days; nor shall there be a man from his offspring who shall sit upon David's throne" (22:30). And a little earlier: "He shall be buried with the burial of a donkey, rotten and cast forth outside the gates of Jerusalem" (22:19). **So Jeremiah took the scroll and gave it to Baruch, who wrote in it from the mouth of Jeremiah all the words of the book that the king burned. And, in addition, many more words were**

added than there had been before, about the tribulation about to come upon the king and his people. For now the sins had been increased, so they deserved greater punishment.

Jehoiakim's Wickedness and a Moral Lesson

Here unbelieving, shameless, and proud people imitate Jehoiakim when they scornfully refuse to endure loving rebukes and loyal warnings and advice. They become even more stubborn when they ought to have changed their ways. Finally, even though they ought to thank the people who are rebuking them and giving advice, they become angry and devise plots against them. Solomon speaks against them in Proverbs [29:1]: "Ruin shall suddenly overtake the man with a stiff neck, who despises the one who reproves him." Indeed, these individuals resemble crazed and raving sick people who push away or bite a parent helping them or a doctor healing them. Whoever discovers that they themselves are like this should change their ways.

Chapter Thirty-Seven

King Zedekiah Asks for Jeremiah's Prayers

37:1–2 Then Josiah's son, King Zedekiah, whom King Nebuchadnezzar appointed as king, reigned instead of Jeconiah [Jehoiachin] son of Jehoiakim. For after Nebuchadnezzar had killed Jehoiakim son of Josiah, he appointed Jehoiakim's son Jeconiah as king in place of his father. When Jeconiah had reigned for three months, Nebuchadnezzar stripped him of his reign and appointed his uncle, Zedekiah, as king (2 Kgs 24:8–17). This phrase is now often repeated: "No work endures very long." **But neither he,** namely, Zedekiah, **nor his servants, nor the people of the land** of Judah **obeyed the words that the Lord spoke through the hand,** that is, through the ministry and actions, **of the prophet Jeremiah.**

37:3–5 And King Zedekiah sent Jehucal son of Shelemiah and the priest Zephaniah to Jeremiah, saying, "Pray to the Lord our God for us." When Zedekiah saw that Jeremiah's prophecies were fulfilled regarding his brother Jehoiakim and Jehoiakim's son, he regarded Jeremiah as a true prophet, servant, and friend of God (Wis 7:27). Therefore he asked for the support of his prayers. Others say, and it seems true enough from the words written above, that Zedekiah himself was fairly pious and peaceable so that he could be considered to be favorably disposed or even friendly toward Jeremiah; but his downfall was caused by the wicked advice of others, just as it happens with rulers all the time.[19] **Now Jeremiah walked freely in the midst of the people** in Jerusalem, **for they had not yet thrown him into prison.** It is clear from this that Zedekiah was more merciful than Jehoiakim. **Then Pharaoh's army came out of Egypt** to help Zedekiah and the Judeans, as Pharaoh had promised him. **And when the Chaldeans who were besieging Jerusalem heard the news about this, they withdrew from Jerusalem,** to attack the Egyptians. When they departed, Zedekiah thought they would not return, and he sent to Jeremiah asking him to pray that the Chaldeans would not return to attack Jerusalem.

37:6–10 And the word of the Lord came to Jeremiah, saying: Thus says the Lord: Say this to the king of Judah who sent you to inquire of me. Jeremiah said these words through the aforementioned messengers of Zedekiah, who sent them to Jeremiah to ask him not only to pray for the people but also to inquire from God whether the Chaldeans would return. The Lord answered this through Jeremiah: **Behold, Pharaoh's army, which came forth to help you, will return to its own land,** because they changed their plan on the way when they considered the power of the Chaldeans, and so they retreated in fear. **Do not deceive yourselves saying, "The Chaldeans shall depart from us and go away** and not return again," **because they shall not go away.** That is, they will not enter Chaldea until they have first devastated this land. **But even if you were to beat the entire army of the Chaldeans and a few wounded ones of them are left, each and every one of them shall rise from his tent and set fire to this city.** That is, however few and weak the Chaldeans might become, they will nonetheless prevail against you, because you deserve to be struck by God's rightful judgment. So even if there were a very small number of these [Chaldeans], God would still terrify your hearts and give the victory to them.

Jeremiah Imprisoned

37:11–15 Now when the army of the Chaldeans had departed from Jerusalem, Jeremiah went forth from Jerusalem; that is, he began to depart,

---

19. Nicholas of Lyra, *Postill on Jeremiah* 37:3.

for he had not completely exited the city, as it will become clear; **to go into the land of Benjamin,** to Anathoth, located in the territory of Benjamin, **in order to divide a possession there in the presence of the citizens.** That is, he was going to take possession of the field that he had purchased from his cousin (Jer 32:9) in the presence of the residents of Anathoth in order to indicate that the field had been divided off from the rest of the seller's land. **But when he arrived at the gate of Benjamin,** the gate of Jerusalem through which there was a road leading from Jerusalem to the land of Benjamin, **the guardian of the gate was there in his turn,** at the time of his shift of duty, **by the name of Jeriah. And he seized Jeremiah, saying, "You are fleeing to the Chaldeans** as traitor to your people." **Then Jeremiah answered, "This is not true. I am not fleeing to the Chaldeans." But he did not hear him.** That is, Jeriah did not believe Jeremiah's explanation. **And he seized Jeremiah and led him to the princes.** Why not instead to the king? Perhaps because the king was rather loyal to the prophet, and Jeriah knew the princes would be harsher toward him. **For this reason the princes were angry with Jeremiah,** for they believed the guardian of the gate rather than the holy prophet. **They beat him** (perhaps whipping him or striking them with their hands) **and sent him into the prison that was in the house of Jonathan the secretary.** This prison, as will soon become apparent, was particularly harsh.

37:16 So Jeremiah entered the house of the cistern, that is, the prison, **and remained many days,** sustained by the bread of tribulation and the water of affliction (1 Kgs 22:27), but he did not lack divine consolations. So let us learn from the example of such a prophet to calmly endure small and insignificant things for a short time, especially when we deserve them, even if, because of our unfortunate imperfection, we are unable to suffer great things for a long time for the sake of justice.

37:17 Then King Zedekiah sent and brought him. He ordered Jeremiah to be taken out of prison and brought to him. It was done stealthily so the king would not offend the princes of his palace. **And he asked him secretly in his house, "Do you think there is a word from the Lord?** That is, has God revealed anything to you about the things that are about to befall us?" **And Jeremiah answered, "There is." Then he said, "You shall be delivered into the hands of the king of Babylon."** By saying this, Jeremiah shows his courage and integrity, because in the midst of such sufferings he fully disclosed to the king the very things that would make him most annoyed. Therefore we should not avoid the truth due to fear or a desire for human favor. Nor should we abandon the path of justice or flatter anyone.

37:18-20 And Jeremiah said to the king, "How have I offended you and your servants the princes, **that you have cast me into prison?"** For the king had permitted the princes to do this. For that reason he addresses this to the king who had an obligation to stop this. For a king ought to be like a living law and the embodiment of justice. He should restrain his subjects from committing injustice, especially oppression of the poor and the righteous. **"Where are your** false **prophets who prophesied to you, 'The king of Babylon will not come against you'?"** It is as though he were saying, "You can see with your own eyes that I myself am speaking on my behalf and those others have lied." **"Therefore, now listen. I beg you, my lord and king, do not send me back to the house of Jonathan the secretary;** I might die there in his prison because of the dreadful and harsh conditions of the cistern." Thus holy men, for their part, are able to ask for a lessening of their persecutions while still preserving the threefold truthfulness of their life, teaching, and just conduct.

37:21 So Zedekiah ordered that Jeremiah be committed into the entrance of the prison, a better location that was more comfortable, **and that they give him each day a piece of bread, except for broth;** they were to give him bread in addition to the broth, so that both were to be served to him every day, **until all the bread in the city** of Jerusalem **was consumed.** This shows there was a certain degree of piety in Zedekiah, but he nevertheless ought to have acted in accordance with genuine justice and released Jeremiah, who was completely innocent. But he did not want to offend his princes, so he confined the prophet in the prison's entrance. There are many such people who wish to serve two masters (Matt 6:24), pleasing both God and the world, and they try to appear agreeable in every circumstance. It is certain that these people wander and stray from the path of impartiality quite frequently.

Chapter Thirty-Eight

Jeremiah Lowered into the Cistern

38:1-3 Now Shephatiah son of Mattan, and Gedeliah, etc., **heard the words that Jeremiah spoke to all the people.** For the residents of Jerusalem were able to approach the prison entrance or enter the area surrounding it. Jeremiah announced to them the evils that were approaching, **saying: Whoever remains in this city,** those who do not flee or surrender themselves to the Chaldeans, **shall die by the sword, and by famine, and by pestilence**—by one of these blows. We should not understand this to apply to absolutely everyone who remained, for certain individuals remained alive, such as King Zedekiah, to whom the prophet had recently said, "You will die in peace" (Jer 34:5). But he is speaking in generalities rather than about every single individual. So when he says, "**whoever,**" he means that a very small number of people will escape but the number would be so small that it could be considered practically none at all. **But whoever flees to the Chaldeans will live. Their souls** (that is, their *lives*—for the souls of the others were also immortal) **will be preserved,** though they themselves will survive **as spoils of war.**

38:4-6 Then the princes said to the king, "We beg you to have this person put to death, for on purpose, craftily and cunningly, **he weakens the hands of our men of war.** He terrifies the hearts of Jerusalem's residents and warriors, thereby weakening their power and causing their hands to tremble." For the emotion of fear weakens men, chills their hearts, and causes trembling. **"For this person,** Jeremiah, **does not seek peace for this people, but evil.** He acts in opposition to the common good." **And the king said, "Behold, he is in your hands.** I give you power over him." By doing this he committed a mortal sin, for he handed over a guiltless man for death, even though he did this out of human fear, so he would not offend his own subjects. But one should obey God rather than humans (Acts 5:29). **"For it is not lawful for** me, **the king, to deny you anything."** This was not true, because one should not agree to anything that is contrary to justice and the will of God, especially by acquiescing to someone of lesser rank who is one's subject. On the contrary, a subject who errs should be instructed and rebuked rather than encouraged in evil. **So they took Jeremiah and threw him into the cistern of Malchiah, and they lowered him with ropes into the cistern, in which there was no water, but mud,** so that there he would die a horrible lengthy death from hunger and from the pressure of the mud. **And Jeremiah sunk into the mire.** See how much this most holy man suffered because of his integrity. Our own miserable impatience should blush with shame!

Jeremiah Rescued from the Cistern

38:8-13 Then Ebedmelech the Ethiopian, a eunuch in the king's house, heard that they had put Jeremiah into the cistern. He said to the king, "My lord and king, these men did evil to Jeremiah. There is no more bread in the city." This clearly refers to the message spoken by Jeremiah, that they would die of hunger. **So the king ordered Ebedmelech the Ethiopian, "Take thirty men from here and lift Jeremiah up from the cistern."** This shows that Zedekiah was a pliable man, quickly bending here and there. **Then Ebedmelech the Ethiopian said to Jeremiah, "Put these old rags under your arms and over the ropes." And Jeremiah did so. Then they drew Jeremiah up from the cistern with the ropes, and Jeremiah remained in the entrance of the prison** so he would not be seen by the princes.

Zedekiah Secretly Consults Jeremiah

38:14-15 Then the king sent and brought Jeremiah to himself at the third entrance that was in the house of the Lord. In fact there were three entrances to the temple. The first, or outer one, was the entrance to the court of the women. The second was for the court of the men. The third one, to which Jeremiah was led, was for the court of the priests. **And the king said to Jeremiah, "I am asking you for a message. Do not hide anything from me." So Jeremiah said, "If I declare it to you, will you not put me to death? And if I give you advice, you will not listen to me."** Jeremiah truly knew through divine revelation that Zedekiah would not be pleased.

38:16-18 So the king swore to Jeremiah in private, saying, "As the Lord lives, the one who made souls for us, the one who created our souls and gave them life and will, **if I kill you,"** which means, "I will not kill you." **And Jeremiah said to Zedekiah, "Thus says the Lord: If you surrender to the princes of the king of Babylon, your soul shall live,** you yourself will remain unharmed, **and this city will not be burned with fire. And you and your house,** your family, **will be safe. But if you do not go out to the princes of the king of Babylon, this city will be delivered into the hands of the Chaldeans. It will be burned with fire, and you will not escape from their hands."**

38:19-20 Then the king said to Jeremiah, "I am disturbed, troubled with fear, **because of the Judeans who have fled to the Chaldeans, for I might**

be handed over to them, by the Chaldeans or in some other way, **and they would abuse me** by shamefully mistreating me or killing me in a vile way." **But Jeremiah answered him,** "The Chaldeans **will not deliver you** into the hands of those Judeans. **I beg you to listen to God's word that I am speaking to you** about going out to the Chaldeans, **and it will be well for you and your soul will live,"** in the manner that was explained earlier (38:17).

38:21–23 "But if you will not go forth, this is the message that the Lord has shown me. The Lord revealed to me that this is what will come to pass for you: **Behold, all the women that remain in the house of the king of Judah,** in your house, O Zedekiah, **will be brought to the princes of the king of Babylon.** For when Jerusalem is captured, the Chaldeans will enter the palace and take your women captive. **And,** when they see you taken captive and your eyes put out, **these [women] will say to you, 'Your men of peace deceived you and prevailed against you.'"** Some people explain that this is about the false prophets who counseled the king to resist the Chaldeans, declaring peace and safety to him.[20] But it is also possible to explain this as being about the king and people of Egypt who promised aid to Zedekiah and the Judeans, but they did not help at all. This could also be understood to refer in a general way to all of the people who persuaded Zedekiah to resist, causing him to be misled and deceived. **"They have plunged you into the mud,** bringing you into despair, **and plunged your feet into a slippery place,** causing you to become unsteady and to fall down." In the moral sense, this can refer to all those who—softened by the flattery, promises, or instigation of others—act unjustly and then fall or perish. They are plunged **into the mud** of filthy sin and they place their affections in **a slippery place,** in the things that are earthly and slip away, not in the highest unchangeable good. So let us pray with the psalmist: "Draw me out of the mire so that I do not become stuck" (Ps 69:13). So the women of Zedekiah's house spoke the preceding words against him, taunting him due to their frustration and sorrow, since they came to such a disaster precisely because of his impiety. For it is the very worst punishment for men when their women are exposed to the lust of their enemies.[21]

---

20. Nicholas of Lyra, *Postill on Jeremiah* 38:22.

21. For medieval commentators' views on sexual assault, including the perception that the rape of a woman is chiefly an offense against her husband or father, see Joy A. Schroeder, *Dinah's Lament: the Biblical Legacy of Sexual Violence in Christian Interpretation* (Minneapolis: Fortress, 2007), 5.

38:24–28 So Zedekiah said to Jeremiah, "Let no one of the people living in Jerusalem at that time **learn these words."** For Zedekiah feared the princes' anger. **"But if the princes hear that I have spoken with you and say to you, 'Tell us what you said to the king,' you shall say, 'I presented my supplication to the king;** I asked him humbly **not to command me to be brought back to the house of Jonathan,** to the prison that is in his house, **to die there.'"** So when Jeremiah answered in this way, he was not lying (38:27). For we must understand that Jeremiah indeed had asked for this, since he had insisted on this very thing in the preceding chapter (37:17–20). **So Jeremiah remained in the entrance of the prison until the day that Jerusalem was captured.**

Chapter Thirty-Nine

The Fall of Jerusalem

39:1–4 In the ninth year of Zedekiah king of Judah, Nebuchadnezzar and all his army came and besieged Jerusalem. In the eleventh year of King Zedekiah, the city was opened, because its outer wall and gates were broken down by the violence of the Chaldeans; the residents of Jerusalem did not open the city. **And the princes of the king of Babylon entered.** But Nebuchadnezzar was not with them, as it will soon become clear. **And they sat in the middle gate** that was between two outer walls. They wanted the rest of the gates to be destroyed. For Jerusalem was surrounded by a triple wall. **And when he saw them, Zedekiah and all the soldiers** still with him at the time **fled. They departed from the city by night by the road of the king's garden** (for there was either a road in his garden or road that led to it) **through a gate that was between two walls** of the city. And many people say that there was a gate there where one could enter an underground passage whose exit was far from the city, through which the king and his officials fled.[22] The fourth book of Kings describes these events fully (2 Kgs 25:1–4).[23] These events were signified prophetically when the Lord ordered Ezekiel to dig through the wall and exit through it, carrying baggage on his shoulders. This is written about at length in Ezekiel [12:5–6].

22. Nicholas of Lyra, *Postill on Jeremiah* 39:4.
23. The books that modern Bibles call 1–2 Samuel and 1–2 Kings were designated as 1–4 Kings.

39:5-7 But the army of the Chaldeans pursued and seized Zedekiah in the plain of the wilderness of Jericho, a desert that was near Jericho. For this reason, it is written in the fourth book of Kings (2 Kgs 25:5) that he was captured in the plains of Jericho. **They took him captive and brought him to Nebuchadnezzar in Riblah,** a city that is also called Antioch, **and he spoke words of judgment to him,** words of rebuke and blame, reproving him for unfaithfulness, rebellion, perjury, and breaking the treaty. It says in the *Scholastic History* that he said to Zedekiah, "Your God, who regards your sin as odious, gave you into my hands."[24] **And the king of Babylon slaughtered Zedekiah's sons before his eyes,** which was unspeakably difficult for him to watch, **as well as all the nobility of Judah,** the elders or princes of Judah captured at the same time as Zedekiah. **And he also,** through his attendants, **put out Zedekiah's eyes and bound him with shackles to be taken to Babylon,** as it was predicted by Ezekiel [12:13]: "He will enter Babylon, but he will not see it."

39:8-10 The Chaldeans also burned the king's house, the palace, **with fire, and the house of the common person,** that is, the houses of the common people. **And they tore down the wall,** the three walls, **of Jerusalem. And Nebuzaradan, the general of the army** of the king of Babylon, **carried away captive into Babylon the remnant of the** Judean **people that remained in the city** of Jerusalem, **and fugitives who had deserted to him,** to the king of Babylon, **as well as the rest of the common people** of Judah. **But Nebuzaradan left some of the poor** Judean **people, who had nothing at all, in the land of Judah** to cultivate the land. **And he gave them vineyards and cisterns at that time,** to serve the king of Babylon and pay him tribute through their governor Gedaliah, as it says below.

Jeremiah Freed from Prison

39:11-14 Now Nebuchadnezzar had given orders to the general of the army regarding Jeremiah: "Take him from the prison entrance **and set your eyes on him;** that is, be merciful to him; **and do him no harm, but do with him as he wishes."** We should assume that the Chaldeans, while their king was absent, entered Jerusalem and when they found an imprisoned man, Jeremiah, and knowing the reason for this, referred this matter to the king

24. Peter Comestor, *Scholastic History, On 2 Kings* 44, PL 198:1426.

himself in Riblah. Then, as God ordained, the king gave the order to the general of the army, as it just said. And then this general and other aristocrats or princes of the king of Babylon **sent** their servants and **took Jeremiah from the prison entrance,** as it says in the text. **And they entrusted him to Gedaliah,** whom the king of Babylon placed as governor over the Judeans, **so he might enter the house** of Gedaliah **and live among the people,** in the midst of the Judeans left behind in the land with Gedaliah.

39:15–18 But the word of the Lord came to Jeremiah while he was still **confined in the prison entrance: Go and tell Ebedmelech the Ethiopian: Thus says the Lord: I, I myself will bring** (that is, I will *fulfill*) **my words,** announced prophetically regarding the devastation of Jerusalem, **upon this city, for evil,** as punishment, **and not for good** or liberation. **On that day these things will happen in your sight.** At the time of the devastation and destruction of Jerusalem, you will see these words fulfilled and you will remember my message. **And I will free you on that day, says the Lord, and I will not give you into the hands of the men,** the Chaldeans, **whom you fear. But, rescuing you, I will deliver you. You will not die by the sword, but your life will be safe;** that is, you will remain physically sound, or you will be saved eternally, **because you put your trust in me.** This was the particular and chief reason for [Ebedmelech's] deliverance—the fact that he placed his trust in God. He also deserved this due to certain good works, especially for taking special care to have Jeremiah freed from the cistern. Moreover, these words are spoken to everyone who hopes in God. Whoever hopes constantly does receive salvation, as it says in the psalm: "And the Lord will help them and deliver them, and will rescue them from the wicked and save them, because they have hoped in the Lord" (Ps 37:40).

Spiritual Interpretation of Zedekiah's Capture

Furthermore, Zedekiah and his princes and officials represent those who are disobedient and are handed over to the devil, who is the king of distress. When they give in to his temptation, they and their spiritual children or subjects are killed by him. The devil also put out the eyes of Zedekiah and bound him with shackles, for he thoroughly blinds the hearts of wicked bishops and leaders of the church, and binds them with the chains of impiety, and sends them to hell.

Bibliography

Primary Sources

Albert the Great. *Opera Alberti Magni.* Vol. 19. Monasterii Westfalorum: Aschendorff, 1952.

Albert the Great and Thomas Aquinas. *Albert and Thomas: Selected Writings.* Translated and edited by Simon Tugwell. Classics of Western Spirituality. Mahwah, NJ: Paulist, 1988.

Ambrose. *De Nabuthae* [= *On Naboth*]. PL 14:765–92.

Aristotle. *De Sensu and De Memoria.* Edited and translated by G. R. T. Ross. Cambridge: Cambridge University Press, 1906.

———. *Metaphysics X–XIV.* Edited and translated by Hugh Tredennick. LCL 287. Cambridge, MA: Harvard University Press, 1977.

———. *The Nicomachean Ethics.* Translated by H. Rackham. LCL 73. Cambridge, MA: Harvard University Press, 2003.

———. *On the Soul. Parva Naturalia. On Breath.* Translated by W. S. Hett. LCL 288. Cambridge, MA: Harvard University Press, 1995.

Augustine. *De Civitate Dei Libri XI–XII* [= *City of God*]. Edited by Bernard Dombart and Alphonsus Kalb. CCSL 48. Turnhout: Brepols, 1955.

———. *De Libero Arbitrio* [= *On Free Choice*]. PL 32:1221–1310.

———. *De Sermone Domini in Monte* [= *On the Lord's Sermon on the Mount*]. CCCM 75. Edited by Almut Mutzenbecher. Turnhout: Brepols, 1967.

———. *De Trinitate* [= *On the Trinity*]. Edited by W. J. Mountain with Fr. Glorie. CCSL 50, 50A. Turnhout: Brepols, 1968.

The Babylonian Talmud, Seder Moʻed. Edited by I. Epstein. Translated by H. Freedman. London: Soncino, 1938.

The Babylonian Talmud, Seder Neziķin, Baba Bathra. Vol. 1. Edited by I. Epstein. Translated by Israel W. Slotki. London: Soncino, 1935.

Biblia Sacra iuxta Vulgatam Versionem. 3rd ed. Edited by Bonifatius Fischer et al. Stuttgart: Deutsche Bibelgesellschaft, 1969.

Birgitta of Sweden. *The Revelations of St. Birgitta of Sweden.* Vol. 2. Translated by Denis Searby. Introduction and notes by Bridget Morris. New York: Oxford University Press, 2008.

Boethius. *De consolatione philosophiae* [= *On the Consolation of Philosophy*]. PL 63:579–870.

Bonaventure. *Opera Omnia.* Vol. 12. Edited by A. C. Peltier. Paris: Ludovicus Vives, 1868.

Cassian, John. *Conferences.* Edited by E. Pichery. SC 54. Paris: Éditions du Cerf, 1958.

Denis the Carthusian. *Enarratio in Jeremiam Prophetam* [= *Exposition on the Prophet Jeremiah*]. In *Opera Omnia,* 9:5–312. Monstrolii: Typis Cartusiae Sanctae Mariae de Pratis, 1900.

———. *Spiritual Writings.* Translated by Íde M. Ní Riain. Dublin: Four Courts Press, 2005.

Glossa Ordinaria on Jeremiah. PL 114:9–62.

Glossa Ordinaria on Matthew. PL 114:63–178.

Gottschalk of Orbais. *Gottschalk and a Medieval Predestination Controversy: Texts Translated from the Latin.* Edited and translated by Victor Genke and Francis X. Gumerlock. Milwaukee: Marquette University Press, 2010.

Gregory the Great. *Liber sacramentorum.* PL 78:25–240.

———. *Moralia on Job.* Edited by Aristide Bocognano. SC 221. Paris: Éditions du Cerf, 1975.

———. *Moralia on Job.* Edited by Marcus Adriaen. CCSL 143, 143A. Turnhout: Brepols, 1979.

———. *Moralia on Job.* PL 75:509–1162; PL 76:9–782.

———. *Règle pastorale* [= *Pastoral Rule*]. Edited by Floribert Rommel. SC 381, 382. Paris: Éditions du Cerf, 1992.

Hildegard of Bingen. *The Letters of Hildegard of Bingen.* Vol. 3. Translated by Joseph L. Baird and Radd K. Ehrman. New York: Oxford University Press, 2004.

Horace. *Satires, Epistles, and Ars Poetica.* Translated by H. Rushton Fairclough. LCL 194. Cambridge, MA: Harvard University Press, 2005.

Hugh of Fleury. *Chronicon.* Edited by Bernhard Rottendorf. Münster: Bernhard Roesfeldt, 1638.

Hugh of St. Cher. *A Commentary on the Parable of the Prodigal Son.* Translated and introduced by Hugh Bernard Feiss. Toronto: Peregrina, 1996.

———. *Postilla super Ieremiam* [= *On Jeremiah*]. In *Opera Omnia in Universum Vetus & Novum Testamentum,* 4:175–282. Lyon: Ioannes Antonius Huguetan and Guillielmus Barbier, 1669.

Isidore of Seville. *Etymologies.* PL 82.

Jeremiah: A New English Translation. 2 vols. Translation of text, Rashi, and commentary by A. J. Rosenberg. New York: Judaica Press, 1985–1989.

Jerome. *Commentarioli in Psalmos* [= *Brief Comments on the Psalms*]. Edited by Germani Morin. CCSL 72:163–245. Turnhout: Brepols, 1959.

———. *Commentariorum in Epistolam Beati Pauli ad Ephesios Libri Tres* [= *Commentary on Ephesians*]. PL 26:439–554.

———. *Commentariorum in Esaiam* [= *Commentary on Isaiah*]. Edited by Marcus Adriaen. CCSL 73, 73A. Turnhout: Brepols, 1963.

———. *Commentariorum in Isaiam Prophetam* [= *Commentary on Isaiah*]. PL 24:17–678.

———. *Commentariorum in Mattheum* [= *Commentary on Matthew*]. Edited by D. Hurst and M. Adriaen. CCSL 77. Turnhout: Brepols, 1969.

———. *Commentary on Jeremiah.* Translated by Michael Graves. Edited by Christopher A. Hall. Ancient Christian Texts. Downers Grove, IL: IVP Academic, 2011.

———. *De viris illustribus.* Edited by Claudia Barthold. Mülheim: Carthusianus Verlag, 1990.

———. *Epistolae* [= *Letters*]. PL 22:325–1224.

———. *In Hieremiam* [= *On Jeremiah*]. Edited by Sigofredus Reiter. CCSL 74. Turnhout: Brepols, 1960.

———. *Liber Interpretationis Hebraicorum Nominum* [= *Interpretation of Hebrew Names*]. Edited by Paul de Lagarde. CCSL 72:57–161. Turnhout: Brepols, 1959.

The Jewish Study Bible. Edited by Adele Berlin and Marc Zvi Brettler. New York: Oxford University Press, 2004.

John of Damascus. *De his qui in fide dormierunt.* PG 95:247–78.

———. *Expositio Fidei Orthodoxae* [= *Exposition of the Orthodox Faith*]. PG 94:789–1228.

Josephus. *Jewish Antiquities, Books IX–XI.* Edited and translated by Ralph Marcus. LCL 326. Cambridge, MA: Harvard University Press, 1995.

Maimonides, Moses. *The Guide for the Perplexed.* Translated by M. Friedländer. 2nd ed. New York: Dover, 1956.

Mechthild of Magdeburg. *The Flowing Light of the Godhead.* Translated by Frank Tobin. Classics of Western Spirituality. Mahwah, NJ: Paulist, 1998.

The New Testament in Scots, Being Purvey's Revision of Wycliff's Version Turned into Scots by Murdoch Nisbet c. 1520. Edited by Thomas Graves Law. Vol. 3. Scottish Text Society 52. Edinburgh: William Blackwood & Sons, 1905.

Nicholas of Lyra. *Postilla super Totam Bibliam—Liber Esaie* [= *Literal Postill on Isaiah*]. In Vol. 2, n.p. Strassburg, 1492. Reprint: Frankfurt am Main: Minerva, 1971.

———. *Postilla super Totam Bibliam—Liber Hieremie* [= *Literal Postill on Jeremiah*]. In Vol. 2, n.p. Strassburg, 1492; reprint: Frankfurt am Main: Minerva, 1971.

Old English Homilies and Homiletic Treatises (Sawles warde, and þe wohunge of Ure

Lauerd: Ureisuns of Ure Louerd and of Ure Lefdi, &c.) of the Twelfth and Thirteenth Centuries. Edited by Richard Morris. Early English Text Society, First Series, 29. London: Trübner, 1868.

Origen. *Homiliae in Ieremiam* [= *Homilies on Jeremiah*]. Edited by Pierre Nautin and Pierre Husson. SC 232, 238. Paris: Éditions du Cerf, 1976–1977.

———. *Homilies on Jeremiah.* Translated by Jerome. PL 25:583–692.

Peter Comestor. *Historia Scholastica—Liber IIII Regum* [= *Scholastic History—The Book of 2 Kings*]. PL 198:1385–1432.

Plato. *Timaeus. Critas. Cleitophon. Menexenus. Epistles.* Translated by R. G. Bury. LCL 234. Cambridge, MA: Harvard University Press, 1999.

Prosper of Aquitaine. *Liber Sententiarum* [= *The Book of Sentences*]. In *Expositio Psalmorum, Liber Sententiarum*, edited by P. Callens, 253–365. CCSL 68A. Turnhout: Brepols, 1972.

Pseudo-Chrysostom. *Fragmenta in Ieremiam.* PG 64:740–1037.

Pseudo-Dionysius. *The Complete Works.* Translated by Colm Luibhéid and Paul Rorem. Classics of Western Spirituality. Mahwah, NJ: Paulist, 1987.

———. *De Divinis Nominibus* [= *Divine Names*]. PG 3:585–996.

Pseudo-Joachim of Fiore. *Abbatis Ioachim Divina prorsus in Ieremiam Prophetam Interpretatio* [= *Super Ieremiam*]. Cologne: Alectorius and haeredes Soteri, 1577.

Rabanus Maurus. *Carmina.* Edited by Ernst Dümmler. MGH Poetae 2. Berlin: Weidmann, 1844.

———. *De institutione clericorum.* Edited by Detlev Zimpel. Freiburger Beiträge zur mittelalterlichen Geschichte: Studien und Texte 7. Frankfurt: Peter Lang, 1996.

———. *De rerum naturis.* PL 111:9–614.

———. *De Universo: The Peculiar Properties of Words and Their Mystical Significance.* Vol. 1. Translated by Priscilla Throop. Charlotte, VT: MedievalMS, 2009.

———. *Epistolae.* Edited by Ernst Dümmler. MGH *Epistolae* 5. Berlin: Weidmann, 1899.

———. *Expositionis Super Jeremiam Prophetam Libri Viginti* [= *Exposition on the Prophet Jeremiah*]. PL 111:797–1272.

Rupert of Deutz. *Commentariorum in Genesim* [= *On Genesis*]. Edited by Hrabanus Haacke. CCCM 21. Turnhout: Brepols, 1971.

———. *In Hieremiam Prophetam Commentariorum Liber Unus* [= *On Jeremiah*]. In *De Sancta Trinitate et Operibus Eius Libros XXVII–XLII*, edited by Hrabanus Haacke, 1572–1642. CCCM 23. Turnhout: Brepols, 1972.

The Targum of Ezekiel. Translated and introduced by Samson H. Levey. The Aramaic Bible 13. Wilmington, DE: Michael Glazier, 1987.

The Targum of Jeremiah. Translated and introduced by Robert Hayward. The Aramaic Bible 12. Wilmington, DE: Michael Glazier, 1987.

Theodoret of Cyrrhus. *Interpretatio in Ieremiam.* PG 81:496–805.

Thomas Aquinas. *In Jeremiam Prophetam Expositio* [= *On Jeremiah*]. In *Opera Omnia*, 14:579–667. Parma: Fiaccadori, 1863.

Bibliography

Virgil. *Eclogues, Georgics, Aeneid I–VI*. Translated by H. Rushton Fairclough. Revised by G. P. Goold. LCL 63. Cambridge, MA: Harvard University Press, 1999.

The Vulgate Bible: Douay-Rheims Translation. Vol. 4, *The Major Prophetical Books*. Edited by Angela M. Kinney. Cambridge, MA: Harvard University Press, 2012.

William of Luxi. *Opera*. Edited by Andrew T. Sulavik. CCCM 219. Turnhout: Brepols, 2005.

The Zohar. Translated by Harry Sperling and Maurice Simon. Vol. 2. London: Soncino, 1956.

Secondary Sources

Abulafia, Anna Sapir. "The Ideology of Reform and Changing Ideas concerning Jews in the Works of Rupert of Deutz and Hermanus Quondam Iudeus." *Jewish History* 7 (1993): 43–63.

Bataillon, Louis-Jacques, Gilbert Dahan, and Pierre-Marie Gy, eds. *Hugues de Saint-Cher (†1263), bibliste et théologien*. Bibliothèque d'Histoire Culturelle du Moyen Âge 1. Turnhout: Brepols, 2004.

Bellamah, Timothy. *The Biblical Interpretation of William of Alton*. Oxford Studies in Historical Theology. New York: Oxford University Press, 2011.

Bennett, R. F. *The Early Dominicans: Studies in Thirteenth-Century Dominican History*. New York: Russell & Russell, 1971.

Bett, Henry. *Joachim of Flora*. Merrick, NY: Richwood, 1976.

Broadie, Alexander. "Maimonides and Aquinas on the Names of God." *Religious Studies* 23 (1987): 157–70.

Chalassery, Joseph. *The Holy Spirit and Christian Initiation in the East Syrian Tradition*. Rome: Mar Thoma Yogam, 1995.

Coogan, Michael D. *A Brief Introduction to the Old Testament: The Hebrew Bible in Its Context*. New York: Oxford University Press, 2009.

Coon, Lynda L. *Dark Age Bodies: Gender and Monastic Practice in the Early Medieval West*. The Middle Ages. Philadelphia: University of Pennsylvania Press, 2011.

Coureas, Nicholas. *The Latin Church in Cyprus, 1195–1312*. Brookfield, VT: Ashgate, 1997.

Dahan, Gilbert, ed. *Nicolas de Lyre: Franciscain du XIVe siècle exégète et théologien*. Collection des Études Augustiniennes. Série Moyen Âge et Temps Modernes 48. Paris: Institut d'Études Augustiniennes, 2011.

Darby, Peter. *Bede and the End of Time*. Burlington, VT: Ashgate, 2012.

De Jong, Mayke. "Exegesis for an Empress." In *Medieval Transformations: Texts, Power, and Gifts in Context*, edited by Esther Cohen and Mayke B. de Jong, 69–100. Cultures, Beliefs and Traditions: Medieval and Early Modern Peoples 11. Boston: Brill 2001.

————. "Old Law and New-Found Power: Hrabanus Maurus and the Old Testament." In *Centres of Learning: Learning and Location in Pre-modern Europe and the Near East,* edited by Jan Willem Drijvers and Alasdair A. MacDonald, 161–76. New York: Brill, 1995.

Elliott, Dyan. "The Physiology of Rapture and Female Spirituality." In *Medieval Theology and the Natural Body,* edited by Peter Biller and A. J. Minnis, 141–73. York Studies in Medieval Theology 1. Rochester, NY: York Medieval Press.

Emery, Kent, Jr. "Denys the Carthusian: The World of Thought Comes to Roermond." In *The Carthusians in the Low Countries: Studies in Monastic History and Heritage,* edited by Krijn Pansters, 255–304. Leuven: Peters, 2014.

Emmerson, Richard Kenneth. *Antichrist in the Middle Ages: A Study of Medieval Apocalypticism, Art, and Literature.* Seattle: University of Washington Press, 1981.

Enos, Theresa, ed. *Encyclopedia of Rhetoric and Composition: Communication from Ancient Times to the Information Age.* New York: Garland, 1996.

Fries, Albert. "Zur Entstehungszeit der Bibelkommentare Alberts des Grossen." In *Albertus Magnus: Doctor Universalis 1280/1980,* edited by Gerbert Meyer and Albert Zimmermann, 119–65. Walberberger Studien: Philosophische Reihe 6. Mainz: Matthias-Grünewald-Verlag, 1980.

Gils, Pierre-Marie. "*Les Collationes* marginales dans l'autographe du commentaire de S. Thomas sur Isaïe." *Revue des sciences philosophiques et théologiques* 42 (1958): 253–64.

Goldfain, Tal. *Word Order and Time in Biblical Hebrew Narrative.* New York: Oxford University Press, 2004.

Grabar, Oleg. "Space and Holiness in Medieval Jerusalem." In *Jerusalem: Its Sanctity and Centrality to Judaism, Christianity, and Islam,* edited by Lee I. Levine, 275–99. New York: Continuum, 1999.

Graves, Michael. *Jerome's Hebrew Philology: A Study Based on His Commentary on Jeremiah.* Supplements to Vigiliae Christianae 90. Boston: Brill, 2007.

Green, Barbara. *Jeremiah and God's Plans of Well-Being.* Columbia, SC: University of South Carolina Press, 2013.

Hall, Joseph, ed. *Selections from Early Middle English 1130–1250.* Part 2, *Notes.* London: Oxford University Press, 1920.

Hartman, Louis F., and S. David Sperling. "God, Names of." In *Encyclopaedia Judaica,* edited by Fred Skolnik and Michael Berenbaum, 7:672–76. 2nd ed. Detroit: Thomson Gale, 2007.

Holladay, William L. *Jeremiah 1: A Commentary on the Book of the Prophet Jeremiah, Chapters 1–25.* Hermeneia. Philadelphia: Fortress, 1986.

————. *Jeremiah: Reading the Prophet in His Time—and Ours.* Philadelphia: Fortress, 1990.

Jacobson, Diane L., and Robert Kysar. *A Beginner's Guide to the Books of the Bible.* Minneapolis: Augsburg, 1991.

Jansen, Katherine Ludwig. *The Making of the Magdalen: Preaching and Popular Devotion in the Later Middle Ages*. Princeton: Princeton University Press, 2000.

Kannengiesser, Charles. *Handbook of Patristic Exegesis: The Bible in Ancient Christianity*. Boston: Brill, 2006.

Keech, Dominic. *The Anti-Pelagian Christology of Augustine of Hippo*. Oxford: Oxford University Press, 2012.

Kienzle, Beverly Mayne, and Pamela J. Walker, eds. *Women Preachers and Prophets through Two Millennia of Christianity*. Berkeley: University of California Press, 1998.

Kottje, Raymund. *Verzeichnis der Handschriften mit den Werken des Hrabanus Maurus*. MGH Hilfsmittel 27. Hannover: Hahnsche Buchhandlung, 2012.

Klepper, Deeana Copeland. *The Insight of Unbelievers: Nicholas of Lyra and Christian Reading of Jewish Text in the Later Middle Ages*. Philadelphia: University of Pennsylvania Press, 2007.

Kovach, Francis J., and Robert W. Shahan, eds. *Albert the Great: Commemorative Essays*. Norman: University of Oklahoma Press, 1980.

Krey, Philip D. W., and Lesley Smith, eds. *Nicholas of Lyra: The Senses of Scripture*. Studies in the History of Christian Thought 90. Boston: Brill, 2000.

Labrosse, Henri. "Oeuvres de Nicholas de Lyre." *Études franciscaines* 19 (1908): 153-75.

Law, Timothy Michael. *When God Spoke Greek: The Septuagint and the Making of the Christian Bible*. New York: Oxford University Press, 2013.

Lerner, Robert E. "Poverty, Preaching, and Eschatology in the Revelation Commentaries of 'Hugh of St. Cher.'" In *The Bible in the Medieval World*, edited by Katherine Walsh and Diane Wood, 157-89. Oxford: Basil Blackwell, 1985.

Levy, Ian Christopher, trans. and ed. *The Letter to the Galatians*. Bible in Medieval Tradition 1. Grand Rapids: Eerdmans, 2011.

Levy, Ian Christopher, Philip D. W. Krey, and Thomas Ryan, trans. and eds. *The Letter to the Romans*. The Bible in Medieval Tradition 2. Grand Rapids: Eerdmans, 2013.

Lewis, Charlton T., and Charles Short, eds. *A Latin Dictionary*. New York: Oxford University Press, 1984.

Linde, Cornelia. *How to Correct the "Sacra Scriptura"? Textual Criticism of the Latin Bible between the Twelfth and Fifteenth Century*. Medium Ævum Monographs 29. Oxford: Society for the Study of Medieval Languages and Literature, 2012.

Lio, Ermenegildo. "Finalmente rintracciata la fonte del famoso testo patristico 'Pasce fame morientem.'" *Antonianum* 27 (1952): 349-66.

Matter, E. Ann. "The Church Fathers and the *Glossa Ordinaria*." In *The Reception of the Church Fathers in the West*, edited by Irena Doreta Backus, 1:83-111. Leiden: Brill, 1997.

McGinn, Bernard. *The Calabrian Abbot: Joachim of Fiore in the History of Western Thought*. New York: Macmillan, 1985.

McKim, Donald K, ed. *Dictionary of Major Biblical Interpreters.* 2nd ed. Downers Grove, IL: IVP Academic, 2007.

Meersseman, G. "De S. Alberti Magni Postilla inedita super Ieremiam." *Angelicum* 9 (1932): 3–20, 236–37.

Morris, David. "The Historiography of the *Super Prophetas* (also known as *Super Esaiam*) of Pseudo-Joachim of Fiore." *Oliviana* 4 (2012): 1–23. http://oliviana .revues.org/512.

Moynihan, Robert. "The Development of the 'Pseudo-Joachim' Commentary 'Super Hieremiam': New Manuscript Evidence." *Mélanges de l'École Française de Rome, Moyen âge-Temps modernes* 98 (1986): 109–42.

Murphy-O'Connor, Jerome. *The Holy Land: An Oxford Archaeological Guide.* 5th ed. New York: Oxford University Press, 2008.

Opper, Thorston. *Hadrian: Empire and Conflict.* Cambridge, MA: Harvard University Press, 2008.

Patterson, Paul A. *Visions of Christ: The Anthropomorphite Controversy of 399 CE.* Studien und Texte zu Antike und Christentum 68. Tübingen: Mohr Siebeck, 2012.

Peter, Carl J. *Participated Eternity in the Vision of God: A Study of the Opinions of Thomas Aquinas and His Commentators on the Duration of the Acts of Glory.* Analecta Gregoriana 142. Rome: Gregorian University Press, 1964.

Pietersma, Albert, and Marc Saunders. "To the Reader of Ieremias." In *A New English Translation of the Septuagint,* edited by Albert Pietersma and Benjamin G. Wright, 876–81. New York: Oxford University Press, 2007.

Raaijmakers, Janneke. *The Making of the Monastic Community of Fulda, c. 744–c. 900.* New York: Cambridge University Press, 2012.

Reeves, Marjorie. *Joachim of Fiore and the Prophetic Future.* New York: Harper, 1977.

Ryan, Thomas F. *Thomas Aquinas as Reader of the Psalms.* Studies in Spirituality and Theology 6. Notre Dame: University of Notre Dame Press, 2000.

Saebø, Magne, ed. *Hebrew Bible/Old Testament: The History of Its Interpretation.* Vol. 1, part 2. Göttingen: Vandenhoeck & Ruprecht, 2000.

Schroeder, Joy A., ed. and trans. *The Book of Genesis.* The Bible in Medieval Tradition 3. Grand Rapids: Eerdmans, 2015.

———. *Dinah's Lament: The Biblical Legacy of Sexual Violence in Christian Interpretation.* Minneapolis: Fortress, 2007.

Smith, Lesley. "Hugh of St. Cher and Medieval Collaboration." In *Transforming Relations: Essays on Jews and Christians throughout History in Honor of Michael A. Signer,* edited by Franklin T. Harkins, 241–64. Notre Dame: University of Notre Dame Press, 2010.

Stump, Eleonore. *Aquinas.* New York: Routledge, 2003.

Sweeney, Marvin A. *Form and Intertextuality in Prophetic and Apocalyptic Literature.* Tübingen: Mohr Siebeck, 2005.

Tarrer, Seth B. *Reading with the Faithful: Interpretation of True and False Prophecy in the Book of Jeremiah from Ancient Times to Modern.* Journal of Theological Interpretation Supplements 6. Winona Lake, IN: Eisenbrauns 2013.

Thompson, J. A. *The Book of Jeremiah.* New International Commentary on the Old Testament. Grand Rapids: Eerdmans, 1980.

Torrell, Jean-Pierre. *Saint Thomas Aquinas.* Vol. 1, *The Person and His Work.* Rev. ed. Translated by Robert Royal. Washington, DC: Catholic University of America Press, 2005.

Van Engen, John. *Rupert of Deutz.* Berkeley: University of California Press, 1983.

Van Henten, Jan Willem. "2 Maccabees." In *The Oxford Encyclopedia of the Books of the Bible,* edited by Michael D. Coogan, 2:15–26. New York: Oxford University Press, 2011.

Van Liere, Frans. *An Introduction to the Medieval Bible.* New York: Cambridge University Press, 2014.

Wasserstein, Abraham, and David J. Wasserstein. *The Legend of the Septuagint from Classical Antiquity to Today.* New York: Cambridge University Press, 2006.

Weisheipl, James A., ed. *Albertus Magnus and the Sciences: Commemorative Essays, 1980.* Studies and Texts—Pontifical Institute of Mediaeval Studies 49. Toronto: Pontifical Institute of Mediaeval Studies, 1980.

Wenthe, Dean O., ed. *Jeremiah, Lamentations.* ACCS Old Testament 12. Downers Grove, IL: InterVarsity Press, 2009.

Wessley, Stephen E. *Joachim of Fiore and Monastic Reform.* New York: Peter Lang, 1990.

Whalen, Brett Edward. *Dominion of God: Christendom and Apocalypse in the Middle Ages.* Cambridge, MA: Harvard University Press, 2009.

Würthwein, Ernst. *The Text of the Old Testament: An Introduction to the "Biblia Hebraica."* 3rd ed. Rev. and expanded by Alexander Achilles Fischer. Translated by Erroll F. Rhodes. Grand Rapids: Eerdmans, 2014.

Young, Spencer E. *Scholarly Community at the Early University of Paris: Theologians, Education and Society, 1215–1248.* New York: Cambridge University Press, 2014.

Zemler-Cizewski, Wanda. "The Literal Sense of Scripture according to Rupert of Deutz." In *The Multiple Meaning of Scripture: The Role of Exegesis in Early-Christian and Medieval Culture,* edited by Ineke van 't Spijker, 203–5. Boston: Brill, 2009.

———. "Rupert of Deutz and the Law of the Stray Wife: Anti-Jewish Allegory in *De Sancta Trinitate et Operibus Eius.*" *Recherches de Théologie et Philosophie Médiévales* 75 (2008): 257–69.

Index of Names

Albert the Great, 5n17, 6, 8, 10, 22–24, 29, 61–72
Alcuin of York, 14–15, 17
Ambrose, 19, 121
Anselm of Canterbury, 19
Aquila, 13, 73n1, 80–81, 86–87, 101, 109, 112, 115, 159
Aquinas. *See* Thomas Aquinas
Aristotle, 24, 30, 42, 67, 69, 258, 269
Augustine, 17, 19, 52n1, 119n3, 123, 128, 137, 146, 150, 207
Averroes, 23

Birgitta of Sweden, 45, 48
Boethius, 24, 41, 42, 72, 278
Bonaventure, 19, 123n8

Cassian, John, 17, 18, 78–79
Celestine V, 47
Chrysostom, John. *See* John Chrysostom
Cicero, 41
Comestor, Peter. *See* Peter Comestor
Cyril of Alexandria, 11

Dante, vii, 19, 46
De Jong, Mayke B., 15–16
Denis the Carthusian, 8–9, 10, 41–45, 260–92

Emery, Kent, 41
Ephrem the Syrian, 11–12

Froehlich, Karlfried, 23

Gilbert the Universal, 26n118
Gils, Pierre-Marie, 34
Gottschalk of Orbais, 16
Gregory XI, 48
Gregory the Great, 11–12, 17, 18, 19, 77, 87, 93, 95, 112, 126n12, 127n14, 148, 152, 163, 207

Hildegard of Bingen, 45, 48–49
Horace, 24, 64
Hugh of Fleury, 255
Hugh of St. Cher, 4, 5n14, 7, 8, 10, 24–29, 37–38, 45, 117–64, 210n2, 230n27, 245n45

Innocent III, 46–47

Jacobinus of Asti, 34
Jacobson, Diane, 3
Jerome, 5, 9–10, 11–14, 38, 50, 213n11, 231n29; cited by Albert the Great, 24, 66–68, 70; cited by Denis the Carthusian, 42, 260n1, 261, 265, 266,

Index of Subjects

Aaron, 126, 152

Abimelech, 249

Abraham, 20, 46, 52–53, 81, 97, 99, 103, 163, 214, 234

Adam, 20, 46, 57, 59, 173, 208, 263

Adultery: literal, 6, 81, 90, 93, 165–66, 217–18, 230; metaphor for idolatry, 93, 97, 99, 100, 115, 217–18

Ages of the world, 20, 46, 52–54

Allegory, 4, 5–6, 14, 17, 25, 42, 115n44, 274–75n15

Amnon, 93

Anagogy, 4, 75, 81, 95, 97

Anathoth: field in, 261, 285; men of, 47, 176

Andrew, 243, 250

Angels, 53, 58, 60, 94, 118, 153, 230, 244, 248, 257, 262–63, 271, 272, 273, 276, 277; as source of inspiration, 7, 226

Anna, 273

Anthropomorphite heresy, 78–79

Anthropopathos, 162

Antichrist, 39, 233–38

Anti-Judaism, 20–21, 38, 211, 245

Aposiopesis, 110, 186

Apostles, 37, 102, 163, 212, 234, 242, 243, 247, 253, 267, 274, 278

Apostrophe, 111

Arabs, 94–95

Ark of the covenant, 102–103, 124

Assyrian Empire, 1, 82–83, 92–93, 97, 101

Baal, 7, 76, 85–86, 89, 90, 97, 136, 212, 217, 265, 266

Babylonian: empire, 1–3, 222; exile, 21, 38, 52, 53, 54, 142, 210, 216, 222, 233, 234, 239, 242, 251, 261, 269; siege and attack on Jerusalem, 28, 32, 49, 55, 110, 113, 115, 153

Baptism, 12, 60, 63, 64, 111, 136, 251

Baruch, 23, 43–44, 262, 279–82

Basilisks, 28, 159–60

Benjamin: territory of, 42, 196, 203, 261, 268, 277, 285; tribe of, 97, 144, 203, 245n45, 268

Bethel, 97

Bethlehem, 12, 39–40, 245, 247n50

Birds, 28, 113–14, 160, 168; allegorical and metaphorical, 54, 140, 141; devouring corpses, 28, 140, 184; object lessons, 28, 142, 148–49, 193

Book of Consolation, 3, 10, 38

Brothers and Sisters of the Common Life, 41

Caiaphas, 47

271, 273; siege of, 2, 3, 10, 140, 153, 155, 230, 260, 265, 268, 284; site of Christ's passion, 4; women of, 32, 169
Jeshua, 53
Jesus Christ, 36, 37, 44, 46, 59, 60, 63–64, 65, 69, 71, 76, 83, 99, 100, 102, 103, 105, 107, 108, 121, 175–76, 186, 202, 276, 281–82; as branch of David, 38, 212–13; as bridegroom, 91, 141, 273; as cornerstone, 254; as good shepherd, 37, 43, 209–12; as sacrifice, 270; conception of, 248; conquering antichrist, 235, 237; cross of, 5, 163, 175, 189; crucifixion of, 122; descended from David, 277–78; descent into hell, 40; divinity of, 213–15, 222; epiphany of, 12; incarnation of, 20, 38, 43, 49, 210, 245, 249, 271; miracles of, 273; passion of, 5, 32, 43, 46, 63, 65, 157, 174, 251, 255; preaching by, 234, 242, 247; predicted in Jeremiah, 39, 233–59; prefigured by prophet Jeremiah, 4–5, 20, 22, 32, 57, 174, 185, 200, 233, 235, 236, 238, 239; priesthood of, 52, 54, 275, 276; resurrection of, 246
Jewish interpreters, 43, 50, 86, 109, 136, 140, 211, 213, 214, 222, 229, 234, 236, 249, 274
Jews, 1, 39, 49, 122, 210–11, 234, 241, 253, 275; as translators of Septuagint, 13, 215; believing in Christ, 36, 37, 250, 251, 253, 254; conversion in the end times, 234–36, 239, 243; dispersion of, 20; expelled from Jerusalem, 21, 255; in Middle Ages, 21, 50; priesthood of, 53; salvation of, 58, 215. *See also* Anti-Judaism; Jewish interpreters
Job, 72, 135, 183, 219
John the Apostle, 91, 204n13
John the Baptist, 8, 23, 46, 60, 64, 91, 248, 273
Jonah, 114, 131, 226
Joseph (husband of the Virgin Mary), 53–54
Joseph (son of Rachel and Jacob), 247, 250

Joshua, 15, 264
Josiah, 2, 15, 96, 98, 203, 279, 282, 283

Land of promise. *See* Promised land
Lateran Council, Fourth, 46, 47
Lent, 162
Levite's concubine, 144, 245n45
Levites, 138, 276–77
Limbo, 40, 246
Literal sense of scripture, viii, 4–5, 8, 9, 12, 14, 20, 23, 25, 26, 27–28, 30, 32, 33, 34, 35–40, 42, 43, 71, 82, 118–19, 120, 128–29, 135, 142, 156, 158, 159, 160, 162, 174, 211, 215, 222, 225, 227, 228, 230, 236, 241–44, 245n45, 248, 249, 255

Maccabean revolt, 31
Marriage, 201, 204; God's marriage to Israel, 83, 96; spiritual marriage, 141
Martyrdom, 98–99, 163; of holy innocents, 40, 246, 248
Mary Magdalene, 137–38n29
Mary of Bethany, 137–38
Mary, Virgin. *See* Virgin Mary
Masoretic text, 13n59, 27, 73–74n2, 92n24, 215n14, 246n49
Matthew, 245, 250
Melchizedek, 53, 266, 276
Menstruation, 86–87, 163
Mercy seat, 181
Merlin, 47
Mirror of eternity, 6–7, 24, 67
Moral sense of scripture. *See* Tropological sense of scripture
Moses, 7n26, 15, 20, 49n221, 52, 68, 71, 72, 91, 105, 125, 134, 144, 163, 214, 222, 240, 263, 264, 271; law of, 98, 102, 229; prayers of, 126, 183
Mourning women, 32, 168–69

Nathanael, 243, 250
Nazarenes, 102
Nebuchadnezzar, 2, 108, 110–11, 119, 122, 140, 143, 149, 153, 156, 174, 201, 230–31, 260, 283, 290, 291; army of, 158; yoke of, 220

Index of Scripture References

Index of Scripture References

Index of Scripture References